A Year of Movies

A Year of Movies

365 Films to Watch
on the Date They Happened

IVAN WALTERS

ROWMAN & LITTLEFIELD
Lanham • Boulder • New York • London

Published by Rowman & Littlefield
A wholly owned subsidiary of The Rowman & Littlefield Publishing Group, Inc.
4501 Forbes Boulevard, Suite 200, Lanham, Maryland 20706
www.rowman.com

Unit A, Whitacre Mews, 26-34 Stannary Street, London SE11 4AB

British Library Cataloguing in Publication Information Available

Library of Congress Cataloging-in-Publication Data

Walters, Ivan, 1963–
  A year of movies : 365 films to watch on the date they happened / Ivan Walters.
    pages cm
  Includes bibliographical references and index.
  ISBN 978-1-4422-4559-4 (hardback : alk. paper) — ISBN 978-1-4422-4560-0 (ebook) 1.
Motion pictures—Catalogs. I. Title.
  PN1998.W28 2016
  791.43'75—dc23

                                                                    2015019467

♾™ The paper used in this publication meets the minimum requirements of American National Standard for Information Sciences—Permanence of Paper for Printed Library Materials, ANSI/NISO Z39.48-1992.

Printed in the United States of America

To Page and the rest of the staff at the York County Library, Rock Hill branch, for their invaluable help in assisting with the research necessary to complete this book

Contents

Reader's Note	ix
January	1
February	31
March	59
April	95
May	131
June	165
July	197
August	231
September	263
October	295
November	327
December	359
Index	393
About the Author	443

Reader's Note

This book is based on a very simple concept. For each day of the year I name a movie in which at least one scene takes place on that date. I got the idea when *Terminator 2: Judgment Day* was shown on television in August and I said to myself, "They're showing it a few days early. They should show it on August 29, because that's Judgment Day" in the film. That got me to thinking about other films that could be shown on the day they occur, like *The Longest Day* and *Back to the Future*. I started to wonder if there was such a film for each day of the year. This book is the result.

In developing this book I was fortunate in that I found a movie relatively easily for practically every day of the year. The only film that had to be "forced" into a date was *Excalibur*. I had a hole on April 25 and put *Excalibur* there because, first, I really like the film, and second, the sword-drawing scene takes place on Easter, which can occur on April 25. The film does not give us the year, so it could have been on that date.

The time references I give for each film indicating the scene or moment in the film where the day of the year is revealed are of course from the version that I watched. As you may be aware, quite a few films have numerous versions of varying length. There has been a recent trend toward release of a "director's cut," which may differ from the regular release. The times given may be different on the version you are watching.

A word of warning: the plot summaries all contain spoilers, so be aware of this from the start.

If you know of a film you think should be listed for a particular day, let me know. If I use this film in a future edition and you are the first person to suggest the film, I will credit your suggestion. Reach me at ivanwalters29@yahoo .com. I also invite additions or corrections.

January

1

ROCKY

Year: 1976
Genre: Drama
Run Time: 1 hour 59 minutes
Date Revealed in Film: 30:21
Availability: DVD, Blu-ray (MGM Home Entertainment)
Director: John G. Avildsen; **Screenplay**: Sylvester Stallone
Cast: Sylvester Stallone ("Rocky" Balboa), Talia Shire (Adrian Pennino), Burt Young (Paulie Pennino), Burgess Meredith (Mickey Goldmill), Carl Weathers (Apollo Creed)

In November 1975 Rocky Balboa is a small-time boxer and a not very effective collection agent for a local loan shark in Philadelphia, where the world heavyweight championship is to be fought on New Year's Day. When the challenger injures his hand, the champion, Apollo Creed, picks a local boy, Rocky, to fight instead. Rocky trains hard, practicing on the carcasses in a meat packing plant where his best friend, Paulie, works. He is dating Adrian, Paulie's shy sister, and the night before the fight Rocky tells Adrian he knows he cannot win, but just wants to "go the distance" and stay on his feet to the end of the bout. When the fight starts on January 1, 1976 (1:39:15 to 1:57:12),

Creed does not take the fight (or Rocky) seriously, but he soon regrets that decision. Rocky and Creed battle it out in a slugfest that will leave you cheering.

One of the classic underdog movies where the little guy gets a shot at greatness. This is also a love story between two almost painfully shy people who find each other. The main cast give understated performances that make it seem even more real, and the fight is well choreographed. A film that leaves you with an "up" feeling.

Awards: *Academy Award Wins*: Best Picture, Best Film Editing, and Best Director. *Academy Award Nominations*: Best Original Screenplay, Best Actor (Sylvester Stallone), Best Actress (Talia Shire), Best Supporting Actor (Burt Young and Burgess Meredith), Best Original Song, and Best Sound. *Golden Globe Win*: Best Motion Picture–Drama. *Golden Globe Nominations*: Best Director–Motion Picture, Best Motion Picture Actor–Drama (Stallone), Best Motion Picture Actress–Drama (Shire), Best Screenplay–Motion Picture, and Best Original Score–Motion Picture

Alternate Film: *Platoon*

2

THE THIN RED LINE

Year: 1998
Genre: War
Run Time: 2 hours 50 minutes
Availability: DVD, Blu-ray (The Criterion Collection)
Director: Terrence Malick; **Screenplay**: Terrence Malick, based on the novel by James Jones
Cast: Sean Penn (1st Sgt. Edward Welsh), Adrien Brody (Cpl. Geoffrey Fife), Jim Caviezel (Pvt. Robert Witt), Ben Chaplin (Pvt. Jack Bell), John Cusack (Capt. John Gaff), Elias Koteas (Capt. Bugger Staros), Nick Nolte (Lt. Col. Gordon Tall)

In the South Pacific during World War II, Private Witt is arrested while living AWOL with the natives and is sent to Guadalcanal with reinforcements. Their commander, Lt. Col. Tall, wants to use this battle to get promoted, but Captain Staros refuses Tall's order to take a strategic Japanese bunker at all costs. On January 2, 1943 (1:29:19 to 1:45:11), a detachment is able to outflank the bunker and capture it, but Staros is relieved of his command for disobeying orders. Witt considers going AWOL again but does not and instead is sent out on a patrol that forces him to decide what kind of a soldier he is.

A very good combat film. Explores combat in an almost mystical way. Tries to get to the inner core of the men who are fighting for their lives.

Awards: *Academy Award Nominations*: Best Cinematography, Best Director (Terrence Malick), Best Editing, Best Original Score, Best Picture, Best Sound, and Best Adapted Screenplay

Source: Morrison, Samuel Eliot. *The Struggle for Guadalcanal.* Boston: Little, Brown and Company, 1959. This book at page 337 gives the date of the attack.

Alternate Film: *Crime of the Century*

3

SHADOWLANDS

Year: 1993

Genre: Drama

Run Time: 2 hours 11 minutes

Availability: DVD (HBO Home Video)

Director: Richard Attenborough; **Screenplay**: William Nicholson, based on his 1983 screenplay

Cast: Anthony Hopkins (C. S. "Jack" Lewis), Edward Hardwicke ("Warnie" Lewis), Debra Winger (Joy Gresham), Joseph Mazzello (Douglas Gresham), James Frain (Peter Whistler), Julian Fellowes (Desmond Arding), Michael Denison (Harry Harrington)

In 1952, author and Christian apologist C. S. Lewis (known as "Jack") lives a very retiring life at "The Kilns" with his brother Warnie and lectures at Oxford University. Then he meets Joy Gresham, an American writer, and Jack invites her and her son to spend Christmas there. Joy confesses to Jack that her husband is a drunken adulterer. After Joy and Douglas leave on January 3, 1953, Jack misses her, even if he won't even admit it to himself (44:45 to 45:35). Joy divorces her husband and moves to England. Joy asks Jack to marry her so she can stay in the United Kingdom, and he agrees. They are married in a civil ceremony and tell no one except Warnie. Then something happens to Joy that will change her life and her relationship with Jack forever. Jack will have to decide if he really believes what he says or not.

A touching, off-key kind of romance. We can see they like each other before they do. An excellent film about faith and love and hope.

Awards: *Academy Award Nominations*: Best Actress (Debra Winger) and Best Adapted Screenplay

Source: Duriez, Colin. *The C. S. Lewis Chronicles*. New York: Bluebridge, 2005. This book at page 253 gives the date Joy and Douglas left the Kilns.

Alternate Film: *In Cold Blood*

4

MY COUSIN VINNY

Year: 1992
Genre: Comedy
Run Time: 2 hours
Date Revealed in Film: 1:13:09
Availability: DVD, Blu-ray (Twentieth Century Fox)
Director: Jonathan Lynn; **Screenplay**: Dale Launer
Cast: Joe Pesci ("Vinny" Gambini), Marisa Tomei (Mona Lisa Vito), Ralph Macchio (Bill Gambini), Mitchell Whitfield (Stan Rothenstein), Fred Gwynne (Judge Haller), Lane Smith (Jim Trotter III), Bruce McGill (Sheriff Farley)

On January 4, 1992, New Yorkers Bill Gambini and Stan Rothenstein are traveling through Beecham County, Alabama, on their way to UCLA and end up getting arrested for murder (00:00:21 to 11:30). Billy's mother sends their cousin Vinny, a neophyte attorney, to represent them. He comes to town with his fiancée, Lisa, and they are two Yankee fish out of water in a small southern town. Vinny's lack of practical legal knowledge gets him into trouble, and he has to deal with his touchy relationship with Lisa. However, when the case comes to trial Vinny and Lisa are able to use their street smarts to ensure that justice is done.

A very funny movie of culture clash. The four Yankees are square pegs in the round holes of this southern town. Their interactions with the locals make this a very amusing movie.

Awards: *Academy Award Win*: Best Supporting Actress (Marisa Tomei)
Alternate Film: *Cromwell*

5

THE TIME MACHINE

Year: 1960
Genre: Science Fiction
Run Time: 1 hour 43 minutes
Date Revealed in Film: 1:35:10
Availability: DVD, VHS (Warner Home Video)
Director: George Pál; **Screenplay**: David Duncan, based on the novel by H. G. Wells
Cast: Rod Taylor (George, the "time traveler"), Alan Young (David Filby and James Filby), Yvette Mimeux (Weena), Sebastian Cabot (Dr. Hillyer), Tom Helmore (Anthony Bridewell), Whit Bissell (Walter Kemp), Doris Lloyd (Mrs. Watchett)

On January 5, 1900, three friends are surprised when their dinner host, George, stumbles in with torn and dirty clothes (02:13 to 06:49). He tells his story. Five days ago, after telling his disbelieving friends that he had invented a time machine, George uses the time machine to travel into the future. Instead of the peaceful future he envisioned, George finds nothing but war. In the far distant future of 802,701 AD, George finds that humanity has split into two species, the apathetic, peaceful Eloi and the Morlocks, on whom the Eloi are dependent. When his machine disappears, George is forced to take action that will reveal the bloody undercurrents of the apparently peaceful world of the future. He returns briefly to January 5, 1900 (1:35:07 to 1:42:19), before returning to the far future.

This is the classic version of this film and the one I grew up with. It is not just an action/adventure film. It addresses pacifism as well as scientific and moral progress.

Awards: *Academy Award Win*: Best Special Effects
Alternate Film: *Dr. No*

6

DOCTOR ZHIVAGO

Year: 1965
Genre: Drama
Run Time: 3 hours 17 minutes

Date Revealed in Film: 1:23:07–08
Availability: DVD, Blu-ray (Warner Home Video)
Director: David Lean; **Screenplay**: Robert Bolt, based on the novel by Boris
  Pasternak
Cast: Omar Sharif (Dr. Zhivago), Julie Christie (Lara), Geraldine Chaplin
  (Tonya Gromeko), Alec Guinness (Yevgraf Zhivago), Rod Steiger (Viktor
  Komarovsky), Tom Courtenay (Pasha [Commissar Strelnikov]), Siobhan
  McKenna (Anna Gromeko)

Orphan Yuri Zhivago grows up to be a doctor and a poet. Meanwhile, Lara
lives with her mother, the mistress of Viktor Komarovsky. Lara loves Pasha,
a left-wing radical. Komarovsky seduces Lara, which causes her mother to
attempt suicide, and Zhivago meets Lara as a result. Komarovsky tries to dissuade Lara from marrying Pasha and then rapes her. On (Orthodox) Christmas Eve, January 6, 1913, Lara takes Pasha's pistol, goes to Yuri and Tonya
Gromeko's engagement party, and shoots Komarovsky in the arm. Pasha
takes Lara away (56:42 to 1:12:35). They are married and move to the Urals.
In the Great War Yuri is an army doctor and meets Lara, who has become a
nurse to look for Pasha, who is missing in action.

One of the classic movie romances. A true epic film with beautiful cinematography. An enthralling, compelling story of great richness.

Awards: *Academy Award Wins*: Best Art Direction, Best Cinematography,
  Best Writing–Adapted Screenplay, Best Costume Design, and Best Score.
  Academy Award Nominations: Best Picture, Best Supporting Actor (Tom
  Courtenay), Best Director, Best Film Editing, and Best Sound. *Golden
  Globe Wins*: Best Motion Picture–Drama, Best Motion Picture Actor–
  Drama (Omar Sharif), Best Motion Picture Director, Best Screenplay, and
  Best Original Score. *Golden Globe Nominations*: Most Promising New-
  comer–Female (Geraldine Chaplin)
Alternate Film: *The Hunchback of Notre Dame*

7

ZORBA THE GREEK
Year: 1964
Genre: Drama
Run Time: 2 hours 22 minutes

Date Revealed in Film: 1:04:22
Availability: DVD, Blu-ray (Twentieth Century Fox)
Director: Michael Cacoyannis; **Screenplay**: Michael Cacoyannis, based on the novel by Nikos Kazantzakis
Cast: Anthony Quinn (Alexis Zorba), Alan Bates (Basil), Irene Papas (Widow), Lila Kedrova (Madame Hortense), Sotiris Moustakas (Mimithos), Anna Kyriakou (Soul), Eleni Anousaki (Lola), Yorgo Voyagis (Pavlo), Takis Emmanuel (Manolakas)

Basil, a tense, repressed Anglo-Greek writer, meets Zorba, a gruff but friendly musician who says he can help run Basil's mine. They stay with an old French war widow, Madame Hortense, with whom Zorba becomes involved. Zorba and Basil meet "the Widow," a young woman tormented by the villagers for not remarrying who is attracted to Basil. On Orthodox Christmas, January 7, Zorba celebrates figuring out the angle for the zip line to bring lumber down the hill to the mine and leaves to buy equipment (1:16:51 to 1:19:59). His letter about a young cabaret singer angers Basil. The night before Zorba's return, Basil makes love to "the Widow," which has consequences.

A very unusual and disturbing film. Both Basil and Zorba seem strangely detached from their surroundings and events.

Awards: *Academy Award Wins*: Best Art Direction–Black-and-White, Best Cinematography, and Best Supporting Actress (Lila Kedrova). *Academy Award Nominations*: Best Picture, Best Director, Best Actor (Anthony Quinn), and Best Adapted Screenplay. *Golden Globe Nominations*: Best Motion Picture–Drama, Best Motion Picture Director, Best Motion Picture Actor–Drama (Quinn), Best Supporting Actress (Kedrova), and Best Original Score
Alternate Film: *The Hoax*

8

BLADE RUNNER
Year: 1982
Genre: Science Fiction
Run Time: 1 hour 57 minutes
Date Revealed in film: 15:16
Availability: DVD, Blu-ray (Warner Home Video)

Director: Ridley Scott; **Screenplay**: Hampton Francher and David Peoples, loosely based on the novel *Do Androids Dream of Electric Sheep?* by Philip K. Dick

Cast: Harrison Ford (Rick Deckard), Rutger Hauer (Roy Batty), Sean Young (Rachael), Edward James Olmos (Gaff), Daryl Hannah (Pris), M. Emmet Walsh (Captain Bryant), Joe Turkel (Dr. Eldon Tyrell), William Sanderson (J. F. Sebastian)

In the future the Tyrell Corporation creates genetically engineered humans with a four-year lifespan called replicants that are used as slaves off world. They are outlawed on Earth and blade runner units find any on Earth and kill them. In November 2019, six replicants steal a shuttle, and flee to Earth. Two are killed and Deckard is ordered to find and kill the others. He goes to Tyrell and meets Rachael, who turns out to be a replicant. Deckard is told to kill Rachel, who has disappeared. After Deckard takes part in a violent confrontation, an unexpected ending on January 8, 2020 (1:27:11 to 1:48:52), takes place.

One of the classic sci-fi films. Explores mortality, humanity, memory, and love.

Awards: *Academy Award Nominations*: Best Art Direction and Best Effects–Visual Effects. *Golden Globe Nomination*: Best Original Score–Motion Picture

Alternate Film: *The Buccaneer*

9

THE ODESSA FILE

Year: 1974
Genre: Action/Thriller
Run Time: 2 hours 10 minutes
Date Revealed in Film: 1:45:15
Availability: DVD, Blu-ray (Image Entertainment)
Director: Ronald Neame; **Screenplay**: Kenneth Ross and George Markstein, based on the novel by Frederick Forsyth
Cast: Jon Voight (Peter Miller), Maximilian Schell (Eduard Roschmann), Maria Schell (Frau Miller), Mary Tamm (Sigi), Derek Jacobi (Klaus Wenzer), Peter Jeffrey (David Porath), Klaus Löwitsch (Gustav Mackensen), Kurt Meisel (Alfred Oster)

David, an Israeli Mossad agent, is told that Egypt's rockets need a guidance system, which is being secretly developed in Germany. Peter Miller, a freelance reporter in Hamburg, obtains a diary from which he learns about the brutal Eduard Roschmann, commandant of the Riga concentration camp, and decides to find him.

With the help of the Mossad, Miller penetrates the ODESSA, the organization that is helping to hide and protect former members of the SS, and uncovers a secret book containing the names and photos of all ODESSA members. Miller heads to Heidelberg on January 9, 1964 (1:45:04 to 1:47:02), where Roschmann now lives as Hans Keifel, head of the electronics firm that is developing the guidance system for the Egyptian rockets. In a surprising climax we learn why Miller was really after Roschmann.

An excellent suspense story. Good action sequences and moments of terror. I love the big plot twist at the end.

Alternate Film: *Monster*

10

COAL MINER'S DAUGHTER

Year: 1980
Genre: Biography
Run Time: 2 hours 5 minutes
Availability: DVD, Blu-ray (Universal Studios)
Director: Michael Apted; **Screenplay**: Thomas Rickman, based on Loretta
    Lynn's autobiography
Cast: Sissy Spacek (Loretta Lynn), Tommy Lee Jones (Mooney Lynn), Beverly
    D'Angelo (Patsy Cline), Levon Helm (Ted Webb), William Sanderson (Lee
    Dollarhide)

The film opens with Loretta Webb and her family living a poverty-stricken nineteenth-century existence in post–World War II Kentucky. She meets and marries (at age thirteen!) Mooney Lynn on January 10, 1948 (28:04 to 31:50). He persuades her to begin singing in honky-tonks and record a single. Their guerilla marketing campaign gets her on the country music charts and leads to an appearance on the Grand Ole Opry, the top of the heap in country music. She acquires a mentor in Patsy Cline and goes on to country music superstardom.

A very good film. Spacek's and Jones's performances make this film seem real. Maintains a good mix of drama and humor.

Awards: *Academy Award Win*: Best Actress (Sissy Spacek). *Academy Award Nominations*: Best Picture, Best Set Decoration, Best Cinematography, Best Film Editing, Best Picture, Best Sound, and Best Adapted Screenplay. *Golden Globe Wins*: Best Motion Picture–Musical/Comedy and Best Motion Picture Actress–Musical/Comedy (Spacek). *Golden Globe Nominations*: Best Motion Picture Actor–Musical/Comedy (Tommy Lee Jones) and Best Motion Picture Supporting Actress–Musical/Comedy (Beverly D'Angelo)

Source: Lynn, Loretta. *Coal Miner's Daughter*. New York: Warner Books, 1976. This book at page 76 gives the date of her wedding.

Alternate Film: *Soul Surfer*

11

THE FIGHTING SULLIVANS

Year: 1944

Genre: Drama

Run Time: 1 hour 52 minutes

Availability: DVD (VCI Entertainment), VHS (IVY Video)

Director: Lloyd Bacon; **Screenwriters**: Edward Doherty, Mary C. McCall Jr., and Jules Schermer

Cast: Anne Baxter (Katherine Mary Sullivan); Thomas Mitchell (Mr. Thomas F. Sullivan), Selena Royle (Mrs. Alleta Sullivan), Edward Ryan (Albert Leo Sullivan), Trudy Marshall (Genevieve Sullivan), John Campbell (Francis Henry Sullivan)

The Sullivans of Waterloo, Iowa, had five children, named George, Frank, Joe, Matt, Al, and Genevieve. The boys engage in the usual childhood shenanigans such as fighting, sailing homemade boats, and sneaking smokes. When Al meets a girl, the family tries to break them up until they realize Al really loves Kathy Mary. They get married and after Pearl Harbor all the brothers enlist in the Navy and serve together on the *Juneau*. The recruiter who swore them into the service comes to the house on January 11, 1943, and has to give the family bad news (1:44:04 to 1:50:03). The USS *The Sullivans*, a destroyer named after the brothers, is launched.

A somewhat romanticized version of the brothers' lives, this entertaining enough movie doesn't quite become a World War II propaganda film. The Sullivans contributed to the adoption of the "sole survivor" policy mentioned in *Saving Private Ryan*.

Awards: *Academy Award Nomination*: Best Writing–Original Story

Source: Satterfield, John. *We Band of Brothers: The Sullivans and World War II*. Parkersburg, IA: Mid-Prairie Books, 1995. This book at pages 1–9 gives the date of the visit.

Alternate Film: *A Song to Remember*

12

THE LORD OF THE RINGS: THE FELLOWSHIP OF THE RING

Year: 2001

Genre: Fantasy

Run Time: 2 hours 58 minutes

Availability: DVD, Blu-ray (New Line Cinema)

Director: Peter Jackson; **Screenplay**: Fran Walsh, Phillipa Boyens, and Peter Jackson, based on the novel by J. R. R. Tolkien

Cast: Elijah Wood (Frodo Baggins), Sean Astin (Samwise Gamgee), Viggo Mortensen (Aragorn), Ian McKellen (Gandalf the Grey), Sean Bean (Boromir), Orlando Bloom (Legolas), John Rhys-Davies (Gimli), Christopher Lee (Saruman the White)

After the Dark Lord Sauron is defeated his ring of power is lost for many years, but eventually ends up in the hands of Frodo Baggins. At the suggestion of the wizard Gandalf, Frodo and his friends Sam, Merry, and Pippin flee with the ring pursued by Black Riders, servants of Sauron. They meet Strider, a friend of Gandalf, who joins them. Frodo is wounded by Black Riders, but reaches Rivendell, where it is decided to destroy the ring. Frodo and eight companions—the three other hobbits; Gandalf; Strider; Gimli, a dwarf; Legolas, an elf; and Boromir, a man from Gondor—are picked for the job. On January 12, 3017, T.A., they are stopped by snow from crossing the Misty Mountains (1:40:07 to 1:42:57). Their "shortcut" through the mines of Moria under the mountains is a disaster, as they are attacked by orcs and Gandalf is killed.

The dark power of the ring produces a confrontation that will change the plans of Frodo and his companions and result in loss and sacrifice.

A mostly faithful adaptation of Tolkien's classic. Beautiful cinematography. Plenty of action and excitement.

Awards: *Academy Award Wins*: Best Cinematography, Best Visual Effects, Best Makeup, and Best Original Music Score. *Academy Award Nominations*: Best Supporting Actor (Ian McKellen), Best Art Direction, Best Director, Best Film Editing, Best Song, Best Picture, Best Sound, Best Costume Design, and Best Writing–Adapted Screenplay. *Golden Globe Nominations*: Best Motion Picture–Drama, Best Director–Motion Picture, Best Original Score–Motion Picture, and Best Original Song–Motion Picture

Source: Tolkien, J. R. R. *The Lord of the Rings*. New York: Houghton Mifflin, 1994. This book at page 1067 gives the date the fellowship tries to climb Caradhas.

Alternate Film: *Since You Went Away*

13

WALK THE LINE

Year: 2005

Genre: Biography

Run Time: 2 hours 15 minutes

Date Revealed in Film: 1:55:34

Availability: DVD, Blu-ray (Twentieth Century Fox)

Director: James Mangold; **Screenplay**: James Mangold and Gill Dennis, based on the autobiographies by Johnny Cash *Man in Black* and *Cash: The Autobiography*

Cast: Joaquin Phoenix (Johnny Cash), Reese Witherspoon (June Carter Cash), Ginnifer Goodwin (Vivian Liberto), Robert Patrick (Ray Cash), Hailey Anne Nelson (Rosanne Cash), Dallas Roberts (Sam Phillips), Johnny Holiday (Carl Perkins)

On January 13, 1968, Johnny Cash is waiting to perform at Folsom Prison (00:37 to 02:50). He thinks back over his life, from growing up poor in Arkansas with a dad who didn't like him, learning to play guitar and write songs while in the Air Force, and his first record contract at Sun Records in Memphis. After an initial rejection by June Carter, Cash became a drug abuser and almost loses June Carter again because of his addictions. However, June eventually was able to detox Cash. A letter from an inmate inspires him to do an album in a prison, leading to the Folsom concert (1:55:46 to 1:59:44). Cash proposes to June on stage and she accepts. They get married and Johnny and his dad work on repairing their relationship.

This is a good biographical film. Reese Witherspoon gives an exceptionally nuanced performance as June Carter. The music is pretty good also.

Awards: *Academy Award Win*: Best Actress (Reese Witherspoon). *Academy Award Nominations*: Best Actor (Joaquin Phoenix), Best Costume Design, Best Film Editing, and Best Sound Mixing. *Golden Globe Wins*: Best Performance by an Actor in a Motion Picture–Comedy or Musical (Phoenix), Best Performance by an Actress in a Motion Picture–Comedy or Musical (Witherspoon), Best Motion Picture–Comedy or Musical

Alternate Film: *Flight 90: Disaster on the Potomac*

14

OUT OF AFRICA

Year: 1985
Genre: Romance
Run Time: 2 hours 41 minutes
Availability: DVD, Blu-ray (Universal Studios)
Director: Sydney Pollack; **Screenplay**: Kurt Luedtke, based on the autographical book by Isak Dinesen and *Isak Dinesen: Life of a Storyteller* by Judith Thurman and *Silence Will Speak* by Errol Trzebinski
Cast: Robert Redford (Denys Finch Hatton), Meryl Streep (Karen Blixen), Klaus Maria Brandauer (Bror Blixen and Hans Blixen), Michael Kitchen (Berkeley Cole), Shane Rimmer (Belknap), Malick Bowens (Farah)

In 1913 Denmark, wealthy Karen Dinesen asks Baron Bror Blixen for a marriage of convenience. They plan to open a dairy farm in Kenya, and on the way there, Karen meets Denys Hatton, a white big game hunter. On January 14, 1914, Karen marries Bror (7:23 to 17:15). She develops a close friendship with Hatton, as her marriage does not turn out as she expected. Bror ignores Karen and cheats on her. He gives Karen syphilis, for which she has to get treatment, and then she and Denys become lovers. Just when it seems happiness is in reach, it is snatched away from her.

One of the classic romantic films of all time. It has fantastic cinematography and a great music score. It is also a very interesting biographical film.

Awards: *Academy Award Wins*: Best Picture, Best Director, Best Art Direction, Best Cinematography, Best Adapted Screenplay, Best Original Score, and Best Sound. *Academy Award Nominations*: Best Actress (Meryl Streep), Best Supporting Actor (Klaus Maria Brandauer), Best Costume Design, and Best Film Editing. *Golden Globe Wins*: Best Director–Motion Picture, Best Performance by an Actor in a Supporting Role in a Motion Picture (Brandauer), Best Original Score–Motion Picture, and Best Motion Picture–Drama. *Golden Globe Nominations*: Best Performance by an Actress in a Motion Picture–Drama (Streep) and Best Screenplay–Motion Picture

Source: Stade, George, ed. *European Writers: The Twentieth Century, Vol. 10.* New York: Charles Scribner's Sons, 1990. This book at page 1285 gives the date of Karen's wedding.

Alternate Film: *The Wrong Man*

15

THE BOUNTY

Year: 1984
Genre: Action/Adventure
Run Time: 2 hours 12 minutes
Availability: DVD (Metro-Goldwyn-Mayer)
Director: Roger Donaldson; **Screenplay**: Robert Bolt, based on the book *Captain Bligh and Mr. Christian* by Richard Hough
Cast: Mel Gibson (Fletcher Christian), Anthony Hopkins (William Bligh), Laurence Olivier (Admiral Hood), Edward Fox (Captain Greetham), Daniel Day-Lewis (John Fryer), Liam Neeson (Charles Churchill)

At the court-martial of Lt. Bligh there is a flashback to the voyage of the *Bounty* to Tahiti to transport breadfruit trees to the West Indies. Bligh asked an old friend, Fletcher Christian, to serve as master's mate. Bligh's harsh discipline causes resentment among the crew, but Christian is promoted to sailing master. In Tahiti the natives receive them enthusiastically. Christian develops an attraction to a native girl, who becomes pregnant. Some of the crew who try and desert to stay in Tahiti are found and whipped. The ship leaves Tahiti, and after Bligh says the ship will return to England by the dangerous Cape Horn route, Christian leads a mutiny. Bligh and those who support him are put in a small boat and set adrift. The *Bounty* returns to Tahiti, picks up some natives, and sets sail to find a refuge. They reach Pitcairn Island on January 15, 1790 (2:02:33 to 2:03:42).

A good movie. Bligh is pig-headed and soft at the wrong times. Christian finds himself a man torn between two worlds and "in Hell" as he says.

Source: Alexander, Caroline. *The Bounty*. New York: Viking, 2003. This book at page 355 gives the date they find Pitcairn Island.

Alternate Film: *Becoming Jane*

16

THE BENNY GOODMAN STORY

Year: 1956
Genre: Biography
Run Time: 1 hour 56 minutes
Availability: DVD (Universal Studios)
Director: Valentine Davies; **Screenplay**: Valentine Davies
Cast: Steve Allen (Benny Goodman), Donna Reed (Alice Hammond), Bertha Gersten (Dora Goodman), Herbert Anderson (John Hammond), Robert F. Simon (Dave Goodman)

In Chicago, young Benny Goodman becomes a clarinet phenom. He learns to play Dixieland jazz and joins a touring band. John Hammond offers the band a job at a club in New York, but his sister, Alice Hammond, doesn't like jazz. Benny talks their Mob boss into letting them go to New York. In New York, Benny meets Alice Hammond again, and she's as dismissive of him as ever until he impresses her with a knockout performance in a classical concert. Benny's band plays on radio and then goes on tour. He meets Alice again, and they admit their attraction for each other. Benny starts to play his own arrangements and is pleased and surprised when they are a big hit. Benny's music finally gets accepted in New York and Hollywood, with a performance at Carnegie Hall on January 16, 1938 (1:42:41 to 1:55:49). Alice is at the show.

A decent film from the golden age of the Hollywood biopic. As with almost all of these films, it's somewhat clichéd at times. However, if you don't expect a classic, it's entertaining enough to hold your interest.

Source: Collier, James L. *Benny Goodman and the Swing Era*. New York: Oxford University Press, 1989. This book at page 218 gives the concert date.
Alternate Film: *The Falcon and the Snowman*

17
REVERSAL OF FORTUNE
Year: 1990
Genre: Mystery/Drama
Run Time: 1 hour 51 minutes
Availability: DVD, VHS (Warner Home Video)
Director: Barbet Schroeder; **Screenplay**: Nicholas Kazan, based on *Reversal of Fortune: Inside the Von Bülow Case* by Alan Dershowitz
Cast: Glenn Close (Sunny von Bülow), Jeremy Irons (Claus von Bülow), Ron Silver (Alan Dershowitz), Uta Hagen (Maria), Annabella Sciorra (Sarah), Fisher Stevens (David Marriott), Jack Gilpin (Peter MacIntosh), Christine Baranski (Andrea Reynolds)

After Sunny von Bülow goes into a coma twice, the second time permanently, her children investigate their stepfather, Claus von Bülow. When drugs are found in Claus's closet, and Sunny's insulin level is fourteen times higher than normal, Claus is charged with attempted murder. After he is convicted, Harvard professor Alan Dershowitz agrees to represent Claus on appeal over the objections of some of his students.

David Marriott claims in a meeting on January 17, 1983, that he sold drugs to Sunny's son, who said he gave some to his mom (28:39 to 32:25). Claus says Sunny took a lot of drugs and that he found her lying on the bathroom floor, passed out. Marriott unsuccessfully tries to use edited tapes of his talks with Dershowitz to try and implicate him in misconduct.

A very interesting movie. Discloses the politics and procedure of a real criminal case. Many people, including me, still can't decide whether Claus is innocent or guilty.

Awards: *Academy Award Win*: Best Actor (Jeremy Irons). *Academy Award Nominations*: Best Director and Best Adapted Screenplay. *Golden Globe Win*: Best Performance by an Actor in a Motion Picture–Drama (Irons). *Golden Globe Nominations*: Best Motion Picture–Drama, Best Director–Motion Picture, and Best Screenplay–Motion Picture

Source: Dershowitz, Alan. *Reversal of Fortune*. New York: Random House, 1986. This book at page 82 gives the date of the meeting.
Alternate Film: *The Executioner's Song*

18

LOGAN'S RUN

Year: 1976
Genre: Science Fiction
Run Time: 1 hour 59 minutes
Date Revealed in Film: 1:48:27
Availability: Blu-ray and DVD (Warner Home Video)
Director: Michael Anderson; **Screenplay**: David Zelag Goodman, based on William F. Nolan and George Clayton Johnson's novel
Cast: Michael York (Logan 5), Richard Jordan (Francis 7), Jenny Agutter (Jessica 6), Farrah Fawcett (Holly 13), Peter Ustinov (Old Man), Roscoe Lee Browne (Box), Michael Anderson Jr. (Doc), Gary Morgan (Billy), Ashley Cox (timid girl)

In a future city sealed away from the world and run by a computer, the inhabitants live a hedonistic lifestyle, but it comes at a price. At age thirty everyone must go onto Carousel, where their bodies are destroyed and they are supposedly renewed. A life crystal is implanted in everyone's palm that turns red when it is time for Carousel. Some people have figured out that there is no renewal and they become "runners." Sandmen track down runners and kill them. Logan 5 and Francis 7 are Sandmen and best friends. After killing a runner, Logan finds an ankh bracelet on the body. Logan meets Jessica 6, who also wears an ankh. When Logan turns in the ankh, he learns the truth that there is no renewal. He is then ordered to leave the city and destroy Sanctuary, the goal of the runners. When his life crystal turns to red four years early he meets Jessica and persuades her to help him. After almost being killed several times, they escape from the city after defeating the robot Box. They emerge outside into the open air and their life crystals are now clear. Reaching the ruins of Washington, D.C., they meet an old man who lives in the U.S. Capitol building. Francis has followed them and Logan now has to kill him. Logan, Jessica, and the old man return to the city on January 18, 2274 (1:43:40 to 1:56:39), for a confrontation that will change their world forever.

A classic sci-fi film. Has an excellent plot and for its time good special effects.

Awards: *Academy Award Win*: Special Achievement for Visual Effects. *Academy Award Nominations*: Best Cinematography and Best Art Direction
Alternate Film: *Black Sunday*

19

FRIED GREEN TOMATOES

Year: 1991
Genre: Drama
Run Time: 2 hours 16 minutes
Availability: Blu-ray and DVD (Universal Home Video)
Director: Jon Avnet; **Screenplay**: Carol Sobieski and Fannie Flagg, based on Flagg's novel *Fried Green Tomatoes at the Whistle Stop Café*
Cast: Kathy Bates (Evelyn Couch), Mary Stuart Masterson (Idgie Threadgoode), Mary-Louise Parker (Ruth Jamison), Jessica Tandy (Ninny Threadgoode), Cicely Tyson (Sipsey), Chris O'Donnell (Buddy Threadgoode), Stan Shaw (Big George)

The story alternates between the present and flashbacks to the 1920s. Evelyn Couch and her husband go to a nursing home to visit his aunt and Evelyn meets an old woman, Ninny Threadgoode, who starts telling her about her sister-in-law, "Idgie." We flash back to the day of Leona Threadgoode's wedding when their brother "Buddy" is killed in front of Idgie and Ruth Jamison in a tragic accident. Evelyn starts attending empowerment classes, but her husband is only interested in baseball. Flashing back, some years later Ruth comes to visit and finds Idgie has become a rabble-rouser. Ruth marries Frank Bennett. Idgie goes to see Ruth, but leaves when she sees Frank has beaten Ruth. When Ruth's mother dies, Idgie brings the pregnant Ruth back home and threatens to kill Frank if he bothers Ruth again.

On January 19, 1986, Evelyn is insulted at the grocery store and goes to the nursing home, where Ninny finds her crying in a wheelchair (51:59 to 57:08). Ninny tells her that Ruth and Idgie opened "the Whistle Stop" café with the African Americans Big George and his mother, Sipsey, as the cooks. The KKK shows up, with Frank Bennett as a member, and he barges in to see his and Ruth's son, but the local police chief is a friend of Ruth and Idgie, so he sends the Klan away. Frank returns to get his son, but is struck by an unseen person.

Back in the present, Evelyn has a run in with two young girls in a grocery store parking lot and rams their car. Idgie tells how Ruth's son, Buddy, lost his arm in a rail accident how Frank Bennett's truck was found in the river near the café. Idgie and Big George were put on trial for Frank Bennett's murder, but after the preacher swears (on what we later learn is a copy of *Moby Dick*) that Idgie and Big George were at the revival when Frank disappeared, they are freed.

In the present, Evelyn becomes a Mary Kay agent, works on rebuilding her house, and learns Ninny's house has been torn down. Idgie tells how after the trial Ruth died of cancer. Ninny's roommate at the nursing home, Mrs. Otis, dies so Idgie leaves and finds out that her house is gone. Evelyn finds Idgie at Whistle Stop and we learn that it was Sipsey who killed Frank Bennett and Idgie went on trial because she knew Sipsey would have been convicted of murder.

A wonderful bittersweet story. Has both comedy and tragedy. An excellent story of two friendships separated by fifty years.

Awards: *Academy Award Nominations*: Best Actress in a Supporting Role (Jessica Tandy) and Best Adapted Screenplay. *Golden Globe Nominations*: Best Motion Picture–Comedy/Musical, Best Performance by an Actress in a Motion Picture–Comedy/Musical (Kathy Bates), and Best Performance by an Actress in a Supporting Role in a Motion Picture–Comedy/Musical (Tandy)

Source: Flagg, Fannie. *Fried Green Tomatoes at the Whistle Stop Café*. New York: McGraw-Hill, 1987. This book at pages 66–69 gives the date of Evelyn's grocery store adventure.

Alternate Film: *The Brink's Job*

20

PATRIOT GAMES

Year: 1992

Genre: Action/Adventure

Run Time: 1 hour 57 minutes

Date Revealed in Film: 27:58

Availability: Blu-ray and DVD (Paramount Home Video)

Director: Phillip Noyce; **Screenplay**: W. Peter Iliff and Donald Stewart, based on the novel by Tom Clancy

Cast: Harrison Ford (Jack Ryan), Anne Archer (Dr. "Cathy" Ryan), Patrick
Bergin (Kevin O'Donnell), Sean Bean (Sean Miller), Thora Birch (Sally
Ryan), James Fox (Lord William Holmes), Ellen Geer (Rose), Samuel L.
Jackson (Robby Jackson)

On January 20, 1992 (05:15 to 12:16), vacationing U.S. Naval Academy professor Jack Ryan disrupts an IRA attack on Lord Holmes in central London.
He kills Patrick Miller and captures his bother, Sean Miller. Ryan testifies
against Miller at his trial, where he is convicted. Miller later escapes. Miller's
group is unsuccessful in an attack on Ryan at the Naval Academy, but Ryan's
wife and daughter are injured in a car crash caused by the terrorists. Miller
is traced to Libya and an attack is launched on his camp. Lord Holmes has
come to America to formally present Ryan with his knighthood at a dinner at
the Ryan home, but unexpected guests make the evening much more exciting
than anyone anticipated.

An outstanding action/adventure film. Maintains a high level of suspense.
The action sequences are very well done.

Alternate Film: *Primary Colors*

21

SWEET DREAMS

Year: 1985
Genre: Biography
Run Time: 1 hour 55 minutes
Availability: DVD (HBO)
Director: Karel Reisz; **Screenplay**: Robert Getchell
Cast: Jessica Lange (Patsy Cline), Ed Harris (Charlie Dick), Ann Wedgeworth
(Hilda Hensley), David Clennon (Randy Hughes), James Staley (Gerard
Cline), Gary Basaraba (Woodhouse), John Goodman (Otis), P. J. Soles
(Wanda)

Charlie Dick goes to a roadhouse and sees Patsy Cline sing. Eventually she
leaves her husband for Charlie. Patsy is on the *Arthur Godfrey Amateur Hour*
on January 21, 1957 (30:21 to 33:35). She has a hit song with "Walking after
Midnight," and then Charlie gets drafted. Patsy continues to tour, but gets
pregnant and moves into base housing. She and Charlie fight, separate, and
reunite. Charlie is carousing when their baby is born, but goes AWOL to see

her when he finds out. Patsy goes to Nashville and teams up with producer Randy Hughes and they hit number one with "I Fall to Pieces." She becomes a regular at the Grand Old Opry and is in a life-threatening car accident. Patsy records her signature song "Crazy." She and Charlie fight and she has him arrested. Patsy records her last hit "Sweet Dreams" and then is killed in a plane crash at the age of thirty.

A Hollywood biopic of one of the true legends of country music. Watchable, but *Coal Miner's Daughter* is more realistic. Still, Jessica Lange does give a compelling performance.

Awards: *Academy Award Nomination*: Best Actress (Jessica Lange)

Source: Nassour, Ellis. *Honky Tonk Angel*. New York: St. Martin's Press, 1993.

This book at page 72 gives the date she was on Arthur Godfrey's show.

Alternate Film: *Carrington*

22

ZULU

Year: 1964

Genre: War

Run Time: 2 hours 19 minutes

Date Revealed in Film: 2:09:13

Availability: Blu-ray (Inspired Studios), DVD (Metro-Goldwyn-Mayer)

Director: Cy Endfield; **Screenplay**: John Prebble and Cy Endfield

Cast: Stanley Baker (Lieutenant John Chard), Michael Caine (Lieutenant Gonville Bromhead), Jack Hawkins (Reverend Otto Witt), Ulla Jacobsson (Margareta Witt), James Booth (Private Henry Hook), Nigel Green (Colour Sergeant Frank Bourne)

After the British defeat at Isandlwana on January 22, 1879 (2:09 to 1:49:45), the Zulus advance on the outpost at Rorke's Drift. Due to the absence of the commanding officer, leadership passes to an engineering officer, who decides to fortify the post using makeshift barricades of grain bags and boxes. The Zulus arrive and attack, setting fire to the hospital building, which has to be abandoned by the British. The Zulus display misguided bravery, charging the British again and again, taking terrible casualties. Early the next day the Zulus sing a war chant and the British respond with "Men of Harlech." The Zulus' last attack is barely beaten off. The Zulus sing to honor their foe and depart.

An action-packed film with spectacular battle scenes. An antiwar film, at least to the extent that the British aren't sure why they are fighting and don't enjoy slaughtering Zulus. Told exclusively from the British viewpoint, with almost no effort to flesh out the Zulus. A "western" set in Africa.
Alternate Film: *Anzio*

23

THE SHOOTIST
Year: 1976
Genre: Western
Run Time: 1 hour 40 minutes
Date Revealed in Film: 18:18
Availability: DVD and VHS (Paramount Home Video)
Director: Don Siegel; **Screenplay**: Miles Swarthout and Scott Hale, based on Glendon Swarthout's novel
Cast: John Wayne (John Bernard "J. B." Books), Lauren Bacall (Bond Rogers), Ron Howard (Gillom Rogers), James Stewart (Dr. E. W. Hostetler), Richard Boone (Mike Sweeney), Harry Morgan (Walter J. Thibido), John Carradine (Hezekiah Beckum)

J. B. Books, a legendary gunfighter, rides into Carson City, Nevada, on a winter's day and gets insulted by Jay Cobb. Books goes to see an old friend, Dr. Hostetler, who confirms that Books has terminal cancer and will soon die a lingering and painful death. Books goes to stay at the widow Bond Rogers's boardinghouse to await his fate. He gives an assumed named, but Gillom Rogers, the widow's son, learns who he really is. The next day, January 23, 1901 (18:15 to 25:48), the widow asks him to leave and calls Marshal Thibido, who lets him stay once he learns Books is dying. Gillom idolizes Books and the violence associated with him. Books meets Mike Sweeney, the brother of a man Books had killed, and that night two men try to kill Books, but are killed by him. After Books learns that a local card dealer is an expert marksman and the pain of his cancer increases, he devises a plan to go out with a bang and teach Gillom a lesson.

A different kind of western. Wayne's final film role is another classic movie.
Awards: *Academy Award Nomination*: Best Set Decoration. *Golden Globe Nomination*: Best Motion Picture Actor in a Supporting Role (Ron Howard)
Alternate Film: *Kramer vs. Kramer*

24

LOVE ACTUALLY

Year: 2003
Genre: Romance
Run Time: 2 hours 16 minutes
Date Revealed in Film: 2:06:35
Availability: Blu-ray and DVD (Universal Studios)
Director: Richard Curtis; **Screenplay:** Richard Curtis
Cast: Alan Rickman (Harry), Emma Thompson (Karen), Hugh Grant (David), Keira Knightley (Juliet), Colin Firth (Jamie), Lúcia Moniz (Aurélia), Liam Neeson (Daniel), Thomas Sangster (Sam), Bill Nighy (Billy Mack), Gregor Fisher (Joe)

Five weeks before Christmas we are introduced to a disparate group of Londoners. Novelist Jamie leaves his unfaithful wife, but eventually finds love with his Portuguese maid, Aurélia. David, the new prime minister, develops an attraction for his assistant, Natalie, and they get together after a few bumps in the road. Daniel is glad that his son Sam is in love with a girl rather than being terminally depressed over the death of his mother and Daniel helps Sam develop a plan to win her. David's sister Karen and her husband, Harry, go through a rough patch due to Harry's infatuation with his new secretary.

John and Judy, the stand-ins in a pornographic film, fall for each other. All these story lines reach their climax on Christmas Eve. Then one month later, on January 24, 2004, everyone converges at Heathrow airport for a generally happy ending (2:06:35 to 2:09:45).

This is a good romantic film. The plot line is complicated, but it's easy to follow while watching it. Also has a great soundtrack.

Awards: *Golden Globe Nominations*: Best Motion Picture–Comedy or Musical and Best Screenplay–Motion Picture
Alternate Film: *The One That Got Away*

25

ANNE OF THE THOUSAND DAYS

Year: 1969
Genre: Period Drama
Run Time: 2 hours 25 minutes

Availability: DVD (Universal Studios Home Video), VHS (MCA Home Video)

Director: Charles Jarrott; **Screenplay**: Bridget Boland, John Hale, and Richard Sokolove, based on Maxwell Anderson's play

Cast: Richard Burton (King Henry VIII), Geneviève Bujold (Anne Boleyn), Anthony Quayle (Thomas Wolsey), Irene Papas (Catherine of Aragon), John Colicos (Thomas Cromwell), Michael Hordern (Thomas Boleyn), Katherine Blake (Elizabeth Boleyn)

Henry VIII dumps both his queen, Catherine of Aragon, and his mistress, Mary Boleyn, in favor of Mary's sister, Anne. She plays hard to get and finally Henry is forced to divorce the queen, setting off the Protestant Reformation in England. Anne finally sleeps with Henry and when she discovers she is pregnant they are married on January 25, 1533 (1:31:05 to 1:32:34). Anne is made queen, but Henry's affections falter when Anne's child is a girl, the future Queen Elizabeth. His attentions wander to Jane Seymour. Henry tells his new chancellor, Thomas Cromwell, to get rid of Anne after a son is born dead. Cromwell uses torture to get false accusations of adultery against Anne. She is convicted and sentenced to death. She refuses to agree to an annulment and is executed. Ten days later Henry marries Jane Seymour.

A mostly accurate tale of the relationship between Henry VIII and Anne. An engrossing depiction of the cynicism that characterized Henry VIII and his "loves."

Awards: *Academy Award Win*: Best Costume Design. *Academy Award Nominations*: Best Actor in a Leading Role (Richard Burton), Best Actress in a Leading Role (Geneviève Bujold), Best Actor in a Supporting Role (Anthony Quayle), Best Art Direction, Best Cinematography, Best Original Score, Best Picture, Best Sound, and Best Adapted Screenplay. *Golden Globe Wins*: Best Motion Picture–Drama, Best Director–Motion Picture, Best Motion Picture Actress–Drama (Bujold), and Best Screenplay. *Golden Globe Nominations*: Best Motion Picture Actor–Drama (Burton), Best Supporting Actor (Quayle), and Best Original Score

Source: Starkey, David. *Six Wives: The Queens of Henry VIII*. New York: HarperCollins Publishers, 2007. This book at page 475 gives the date of the marriage

Alternate Film: *The Last King of Scotland*

26

KHARTOUM

Year: 1966
Genre: War/Drama
Running Time: 2 hour 8 minutes
Availability: Blu-ray (Twilight Time), DVD (Metro-Goldwyn-Mayer Home Entertainment)
Directors: Basil Dearden and Eliot Elisofon; **Screenplay**: Robert Ardrey
Cast: Charlton Heston (Charles Gordon), Laurence Olivier (The Mahdi), Ralph Richardson (William Gladstone), Richard Johnson (Colonel Stewart), Alexander Knox (Sir Evelyn Baring), Nigel Green (General Wolseley), Michael Hordern (Lord Grenville)

In the 1880s an Islamic religious leader, the Madhi, seized power, destroying an Egyptian army sent to defeat him. The British cabinet sends General "Chinese" Gordon to the Sudan. Gordon is received as a hero, since in a previous stint as governor of Sudan he ended slavery there. Gordon meets the Madhi, and learns the Madhi will not let him evacuate the Egyptians out of the country since the Madhi plans to kill them all to prove his ruthlessness. Gordon fortifies Khartoum, digs a moat, seizes all available food from the countryside, and waits. A boat evacuating a few Europeans from the city is attacked by the Madhi's forces and destroyed. When the citizens begin to despair of the existence of a relief force, many leave the town. A relief force is being sent but moving slowly. The Madhi offers Gordon a chance to leave the city, but he refuses. On January 26, 1885, the Madhi's army attacks Khartoum and Gordon is killed (1:59:59 to 2:07:12). The relief force reaches Khartoum two days later.

Interesting bio. Presents both Gordon and the Madhi as mystics. The action sequences are good.

Awards: *Academy Award Nomination*: Best Original Screenplay
Source: Dupuy, R. Ernest, and Dupuy, Trevor N. *The Encyclopedia of Military History from 3500 B.C. to the Present*. New York: Harper & Row, 1977. This book at page 848 gives day of the assault.
Alternate Film: *The Dead Zone*

27

DRIVING MISS DAISY

Year: 1989
Genre: Comedy/Drama
Run Time: 1 hour 39 minutes
Availability: Blu-ray and DVD (Warner Home Video)
Director: Bruce Beresford; **Screenplay**: Alfred Uhry, based on his play
Cast: Jessica Tandy (Miss Daisy), Morgan Freeman (Hoke), Dan Aykroyd (Boolie), Esther Rolle (Idella)

In 1948 Atlanta widow Daisy Werthern totals her car and her son forces her to get a chauffeur. Her son hires Hoke, an older African American man, to drive her. She tries to ignore Hoke, but finally comes to accept him and even teaches him how to read. Her synagogue is bombed and Miss Daisy realizes that prejudice affects her as well. When Miss Daisy is invited to a dinner honoring Dr. Martin Luther King Jr. on January 27, 1964, her son can't attend, but she only invites Hoke on the way to the dinner, upsetting him (1:18:15 to 1:22:30). In 1971 Miss Daisy has a stroke and she tells Hoke he's her best friend. Miss Daisy goes to a nursing home, where her son and Hoke visit her.

A sweet film. Miss Daisy and Hoke are cantankerous and their interaction makes this a funny movie. Serious issues such as prejudice and aging are touched on also.

Awards: *Academy Award Wins*: Best Picture, Best Actress (Jessica Tandy), Best Makeup, and Best Adapted Screenplay. *Academy Award Nominations*: Best Actor (Morgan Freeman), Best Supporting Actor (Dan Aykroyd), Best Art Direction, Best Costume Design, and Best Film Editing. *Golden Globe Wins*: Best Performance by an Actress in a Motion Picture–Comedy or Musical (Tandy), Best Performance by an Actor in a Motion Picture–Comedy or Musical (Freeman), and Best Motion Picture–Comedy or Musical

Source: Garrow, David J. *Bearing the Cross*. New York: William Morrow, 1986. This book at page 381 gives the date of the banquet.

Alternate Film: *Dreamchild*

28
ARGO
Year: 2012
Genre: Drama
Run Time: 2 hours
Date Revealed in Film: 1:27:14
Availability: Blu-ray and DVD (Warner Home Video)
Director: Ben Affleck; **Screenplay:** Chris Terrio, based on Tony Mendez's
  book *The Master of Disguise* and a *Wired* magazine story, "The Great Es-
  cape" by Joshuah Bearman
Cast: Ben Affleck (Tony Mendez), Bryan Cranston (Jack O'Donnell), Alan
  Arkin (Lester Siegel), John Goodman (John Chambers), Victor Garber
  (Ken Taylor), Kyle Chandler (Hamilton Jordan), Bob Gunton (Cyrus
  Vance)

In November 1979, Iranian militants storm the American embassy in Tehran
demanding the return of the exiled Shah. Six employees escape and go to the
home of the Canadian ambassador, Ken Taylor. Tony Mendez of the CIA
goes to a State Department meeting to devise a plan to get the six out, but
all options seem bad. Tony gets the idea to document the six as Canadian
members of a film crew who are in Iran scouting locations for a science fiction
movie. John Chambers, a Hollywood makeup artist who had worked for the
CIA, gets producer Lester Siegel to set up a fake film company, find a script,
and publicize the movie.

Mendez flies to Iran and gives the six their cover stories. The six survive
a trip to the Grand Bazaar. Then Mendez is told the plan has been canceled
to avoid derailing a planned military rescue operation, but he decides to go
ahead anyway and they reach the airport on January 28, 1980 (1:22:57 to
1:44:46). However, their troubles are just beginning.

An exciting film. Many details were altered for this movie, mainly to increase the dramatic suspense. Does an excellent job of re-creating the look
and feel of the era.

Awards: *Academy Award Wins:* Best Picture, Best Adapted Screenplay, and
  Best Film Editing. *Academy Award Nominations:* Best Supporting Actor
  (Alan Arkin), Best Sound Editing, Best Sound Mixing, and Best Original
  Score. *Golden Globe Wins:* Best Motion Picture–Drama and Best Director–
  Motion Picture. *Golden Globe Nominations:* Best Performance by an Actor

in a Supporting Role in a Motion Picture (Arkin), Best Screenplay–Motion
Picture, and Best Original Score–Motion Picture
Alternate Film: *W*

29

THE GREAT RAID

Year: 2005
Genre: War
Run Time: 2 hours 12 minutes
Date Revealed in Film: 39:00
Availability: Blu-ray and DVD (Miramax)
Director: John Dahl; **Screenplay**: Carlo Bernard and Doug Miro, based on
    William B. Breuer's book *The Great Raid on Cabanatuan*, with additional
    material from Hampton Sides's book *Ghost Soldiers*
Cast: Benjamin Bratt (Lt. Col. Henry Mucci), James Franco (Capt. Robert
    Prince), Sam Worthington (Pfc. Lucas), Robert Mammone (Capt. Fisher),
    Joseph Fiennes (Maj. Gibson), Connie Nielsen (Margaret Utinsky), Dale
    Dye (Lt. Gen. Walter Krueger)
The Americans have landed on Luzon, and the Japanese plan on killing all
POWs. In January 1945, the rangers are ordered to free the POWs at Camp
Cabanatuan. Margaret, a former army nurse, lives in Manila and pretends to
be Lithuanian so the Japanese will leave her alone. She works with the underground to get medicines, especially quinine, to the POWs. The rangers move
out and spend the day dodging Japanese forces. That same day, the army
guards abandon the camp, but the Kemepiti (Japanese Secret Police) arrive
and take over the camp. In the camp things are getting tense. The senior officer, Gibson, refuses quinine, ordering it given to others. He is in love with
Margaret, whom he had known before the war.
    On January 29, 1945, in Manila, a collaborator identifies some members
of the underground and they are executed. The rangers link up with Filipino
guerillas and agree to delay the attack for one night so transport can be arranged for the POWs. Margaret is betrayed to the Japanese, but released after
two of her comrades are shot (38:55 to 1:05:03). The rangers and guerillas
attack the camp the next day and after heavy combat liberate it. However,
during the rescue Gibson dies of malaria.

A movie based on fact. The raid did free over five hundred American POWs. The movie relates that they felt "abandoned" by the United States adopting a Germany-first policy. This is revisionist nonsense. In May 1942, when Corregidor fell, there was nothing the United States could have done to prevent it, even if it had adopted a "Japan-first" policy. Japanese military supremacy was absolute in the area at that moment.

Alternate Film: *The Company You Keep*

30

GANDHI

Year: 1982
Genre: Biography
Run Time: 3 hours 11 minutes
Date Revealed in Film: 01:35
Availability: Blu-ray (Sony Pictures), DVD (Columbia/TriStar)
Director: Richard Attenborough; **Screenplay**: John Briley
Cast: Ben Kingsley (Mohandas Gandhi), Candace Bergen (Margaret Bourke-White), Edward Fox (Reginald Dyer), John Gielgud (Baron Irwin), Trevor Howard (Judge Broomfield), Martin Sheen (Vince Walker), Ian Charleson (Rev. Andrews), Daniel Day-Lewis (Colin)

On January 30, 1949 (01:35 to 03:57), Gandhi is assassinated. We then flash back to 1893 when Gandhi, then a barrister living in Natal, is thrown off a train because he is an Indian. He organizes a campaign of nonviolent resistance to discrimination. He returns to India as a hero and continues a campaign of nonviolent resistance to British rule there, getting arrested many times by the British. Gandhi opposes the partition of India but works for peace between India and Pakistan. This angers extremists on both sides, leading to his death by assassination (2:59:19 to 3:02:23).

A good film, but it is an homage rather than a completely honest and thorough assessment. The film mainly sticks to the actual history and doesn't create events.

Awards: *Academy Award Wins*: Best Picture, Best Actor (Ben Kingsley), Best Director, Best Art Direction, Best Cinematography, Best Costume Design, Best Film Editing, and Best Original Screenplay. *Academy Award Nominations*: Best Makeup, Best Original Music Score, and Best Sound. *Golden Globe Wins*: Best Foreign Film, Best Director–Motion Picture, Best Actor

in a Motion Picture–Drama (Ben Kingsley), Best New Star of the Year in a Motion Picture–Male (Kingsley), and Best Screenplay–Motion Picture
Alternate Film: *Full Metal Jacket*

31

LINCOLN

Year: 2012
Genre: Historical Drama
Run Time: 2 hours 30 minutes
Date Revealed in Film: 1:46:38
Availability: Blu-ray (Disney/Buena Vista), DVD (DreamWorks)
Director: Steven Spielberg; **Screenplay**: Tony Kushner, based on Doris Kearns Goodwin's book *Team of Rivals: The Political Genius of Abraham Lincoln*
Cast: Daniel Day-Lewis (President Abraham Lincoln), Sally Field (First Lady Mary Todd Lincoln), Joseph Gordon-Levitt (Robert Todd Lincoln), David Strathairn (Secretary of State William H. Seward), Tommy Lee Jones (Congressman Thaddeus Stevens)

President Abraham Lincoln uses political horse trading to get the votes needed to pass the Thirteenth Amendment abolishing slavery, both by offering government jobs to defeated lame-duck Democratic congressmen and letting the conservative wing of the Republican Party send a representative to the Confederacy to start talks to end the war. Abolitionist Republicans think a vote now is part of a plot to end the war without abolishing slavery. Lincoln agrees to meet with the delegates sent by the Confederate government. Thaddeus Stevens, an abolitionist, switches his support to the amendment. On January 31, 1865 (1:46:31 to 2:05:00), the amendment comes up for a vote. The Democrats say a vote is unnecessary, as Confederate delegates are in the city with a peace offer. Lincoln gives a politician's answer to the question to force a vote.

A film showing that, among his other attributes, Lincoln was a consummate politician.

Awards: *Academy Award Wins*: Best Actor (Daniel Day-Lewis) and Best Production Design. *Academy Award Nominations*: Best Picture, Best Director, Best Supporting Actor (Tommy Lee Jones), Best Supporting Actress (Sally Field), Best Adapted Screenplay, Best Original Score, Best Sound Mixing, Best Cinematography, Best Costume Design, and Best Film Editing
Alternate Film: *The Victors*

February

1

CHARLIE AND THE CHOCOLATE FACTORY

Year: 2005
Genre: Comedy
Run Time: 1 hour 55 minutes
Date Revealed in Film: 31:13
Availability: Blu-ray and DVD (Warner Home Video)
Director: Tim Burton; **Screenplay**: John August, based on Roald Dahl's book
Cast: Johnny Depp (Willie Wonka), Freddie Highmore (Charlie Bucket), Helena Bonham Carter (Mrs. Bucket), Annasophia Robb (Violet Beauregarde), Christopher Lee (Wilbur Wonka), David Kelly (Grandpa Joe), Missi Pyle (Mrs. Beauregarde)

When the mysterious Willie Wonka announces a contest for five children to win a tour of his candy factory, the winners are poor Charlie Bucket and four other obnoxious children. During the tour on February 1, 2005 (from 33:01 to 1:40:43), all the children, except Charlie, defy Wonka's instructions and suffer the consequences, as explained by the Oompa-Loompas, the midget workers, in their songs. However, getting a tour of the factory was not the real purpose of the contest. Wonka has to face the demons of his past to reach a resolution.

This is one of the very few movies where I can't decide whether I like the original or the remake better. In this one Charlie seems to be a more well-rounded character, and Wonka to be zanier. I like the special effects and songs in both.

Awards: *Academy Award Nomination*: Best Costume Design. *Golden Globe Nomination*: Best Performance by an Actor in a Motion Picture–Comedy or Musical (Johnny Depp)

Alternate Film: *Swiss Family Robinson*

2

GROUNDHOG DAY

Year: 1993
Genre: Comedy/Drama
Run Time: 1 hour 41 minutes
Date Revealed in Film: 14:18
Availability: Blu-ray and DVD (Sony Pictures)
Director: Harold Ramis; **Screenplay**: Danny Rubin and Harold Ramis
Cast: Bill Murray (Phil Connors), Andie MacDowell (Rita Hanson), Chris Elliott (Larry), Stephen Tobolowsky (Ned Ryerson), Brian Doyle-Murray (Buster Green), Angela Paton (Mrs. Lanchester), Rick Ducommun (Gus), Rick Overton (Ralph)

Unliked (and unlikable) weatherman Phil Conners; his assistant, Rita; and Larry, their cameraman, travel from Pittsburgh to Punxsutawney to cover Groundhog Day on February 2, 1993 (07:24 to 1:34:38). A blizzard forces the crew to spend the night in the town. When Phil wakes up, every day is now February 2. Phil goes through an emotional roller coaster of repeating the same day over and over, while he tries to figure out how to get off this ride and win Rita's heart.

A sweet, funny movie about the power of a second chance.

Alternate Film: *Dragon: The Bruce Lee Story*

3

LA BAMBA

Year: 1987
Genre: Biography
Run Time: 1 hour 48 minutes
Availability: DVD (Sony Pictures), VHS (PCA/Columbia Pictures Home Video)

Director: Luis Valdez; **Screenplay:** Luis Valdez

Cast: Lou Diamond Phillips (Ritchie Valens), Esai Morales (Bob Morales), Rosanna DeSoto (Connie Valenzuela), Elizabeth Peña (Rosie Morales-Valenzuela), Danielle von Zerneck (Donna Ludwig), Joe Pantoliano (Bob Keane)

Ritchie Valens, a rock-n-roll-loving Chicano, and his family leave the migrant work camps in California and move to Los Angeles, where Ritchie works his way into performing rock and roll while trying to handle teenage love and family problems. Ritchie becomes a superstar, but then he goes on the "Winter Dance Party" tour with Buddy Holly and the "Big Bopper." When the bus breaks down in Clear Lake, Iowa, Holly hires a plane to fly them to the next tour stop. Ritchie wins the toss to get a seat on the plane that takes off in the early morning hours of February 3, 1959 (1:39:45 to 1:44:00).

A good, if somewhat fictionalized, biopic. Phillips is very good as Ritchie. The movie is almost as much about his brother, Bob. The music is great.

Awards: *Golden Globe Nomination*: Best Motion Picture–Drama

Source: Waterkeyn, Xavier. *Air and Space Disasters of the World.* London: New Holland Publishers, 2007. This book at page 212 gives the date of the crash.

Alternate Film: *Serpico*

4

PATTY HEARST

Year: 1988

Genre: Biography

Run Time: 1 hour 48 minutes

Date Revealed in Film: 00:35

Availability: DVD (Metro-Goldwyn-Mayer), VHS (Media Home Entertainment)

Director: Paul Schrader; **Screenplay:** Nicholas Kazan, based on the Patricia Hearst and Alvin Moscow's book, *Every Secret Thing*

Cast: Natasha Richardson (Patricia Hearst), William Forsythe (Teko), Ving Rhames (Cinque), Frances Fisher (Yolanda), Jodi Long (Wendy Yoshimura), Olivia Barash (Fahizah), Dana Delany (Gelina), Marek Johnson (Zoya), Kitty Swink (Gabi)

Patty Hearst is kidnapped by the SLA on February 4, 1974 (00:16 to 7:30). She's locked in a closet that's only opened so the kidnappers can spout revolutionary nonsense or threats. Efforts to secure her release don't satisfy the SLA. Eventually Patty joins the SLA, calling herself Tanya, and takes part in a bank robbery. Finally, when she's arrested, she states her profession as "urban guerilla."

An interesting biopic. Richardson plays Patty as a confused young woman who in some ways had great inner strength but in others didn't know herself. Holds your interest.

Alternate Film: *The Social Network*

5

GHOSTS OF MISSISSIPPI

Year: 1996
Genre: Drama
Run Time: 2 hours 10 minutes
Availability: DVD (Warner Home Video), VHS (Columbia TriStar Home Video)
Director: Rob Reiner; **Screenplay**: Lewis Colick
Cast: Alec Baldwin (Bobby DeLaughter), Whoopi Goldberg (Myrlie Evers-Williams), James Woods (Byron De La Beckwith), Virginia Madsen (Dixie DeLaughter), Susanna Thompson (Peggy Lloyd), Craig T. Nelson (Ed Peters), Lucas Black (Burt DeLaughter)

Medgar Evers is assassinated. Byron De La Beckwith is arrested and charged with the murder, but there are two mistrials. Twenty-five years later Evers's widow wants the case reopened. The district attorney, Bobby DeLaughter, reluctantly agrees, even though his wife leaves him. A former undercover FBI agent who infiltrated the KKK heard Beckwith confess to shooting Evers and agrees to testify. Beckwith is put on trial, with the verdict coming down on February 5, 1994 (2:01:38 to 2:05:49).

A good police procedural film. It develops DeLaughter as a person, not just a prosecutor. James Woods plays Beckwith as an arrogant man who thinks he is above the law.

Awards: *Academy Award Nominations*: Best Supporting Actor (James Woods) and Best Makeup. *Golden Globe Nomination*: Best Performance by an Actor in a Supporting Role (Woods)

Source: Vollers, Margaret. *Ghosts of Mississippi*. New York: Little, Brown & Co., 1995. This book at page 377 gives the date of the verdict.
Alternate Film: *A Child's Wish*

6
THE ANDROMEDA STRAIN
Year: 1971
Genre: Science Fiction
Run Time: 2 hours 10 minutes
Date Revealed in Film: 5:25
Availability: DVD and VHS (Universal Pictures)
Director: Robert Wise; **Screenplay**: Nelson Gidding, based on Michael Crichton's novel
Cast: Arthur Hill (Dr. Jeremy Stone), David Wayne (Dr. Charles Dutton), James Olson (Dr. Mark Hall), Kate Reid (Dr. Ruth Leavitt), Paula Kelly (Karen Anson), George Mitchell (Peter Jackson), Ramon Bieri (Major Manchek), Peter Hobbs (General Sparks)

A two-man team enters the tiny town of Piedmont, New Mexico, to recover the *Scoop VII* satellite that crashed near there. They find everyone dead and order an alert. Jeremy Stone, Ruth Leavitt, Mark Hall, and Charles Dutton are the science team that has been selected to deal with a problem like this. Stone and Hall fly to Piedmont on February 6, 1971, and confirm everyone is dead from an alien germ, brought back by *Scoop VII*, that causes instant blood clotting in the whole body. They find two survivors, an old man and a baby, and take them to their base, "Wildfire." Hall is to decide, in case the organism escapes, whether to cancel an automatic detonation of an atomic bomb self-destruct system (16:15 to 54:43). They discover how the germ infects the body and isolate it. But when a seal breaks, the countdown to atomic self-destruct is activated, leading to a nail-biting climax.

Almost presented as a docudrama. Doesn't talk down to the audience, but keeps it entertaining. A great scientific mystery film.
Awards: *Academy Award Nominations*: Best Art Direction and Best Film Editing. *Golden Globe Nomination*: Best Original Score
Alternate Film: *Klimt*

7

THE LIFE OF EMILE ZOLA

Year: 1937
Genre: Biography
Run Time: 1 hour 56 minutes
Availability: DVD (Warner Home Video), VHS (MGM/UA Home Video)
Director: William Dieterle; **Screenplay**: Norman Reilly Raine, Heinz Herald, and Geza Herczeg, based on Matthew Josephson's book, *Zola and His Time*
Cast: Paul Muni (Emile Zola), Gale Sondergaard (Lucie Dreyfus), Joseph Schildkraut (Alfred Dreyfus), Gloria Holden (Alexandrine Zola), Donald Crisp (Maitre Labori), Erin O'Brien-Moore (Nana), John Litel (Charpentier), Morris Carnovsky (Anatole France)

Idealistic Emile Zola is the writer of a series of popular but controversial novels in nineteenth-century France. Col. Dreyfus, a Jewish French officer, is found guilty of betraying military secrets and sent to Devil's Island. When it is learned that Col. Esterhazy is actually the guilty officer, the high command does nothing, as reversing Dreyfus's conviction would embarrass the army. Mrs. Dreyfus persuades Zola to help, and he becomes convinced Dreyfus is innocent. Zola writes an open letter saying the government is involved in a cover-up. He is brought to trial for criminal libel on February 7, 1898 (1:09:05 to 1:11:36), in a kangaroo court and convicted. However, others continue to fight for the truth.

In my opinion Zola is a great Frenchman. He was a tireless pursuer of the truth. He is to be praised even more for doing it in this case where he had no personal interest.

Awards: *Academy Award Wins*: Best Picture, Best Supporting Actor (Joseph Schildkraut), and Best Screenplay. *Academy Award Nominations*: Best Actor (Paul Muni), Best Art Direction, Best Director, Best Assistant Director, Best Score, Best Sound, and Best Screenplay
Source: Begley, Louis. *Why the Dreyfus Affair Matters*. New Haven, CT: Yale University Press, 2009. This book at page 140 gives the trial's start date.
Alternate Film: *Death on the Nile* (1978)

8

LOVE AFFAIR

Year: 1995
Genre: Romantic Drama
Run Time: 1 hour 48 minutes
Date Revealed in Film: 53:57–54:08
Availability: DVD and VHS (Warner Home Video)
Director: Glenn Gordon Caron; **Screenplay:** Robert Towne and Warren Beatty
Cast: Warren Beatty (Mike Gambril), Annette Bening (Terry McKay), Katharine Hepburn (Ginny), Garry Shandling (Kip DeMay), Chloe Webb (Tina Wilson), Pierce Brosnan (Ken Allen), Kate Capshaw (Lynn Weaver)

A womanizing ex-quarterback, Mike Gambril, and singer Terry McKay meet on a flight to Australia. When the plane has to make a forced landing in a storm, they sail together on a Russian cruise liner. They go to see Gambril's aunt, then fly back to New York. As they arrive on February 8, 1995, they agree to meet at the top of the Empire State Building in three months if they can, as they have fallen in love with each other (50:47 to 58:16). Mike and Terry both break it off with their respective fiancées. Mike tries to get his life in order, becomes the football coach at a small college and takes up painting again. Terry becomes a music teacher at an elementary school. On the day of the rendezvous, she is paralyzed from the waist down in an accident, while Mike waits at the top of the Empire State Building all evening. Mike gives the painting he was going to give Terry to a restaurant. Months pass and Mike sees her (seated) at a concert. Mike finally gets up the courage to pay Terry a visit, which will reveal a great deal to both of them.

This film is not as bad as some of the critics would have you believe. It is actually a decent romantic drama. Notable as Katharine Hepburn's last film.
Alternate Film: *Elizabeth: The Golden Age*

9

I WANNA HOLD YOUR HAND

Year: 1978
Genre: Comedy
Run Time: 1 hour 44 minutes
Availability: DVD (Universal Studios), VHS (Warner Home Video)

Director: Robert Zemekis; **Screenplay**: Bob Gale and Robert Zemekis

Cast: Nancy Allen (Pam Mitchell), Bobby Di Cicco (Tony Smerko), Marc McClure (Larry Dubois), Susan Kendall Newman (Janis Goldman), Theresa Saldana (Grace Corrigan), Wendie Jo Sperber (Rosie Petrofsky), Eddie Deezen (Richard "Ringo" Klaus)

Rosie, Pam, Janet, and Grace are four friends in Maplewood, New Jersey. They recruit shy Larry Dubois, the local undertaker's son, to get a limo to take them to the Beatles' appearance on the *Ed Sullivan Show*. On the morning of February 9, 1964, they pull up at the hotel where the Beatles are staying and Grace, Rosie, and Pam sneak in. Grace and Rosie get caught, but Pam is able to get into the Beatles' suite. Janet is caught too, and she goes to CBS studios, where a guard tells her that for $50 he will let her in backstage during the show so she can get exclusive photos of the band. All the girls pursue various schemes to try and get tickets to the show. Rosie wins tickets on a radio call-in show. Pam is caught, but the Beatles' roadie Neil Aspinell gives her a ticket to see the show. Larry parks the limo beside CBS in an alley and is almost arrested for improper parking and driving without a license. Grace uses her $50 to bribe the cop into letting him go, but now she can't get backstage and get her photos. However, a case of mistaken identity saves the day (17:08 to 1:37:12).

A funny movie. A behind-the-scenes paean to Beatlemania. The music is great!

Source: Gould, Jonathan. *Can't Buy Me Love*. New York: Harmony Books, 2007. This book at page 3 gives the date of their appearance.

Alternate Film: *Mr. Saturday Night*

10

GRAN TORINO

Year: 2008

Genre: Drama

Run Time: 1 hour 56 minutes

Date Revealed in Film: 1:02:37

Availability: Blu-ray and DVD (Warner Home Video)

Director: Clint Eastwood; **Screenplay**: Nick Schenk

Cast: Clint Eastwood (Walt Kowalski), Bee Vang (Thao Vang Lor), Ahney Her (Sue Lor), Christopher Carley (Father Janovich), Doua Moua (Fong

"Spider"), Choua Kue (Youa), Brian Howe (Steve Kowalski), Brian Haley
(Mitch Kowalski)

Crabby widower Walt Kowalski is a Korean War veteran and former auto-
worker who does not relate to his family or his Asian immigrant neighbors.
Thao Vang Lor, a Hmong who lives next door, tries to steal Walt's pride and
joy, his 1972 Ford Gran Torino, as part of a gang initiation. When he fails, the
gang tries to beat him up, but Walt stops them. This makes Walt a hero to the
Hmong, which annoys him, as the community keeps bringing him gifts. On
an unseasonably warm February 10, 2008 (38:17 to 53:47), after Walt's family
leaves, Thao's sister Sue invites Walt to celebrate his birthday with her family. Later, Thao works for Walt to make amends, and Walt takes an interest
in Thao by getting him a job; he even allows him to use the Gran Torino on
a date. Then the gang does a drive-by shooting on the Lors' house and they
beat and rape Sue. This leads to a surprising final confrontation between Walt
and the gang.

Eastwood gives a fantastic performance as the cranky, racist Walt. This
film has a well-thought-out plot. Unbelievable that this movie did not get one
Oscar nomination.

Awards: *Golden Globe Nomination*: Best Original Song
Alternate Film: *Mary, Queen of Scots*

11

THE SONG OF BERNADETTE

Year: 1943
Genre: Drama
Run Time: 2 hours 36 minutes
Date Revealed in Film: 1:40
Availability: Blu-ray (Twilight Time), DVD (Twentieth Century Fox Home
Video)
Director: Henry King; **Screenplay**: George Seaton, based on the Franz Werfel
novel
Cast: Jennifer Jones (Bernadette), Charles Bickford (Father Peyramale),
Gladys Cooper (Sister Marie Therese Vauzous), Anne Revere (Louise Sou-
birous), Vincent Price (Vital Dutour), Lee J. Cobb (Dr. Dozous), Patricia
Morison (Empress Eugenie)

On February 11, 1858, Bernadette, a not very religious French peasant girl, has a vision of a lady, but her family thinks she made it up (1:42 to 28:13). Local politicians and the church try to persuade her to forget about it. When Bernadette gets a message from the lady that a chapel should be built, she begins to dig a foundation, causing a spring to appear. The villagers build a pool, and the water miraculously heals a crippled infant. The villagers say the lady is the Virgin Mary. The government closes the grotto, but the church has decided to support Bernadette. Then the water heals the son of the emperor and the grotto is reopened. Bernadette goes to a convent, where she suffers from a painful illness for years and finally dies.

A good 1940s biopic. Sticks mainly with the facts. Interesting for its discussion of the relationship between faith and science.

Awards: *Academy Award Wins*: Best Actress (Jennifer Jones), Best Art Direction, Best Cinematography, and Best Original Music Score. *Academy Award Nominations*: Best Supporting Actor (Charles Bickford), Best Actress in a Supporting Role (Gladys Cooper and Anne Revere), Best Director, Best Film Editing, Best Picture, Best Sound, and Best Screenplay. *Golden Globe Wins*: Best Motion Picture–Drama, Best Motion Picture Actress (Jones), and Best Director

Alternate Film: *The Color of Freedom*

12

A MIGHTY HEART

Year: 2007
Genre: Drama
Run Time: 1 hour 48 minutes
Availability: Blu-ray (Warner Home Video), DVD (Paramount)
Director: Michael Winterbottom; **Screenplay**: John Orloff, based on Mariane Pearl's memoir
Cast: Dan Futterman (Daniel Pearl), Angelina Jolie (Mariane Pearl), Will Patton (Special Agent Randall Bennett), Archie Panjabi (Asra Nomani), Irfan Khan (Mir Zubair Mahmood), Alyy Khan (Ahmed Omar Saeed Sheikh), Daniel O'Hare (John Bussey)

Wall Street Journal reporter Danny Pearl goes to a meeting in Karachi, Pakistan, with Sheik Mubarak Ali Gilani and is kidnapped by Islamic militants.

Pearl's wife, the Pakistani police, and the FBI and Diplomatic Security Service hunt for him. His wife reflects on her life with Danny. An article appears that the *Wall Street Journal* turned over files to the CIA about the "Shoebomber," Richard Reed. Omar Saeed Sheikh, who was responsible for the kidnapping, turns himself in to the secret police and is then "arrested" by the regular police on February 12, 2002 (1:16:04 to 1:18:39). A tape showing Danny's murder is delivered and his body is found. His wife gives birth to their son.

A tragic story. A film that may be hard to watch, but you should.

Awards: *Golden Globe Nomination*: Best Performance by an Actress in a Motion Picture–Drama (Angelina Jolie)

Source: *The New York Times*, February 13, 2002, p. A15. A story by Douglas Jehl bylined "Islamabad, February 12," reports that Omar Saeed was arrested "today."

Alternate Film: *Black Swan*

13
ETERNAL SUNSHINE OF THE SPOTLESS MIND

Year: 2004
Genre: Science Fiction/Romance
Run Time: 1 hour 43 minutes
Date Revealed in Film: 20:08
Availability: Blu-ray and DVD (Universal Studios)
Director: Michel Gondry; **Screenplay**: Charlie Kaufman
Cast: Jim Carrey (Joel Barish), Kate Winslet (Clementine Kruczynski), Kirsten Dunst (Mary Svevo), Mark Ruffalo (Stan Fink), Elijah Wood (Patrick), Tom Wilkinson (Dr. Howard Mierzwiak), Jane Adams (Carrie), David Cross (Rob)

Joel and Clementine were lovers who lived together for two years. After a huge fight Clem goes to Lacuna, Inc., and has all memory of Joel "erased" from her mind. Joel finds out about this when he goes to give her an early Valentine's present and she appears not to know him. Joel decides to have Clem "erased" from his memory on February 13, 2004 (17:37 to 1:31:37). When he starts reliving memories of his relationship in reverse order he realizes he doesn't want to forget her. He and the memory of Clem try to hide her in Joel's other memories, where she can't be found and erased, but she finally is completely erased. On Valentine's Day Joel wakes up with no memory of Clem, but meets her again and they become lovers again. Then they get a package in the mail that may change everything.

A very unique film. Explores the relationship of love and memory. Very interesting cinematography.

Awards: *Academy Award Win*: Best Original Screenplay. *Academy Award Nomination*: Best Actress (Kate Winslet). *Golden Globe Nominations*: Best Performance by an Actor in a Motion Picture–Comedy or Musical (Jim Carrey), Best Performance by an Actress in a Motion Picture–Comedy or Musical (Kate Winslet), Best Screenplay–Motion Picture, and Best Motion Picture–Comedy or Musical

Alternate Film: *Young Bess*

14

SLEEPLESS IN SEATTLE

Year: 1993

Genre: Romance

Run Time: 1 hour 45 minutes

Date Revealed in Film: 1:19:05

Availability: Blu-ray (Sony Pictures), DVD (Columbia/TriStar)

Director: Nora Ephron; **Screenplay**: Jeff Arch, Nora Ephron, and David Ward

Cast: Tom Hanks (Sam Baldwin), Meg Ryan (Annie Reed), Bill Pullman (Walter), Rosie O'Donnell (Becky), Gaby Hoffmann (Jessica), Victor Garber (Greg), Ross Malinger (Jonah Baldwin), Rita Wilson (Suzy), Barbara Garrick (Victoria)

Jonah Baldwin calls a national radio talk show and gets his father, Sam, to talk about how much he misses his deceased wife, and thousands of women send him letters. One comes from Annie Reed, an engaged journalist from Baltimore. Jonah likes Annie's letter, but his father won't agree to meet her on the top of the Empire State Building on Valentine's Day. Sam begins dating Victoria, whom Jonah cannot stand. Jonah sends a letter in his father's name to Annie agreeing to the meeting. With the help of a friend whose mother is a travel agent, Jonah flies to New York and goes to the Empire State Building. Sam discovers this and follows him. Meanwhile, Annie finally confronts her feelings and heads to an unexpected encounter on top of the Empire State Building.

A great and unpredictable romance movie. More a story of their private struggles to accept the possibility of love and not their romance.

Awards: *Academy Award Nominations*: Best Original Song and Best Original Screenplay. *Golden Globe Nominations*: Best Motion Picture–Comedy or Musical, Best Performance by an Actor in a Motion Picture–Comedy or Musical (Tom Hanks), and Best Performance by an Actress in a Motion Picture–Comedy or Musical (Meg Ryan)

Alternate Film: *Picnic at Hanging Rock*

15

SOME LIKE IT HOT

Year: 1959
Genre: Comedy
Run Time: 2 hours
Date Revealed in Film: 17:05
Availability: Blu-ray and DVD (Metro-Goldwyn-Mayer)
Director: Billy Wilder; **Screenplay**: Billy Wilder and I. A. L. Diamond, suggested by a story by Robert Thoeren and Michael Logan
Cast: Marilyn Monroe ("Sugar" Kane Kowalczyk), Jack Lemmon (Jerry/"Daphne"), Tony Curtis (Joe/"Josephine"/"Junior"), Pat O'Brien (Detective Mulligan), Edward G. Robinson Jr. (Johnny Paradise), Joe E. Brown (Osgood Fielding III)

Jerry and Joe witness the St. Valentine's Day massacre. To avoid the Mob, they disguise themselves as women, join an all-girl band, and leave town. They arrive in Florida on February 15, 1929. Both men fall for "Sugar" Kane, the band's lead vocalist. In Florida Joe woos Sugar by also pretending to be a millionaire, while an actual millionaire, Osgood, falls for Jerry's alter ego, "Daphne," and proposes. Jerry accepts, thinking he can extort cash out of him after their "wedding." The Mob arrives and chaos ensues, but Joe, Jerry, Sugar, and Osgood reach Osgood's yacht. Joe tells Sugar who he really is, but she agrees to marry him anyway. Osgood rejects all of Daphne's reasons for breaking their engagement, even after Jerry has revealed he's a man, replying, "Well nobody's perfect" (37:12 to 1:29:03).

A hilarious film. Almost goes over the top at times. If nothing else, it's an excuse to look at Marilyn Monroe for two hours.

Awards: *Academy Award Win*: Best Costume Design–Black-and-White. *Academy Award Nominations*: Best Actor (Jack Lemmon), Best Art Direction, Best Cinematography–Black-and-White, Best Director, and Best Adapted Screenplay. *Golden Globe Wins*: Best Motion Picture–Comedy, Best Motion Picture Actress–Musical or Comedy (Marilyn Monroe), and Best Motion Picture Actor–Musical or Comedy (Lemmon)

Alternate Film: *Conspiracy*

16

CORALINE

Year: 2009

Genre: Fantasy

Run Time: 1 hour 40 minutes

Date Revealed in Film: 41:18

Availability: Blu-ray and DVD (Universal Studios)

Director: Henry Selick; **Screenplay**: Henry Selick, based on Neil Gaiman's novella

Voice Cast: Dakota Fanning (Coraline Jones), Teri Hatcher (Mel Jones), John Hodgman (Charlie Jones), Keith David (the cat), Robert Bailey Jr. (Wybie Lovat), Jennifer Saunders (Miss Spink), Dawn French (Miss Forcible), Ian McShane (Mr. Bobinsky)

Coraline Jones and her self-absorbed parents move to the Pink Palace Apartments, where she goes through a tunnel behind a door that has been wallpapered over to a near duplicate world inhabited by her "other" mother and father, who have buttons for eyes. They are nicer to Coraline than her real parents are. Coraline is warned not to go through the door again, but she does anyway. Coraline and her mom visit the President's Day sale on February 16, 2009, and argue about what to buy (40:38 to 44:07). In the "other" world Coraline is told she can stay forever if she has buttons sewn in her eyes. She refuses, and is imprisoned by the "other mother." Coraline escapes, but finds that her parents have vanished. She goes back and challenges the "other mother." If she finds the eyes of the three kids who were trapped with her, they all can leave; otherwise, Coraline will stay. She uses a ring given to her by

Misses Spink and Forcible to find the eyes. Coraline escapes with her parents. However, the other mother forces a final confrontation with Coraline.

A quirky story. The 3D graphics are very good, creating a world that looks and feels real. This film is for both kids and adults. Parents should watch it to be reminded not to act like Coraline's parents, while kids need to be reminded to be careful what you wish for, as you might get it!

Awards: *Academy Award Nomination*: Best Animated Feature Film of the Year. *Golden Globe Nomination*: Best Animated Feature Film

Alternate Film: *The Boys from Brazil*

17
THREE CAME HOME

Year: 1950

Genre: Biographical Drama

Run Time: 1 hour 46 minutes

Date Revealed in Film: 1:17:44

Availability: DVD (VCI), VHS (Madacy Video)

Director: Jean Negulesco; **Screenplay**: Nunnally Johnson, based on Agnes Newton Keith's memoirs

Cast: Claudette Colbert (Agnes Newton Keith), Patric Knowles (Harry Keith), Florence Desmond (Betty Sommers), Sessue Hayakawa (Colonel Suga), Sylvia Andrew (Henrietta), Mark Keuning (George Keith), Phyllis Morris (Sister Rose)

Agnes Keith is living with her husband, Harry, and young son, George, in British North Borneo in 1941. The Japanese arrive and occupy the country, and for a while things continue as almost normal. Then the Europeans are sent to separate camps, one for men and the other for women and children. One night, even though she is very sick with malaria, Agnes sneaks out of the camp to try and meet with her husband and just escapes being caught and punished. Later the women and children are moved to another camp far away. When some Australian POWs sneak up outside the fence so they can just talk to some women, they are discovered by the Japanese and killed. Then on February 17, 1945, a Japanese guard attacks Agnes (1:07:18 to 1:12:21). Although Col. Suga believes her report, other officers try to torture her into renouncing her accusation. Since this would leave her open to the capital charge of falsely accusing a Japanese soldier, she refuses to sign. Eventually, the Japanese allow her to drop the accusation without saying it was false. At the end of the war, George and two other children go with Col. Suga to his house, where he gives them a meal, even though Suga believes his family was killed in the atomic bombing of Hiroshima. One morning the internees awake to find the guards have abandoned the camp.

This is an exciting yet heartfelt film. A little gem that is well worth watching.

Alternate Film: *Days of Thunder*

18

BREACH

Year: 2007
Genre: Drama
Run Time: 1 hour 50 minutes
Date Revealed in Film: 1:32:15
Availability: DVD (Universal Studios)
Director: Billy Ray; **Screenplay**: Billy Ray, William Rotko, and Adam Mazer
Cast: Chris Cooper (Robert Hanssen), Ryan Phillippe (Eric O'Neill), Laura
    Linney (Kate Burroughs), Caroline Dhavernas (Juliana O'Neill), Dennis
    Haysbert (Dean Plesac), Gary Cole (Rich Garces), Kathleen Quinlan (Bon-
    nie Hanssen), Bruce Davison (John O'Neill)
Eric O'Neill is an FBI employee who is assigned as assistant to Robert Hanssen so that he can spy on him. He eventually learns this is because it is feared Hanssen is a spy. Hanssen becomes friends with O'Neill and his wife, and O'Neill grows to admire Hanssen. In the effort to catch Hanssen the FBI plants bugs in his car, but Hanssen becomes suspicious and signals the Russians that he won't pass them any more information. O'Neill reassures Hanssen that he is not being followed by anybody, so Hanssen makes one last dead drop of classified material and is arrested on February 18, 2001 (1:32:21 to 1:40:16). Afterward O'Neill leaves the agency.

A compelling true story of espionage. It is also a character study of both Hanssen and O'Neill. Slightly deviates from the real facts, but interesting in that it points out errors made by the FBI in this case and doesn't paint the bureau in a very good light.

Alternate Film: *Hanna*

19
YOU'VE GOT MAIL
Year: 1998
Genre: Romantic Comedy
Run Time: 1 hour 59 minutes
Date Revealed in Film: 1:10:34
Availability: Blu-ray and DVD (Warner Home Video)
Director: Nora Ephron; **Screenplay**: Nora Ephron and Delia Ephron
Cast: Tom Hanks (Joe "NY152" Fox), Meg Ryan (Kathleen "Shopgirl" Kelly), Parker Posey (Patricia Eden), Jean Stapleton (Birdie Conrad), Greg Kinnear (Frank Navasky), Steve Zahn (George Pappas), Dabney Coleman (Nelson Fox)

Kathleen Kelly, the owner of the kid's book store The Shop Around the Corner, and Joe Fox, executive for a big chain store, Fox Books, are both in relationships. In spite of this, the two begin corresponding by e-mail, Kathleen using the name "Shopgirl" and Joe as "NY152." They agree to never talk specifics about their lives. Kathleen learns Fox Books is opening a superstore near her, but doesn't think it will affect her. Joe meets Kathleen at her store and they like each other. The Fox Books store opens and immediately affects sales at The Shop Around the Corner. At a party Kathleen meets Joe again and is horrified to learn he is behind her business troubles. They try to avoid each other since they live in the same neighborhood, but Shopgirl asks NY152 for business advice. Joe advises war, so she organizes a boycott of Fox Books and gives interviews opposing them. Shopgirl and NY152 finally agree to meet. When Joe goes to their date, he discovers Shopgirl is Kathleen. Without letting on his identity as NY152, he goes in and they exchange spiteful remarks. The next day, February 19, 1998 (1:09:17 to 1:16:39), Kathleen's staff tries to convince her that NY152 is actually the rooftop killer. Shopgirl and NY152 make up about the missed date, and Kathleen decides to close the store. Kathleen and Joe both end their current relationships. Joe drops by to see Kathleen while she is sick and they have a friendly meeting. Shopgirl and NY152 finally agree to meet in person.

A decent romantic comedy. Joe is a bit of a cad, toying with her after he learns her identity, but she doesn't know his. Still all in all a very enjoyable film.

Awards: *Golden Globe Nomination*: Best Performance by an Actress in a Motion Picture–Comedy/Musical (Meg Ryan)
Alternate Film: *Flags of Our Fathers*

20

THE MATRIX

Year: 1999
Genre: Science Fiction
Run Time: 2 hours 16 minutes
Date Revealed in Film: 00:50
Availability: Blu-ray and DVD (Warner Home Video)
Directors: Andy Wachowski and Larry Wachowski; **Screenplay**: Andy Wachowski and Larry Wachowski
Cast: Keanu Reeves (Neo/Thomas Anderson), Laurence Fishburne (Morpheus), Carrie-Anne Moss (Trinity), Hugo Weaving (Agent Smith), Joe Pantoliano (Cypher), Julian Arahanga (Apoc), Anthony Ray Parker (Dozer), Marcus Chong (Tank)

Computer hacker Thomas Anderson, known as "Neo," meets Trinity, who tells him about Morpheus, who has been trying to answer the same questions about life as Neo. The next day, February 20, 1998, Thomas is late for work (11:57 to 32:27). In spite of help from Morpheus, Neo is arrested. The people arresting Neo offer a "deal," which he declines, and then implant a probe in him. He wakes up convinced it was a dream. Trinity removes the probe. Neo meets Morpheus, who offers him a choice: take a blue pill and return to his old life or a red one and join him. Neo takes the red one and wakes up in a fluid-filled pod, attached to wires. Neo is told that it is 2199 and that Artificial Intelligence has developed to the point that it has taken over and imprisoned people in pods to harvest their bioelectrical energy and body heat. The world Neo knew as real is actually a computer program, "the Matrix," designed to simulate 1998 and keep people docile. Morpheus and others are aware of this and are fighting to defeat the machines. Neo uploads combat training's brain and learns that death in the Matrix will kill his real body. In the Matrix they walk into a trap created by a traitor in Morpheus's group. Morpheus allows himself to be captured so the others can escape. Neo and Trinity rescue Morpheus. An agent shoots Neo, but Trinity's kiss and declaration of love revive him in the Matrix, and he now easily wins in both the Matrix and reality.

Fantastic special effects. Real characters are used to make this story believable and interesting. This film grabs your attention and doesn't let go.

Awards: *Academy Award Wins*: Best Film Editing, Best Sound, Best Sound Effects, and Best Visual Effects

Alternate Film: *The Prince and the Pauper* (1937)

21

MALCOLM X

Year: 1992

Genre: Biography

Run Time: 3 hours 22 minutes

Availability: Blu-ray and DVD (Warner Home Video)

Director: Spike Lee; **Screenplay**: Spike Lee and Arnold Perl, based on *The Autobiography of Malcolm X* by Malcolm X and Alex Haley

Cast: Denzel Washington (Malcolm X), Angela Bassett (Betty Shabazz), Albert Hall (Baines), Al Freeman Jr. (Elijah Muhammad), Spike Lee (Shorty), Bobby Seale (Street Preacher), Al Sharpton (Street Preacher), Christopher Plummer (Chaplain Gill)

African American Malcolm Little has a troubled childhood, as his father is murdered and his mother goes insane. He works as a Pullman porter, but later becomes a burglar, is arrested, and is sentenced to ten years. In prison he joins the Nation of Islam, which preaches separation from white society. He becomes an outstanding and well-known speaker for the movement. When Malcolm discovers the group's leader, Elijah Muhammad, is having extramarital affairs, he is very upset. His attitude toward whites softens after a trip to Mecca when he realizes Muslims come from all races. His attempt to deliver this message creates enemies, who murder Malcolm X in front of his family on February 21, 1965 (2:56:26 to 3:06:54).

An interesting movie about a controversial figure. There was more controversy about the creation of the film than the subject matter. Holds your interest.

Awards: *Academy Award Nominations*: Best Actor (Denzel Washington) and Best Costume Design. *Golden Globe Nomination*: Best Performance by an Actor in a Motion Picture–Drama (Washington)

Source: *The Sixties Chronicle*. Lincolnwood, IL: Legacy Publishing, 2004. This book at page 224 gives the date of the assassination.

Alternate Film: *The Verdict*

22

MIRACLE

Year: 2004
Genre: Sports/Drama
Run Time: 2 hours 15 minutes
Availability: Blu-ray and DVD (Disney/Buena Vista)
Director: Gavin O'Connell; **Screenplay**: Eric Guggenheim
Cast: Kurt Russell (Herb Brooks), Patricia Clarkson (Patti Brooks), Noah Emmerich (Craig Patrick), Eric Peter-Kaiser (Mark Johnson), Eddie Cahill (Jim Craig), Kenneth Welsh (Doc Nagobads), Sean McCann (Walter Bush), Bobby Hanson (Dave Silk)

The U.S. Olympic committee picks Herbert Brooks to be the coach of the 1980 U.S. Olympic hockey team. He takes charge, picking the roster without tryouts. He pushes exhausting conditioning drills on the team. After an exhibition game that ends in a tie, Brooks thinks the team is distracted and makes them run drills until they say they are playing for the USA, but they are still beaten by the Soviets in another exhibition game. They trail in the first Olympic game, but when an injured teammate puts aside his pain to play, the team rallies and ties the score. They win the next four games. In the semi-final game with the Soviets on February 22, 1980, the game goes back and forth, but the U.S. team holds on to win 4–3 (1:35:01 to 2:07:23). It is anticlimactic when they beat Finland to win the gold.

An inspirational film. Takes some dramatic liberties, but on the whole faithfully follows the story. One of the best sports movies.
Source: Garner, Joe. *Stay Tuned*. Kansas City, KS: Andrews McMeel Publishing, 2002. This book at page 160 gives date of the match.
Alternate Film: *The Assassination of Richard Nixon*

23

SANDS OF IWO JIMA

Year: 1949
Genre: War/Drama
Run Time: 1 hour 40 minutes
Availability: DVD and VHS (Republic Pictures)
Director: Allan Dwan; **Screenplay**: Harry Brown and James Edward Grant

Cast: John Wayne (Sergeant Stryker), John Agar (PFC Peter Conway), Julie Bishop (Mary), Forrest Tucker (PFC Al Thomas), Arthur Franz (Corporal Robert Dunne), Adele Mara (Allison Bromley), Wally Cassell (PFC Benny Regazzi)

Marine Sergeant John Stryker is thoroughly hated by his squad, especially Peter Conway, the arrogant son of Stryker's former commander, and Al Thomas, who blames Stryker for his being demoted because he forces them to go through extensive hard training. When the Marines land on Tarawa the squad starts to appreciate Stryker, except Conway. Thomas causes the death of two men by lingering when he is sent to get ammunition. Stryker fights Thomas because of this, but Thomas absolves Stryker of disciplinary action by claiming they were practicing judo. Stryker picks up a girl while on leave, but when he sees she is a war widow, he gives her all his cash and leaves. Stryker saves Conway's life during a training exercise, and their relationship improves. Stryker's squad lands on Iwo Jima, where they are ordered to raise the flag on Mount Surabachi on February 23, 1945 (1:40:21 to 1:49:15), and then tragedy strikes.

A war film that accurately portrays the Pacific war. It uses some actual combat footage. The flag used in the scene on Mount Surabachi is the actual flag used in the famous photo, on loan from the Marines.

Awards: *Academy Award Nominations*: Best Actor (John Wayne), Best Sound Recording, Best Film Editing, and Best Original Screenplay

Source: Bradley, James. *Flags of Our Fathers*. New York: Bantam Books, 2000. This book at page 201 gives the date of the flag raising on Mount Surabachi.

Alternate Film: *Rogue Trader*

24

THE ALAMO

Year: 2004
Genre: War
Run Time: 2 hours 17 minutes
Availability: Blu-ray and DVD (Disney/Buena Vista)
Director: John Lee Hancock; **Screenplay**: Leslie Bohem, Stephen Gaghan, and John Lee Hancock

Cast: Dennis Quaid (Sam Houston), Jordi Mollà (Juan Seguin), Billy Bob
Thornton (Davy Crockett), Jason Patric (James Bowie), Mark Blucas
(James Bonham), Patrick Wilson (William Barret Travis), Emilio Eche-
varría (Santa Ana)

Sam Houston, commander of the Texan Revolutionary Army, asks Jim Bowie
to go to the Alamo for the army. Bowie travels to San Antonio and reminisces
about meeting his now deceased wife there. William Travis and his troops
reach San Antonio and he assumes command of all forces, but Bowie and
Travis argue about who is in charge. Santa Ana reaches San Antonio, and the
Texans hole up in the Alamo. Travis sends out couriers to ask for aid. The
Mexicans raise the red flag and play the dueguello, meaning no quarter will
be offered. The next day, February 24, 1836, Travis and Bowie reconcile. Davy
Crockett takes a long shot at Santa Ana, but just clips his uniform (46:03 to
1:00:24). The Texans try to strengthen the Alamo while Houston tries to raise
a relief force. Travis tells the men no aid is coming and offers them a chance
to leave, but no one does. Early one morning the attack begins and though
the Texans fight bravely and ferociously, they are overwhelmed. Crockett
is knocked out and captured. Santa Ana wants him to beg for his life, but
Crockett tells him off and is executed. Houston and the Texans retreat, but
later they return and take on Santa Ana, shouting, "Remember the Alamo!"

This version is somewhat more historically accurate than the 1960 version.
This version shows the controversial story that Crockett was captured and not
killed outright in the fighting.

Source: Roberts, Randy, and Olson, James S. *A Line in the Sand: The Alamo
in Blood and Memory*. New York: The Free Press, 2001. This book at page
130 gives the date Santa Ana rode close to the walls.

Alternate Film: *Amistad*

25

ALI

Year: 2001

Genre: Biography

Run Time: 2 hours 37 minutes

Availability: DVD (Sony Pictures), VHS (Columbia/TriStar Home Entertainment)

Director: Michael Mann; **Screenplay**: Michael Mann, Eric Roth, Stephen J. Rivele, and Christopher Wilkinson

Cast: Will Smith (Muhammad Ali), Jon Voight (Howard Cosell), Jamie Foxx (Drew Bundini Brown), Ron Silver (Angelo Dundee), Mario Van Peebles (Malcolm X), Jada Pinkett Smith (Sonji Roi), LeVar Burton (Martin Luther King Jr.)

Cassius Clay beats Sonny Liston for the world heavyweight boxing title on February 25, 1964 (8:55 to 26:17), and later adopts the name Muhammad Ali. Ali beats Liston again, but when he refuses to be inducted into the army Ali is arrested. Ali refuses to apologize and get a sweetheart assignment. He is tried and found guilty. Ali can't box and is stripped of his title while he appeals his conviction all the way to the U.S. Supreme Court. The new champ, Joe Fraser, agrees to fight him. The Supreme Court reverses his conviction. He fights Fraser, but loses by decision. Ali faces Fraser in the famous "Rumble in the Jungle."

An interesting biopic. Has an unusual style; for example, the first part of the film concentrates as much on Malcolm X as Ali. Will Smith is very convincing as Ali.

Awards: *Academy Award Nominations*: Best Actor (Will Smith) and Best Supporting Actor (Jon Voight). *Golden Globe Nominations*: Best Performance by an Actor in a Motion Picture–Drama (Smith), Best Performance by an Actor in a Supporting Role in a Motion Picture–Drama (Voight), Best Original Score–Drama

Source: Roberts, James B., and Skutt, Alexander G. *The Boxing Register*. Ithaca, NY: McBooks Press, 1997. The book at page 289 gives the date of this bout.

Alternate Film: *Courage under Fire*

26

SELENA

Year: 1997
Genre: Biography
Run Time: 2 hours 7 minutes
Date Revealed in Film: 2:35
Availability: Blu-ray and DVD (Warner Home Video)

Director: Gregory Nava; **Screenplay**: Gregory Nava
Cast: Jennifer Lopez (Selena), Jackie Guerra (Suzette Quintanilla), Constance
Marie (Marcella Quintanilla), Alex Meneses (Sara), Jon Seda (Chris Pérez),
Edward James Olmos (Abraham Quintanilla Jr.), Jacob Vargas (A. B.
Quintanilla), Lupe Ontiveros (Yolanda Saldivar)
Selena gives a sold-out concert at the Houston Astrodome on February 26,
1995 (00:33 to 7:17). Her father flashes back to 1961 when his band lost one job
because they were Mexican American and another because they didn't know
any Mexican music. Twenty years later he starts a band with his kids. He opens
a Mexican restaurant to provide them a performance venue. It is a success for
a while but eventually goes belly up. As the band performs across Texas their
popularity increases. Selena has a number-one song on the Latin chart and
when she performs in Mexico, there is almost a riot by the fans when ten times
as many people as expected show up. In spite of disapproval from her controlling father, Selena marries the guitarist in her band. She wins the Grammy and
opens a series of boutique shops, which are managed by Yolanda, the president
of her fan club. Selena and her father confront Yolanda over financial irregu-
larities, which ends in a cataclysmic confrontation.
   A feel good kind of bio. Concentrates much more on her personal life than
her career. Somewhat melodramatic.
Awards: *Golden Globe Nomination*: Best Performance by an Actress in a Motion Picture–Comedy/Musical (Jennifer Lopez)
Alternate Film: *Bright Star*

27
BREAKER MORANT
Year: 1980
Genre: Courtroom Drama
Run Time: 1 hour 47 minutes
Availability: Blu-ray (Image Entertainment), DVD (Lorber Films)
Director: Bruce Beresford; **Screenplay**: Jonathan Hardy, David Stevens, and
Bruce Beresford, based on Kenneth G. Ross's play, with additional material
from *The Breaker* by Kit Dentom
Cast: Edward Woodward (Lt. Harry "Breaker" Morant), Bryan Brown (Lt.
Peter Handcock), Lewis Fitz-Gerald (Lt. George Witton), Jack Thompson

(Maj. J. F. Thomas), John Waters (Capt. Alfred Taylor), Alan Cassell (Lord Kitchener)

During the Boer War three Australian officers, Harry "Breaker" Morant, Peter Handcock, and George Witton, are on trial for murdering Boer POWs and a German missionary. Their defense counsel, J. F. Thomas, has been given one day to prepare their defense. The British commander, Lord Kitchner, wants a guilty verdict and appoints a court to accomplish this. Thomas hears the story of why the three are on trial. In a raid, Capt. Hunt, the men's commander, was killed and his body mutilated. When six Boers, part of the commando group that killed Hunt, surrender under a white flag, Morant has them executed. Handcock kills a German missionary who talked to the prisoners. The defendants say they were ordered to "take no prisoners." They are found guilty and sentenced to be shot. Morant and Handcock are executed on February 27, 1902 (1:37:06 to 1:44:26). Witton's sentence is commuted to life and he is released three years later.

One of the great trial movies. Shows that this trial was a farce, with the verdict predetermined. The three were offered up as sacrifices to save the high command from embarrassment.

Awards: *Academy Award Nomination*: Best Adapted Screenplay. *Golden Globe Nomination*: Best Foreign Film

Source: Bleszynski, Nick. *Shoot Straight, You Bastards!* New York: Random House, 2002. This book at pages xxix–xliii and 263–78 gives the execution date.

Alternate Film: *Why Do Fools Fall in Love*

28

THE COUNT OF MONTE CRISTO

Year: 2002

Genre: Action

Run Time: 2 hours 11 minutes

Availability: Blu-ray (Disney/Buena Vista), DVD (Touchstone Pictures)

Director: Kevin Reynolds; **Screenplay**: Jay Wolpert, based on Alexandre Dumas's novel

Cast: James Caviezel (Edmond Dantès), Richard Harris (Abbé Faria), Guy Pearce (Fernand Mondego), Luis Guzmán (Jacopo), James Frain (J. F.

Villefort), Dagmara Dominczyk (Mercedès Iguanada), Michael Wincott
(Armand Dorleac)
When merchant seaman Edmund Dantès agrees to deliver a letter from the
exiled Napoleon to Clarion, he ends up arrested for treason on February 28,
1815, but the Bourbon prosecutor Villefort is willing to let him go until he
learns the letter's addressee (15:22 to 25:39). Clarion turns out to be Villefort's father, so he keeps Dantès locked up to protect his job. Fellow crewman
Mondego, Dantès's rival in love, tells Mercedès that Dantès is dead, so she
weds Mondego. After seven years in jail, another prisoner, the Abbé Faria,
digs into Dantès's cell. They begin digging a new tunnel while the Abbé
teaches Dantès fencing. Dantès swears revenge on Villefort and Mondego.
The tunnel collapses and Abbé Faria is fatally injured. Before he dies he tells
Dantès where the treasure of Count Sparta is located. Dantès puts himself
into Faria's shroud and escapes when it is thrown into the sea. After Dantès
beats the smuggler, Jacopo, in a fight, Jacopo becomes his servant. They go
to Marseille, where Dantès learns of Mercedès's marriage. Dantès and Jacopo
find the treasure, and Dantès goes to Paris, where he buys an estate, assum-
ing the title "Count of Monte Cristo." Villefort and Mondego try to get the
treasure for themselves and arrest Monte Cristo. Mercedès learns that Monte
Cristo is Dantès. Monte Cristo tells Villefort that he knows Villefort killed
Mondego's father, while Mondego killed Villefort's father, and Villefort is
arrested for murder. Dantès has a confrontation with Mondego during which
many secrets are revealed.

A classic adventure story. Has it all: love, betrayal, loyalty, and lots of action.

Source: Dumas, Alexandre. *The Count of Monte Cristo*. New York: The Modern Library, 1996. This book at page 142 gives the date on Dantès's arrest.

Alternate Film: *44 Minutes: The North Hollywood Shootout*

29

LEAP YEAR

Year: 2010
Genre: Romantic Comedy
Run Time: 1 hour 40 minutes
Date Revealed in Film: 1:01:07–09

Availability: Blu-ray and DVD (Universal Studios)
Director: Anand Tucker; **Screenplay**: Deborah Kaplan and Harry Elfont
Cast: Amy Adams (Anna Brady), Matthew Goode (Declan O'Callaghan), Adam Scott (Jeremy Sloane), John Lithgow (Jack Brady), Kaitlin Olson (Libby), Noel O'Donovan (Seamus), Tony Rohr (Frank), Pat Laffan (Donal), Alan Devlin (Joe)

Anna Brady and her boyfriend, Dr. Jeremy Sloane, have applied for a space in an exclusive Boston condo. She later decides to follow an old Irish custom and proposes to Jeremy on Leap Year's Day in Dublin. However, bad weather diverts her to Dingle. She stumbles into Declan O'Callaghan's bar. After some misadventures, he agrees to drive her to Dublin. On the way there Anna manages to wreck the car. She tries to hitch a ride with someone, who steals her luggage, but Declan later beats them up and retrieves it. They miss the train and have to stay at a bed and breakfast, where they are forced to pretend to be married. Anna and Declan refuse to acknowledge their growing attraction to each other. On February 29, 2008, they ride the bus to Dublin. She finds Jeremy, who proposes to her (1:11:45 to 1:22:48). At Anna and Jeremy's engagement party, she learns he only proposed because the owner's committee refused to sell to an unmarried couple. Anna returns to Ireland, where she becomes engaged to Declan, and the film ends as they set out on their honeymoon.

A rare, clean, but sweet and funny modern romantic comedy. This one could have been made in the golden age of Hollywood. Well written, acted, and directed.

Alternate Film: *Karol: A Man Who Became Pope*

March

1
THE LORD OF THE RINGS: THE TWO TOWERS
Year: 2002

Genre: Action/Fantasy

Run Time: 2 hours 59 minutes

Availability: Blu-ray and DVD (New Line Cinema)

Director: Peter Jackson; **Screenplay**: Peter Jackson, Frances Walsh, Phillipa Boynes, and Stephen Sinclair, based on the novel by J. R. R. Tolkien

Cast: Elijah Wood (Frodo Baggins), Sean Astin (Samwise Gamgee), Viggo Mortensen (Aragorn), Ian McKellen (Gandalf), Orlando Bloom (Legolas), John Rhys-Davies (Gimli), Christopher Lee (Saruman), Liv Tyler (Arwen), Miranda Otto (Éowyn)

Gandalf narrates that he fell with the balrog into the pit, where they fought, and then he climbed to the mountaintop, where he was killed. He was then brought back to complete his mission. Frodo and Sam get lost in the hills on the way to Mordor. They capture Gollum, who has been stalking them, and he swears on "The Precious" to obey Frodo. Aragorn, Gimli, and Legolas pursue the orcs who have taken Merry and Pippin. Saruman attacks Rohan, but the king (who is under Saruman's control) does nothing. Merry and Pippin escape during an attack by the riders of Rohan on the orcs' camp on the edge of Fangorn Forest. The Riders tell Aragorn, Gimli, and Legolas they left no survivors, but Aragorn's superior tracking abilities show the hobbits escaped. In Fangorn, Merry and Pippin meet Treebeard, an ent (a treelike creature). Frodo, Sam, and Gollum leave the hills and enter the Dead Marshes on March 1, 3017 T.A. (34:15 to 39:20). Aragorn, Gimli, and Legolas enter Fangorn and meet Gandalf, now "the White." The four go to Edoras, seat of the King of Rohan. Frodo reaches the Black Gate of Mordor and finds it impenetrable, but Gollum says he knows another way in. Gandalf, Aragorn, Gimli, and Legolas reach Edoras and exorcise the king. Aragorn thinks about Arwen, his fiancée. The riders of Rohan retreat to their stronghold, Helm's Deep, and are attacked by orcs. Aragorn is attacked but finally arrives. Arwen prepares to depart across the sea to Valinor. Faramir captures Frodo, Sam, and Gollum and is going to take them to Gondor. A Nazgul attacks, and the weary Frodo almost gives up the ring to it before Sam and Faramir kill it. The ents attack Isengard and destroy it.

Good action scenes. I didn't like how they deviated from the book. It's a classic, so why did they need to mess with it? Still very much worth watching.

Awards: *Academy Award Wins*: Best Visual Effects and Best Sound Editing. *Academy Award Nominations*: Best Picture, Best Art Direction, Best Film Editing, and Best Sound Mixing. *Golden Globe Nominations*: Best Motion Picture–Drama and Best Director–Motion Picture

Source: Tolkien, J. R. R. *The Lord of the Rings: The Return of The King*. New York: Houghton Mifflin, 1994. This book at page 1,067 gives the date they entered the swamps.

Alternate Film: *JFK*

2

SEABISCUIT

Year: 2003
Genre: Sports/Drama
Run Time: 2 hours 20 minutes
Availability: Blu-ray and DVD (Universal Studios)
Director: Gary Ross; **Screenplay:** Gary Ross, based on Laura Hillenbrand's book *Seabiscuit: An American Legend*
Cast: Tobey Maguire (Red Pollard), Jeff Bridges (Charles S. Howard), Chris Cooper (R. Thomas Smith), William H. Macy (Tick Tock McGlaughlin),

Elizabeth Banks (Marcela Howard), Gary L. Stevens (George Woolf), Eddie Jones (Samuel D. Riddle)

These are the converging stories of three men and a horse. Charles Howard was a bicycle repairman who became the largest car dealer in the San Francisco Bay area, but when his son is killed he falls into depression. Red Pollard was the son of a family ruined by the Depression who became a boxer and jockey. Tom Smith worked as a cowboy. Charles Howard gets married again after a divorce from his first wife. His new bride encourages him to buy horses. Charles Howard hires Tom Smith as a trainer.

Seabiscuit was considered a "lazy" horse and was trained to lose in races with more important horses. Smith sees a similarity of temperament between Seabiscuit and Red Pollard and makes him a jockey. Seabiscuit is retrained to win and wins several races in a row, becoming a media sensation. Howard challenges the owner of War Admiral, the best-known horse of the era, to a race, but he is refused. Seabiscuit loses the hundred-thousand-dollar challenge by a nose because Pollard can't see the other horse coming up on the right, being blind in that eye from an injury incurred in his boxing days.

War Admiral's owner finally accepts the challenge to race. Seabiscuit is retrained to jump off to a lead instead of coming from behind in his usual style. Pollard injures his leg though, so George Woolf, the greatest jockey of the era, rides Seabiscuit. In the race with War Admiral, Seabiscuit jumps out to a lead. War Admiral comes alongside, but then Seabiscuit pulls away to win. Seabiscuit is injured, but Pollard nurses him back to full health. In his last race on March 2, 1940, Pollard wears a special brace and guides Seabiscuit to victory (2:04:08 to 2:12:13).

An underdog story. You want Seabiscuit and Pollard to prevail. Sweet without being saccharine.

Awards: *Academy Award Nominations*: Best Picture, Best Adapted Screenplay, Best Art Direction, Best Cinematography, Best Costume Design, Best Film Editing, and Best Sound Mixing. *Golden Globe Nominations*: Best Motion Picture–Drama and Best Performance by an Actor in a Supporting Role in a Motion Picture (William H. Macy)

Source: Hillenbrand, Laura. *Seabiscuit: An American Legend.* New York: Random House, 2001. This book at page 304 gives the date of his last race.

Alternate Film: *Working Girl*

3
THE MIRACLE WORKER
Year: 1962
Genre: Biographical Drama
Run Time: 1 hour 46 minutes
Availability: DVD (Metro-Goldwyn-Mayer), VHS (MGM/UA Home Video)
Director: Arthur Penn; **Screenplay**: William Gibson, based on his play
Cast: Anne Bancroft (Annie Sullivan), Patty Duke (Helen Keller), Victor Jory
    (Captain Keller), Inga Swenson (Kate Keller), Andrew Prine (James Keller)
Young Helen Keller gets sick and as a result becomes blind and deaf. When
she is seven there is talk of putting her into an asylum, but her mother con-
vinces her father to write to the Perkins School for the Blind in Boston, and
they send Annie Sullivan, who arrives on March 3, 1887 (13:45 to 29:47). She
tries to teach Helen sign language, but Helen behaves very badly and locks
Miss Sullivan in her room and hides the key. They have "the battle of the
breakfast table" in which Miss Sullivan forces her to eat correctly.

A moving and touching biopic. Some scenes, such as "the battle of the
breakfast table," are classics. Patty Duke does a great acting job without ever
speaking.

Annie persuades the Kellers to let her spend a week alone with Helen in a
cottage on their property. Helen finally gets to the point where she will work
with Annie to try and learn. When they return, even though Helen doesn't
want to behave at dinner, she finally has a breakthrough as she associates the
hand sign for "water" with water and starts to learn many words now that she
has grasped the concept.

A moving and touching biopic. Some scenes, such as "the battle of the
breakfast table," are classics. Patty Duke does a great acting job without ever
speaking.

Awards: *Academy Award Wins*: Best Actress (Anne Bancroft) and Best Sup-
porting Actress (Patty Duke). *Academy Award Nominations*: Best Direc-
tor, Best Adapted Screenplay, and Best Costume Design. *Golden Globe
Nominations*: Best Motion Picture–Drama, Best Motion Picture Actress–
Drama (Bancroft), and Best Supporting Actress (Duke)
Source: Keller, Helen. *The Story of My Life*. New York: W.W. Norton and
Co., 2003. This book at page 25 gives the date of Annie Sullivan's arrival.
Alternate Film: *Dark Blue*

4

A STAR IS BORN

Year: 1954

Genre: Musical/Romance

Run Time: 2 hours 34 minutes (theatrical release), 2 hours 56 minutes (restored)

Date Revealed in Film: 2:02:54

Availability: Blu-ray and DVD (Warner Home Video)

Director: George Cukor; **Screenplay**: Moss Hart, based on Dorothy Parker, Alan Campbell, and Robert Carson's screenplay

Cast: Judy Garland (Esther Blodgett/Vicki Lester), James Mason (Norman Maine), Jack Carson (Matt Libby), Charles Bickford (Oliver Niles), Tommy Noonan (Danny McGuire), Amanda Blake (Susan Ettinger), James Brown (Glenn Williams)

Alcoholic Norman Maine is a well-known movie actor who after being saved from a very public embarrassment by singer Esther Blodgett promises to get her a movie audition. Due to events beyond his control, Maine can't immediately keep his promise and Esther thinks he was just trying to seduce her. Eventually Maine does get her a bit part, and the studio changes her name to Vicki Lester. Maine convinces the studio head to cast Vicki as a replacement in a major musical film that turns out to be a huge success. Vicki and Maine fall in love and elope. Then the studio fires Maine because of his alcoholism. Vicki's career continues to flourish, and on March 4, 1943 (2:02:50 to 2:09:11), she wins the Best Actress Oscar. Maine shows up at the ceremony drunk, and his life goes downhill from there, involving detox efforts, fights, and car crashes. When Maine overhears Vicki and Niles discuss her plans to give up her career to care for him, he takes a radical step to solve the problem.

One of the classic golden age of Hollywood musicals. This film is the high point of Garland's career. She should have won the Oscar for this role.

Awards: *Academy Award Nominations*: Best Actress (Judy Garland), Best Actor (James Mason), Best Color Art Direction, Best Color Costume Design, Best Original Song, and Best Original Score. *Golden Globe Wins*: Best Motion Picture Actress–Musical/Comedy (Garland) and Best Motion Picture Actor–Musical/Comedy (Mason)

Alternate Film: *The Other Boleyn Girl* (2008)

5
JUDGMENT AT NUREMBURG
Year: 1961
Genre: Drama
Run Time: 3 hours 6 minutes
Availability: DVD (Metro-Goldwyn-Mayer), VHS (MGM/UA Home Video)
Director: Stanley Kramer; **Screenplay**: Abby Mann
Cast: Spencer Tracy (Chief Judge Dan Haywood), Burt Lancaster (Dr. Ernst
Janning), Richard Widmark (Tad Lawson), Marlene Dietrich (Mrs. Ber-
tholt), Maximilian Schell (Hans Rolfe), Judy Garland (Irene Hoffman),
Montgomery Clift (Rudolph Peterson)
The film begins with the opening statements in the trial on March 5, 1947,
where Nazi judges and prosecutors are put on trial for crimes against humanity (11:50 to 31:45). Ernst Janning is the main defendant. The prosecution
presents evidence of the Nazi's eugenics program of sexual sterilization. The
defense tries to counter by showing that other countries, including the United
States, had similar laws. Evidence is then presented about the "Feldenstein"
case, where an elderly Jew was accused of having sex with a young Aryan girl
and put to death. The defense tries to intimidate the "victim" into admitting
that they actually were intimate. This causes Janning to get angry and he gets
on the stand and confesses his guilt.

The defense counters that if Janning is guilty, others, including the USSR,
Churchill, and American industrialists, are guilty also. Pressure is put on the
prosecutor to seek only light sentences, as the United States needs the support
of the German people against the Russians. The judge resists this idea, and
while agreeing that the defense arguments have some merit, finds all defendants guilty and sentences them all to life imprisonment.

One of the great trial films. Explores the concepts of justice and justifica-
tion. The Germans argue they merely followed the law, but this is rejected as
a defense.

Awards: *Academy Award Wins*: Best Actor (Maximilian Schell) and Best
Adapted Screenplay. *Academy Award Nominations*: Best Actor (Spen-
cer Tracy), Best Supporting Actor (Montgomery Clift), Best Supporting
Actress (Judy Garland), Best Art Direction–Black-and-White, Best Cin-
ematography–Black-and-White, Best Costume Design–Black-and-White,
Best Director, Best Film Editing, and Best Picture. *Golden Globe Wins*:

Best Motion Picture Director and Best Motion Picture Actor (Schell). *Golden Globe Nominations*: Best Motion Picture–Drama, Best Supporting Actress–Drama (Garland), Best Supporting Actor (Clift), and Best Film Promoting International Understanding

Source: *Trials of War Criminals before the Nuremberg Military Tribunals under Control Council Law No. 10, Vol III.* Washington: U.S. Government Printing Office, 1951. This book at page 5 gives the date of the trial's opening.

Alternate Film: *Lenny*

6

THE ACCUSED

Year: 1988
Genre: Drama
Run Time: 1 hour 51 minutes
Availability: DVD and VHS (Paramount Pictures)
Director: Jonathan Kaplan; **Screenplay**: Tom Topor
Cast: Kelly McGillis (Kathryn Murphy), Jodie Foster (Sarah Tobias), Bernie Coulson (Kenneth Joyce), Leo Rossi (Cliff "Scorpion" Albrect), Ann Hearn (Sally Fraser), Carmen Argenziano (Paul Rudolph), Steve Antin (Bob Joiner), Tom O'Brien (Larry)

On March 6, 1983, Sarah Tobias is gang-raped in a bar while drunken patrons cheer the rapists on (00:28 to 15:32 and 1:20:00 to 1:33:54). The prosecutor assigned to the case is persuaded to let them plead guilty to a lesser charge that could get them out of jail in a year. The victim becomes enraged about this. When the victim is hospitalized after ramming the truck of one of the witnesses who had propositioned her, the prosecutor decides to charge those who cheered on the rapists with criminal solicitation. At trial they are convicted.

A brutally honest film. Almost painful in its portrayal of events. One of those films you really don't want to see, but should.

Awards: *Academy Award Win*: Best Actress (Jodie Foster). *Golden Globe Win*: Best Performance by an Actress in a Motion Picture–Drama (Foster)

Source: *The Providence Journal*, November 1, 1999, a story called "Big Dan's rape case" by Paul Edward Parker gives the date of the real-life assault on which the film is based.

Alternate Film: *Testimony*

7
THE BRIDGE AT REMAGEN
Year: 1969
Genre: War
Run Time: 1 hour 55 minutes
Availability: Blu-ray (Metro-Goldwyn-Mayer), VHS (MGM/UA Home Video)
Director: John Guillermin; **Screenplay**: William Roberts and Richard Yates
Cast: George Segal (Lt. Phil Hartman), Robert Vaughn (Maj. Paul Kruger), Ben Gazzara (Sgt. Angelo), Bradford Dillman (Maj. Barnes), E. G. Marshall (Gen. Shinner), Peter van Eyck (Gen. von Brock), Hans Christian Blech (Karl Schmidt), Bo Hopkins (Cpl. Grebs)

This movie contains intersecting stories. The first concerns German Major Kruger, who is sent to destroy the bridge but at the same time is secretly acting to keep it intact as long as possible to allow the escape of thousands of German soldiers caught on the wrong side of the river Rhine. The second concerns an irreverent and war-weary American army squad sent to capture Remagen and the bridge. They advance onto the bridge on March 7, 1945, at which point Major Kruger blows the bridge, but it stays up due to the inferior-grade explosives used. The Americans race across. After a counterattack fails, Major Kruger goes for reinforcements, but he is arrested for desertion and shot (42:40 to 1:33:40).

An interesting film. The cynical attitudes of the American squad probably better represent the mind-set of the average soldier better than most gung-ho war films. They are doing a job, not trying to be heroes, in contrast to their battalion commander, who wants to get promoted through their accomplishments. The action sequences are well done.

Source: Sylvan, William C., and Smith, Francis G. Jr. *Normandy to Victory*. Lexington: University Press of Kentucky, 2008. This book at page 324 gives the date of the bridge's capture.

Alternate Film: *Mommie Dearest*

8

LOVE STORY

Year: 1970
Genre: Romance
Run Time: 1 hour 39 minutes
Availability: Blu-ray (Warner Home Video), DVD (Paramount Pictures)
Director: Arthur Hiller; **Screenplay**: Erich Segal, based on his novel
Cast: Ali MacGraw (Jennifer Cavilleri), Ryan O'Neal (Oliver Barrett IV), John Marley (Phil Cavilleri), Ray Milland (Oliver Barrett III), Russell Nype (Dean Thompson), Katharine Balfour (Mrs. Barrett), Tommy Lee Jones (Hank Simpson)

Oliver Barrett IV, Harvard pre-law, meets poor Radcliffe music student Jennifer Cavilleri and they begin a relationship. She stays in Boston on March 8, 1969, when the Harvard ice hockey team travels to Ithaca and loses the Ivy League title game to Cornell. Afterward, Oliver, who is on the team, meets his father, and it's obvious they have a very frosty relationship (8:57 to 13:17). Oliver and Jennifer's relationship becomes intimate. He proposes and she accepts. They go to see his parents, and it doesn't turn out well. His father wants them to wait until Oliver finishes law school, and when Oliver refuses, his father cuts him off financially. The trip to see her father goes better. They get married. He goes to Harvard law school, while she teaches music to support them. They have a huge fight when Oliver refuses to attend his father's sixtieth birthday party. They make up after Jennifer pronounces the iconic line "Love means never having to say you're sorry." Oliver graduates and goes to work for a big New York law firm. They try to have a baby and get some bad news.

Watching this movie for the first time I decided it wasn't as bad as I thought it might be. It's been (badly) copied so many times that I was prejudiced against the original. Actually it's not a bad romance film. However, for the most part current audiences know the story and how everything turns out, which may affect their view of the film, making it seem more poignant than it might otherwise.

Awards: *Academy Award Win*: Best Original Score. *Academy Award Nominations*: Best Picture, Best Director, Best Original Screenplay, Best Actor (Ryan O'Neal), Best Actress (Ali MacGraw) and Best Supporting Actor (John Marley)

Source: http://www.ecahockey.com/men/history/Summaries-I.pdf
Alternate Film: *Lonely Hearts*

9

GOODNIGHT, AND GOOD LUCK

Year: 2005
Genre: Drama
Run Time: 1 hour 33 minutes
Availability: Blu-ray and DVD (Warner Home Video)
Director: George Clooney; Screenplay: George Clooney and Grant Heslov
Cast: David Strathairn (Edward R. Murrow), George Clooney (Fred Friendly),
Robert Downey Jr. (Joseph Wershba), Patricia Clarkson (Shirley Wershba),
Frank Langella (William S. Paley), Jeff Daniels (Sig Mickelson), Tate
Donovan (Jesse Zousmer)

In the early 1950s CBS requires a "loyalty oath," the need for which is questioned by some employees. Ed Murrow, through his show, *See It Now*, supports Mila Radulovich, a member of the Air Force who is being forced out because of his family's political views. At Radulovich's hearing a sealed envelope was used as evidence, but Radulovich wasn't allowed to see it, and Murrow considers this a due process violation. The show results in Radulovich being retained. Senator Joe McCarthy hands Joseph Wershba, a reporter for the show, an envelope that contains "evidence" that Murrow is a secret communist, and the show's staff interpret this as a covert attack on Murrow.

CBS head Bill Paley pressures Murrow to leave McCarthy alone, but Murrow decides to attack him directly in a show that airs on March 9, 1954, and gets generally positive reviews (39:24 to 47:25). McCarthy later appears on the show and makes allegations about Murrow that Murrow says are false. One of the other CBS broadcasters commits suicide after being accused of being a communist. Wershba and his new wife hide their marriage rather than run afoul of CBS policy that forbids spouses from working together there. When this is discovered, he resigns to look for another job. Paley moves Murrow's show to a dead time slot in order to kill it. In 1958 Murrow is honored at a banquet, where he gives a speech to his fellow TV newsmen encouraging them to use TV for education and not just entertainment.

An interesting drama about a little-explored episode of American history. Murrow and his colleagues actually investigated the news instead of being mouthpieces. Unfortunately, Murrow wasn't able to kill off the idea of the unsupported allegation as a political weapon.

Awards: *Academy Award Nominations*: Best Picture, Best Director, Best Actor (David Strathairn), Best Original Screenplay, Best Achievement in Art Direction, and Best Cinematography. *Golden Globe Nominations*: Best Motion Picture–Drama, Best Performance by an Actor in a Motion Picture–Drama (David Strathairn), Best Director–Motion Picture, and Best Screenplay–Motion Picture

Source: Sperber, A. M. *Murrow: His Life and Times*. New York: Freundlich Books, 1986. This book at page 424 gives the date of the broadcast.

Alternate Film: *The Onion Field*

10

LOST HORIZON

Year: 1937

Genre: Drama

Run Time: 1 hour 37 minutes

Date Revealed in Film: 3:03

Availability: DVD (Sony Pictures), VHS (RCA/Columbia Pictures Home Entertainment)

Director: Frank Capra; **Screenplay**: Robert Riskin, based on James Hilton's novel

Cast: Ronald Colman (Robert Conway), Jane Wyatt (Sondra Bizet), Sam Jaffe (High Lama), H. B. Warner (Chang), Edward Everett Horton (Alexander P. Lovett), Thomas Mitchell (Henry Barnard), Margo (Maria), Isabel Jewell (Gloria Stone), Richard Loo (Shanghai Airport Official)

Robert Conway has been recalled to Britain to become foreign secretary. First he has to get the last foreigners out of Baskul, China, before a warlord's army kills them. Conway, his brother George, Alexander P. Lovett, Henry Barnard, and Gloria Stone get on the last plane out on March 10, 1937 (3:05 to 14:45). In the confusion of the escape, they don't notice their pilot has been replaced until they realize they are flying the wrong way. They are refueled on the Tibetan Plateau, but make a crash landing in the Himalayas that kills the pilot. Gloria Stone has a fatal disease, but has outlived her diagnosis.

They meet a group of porters, led by Chang, who leads them to Shangri-La, an enclosed valley in the mountains that is a peaceful and tranquil place.

George meets a woman, Maria, and they are attracted to each other. Robert Conway learns Shangri-La is entirely peaceful and without crime. The valley causes perfect health and very slow aging in its inhabitants. A priest, Father Perrot, founded it in 1713. Gloria Stone's health starts to improve. Father Perrot used the gold found in the valley to buy books and artworks and bring them to Shangri-La. Robert becomes fascinated with Sondra Bizet, a woman of Shangri-La. George says they have been kidnapped and held against their will.

Chang takes Robert to meet the High Lama, who is Father Perrot, still alive after two centuries. The High Lama says that they were brought there deliberately. He created Shangri-La as a repository of culture. After the "civilized" world finally destroys itself in warfare, Shangri-La's doctrine of peace and nonviolence can spread over the world. Maria is seventy, but looks twenty, and her appearance will quickly revert to that of her real age if she ever leaves. Robert and Sondra become closer and all the newcomers except George adapt to life in Shangri-La, and now want to stay. George becomes determined to leave with Maria. The High Lama tells Robert that he is dying and plans to make him leader. However, the death of the High Lama sets in action a chain of events that forces Robert Conway to decide what he really values.

An interesting film. It is part action/adventure and part pacifist propaganda. However, even Shangri-La can't keep jealousy and envy out entirely.

Awards: *Academy Award Wins*: Best Art Direction and Best Film Editing. *Academy Nominations*: Best Picture, Best Supporting Actor (H. B. Warner), Best Original Score, Best Sound, and Best Assistant Director

Alternate Film: *The Story of Alexander Graham Bell*

11
THEY WERE EXPENDABLE
Year: 1945
Genre: War/Drama
Run Time: 2 hours 15 minutes
Availability: DVD (Warner Home Video), VHS (MGM/UA Home Video)
Director: John Ford; **Screenplay**: Frank Wead, based on William L. White's book
Cast: Robert Montgomery (Lt. John Brickley), John Wayne (Lt. J. G. "Rusty" Ryan), Donna Reed (2nd Lt. Sandy Davyss), Jack Holt (General Martin),

Ward Bond ("Boats" Mulcahey), Marshall Thompson ("Snake" Gardner),
Paul Langton ("Andy" Andrews)

Two Navy lieutenants, John Brickley and "Rusty" Ryan, try to deal with the
Navy's disdain for their PT boats, as shown by the fact that on the day after
Pearl Harbor, they were ordered to be couriers instead of being given a combat assignment. The base gets bombed by the Japanese. Rusty is injured and
sent to the hospital, where he meets an army nurse, Sandy. They finally convince the brass to give them a shot and they sink several Japanese ships. Ryan
develops a relationship with Sandy. They leave Bataan with Gen. MacArthur
on March 11, 1942 (1:12:44 to 1:22:58) and take him to Mindanao. The crews
keep fighting the Japanese until all their boats are lost. Brick and Ryan are
ordered to return to the States to train others in PT tactics. Ryan considers
staying to find Sandy, but is persuaded to do his duty and they fly out in the
last places in the last plane.

A practical, non-romantic look at the war. No melodrama, just real heroics
of the men who laid down a bunt, as Admiral Hart puts it, to stall the Japanese
as long as possible. The action scenes are very realistic.

Awards: *Academy Award Nominations*: Best Visual Effects and Best Sound
Recording

Source: Salmaggi, Cesare, and Pallavisini, Alfredo. *2,194 Days of War*. New
York: Gallery Books, 1977, at page 224 gives the date MacArthur evacuated.

Alternate Film: *The Fighter*

12
THE SHAWSHANK REDEMPTION

Year: 1994

Genre: Drama

Run Time: 2 hours 22 minutes

Availability: Blu-ray and DVD (Warner Home Video)

Director: Frank Darabont; **Screenplay**: Frank Darabont, based on the Stephen King short story "Rita Hayworth and the Shawshank Redemption"

Cast: Tim Robbins (Andy Dufresne), Morgan Freeman ("Red" Redding), Bob
Gunton (Warden Samuel Norton), William Sadler (Heywood), Clancy
Brown (Capt. Byron Hadley), Gil Bellows (Tommy Williams), James
Whitmore (Brooks Hatlen)

Andy Dufresne's wife and her lover are murdered. Andy is convicted of the crime and sentenced to two life terms at Maine's Shawshank prison, where he becomes friends with "Red" Redding, who smuggles in items for Andy. Andy uses his financial skills to help the guards and is picked to work in the library with Brooks, who has been in for fifty years. Brooks is paroled but wants to stay, and when released he can't adapt to the outside and commits suicide. Andy gets books and records he had requested from the legislature and, taking advantage of being in the prison office, broadcasts Mozart's "Sull'aria" over the intercom, and is punished.

The warden starts the "Inside Out" program, using prison labor outside the walls and getting kickbacks from contractors who pay to have him not compete with them for jobs. He uses Andy's financial skills to launder the money. In 1965, a new convict, Tommy Williams, arrives. After hearing Andy's story, Tommy says that a man in another prison confessed to the crime Andy was convicted of. The warden reacts to this story by throwing Andy in solitary for two months and having Tommy "shot while trying to escape."

When he gets out Andy tells Red of his dream of living in Zihuatanejo, Mexico, and that if Red ever gets out he should look in a certain field near Buxton, Maine, for something Andy had left there. The next morning, March 12, 1967, when Andy does not appear at roll call, Red fears Andy has killed himself in his cell (1:50:25 to 1:54:37, 2:00 to 2:01:17) But what actually happened the night before and its repercussions are far more powerful. It is just the start of a journey to freedom and self-discovery for Red.

A very good dramatic film. Right up there with *Gone with the Wind*, *Casablanca*, and *Chariots of Fire*.

Awards: *Academy Award Nominations*: Best Picture, Best Actor (Morgan Freeman), Best Adapted Screenplay, Best Cinematography, Best Editing, Best Original Score, and Best Sound Mixing. *Golden Globe Nominations*: Best Performance by an Actor in a Motion Picture–Drama (Morgan Freeman) and Best Screenplay–Motion Picture

Source: King, Stephen. *Different Seasons*. New York: The Viking Press, 1982. This book at page 77 gives the date of the escape.

Alternate Film: *The Linda McCartney Story*

13
SCHINDLER'S LIST
Year: 1993
Genre: Drama
Run Time: 3 hours 15 minutes
Date Revealed in Film: 56:55
Availability: Blu-ray and DVD (Universal Studios)
Director: Steven Spielberg; **Screenplay**: Steven Zaillian, based on the novel *Schindler's Ark* by Thomas Keneally
Cast: Liam Neeson (Oskar Schindler), Ben Kingsley (Itzhak Stern), Ralph Fiennes (Amon Goeth), Caroline Goodall (Emilie Schindler), Jonathan Sagall (Poldek Pfefferberg), Embeth Davidtz (Helen Hirsch), Mark Ivanir (Marcel Goldberg)

Early in World War II Oskar Schindler arrives in Krakow, Poland. He suggests to Itzhak Stern that he find Jews to put up the money to buy a metal enamelwork factory in Schindler's name, so they get a cut of the profits, as Jews can't legally own a business. After all Jews are forced to move to the ghetto, two men decide to "invest." Schindler decides to use Jews to work in the factory. Stern, who actually runs things for Schindler, forges documents to have as many Jews as possible declared "essential" to the war effort and safe from deportation. Schindler uses his military contacts to get a lot of business for the factory. Amon Goeth takes over the Plaszow camp.

On March 13, 1943, Goeth sends in troops to liquidate the Krakow ghetto. Schindler witnesses these atrocities (55:05 to 1:10:30). Schindler persuades Goeth to let the Plaszow inmates work in his factory. Goeth is ordered to dig up and burn the bodies of those Jews who were killed earlier. The factory is relocated, and Schindler takes his workers with him. The train carrying the women and children is accidentally rerouted to Auschwitz. Schindler goes there and pays massive bribes to free them. At the end of the war Schindler is broke, but he talks the SS guards into not shooting the Jews. As the Red Army arrives, Schindler flees with his wife. The film ends with a very moving scene of the real people saved by Schindler placing a memorial stone on his grave in Jerusalem.

A very powerful and moving film. The story of one man who did the right thing.

Awards: *Academy Award Wins*: Best Picture, Best Adapted Screenplay, Best Director, Best Set Decoration, Best Cinematography, Best Film Editing, and Best Original Score. *Academy Award Nominations*: Best Actor (Liam Neeson), Best Supporting Actor (Ralph Fiennes), Best Costume Design, Best Makeup, and Best Sound. *Golden Globe Wins*: Best Motion Picture–Drama, Best Screenplay–Motion Picture. *Golden Globe Nominations*: Best Performance by an Actor in a Motion Picture–Drama (Neeson), Best Performance by an Actor in a Supporting Role in a Motion Picture (Fiennes), Best Original Score–Motion Picture
Alternate Film: *Gotti*

14

RAGING BULL

Year: 1980
Genre: Biography
Run Time: 2 hours 9 minutes
Availability: Blu-ray and DVD (Metro-Goldwyn-Mayer)
Director: Martin Scorsese; **Screenplay**: Paul Schrader, Mardik Martin, and Martin Scorsese, based on the autobiography *Raging Bull: My Story* by Jake LaMotta with Joseph Carter and Peter Savage
Cast: Robert De Niro (Jake LaMotta), Cathy Moriarty (Vikki LaMotta), Joe Pesci (Joey LaMotta), Nicholas Colasanto (Tommy Como), Theresa Saldana (Lenora LaMotta), Frank Vincent (Salvy "Batts"), Mario Gallo (Mario), Frank Adonis (Patsy)

In 1941 Jake LaMotta loses his first major boxing match. His brother Joey tries to get him a shot at the middleweight title by talking to the Mob. Jake meets and falls for a fifteen-year-old named Vikki (even though he's already married). His wife leaves him. Jake beats and later loses to Sugar Ray Robinson. Jake wins a couple of fights and he and Vikki get married.

Jake continues to win, including beating Tommy Bell on March 14, 1947 (43:44 to 43:48). He and Vikki have started a family, and Jake develops a jealous streak about her. After Jake wins a fight against Bobby Janiro, Joey sees Vikki with one of his Mob pals and Joey beats him up. The Mob has Joey tell Jake that if Jake wants a shot at the title, he first has to take a dive in a fight so the Mob can make a bundle on gambling. Jake does this, but is suspended from boxing. When he finally gets his suspension lifted he wins the middle-weight title. Jake's jealousy spills over and he accuses his brother of having an affair with Vikki. He accuses Vikki also, and she (sarcastically?) replies that she's slept with a lot of people. Jake beats up his brother in front of his wife. Jake loses his title to Sugar Ray Robinson. Later he opens a nightclub in Miami and Vikki divorces him. He is arrested for introducing fifteen-year-old girls to men and serves time in jail. Joey forgives him.

A good biopic about a man who could not control his passions. Almost has a documentary feel.

Awards: *Academy Award Wins*: Best Actor (Robert De Niro) and Best Film Editing. *Academy Award Nominations*: Best Picture, Best Director, Best Supporting Actress (Cathy Moriarty), Best Supporting Actor (Joe Pesci), Best Cinematography, Best Sound, and Best Film Editing. *Golden Globe Win*: Best Actor in a Motion Picture–Drama (De Niro). *Golden Globe Nominations*: Best Motion Picture–Drama, Best Director–Motion Picture, Best Motion Picture Actress in a Supporting Role (Moriarty), Best Motion Picture Actor in a Supporting Role (Pesci), New Star of the Year in a Motion Picture–Female (Moriarty), Best Screenplay–Motion Picture

Source: Roberts, James B., and Skutt, Alexander G. *The Boxing Register*. Ithaca, NY: McBooks Press, 1997. The book at page 286 gives the date of this bout.

Alternate Film: *Julius Caesar* (1953)

15

THE DEPARTED

Year: 2006
Genre: Crime/Thriller
Run Time: 2 hours 31 minutes
Date Revealed in Film: 44:36
Availability: Blu-ray and DVD (Warner Brothers)
Director: Martin Scorsese; **Screenplay**: William Monahan, based on the film *Internal Affairs* by Alan Mak and Felix Chong
Cast: Leonardo DiCaprio (William "Billy" Costigan Jr.), Matt Damon (Colin Sullivan), Jack Nicholson (Francis "Frank" Costello), Mark Wahlberg (Sean Dignam), Martin Sheen (Oliver Charles Queenan), Vera Farmiga (Dr. Madolyn Madden)

Mob Boss Frank Costello gets Colin Sullivan to become a mole in the State Police. Captain Queenan and Staff Sergeant Dignam ask police academy student Billy Costigan to infiltrate the Mob. Costigan agrees. Costigan eventually gets introduced to Costello and persuades him he's not a cop. Sullivan begins a romance with psychiatrist Madolyn Madden.

On March 15, 2006, Costigan goes along on his first "job" for Costello (42:00 to 44:51). The pressure of living a double life starts to get to Costigan. When Costello eludes surveillance Costigan's fears that there is a mole in the State Police are confirmed. The fact that the police knew about his meeting convinces Costello and Sullivan that the police have a mole inside the Mob. Costello gets personal data on his "crew" that will help Sullivan find the mole. This data is put in an envelope that Costigan writes on. Costigan hears that Costello is an FBI informant and tells this to Queenan.

The relationship between Dr. Madden and Costigan becomes a sexual one. Costello gives Sullivan the envelope with his crews' personal info. When Queenan is killed, Sullivan learns Costello is an FBI informant and kills him to ensure his identity won't ever make it back to the State Police. With Costello dead, everyone on the force applauds Sullivan the next day.

Costigan learns Sullivan is the mole when he sees Sullivan has the envelope he wrote on. He makes a plan to arrest Sullivan. However, this leads to the explosive climax, where only the unexpected happens.

A twisty, turny battle of wits. Both moles slide from point of danger to point of danger. Interesting exploration of the psychology of honesty and lying.

Awards: *Academy Award Wins*: Best Director, Best Film Editing, Best Picture, and Best Adapted Screenplay. *Academy Award Nomination*: Best Supporting Actor (Mark Wahlberg). *Golden Globe Win*: Best Director–Motion Picture. *Golden Globe Nominations*: Best Motion Picture–Drama, Best Performance by an Actor in a Motion Picture–Drama (Leonardo DiCaprio), Best Performance by an Actor in a Supporting Role in a Motion Picture (Jack Nicholson), Best Performance by an Actor in a Supporting Role in a Motion Picture (Wahlberg) and Best Screenplay–Motion Picture

Alternate Film: *Eddie and the Cruisers*

16
THE FUGITIVE
Year: 1993
Genre: Action/Adventure
Run Time: 2 hours 10 minutes
Date Revealed in Film: 1:10:52
Availability: Blu-ray (Warner Home Video)
Director: Andrew Davis; **Screenplay**: Jeb Stuart, David Twohy, and Roy Huggins
Cast: Harrison Ford (Dr. Richard Kimble), Tommy Lee Jones (Deputy Samuel Gerard), Jeroen Krabbé (Dr. Charles Nichols), Andreas Katsulas (Frederick Sykes), Joe Pantoliano (Agent Cosmo Renfro), Sela Ward (Helen Kimble), Julianne Moore (Dr. Anne Eastman)

While Dr. Richard Kimble is performing an emergency operation, a one-armed man attacks his wife at their house. When Kimble returns home, his wife hears him and says his name to 911. The one-armed man attacks Kimble and gets away, but his prosthetic arm is damaged. Due to the 911 call and other circumstantial matters, the police suspect Kimble, who is arrested, tried, and convicted of his wife's murder.

On the way to state prison by bus, an attempted escape causes the bus to end up wrecked on a railroad track. Kimble, who was unlocked to assist with a wounded guard, escapes. U.S. Deputy Marshal Gerard arrives to round up the convicts. Gerard tries to trap Kimble in a tunnel at a dam, but he gets away by making a death-defying leap off the dam. Kimble goes back to Chicago's Cook County Hospital and gets a list of people who had their prosthetic arm repaired shortly after his wife's murder. The next day, March 16, 1993, at the hospital, Gerard figures out that Kimble is looking for a man with a prosthetic arm (1:12:55 to 1:15:37). Kimble is almost caught by Gerard. At the home of the next person on his list, Frederick Sykes, Kimble finds evidence that his friend, Dr. Nichols, had put a hit on Kimble to cover up his involvement in a defective drug case and Kimble's wife's death was purely coincidental. Kimble heads to meet Nichols in a final showdown.

Wow! Nonstop action! A fast paced, don't-blink-or-you'll-miss-something kind of movie. This tale of the pursuit of justice is not to be missed.

Awards: *Academy Award Win*: Best Supporting Actor (Tommy Lee Jones). *Academy Award Nominations*: Best Picture, Best Cinematography, Best

Sound Editing, Best Film Editing, Best Original Score, and Best Sound. *Golden Globe Win*: Best Performance by an Actor in a Supporting Role in a Motion Picture (Jones). *Golden Globe Nominations*: Best Performance by an Actor in a Motion Picture–Drama (Harrison Ford) and Best Director–Motion Picture

Alternate Film: *Capricorn One*

17

GLADIATOR

Year: 2000

Genre: Period Drama

Run Time: 2 hours 35 minutes

Availability: Blu-ray and DVD (Warner Home Video)

Director: Ridley Scott; **Screenplay**: David Franzoni, John Logan, and William Nicholson

Cast: Russell Crowe (Maximus Decimus Meridius), Joaquin Phoenix (Commodus), Connie Nielsen (Lucilla), Djimon Hounsou (Juba), Oliver Reed (Antonius Proximo), Derek Jacobi (Gracchus), Ralf Möller (Hagen), Richard Harris (Marcus Aurelius)

Emperor Marcus Aurelius tells Maximus, a victorious Roman general, that he wants him to be emperor when he dies so he can hand power back to the Senate. When Marcus Aurelius tells his son Commodus he is not to be emperor, Commodus kills him on March 17, 180 (31:47 to 39:16).

Commodus becomes emperor and orders Maximus and his family to be arrested and executed. Maximus escapes and races home to find his family already dead. Slavers take him to Africa, where Proximo, a gladiator trainer and promoter, buys him. Under the name of "the Spaniard," Maximus wins many fights and returns with Proximo to Rome. Commodus is introduced to "the Spaniard," who reveals himself as Maximus. Commodus considers having Maximus killed in the arena, but under pressure from the crowd, relents. Commodus brings the only undefeated gladiator out of retirement to beat Maximus in a fight, but Maximus wins anyway. When he refuses to deliver the deathblow, the crowd dubs him "Maximus the Merciful." This annoys Commodus, as he can't have Maximus killed.

Maximus meets his former servant, Cicero, who tells him his army is still loyal to him. Commodus's sister, Lucilla, who is Maximus's former lover, brings Senator Gracchus to meet with Maximus. She does not like Commodus because she knows Commodus killed their father. Maximus tells the senator that with his help he can bring his army to Rome, kill Commodus, and restore the Senate to power. Gracchus agrees. But Commodus, suspicious, indirectly threatens Lucilla's son and forces her to reveal the plot. Troops attack the gladiator barracks. They fight to hold off the troops so Maximus can get away, but in the end Maximus is captured and Gracchus arrested. Commodus stabs Maximus with a knife and then fights him in the arena hand to hand. But Maximus is able to kill Commodus despite his mortal stab wound. With his dying breath, Maximus directs that Gracchus be freed and that power be restored to the Senate.

A good revival of the 1950s sword-and-sandal epics. Plenty of action and skullduggery. Not strictly historically accurate, but still good.

Awards: *Academy Award Wins*: Best Picture, Best Actor (Russell Crowe), Best Costume Design, Best Sound, and Best Visual Effects. *Academy Award Nominations*: Best Supporting Actor (Joaquin Phoenix), Best Art and Set Decoration, Best Cinematography, Best Director, Best Editing, Best Original Score, and Best Screenplay. *Golden Globe Wins*: Best Motion Picture–Drama and Best Original Score–Motion Picture. *Golden Globe Nominations*: Best Director–Motion Picture, Best Performance by an Actor in a Motion Picture–Drama (Crowe) and Best Performance by an Actor in a Supporting Role in a Motion Picture (Phoenix)

Source: McLynn, Frank. *Marcus Aurelius: A Life*. Cambridge, MA: Da Capo Press, 2009. This book at page 418 gives the date of his death.

Alternate Film: *Flight of the Phoenix* (1965)

18
THE LORD OF THE RINGS: RETURN OF THE KING

Year: 2003
Genre: Fantasy/Action
Run Time: 3 hours 21 minutes
Availability: Blu-ray and DVD (New Line Cinema)
Director: Peter Jackson; **Screenplay**: Fran Walsh, Peter Jackson, and Phillipa Boyens, based on the novel by J. R. R. Tolkien
Cast: Elijah Wood (Frodo Baggins), Sean Astin (Samwise Gamgee), Viggo Mortensen (Aragorn), Ian McKellen (Gandalf), Orlando Bloom (Legolas),

John Rhys-Davies (Gimli), Miranda Otto (Éowyn), Karl Urban (Éomer), Liv Tyler (Arwen)

Gollum flashes back to when he acquired the ring after murdering Deagol long ago. Aragorn, Gandalf, Gimli, and Legolas reach Isengard and view the destruction there. They retrieve Merry and Pippin and return to Edoras, capital of Rohan. Pippin and Gandalf reach Minas Tirith, while Frodo, Sam, and Gollum reach Minas Morgul. The orcs attack and capture Osgiliath from the forces of Gondor. Pippin accidentally lights the first beacon that requests aid from Rohan. The Rohirrim leave for Minas Tirith, with Merry riding behind "Dernhelm."

Faramir's forces, retreating from Osgiliath, reach Minas Tirith. Frodo, Sam, and Gollum reach the pass into Mordor. Aragorn takes the path of the dead and agrees to release the dead if they will help him seize the pirate fleet of Umbar. Faramir is wounded and the orcs attack Minas Tirith. Frodo, Sam, and Gollum enter a cave, where Gollum disappears while they are attacked by a giant spider. Sam kills it, and orcs capture Frodo, but Sam gets the ring. The Rohrrim attack in the Battle of the Pellanor Fields. The chief Nazgul, who cannot be killed by any man, kills Theoden, King of Rohan, but is killed by "Dernhelm," who is revealed to be Eowyn, daughter of Theoden. The oliphants are defeated and Aragorn's arrival with the dead helps finish off the orc attack. Sam rescues Frodo from the orcs.

Aragorn leads the Host of the West out of Minas Tirith on March 18, 3017, T.A. (2:26:08 to 2:26:25) to draw out Sauron's armies so Frodo can complete his mission. The Host reaches the Black Gate and appears about to be annihilated. Frodo and Sam reach Mount Doom, but at the last second Frodo cannot bring himself to destroy the ring. Gollum appears and bites off the finger with the ring and it falls into the fire, destroying the ring. Sauron is destroyed and Frodo, Sam, and the army are saved. Aragorn is crowned King Elessar of Gondor and marries Arwen. The hobbits return to the Shire. Frodo, Bilbo, and Gandalf leave on the last ship to depart Middle Earth.

A great action/adventure story. Even if you've read the book it keeps you interested. Great special effects and cinematography.

Awards: *Academy Award Wins*: Best Picture, Best Director, Best Adapted Screenplay, Best Original Score, Best Song, Best Visual Effects, Best Art

Direction, Best Costume, Best Makeup, Best Sound Mixing, and Best Film Editing. *Golden Globe Wins*: Best Director–Motion Picture, Best Original Score–Motion Picture, Best Original Song–Motion Picture, and Best Motion Picture–Drama

Source: Tolkien, J. R. R. *The Lord of the Rings*. New York; Houghton Mifflin, 1994. This book at page 1067 gives the date the host leaves Minas Tirith.

Alternate Film: *Tombstone*

19

GLORY ROAD

Year: 2006
Genre: Sports/Drama
Run Time: 1 hour 58 minutes
Availability: Blu-ray (Disney/Buena Vista)
Director: James Gartner; **Screenplay**: Chris Cleveland and Bettina Gilois
Cast: Josh Lucas (Don Haskins), Derek Luke (Bobby Joe Hill), Austin Nichols (Jerry Armstrong), Jon Voight (Adolph Rupp), Evan Jones (Moe Ibal), Schin A. S. Kerr (David Lattin), Alphonso McAuley (Orsten Artis), Emily Deschanel (Mary Haskins)

Don Haskins is named head basketball coach at Texas Western University. He recruits the best players regardless of race. Haskins starts playing an integrated squad, which generates success on the court and racial hatred off court. They finish the year ranked third in the country. In the NCAA tournament they face the all-white Kentucky squad. Haskins decides to play an all–African American team. On March 19, 1966, they win the title (1:30:30 to 1:46:23).

A good basketball film. Takes a few liberties with the facts, but still good. A film about the cost of racism.

Source: Douchant, Mike (ed.). *Encyclopedia of College Basketball*. Detroit, MI: Gale Research, Inc., 1995. This book at page 128 gives the date of this game.

Alternate Film: *The Mighty Macs*

20

AMELIA

Year: 2009
Genre: Biographical Drama
Run Time: 1 hour 51 minutes
Date Revealed in Film: 1:44:21
Availability: Blu-ray and DVD (Twentieth Century Fox)
Director: Mira Nair; **Screenplay**: Ronald Bass and Anna Hamilton Phelan
Cast: Hilary Swank (Amelia Earhart), Richard Gere (George P. Putnam), Ewan McGregor (Gene Vidal), Christopher Eccleston (Fred Noonan), William Cuddy (Gore Vidal), Mia Wasikowska (Elinor Smith), Cherry Jones (Eleanor Roosevelt)

As a young child, when Amelia Earhart saw an airplane, she wanted to fly. After Amelia learned how to pilot an airplane she visited George Putnam, a publisher, to get herself selected as the first woman to fly across the Atlantic as a passenger. After she orders fuel dumped in Newfoundland to lighten the plane they finally manage to take off. They fly right across Ireland and land in Wales. She becomes an instant celebrity, dubbed "Lady Lindy." She gets a ticker-tape parade on her return to New York and sets the autogiro altitude record.

An attraction develops between Amelia and George Putnam, and he finally convinces her to marry him. Amelia finishes third in a cross-country airplane race. She then becomes the first woman to fly across the Atlantic solo. George organizes a publicity and endorsement campaign, and she takes Eleanor Roosevelt up on a flight. George persuades Purdue University to foot the bill for an around-the-world flight.

Amelia flies to Hawaii on the first leg of the flight. On March 20, 1937, she crashes the plane in a takeoff attempt (1:14:21 to 1:17:44). The plane has to be shipped back to California and repaired. She now flies east to Florida, to Africa, to India, and on to New Guinea. From there she takes off for tiny Howland Island, but vanishes over the Pacific.

Although somewhat formulaic, it is still an engaging film. Swank captures the essence of Amelia Earhart in looks and personality.

Alternate Film: *Phar Lap*

21
THX 1138

Year: 1971

Genre: Science Fiction

Run Time: 1 hour 26 minutes (theatrical release), 1 hour 29 minutes (director's cut)

Date Revealed in Film: 13:50

Availability: Blu-ray ad DVD (Warner Home Video)

Director: George Lucas; **Screenplay**: George Lucas and Walter Murch

Cast: Robert Duvall (THX 1138), Donald Pleasence (SEN 5241), Don Pedro Colley (the hologram SRT), Maggie McOmie (LUH 3417), Ian Wolfe (the old prisoner PTO), Marshall Efron (prisoner TWA), Sid Haig (prisoner NCH)

On March 21 in a year of the twenty-fifth century (2:57 to 16:44) in an underground city, the population is controlled by drugs and sex is outlawed. SEN 5241 (a man) and LUH 3417 (a woman) work in the surveillance center. LUH 3417 has a male roommate, THX 1138, who works in an android robot factory. At home he takes his drugs and watches mindless entertainment. LUH 3417 switches her drugs for THX 1138's drugs, which cause him to have emotional feelings, and he and LUH 3417 have sex. She suggests they escape, but he declines. THX 1138 stops taking his drugs. SEN 5241 tries to talk THX 1138 into becoming his roommate, so THX 1138 files a complaint against SEN 5241. The control center mentally immobilizes THX 1138 prior to his arrest for non-drug use. This occurs at a critical time and almost causes a nuclear accident. THX 1138 and LUH 3417 are arrested and she tells him she is pregnant. THX 1138 is sent to limbo. He refuses to accept his fate and makes a bold try for freedom.

A classic dystopian film with a message about totalitarian control and the human spirit.

Alternate Film: *Doomsday Gun*

22
CINDERELLA MAN

Year: 2005

Genre: Biography

Run Time: 2 hours 24 minutes

Date Revealed in Film: 1:18:09

Availability: Blu-ray and DVD (Universal Studios)

Director: Ron Howard; **Screenplay**: Cliff Hollingsworth and Akiva Goldsman

Cast: Russell Crowe (James J. Braddock), Renée Zellweger (Mae Braddock), Paul Giamatti (Joe Gould), Bruce McGill (James Johnston), Craig Bierko (Max Baer), Paddy Considine (Mike Wilson), David Huband (Ford Bond), Connor Price (Jay Braddock)

In 1928 Jim Braddock knocks out Tuffy Griffith in a bout at Madison Square Garden, winning a big purse and setting him on course for a shot at the heavyweight title. We jump ahead five years. Braddock has lost the title bout and suffered various injuries. As a result the family is reduced to living in a basement in a New Jersey slum and is practically starving. His son steals food and Jim promises him he will never send the children to live with relatives.

Braddock's license to box is revoked. His hand is broken, but he gets occasional work on the loading docks. They are still in dire financial straits and are reduced to scavenging. When the power is cut off, Braddock's wife, Mae, sends the kids to live with her parents. This upsets Jim, who goes and signs up for Public Relief. He goes to Madison Square Garden and begs for help from the writers and promoters there, and some do help. He gets the kids back. His longtime manager gets him a fight against Corn Griffin as a replacement opponent. Jim knocks him out. His manager arranges a second bout for him and comes up with enough money so Jim can skip work and train.

Jim beats John Henry Lewis and later beats Art Lasky on March 22, 1935 (1:18:03 to 1:22:46). He pays back the welfare money he received. A title fight against Max Baer is arranged, but people try to talk Jim out of it since Baer has killed two men in the ring. All the poor people in the country see Jim as representing them and are pulling for him. Braddock beats Baer in the title bout.

A great story of the underdog. Also a story of faith and hanging on until things turn around. Zellweger and Crowe give sincere, believable performances.

Awards: *Academy Award Nominations*: Best Editing, Best Makeup, and Best Supporting Actor (Paul Giamatti). *Golden Globe Nominations*: Best Performance by an Actor in a Motion Picture–Drama (Russell Crowe) and

Best Performance by an Actor in a Supporting Role in a Motion Picture–
Drama (Giamatti)
Alternate Film: *Chocolat*

23

SINGIN' IN THE RAIN
Year: 1952
Genre: Musical/Comedy
Run Time: 1 hour 43 minutes
Date Revealed in Film: 1:01:32–39
Availability: Blu-ray and DVD (Warner Home Video)
Directors: Gene Kelly and Stanley Donen; **Screenplay**: Betty Comden and
Adolph Green
Cast: Gene Kelly (Don Lockwood), Donald O'Connor (Cosmo Brown), Deb-
bie Reynolds (Kathy Selden), Jean Hagen (Lina Lamont), Millard Mitchell
(R. F. Simpson), Cyd Charisse (Lockwood's dance partner), Rita Moreno
(Zelda Zanders)
Don Lockwood is a popular silent film star who came up through the ranks as
a singer, dancer, and stuntman. He's usually teamed in period swashbuckler
films with Lina Lamont, a shallow and self-centered actress. The studio has
paired the two romantically for publicity purposes and while Lina believes
Don really loves her, he does not. On the way to a party, in order to escape
some fans Don jumps in a car driven by Kathy Selden, an aspiring stage
actress who's disdainful of movie stars. At the party R. F., the head of Don's
studio, demonstrates a talking film, but his guests are dismissive of the new
technology. When Kathy pops out of a cake at the party, Don is amused and
she is humiliated and flees after tossing a cake targeted at Don into the face
of Lina. Lina is so furious she goes out of her way to get Kathy fired from her
chorus girl job. After much searching, Don finds Kathy working on another
film at the studio and they strike up a relationship.

After *The Jazz Singer*, a "talkie," is a huge hit, R. F. converts all his films, including the new Lockwood-Lamont vehicle, *The Dueling Cavalier*, into talkies. They have problems with Lina's grating voice and inability to speak into
the microphone. The premiere on March 23, 1930, is a disaster. The audience
laughs at Lina's voice and the sound goes out of synchronization (55:08 to

59:29). Cosmo Brown, Don's best friend, suggests converting the film into a musical, *The Dancing Cavalier*, and have Kathy dub Lina's lines. After filming is completed, but before release, Lina finds out about this and Don's romance with Kathy. Lina is very angry. R. F. had planned to give Kathy screen credit and promote her as a "talkies" star. Lina, relying on her contract, tells R. F. he has to drop all ideas of promoting Kathy and make Kathy (without credit) continue to dub Lina. R. F. reluctantly agrees.

The Dancing Cavalier's premiere is a success. When Lina praises her own "performance" in the film, the audience wants her to sing live. Don, Cosmo, and R. F. convince her to lip-synch a song while Kathy, hidden behind the curtain actually sings for her, but they raise the curtain, revealing the deception to the crowd. Lina flees in embarrassment and Don introduces Kathy, "the real star of the film," to an appreciative audience. Don and Kathy then star in a new movie, *Singin' in the Rain*.

One of the classic Hollywood musicals. Has the right mixture of comedy and music to make this a smash. All the performances are good and the songs are excellent, including Gene Kelly's iconic performance of the title song, "Singin' in the Rain."

Awards: *Academy Award Nominations*: Best Supporting Actress (Jean Hagen) and Best Original Music Score. *Golden Globe Win*: Best Motion Picture Actor–Musical/Comedy (Donald O'Connor). *Golden Globe Nomination*: Best Motion Picture–Musical/Comedy

Alternate Film: *September Dawn*

24

THE BREAKFAST CLUB
Year: 1985
Genre: Comedy/Drama
Run Time: 1 hour 37 minutes
Date Revealed in Film: 2:08–11
Availability: Blu-ray and DVD (Universal Studios)
Director: John Hughes; **Screenplay**: John Hughes
Cast: Emilio Estevez (Andrew "Andy" Clark), Paul Gleason (Richard "Dick" Vernon), Anthony Michael Hall (Brian Ralph Johnson), Judd Nelson (John Bender), Molly Ringwald (Claire Standish), Ally Sheedy (Allison Reynolds), John Kapelos (Carl Reed)

On Saturday, March 24, 1984, five students—Claire Standish, John Bender, Brian Johnson, Andy Clark, and Allison Reynolds—are in detention at Shermer High School. The principal, Dick Vernon, directs each of them to write a thousand-word essay about who they think they are. Since Vernon leaves them alone, they end up opening up to each other, revealing their secrets and becoming friends. Andy hates his overbearing father; John's father abuses him; Allison is a liar; Claire is a virgin; and Brian has considered suicide. Claire and John and Allison and Andy become couples. The five vow to remain friends. Brian writes a letter to Vernon saying his essay assignment is ridiculous, as he has already decided who they are, a criminal (John), an athlete (Andy), a brain (Brian), a princess (Claire), and a basket case (Allison). They all head home.

An interesting character-driven movie. There's little real action, but a lot of thoughtful conversation.

Alternate Film: *Romero*

25

THE GREAT ESCAPE

Year: 1963
Genre: Adventure
Run Time: 2 hours 52 minutes
Availability: Blu-ray and DVD (Metro-Goldwyn-Mayer)
Director: John Sturges; **Screenplay**: James Clavell and W. R. Burnett
Cast: Steve McQueen (Hilts "The Cooler King"), James Garner (Hendley "The Scrounger"), Richard Attenborough (Bartlett "Big X"), James Donald (Ramsey "The SBO"), Charles Bronson (Danny "Tunnel King"), Hannes Messemer (Von Luger)

In World War II a group of Allied air force officers are prisoners in the new "secure" German camp of Stalag III. They work together to dig three escape tunnels and prepare disguises and paperwork to use in escapes. Equipment is obtained by blackmailing some German guards. Even though one tunnel is discovered, they break out in another tunnel, with the last men leaving early on the morning of March 25, 1944 (2:01:38 to 2:16:31). Seventy-six men escape, even though the tunnel exit is exposed in the space between the fence and the sheltering woods. The men now engage in a desperate attempt to get out of Nazi-occupied territory alive.

A great action/adventure story largely based on actual events. Some scenes, such as Steve McQueen's attempt to escape on a motorcycle, have become iconic.

Awards: *Academy Award Nomination*: Best Film Editing

Source: Carroll, Tim. *The Great Escape from Luft Stalag III*. New York: Pocket Books, 2004. This book at pages 195–96 and 208–9 gives the date the last men left the tunnel.

Alternate Film: *Men of Honor*

26

THE WORLD'S FASTEST INDIAN

Year: 2005

Genre: Biography

Run Time: 2 hours 7 minutes

Availability: Blu-ray and DVD (Magnolia Pictures)

Director: Roger Donaldson; **Screenplay**: Roger Donaldson

Cast: Anthony Hopkins (Burt Munro), Jessica Cauffiel (Wendy), Joe Howard (Otto), Chris Williams (Tina), Paul Rodriguez (Fernando), Christopher Lawford (Jim Moffet), Annie Whittle (Fran), Aaron J. Murphy (Tom), Chris Bruno (Bob), Diane Ladd (Ada)

Burt Munro has spent years rebuilding his 1920 Indian motorcycle to make it the fastest one in Australasia, and it gets mentioned in *Popular Mechanics*. This makes him a folk hero to some extent, but he still annoys his neighbors with some of his idiosyncrasies. At his birthday party, some local bikers challenge him to a race the next day. On March 26, 1967 (14:47 to 19:31), Munro easily outpaces the bikers on the first leg, but loses when he turns over during a turn. Munro mortgages his house so he can travel to the Bonneville Salt Flats in Utah to see how fast he can go. In the United States he has many problems, including a damaged bike and failure to have preregistered. However, Munro's gregarious nature compels people to help him overcome his problems. After his first run, Munro realizes he still has one problem to overcome before he tries to break the record.

Source: Hanna, Tim. *One Good Run*. New York, Penguin Books, 2005. This
   book at page 27 gives his birth date and the race is the next day.
Alternate Film: *Letters from Iwo Jima*

27
PLANET OF THE APES
Year: 1968
Genre: Science Fiction
Run Time: 1 hour 52 minutes
Date Revealed in Film: 2:17
Availability: Blu-ray and DVD (Twentieth Century Fox)
Director: Franklin J. Schaffner; **Screenplay**: Michael Wilson and Rod Serling,
   based on Pierre Boulle's novel
Cast: Charlton Heston (George Taylor), Roddy McDowell (Cornelius), Kim
   Hunter (Dr. Zira), Maurice Evans (Dr. Zaius), James Whitmore (President
   of the Assembly), Linda Harrison (Nova), Robert Gunner (Landon), Lou
   Wagner (Lucius), Jeff Burton (Dodge)
Astronaut George Taylor records a log entry on Earth date March 27, 2673,
before putting himself in hibernation (2:17). He is on a ship traveling through
space at near light speed such that while two thousand years pass on Earth,
only eighteen months pass for the crew. They awaken when their ship crashes
in a lake on an unknown planet and sinks.

Taylor, Landon, and Dodge escape. They trek through the desert and when
they find water go for a swim. Primitive humans steal their clothes. Suddenly
gorillas on horseback charge. They kill Dodge, knock Landon unconscious,
and shoot Taylor in the throat. Landon and Taylor along with many of the
primitive humans are captured. A chimp scientist, Zira, saves Taylor's life.
Taylor, who has been rendered temporarily mute by his wound, discovers
that simians are civilized, while mute humans are considered wild animals.
Taylor tries to mouth words to Zira and eventually steals paper and writes
her a note. She and her fiancé, Cornelius, an archaeologist, become convinced
Taylor is intelligent. When their boss, Dr. Zaius, learns of this he orders Taylor castrated. Taylor escapes, but is recaptured, uttering the classic line, "Take
your stinking paws off me, you damned dirty ape!"

A trial is held to determine where Taylor is from and what to do with him. They refuse to believe his story of coming from another planet and bring in a lobotomized Landon to "prove" Taylor is a freak. Zira and Cornelius kidnap Taylor and his female companion, Nova, and take them to "the Forbidden Zone," the desert area where Taylor's ship crashed. Cornelius had previously conducted a dig there and found artifacts that seemed to establish a pre-simian society. Dr. Zaius appears with his soldiers and after viewing artifacts in a seaside cave admits that he knew all along that people were dominant before apes. He expels Taylor and Nova. They travel up the coast until they make a startling discovery.

One of the classic sci-fi films. Good even though it does use the B-movie cliché of the apes speaking English. Also works as a pacifist film.

Awards: *Academy Award Wins*: Best Costume Design and Best Original Score
Alternate Film: *Heavens Fall*

28

CAPTAIN PHILLIPS

Year: 2013
Genre: Action/Drama
Run Time: 2 hours 14 minutes
Date Revealed in Film: 00:45
Availability: Blu-ray and DVD (Sony Pictures)
Director: Paul Greengrass; **Screenplay**: Billy Ray, based on Richard Phillips
 and Stephen Talty's book, *A Captain's Duty: Somali Pirates, Navy SEALS
 and Dangerous Days at Sea*
Cast: Tom Hanks (Captain Richard Phillips), Barkhad Abdi (Abduwali
 Muse), Catherine Keener (Andrea Phillips), Faysal Ahmed (Najee), Mi-
 chael Chernus (Shane Murphy), David Warshofsky (Mike Perry), Corey
 Johnson (Ken Quinn)

On March 28, 2009 (00:38 to 4:05), Captain Richard Phillips leaves home and travels to his cargo ship, the MV *Maersk Alabama*, which is to sail from Oman to Tanzania. A group of Somali pirates set sail. Captain Phillips wants security on the ship increased after he receives a pirate warning. The pirates, led by Abduwali Muse, notice that the *Maersk Alabama* is sailing alone. The crew scares off the pirates the first time, but on their second attempt they get aboard. Some crew and Phillips are captured, but the crew captures Muse, the pirate leader, and proposes to trade him for Phillips, $30,000, and a lifeboat. When the pirates leave in the lifeboat, they take Phillips with them. The USS *Bainbridge* arrives and begins negotiations. Costellano has orders to do whatever is necessary to ensure the lifeboat does not reach Somalia. The Navy agrees to tow the lifeboat. Phillips briefly escapes, but is recaptured. Muse is tricked on board the *Bainbridge*. This precipitates the dangerous end game.

A very good action/adventure based on true events. Maintains a high level of tension. The four Somalis who portray the pirates give very good performances for non-professional actors.

Awards: *Academy Award Nominations*: Best Picture, Best Supporting Actor (Barkhad Abdi), Best Film Editing, Best Sound Editing, Best Sound Mixing, Best Adapted Screenplay. *Golden Globe Nominations*: Best Motion Picture–Drama, Best Performance by an Actor in a Motion Picture–Drama (Tom Hanks), Best Performance by an Actor in a Supporting Role in a Motion Picture (Abdi), Best Director–Motion Picture

Alternate Film: *Frost/Nixon*

29

THE ADVENTURES OF ROBIN HOOD

Year: 1938
Genre: Adventure
Run Time: 1 hour 42 minutes
Availability: Blu-ray and DVD (Warner Home Video)
Directors: Michael Curtiz and William Keighley; **Screenplay**: Norman Raine and Seton Miller
Cast: Erroll Flynn (Robin Hood), Olivia de Havilland (Maid Marian), Basil Rathbone (Guy of Gisbourne), Claude Rains (Prince John), Patric Knowles (Will Scarlett), Eugene Pallette (Friar Tuck), Alan Hale Sr. (Little John), Herbert Mundin (Much)

Richard the Lion-Hearted is taken prisoner by the Duke of Austria while returning from the Third Crusade. His brother, Prince John, uses this as an excuse to seize the regency for himself. He enforces an oppressive taxation, ostensibly to raise the ransom for the king, but he intends to continue ruling and keep the money for himself. Robin of Locksley, a Saxon, saves a man (Much) from being killed by Sir Guy of Gisbourne for poaching a royal deer to stay alive. At a banquet Robin tells Prince John of his plan to organize a revolt, and in spite of the efforts of the Sheriff of Nottingham and his men, Robin escapes and is declared an outlaw.

Robin gathers the Merry Men, who hide in Sherwood Forest and harass the Normans. One day they capture a party transporting taxes. Guy of Gisbourne, the Sheriff of Nottingham, and Maid Marian, the king's ward who thought Robin haughty and uncouth at the banquet, are among the party. Robin convinces her of his good intentions when the Merry Men are incensed at Robin's satirical "suggestion" that they keep the tax money for themselves instead of using it for the king's ransom. After their release, the sheriff holds an archery tournament that traps Robin, who is sentenced to hang. Marian has fallen in love with Robin and uses her maid's friendship with Much to contact Robin's men. Together they hatch a plan to save Robin at the last minute. Robin later risks his life to enter the castle and profess his love for Marian.

King Richard is released and secretly returns to England. A supporter of Prince John, the Bishop of the Black Canons, recognizes the king and John sends an assassin to kill Richard. Maid Marian overhears this conversation. Guy finds a note she has written, and Prince John sentences her to death. Richard, disguised as a monk, enters Sherwood Forest on March 29, 1194, and encounters Robin (1:24:11 to 1:29:46). Much stops the assassin from carrying out his task. Robin and his men come up with a plan to stop Prince John for good.

A great action/adventure film. This one set the standard. The climactic melee is a classic. The resemblance of the film's action to historical events is minimal.

Awards: *Academy Award Wins*: Best Art Direction, Best Film Editing, and Best Original Score. *Academy Award Nomination*: Best Picture

Source: Norgate, Kate. *Richard the Lion Heart*. London: Macmillan, 1924.
This book at page 289 gives the date Richard entered Sherwood.

Alternate Film: *Scott of the Antarctic*

30

SECRETARIAT

Year: 2010

Genre: Drama

Run Time: 2 hours 3 minutes

Availability: Blu-ray and DVD (Disney/Buena Vista)

Director: Randall Wallace; **Screenplay**: Mike Rich and Sheldon Turner, based on the book by William Nack

Cast: Diane Lane (Penny Chenery Tweedy), John Malkovich (Lucien Laurin), Amanda Michalka (Kate Tweedy), Graham McTavish (Charles Hatton), Marissa Capobianco (Sarah Tweedy), Scott Glenn (Christopher Chenery), James Cromwell (Ogden Phipps)

Penny Tweedy travels to her family's horse farm in Virginia when her mother dies. Her father has Alzheimer's, and she takes over running the farm. Her father had agreed with another owner, Ogden Phipps, to mate two of his mares to another owner's stud, with the winner of a coin toss getting to pick one of the foals to take. When the coin toss is held, Penny loses the toss. She hires Lucien Laurin as her trainer.

Secretariat is born on March 30, 1970 (24:25 to 25:33), but does not impress his trainer. In his first race Secretariat finishes fourth and Ron Turcotte is hired as jockey. Secretariat runs at Saratoga and with a come-from-behind win is named horse of the year. Penny's father dies and the estate taxes are $6 million. Her brother and husband want to sell Secretariat to pay them, but she says no. Her effort to sell Secretariat's future breeding rights fails until she talks Ogden Phipps into investing and then enough money is raised. At the Woods Memorial Race Secretariat finishes third and questions are raised about his future. Secretariat develops a mouth abscess and doesn't eat very much but recovers the day before the Derby. Secretariat comes from behind and wins in the Derby, the Preakness, and the Belmont to win the Triple Crown.

A fun movie. Penny Tweedy is a strong woman who takes charge and does great things. She lives by the adage "Nothing ventured, nothing gained." You can see that she feels she did miss out on some of her family's life.

Source: Simon, Mary. *Racing through the Century*. Irvine, CA: BowTie Press, 2002. This book at page 222 gives Secretariat's birth date.

Alternate Film: *Introducing Dorothy Dandridge*

31

PERSEPOLIS

Year: 2007
Genre: Biographical Drama
Run Time: 1 hour 35 minutes
Availability: Blu-ray and DVD Sony Pictures
Directors: Marjane Satrapi and Vincent Paronnaud; **Screenplay**: Marjane
   Satrapi and Vincent Paronnaud, based on Satrapi's graphic novel
Cast: Chiara Mastroianni (teenage and adult Marjane), Amethyste Frezignac
   (child Marjane), Catherine Deneuve (Mother), Gena Rowlands (Grand-
   mother), Sean Penn (Father), Iggy Pop (Uncle Anouche)
Marjane is a normal little girl in 1978 Iran who loves Adidas sneakers and
Bruce Lee. As protests rise against the Shah, who had replaced the former
Kajar dynasty, the Shah is overthrown. Marjane's uncle Anouche is released
from jail. The Islamist victory in the National Referendum is announced on
March 31, 1979 (18:56 to 19:13). Anouche is soon rearrested and executed.
Then Iraq attacks, resulting in political repression, food shortages, and missile
attacks. Marjane defies the repressive societal rules. After Marjane contradicts
her teacher's political propaganda her family sends her to school in Vienna.
After a difficult time there, she eventually returns to Iran. Marjane is married
off to a man who is soon revealed as an idiot. Marjane is forced by the repressive government to make a difficult decision about her future.

A refreshingly different animated movie. Has a simple black-and-white
design as in the graphic novel. Maintains the right balance between political
lecture and comedy.

Awards: *Academy Award Nomination*: Best Animated Film
Source: Fisher, Michael. *Iran: From Religious Dispute to Revolution.* Cambridge, MA: Harvard University Press, 1980. At page 220 this book gives
   the date of the referendum.
Alternate Film: *Kundun*

April

1

GOODBYE, MR. CHIPS

Year: 1939
Genre: Drama
Run Time: 1 hour 54 minutes
Date Revealed in Film: 1:13:16
Availability: Blu-ray (Warner Home Video), VHS (MGM/UA Home Video)
Director: Sam Wood; **Screenplay**: R. C. Sheriff, Claudine West, and Eric
  Maschwitz, based on the novella by James Hilton
Cast: Robert Donat (Mr. Chips), Greer Garson (Katherine), Lyn Harding
  (Wetherby), Paul Henreid (Max Staeffel), Terry Kilburn (John Colley, Pe-
  ter Colley I, II, and III), John Mills (adult Peter Colley), Scott Sunderland
  (Sir John Colley)

Edward Chipping ("Mr. Chips") starts teaching at Brookfield, an English
public school in 1870. He becomes a target of the students' practical jokes, to
which he responds by imposing strict discipline. He becomes respected, but
not liked. Chips goes on holiday and meets and falls in love with Katherine
Ellis, a vacationing English suffragette. They marry, and she wins over the
school with her friendly personality.

Katherine dies in childbirth on April 1, 1898 (1:12:57 to 1:18:28). After her
death, Chips comes out of his shell and becomes a very popular teacher, often

teaching the children of prior students. He retires at the start of World War I, but is recalled to serve as interim headmaster. He permanently retires in 1918. When he dies he looks back fondly on his career, thinking he had thousands of children, "all boys."

A good period piece with romance and touching sentiment. Chips also promotes a message of tolerance, trying to prevent the demonizing of the enemy in World War I. A very touching story.

Awards: *Academy Award Win*: Best Actor (Robert Donat). *Academy Award Nominations*: Best Picture, Best Director, Best Actress (Greer Garson), Best Adapted Screenplay, Best Film Editing, and Best Sound

Alternate Film: *Dirty Harry*

2

PRESUMED INNOCENT

Year: 1990
Genre: Courtroom Drama
Run Time: 2 hours 7 minutes
Date Revealed in Film: 1:13:23 and 5:48
Availability: Blu-ray and DVD (Warner Home Video)
Director: Alan J. Pakula; **Screenplay**: Frank Pierson and Alan J. Pakula, based on the novel by Scott Turow
Cast: Harrison Ford (Rozat "Rusty" Sabich), Brian Dennehy (Raymond Horgan), Raúl Juliá (Sandy Stern), Bonnie Bedelia (Barbara Sabich), Paul Winfield (Judge Lyttle), Greta Scacchi (Carolyn Polhemus), John Spencer (Det. Lipranzer)

"Rusty" Sabich goes to work in the Kendall County prosecutor's office on April 2, 1990, and learns a colleague, Carolyn Polhemus, was found raped and murdered the previous night (2:35 to 14:25). His boss, District Attorney Raymond Horgan, who's running for reelection, asks him to head the investigation. There is a file about bribery of government officials missing from her office and we learn Polhemus and Sabich once had an affair. The bribery file reveals that five years ago a guy named Leon paid to have his case dismissed. The probation officer was Polhemus, and the prosecutor was Malto, who has quit to work for Della Guardia, Horgan's opponent in the election. Polhemus's autopsy shows that the sperm in the sample taken from her body were dead and that she was tied up after she was dead. Horgan confesses to having an affair with Polhemus, which leads Rusty to think back about his own affair with her. Horgan loses the election. Della Guardia takes over the case, and says Rusty's prints were found on a glass in Polhemus's apartment.

Rusty is charged with her murder, and his house is searched. Rusty hires Sandy Stern as his attorney. At the grand jury he takes the Fifth and is indicted. Horgan turns against him. The trial begins and some big surprises are revealed during the course of testimony. However, the ending of the trial is not the biggest surprise in this film.

An excellent courtroom murder case. Keeps you guessing until the big twist at the end. A must-see film for mystery buffs.

Alternate Film: *An Ungentlemanly Act*

3

A PASSAGE TO INDIA

Year: 1984
Genre: Period Drama
Run Time: 2 hours 44 minutes
Date Revealed in Film: 1:57:53–54
Availability: Blu-ray and DVD (Sony Pictures)
Director: David Lean; **Screenplay**: David Lean, based on the novel by E. M. Forster and the play by Santha Rama Rau
Cast: Judy Davis (Adela Quested), Peggy Ashcroft (Mrs. Moore), Victor Banerjee (Dr. Aziz Ahmed), James Fox (Richard Fielding), Alec Guinness (Professor Godbole), Nigel Havers (Ronny Heaslop)

Adela Quested and Mrs. Moore sail to India to meet Ronny Heaslop, Mrs. Moore's son and Adela's fiancé, the city magistrate in Chandrapore. Muslim physician Dr. Aziz meets Mrs. Moore. On April 3, 1924, at a garden party, Adela meets Mr. Fielding, director of the local English school, who invites her and Mrs. Moore to meet with Dr. Aziz and the Brahmin Professor Godbole at tea (27:55 to 32:33). Dr. Aziz impulsively proposes a day trip to the Marabar caves for the group. Ronnie's anti-Indian attitude, in part, compels Adela to end their engagement, but she later changes her mind.

On the day of the trip to the caves, Fielding and Godbole miss the train carrying Aziz, Adela, and Mrs. Moore. They tour the first cave, but Mrs. Moore suggests Aziz and Adela continue the tour with just the guide. Aziz stops to smoke, then looks for Adela, but only finds her broken field glasses and sees her leave in a car. Back in Chandrapore, Adela, bloody and disheveled, is persuaded to accuse Dr. Aziz of assaulting her.

Upon his return Aziz is arrested, but Fielding is convinced he's innocent. The case becomes a cause célèbre, and Fielding resigns from the local British club when it becomes clear he is the only European who thinks Aziz is innocent. The trial begins. Ronny arranges for Mrs. Moore to leave India, so she can't testify on Aziz's behalf. Mrs. Moore dies on the ship and is buried at sea. When Adela takes the stand, to the unexpected joy of the Indians and the horror of the Europeans, she withdraws her charges. Aziz is freed. The European community turns on Adela, but she is rescued by Dr. Fielding and also has to deal with the news of Mrs. Moore's death. Aziz wants to seek damages from Adela, but Fielding talks him out of this, at the cost of their friendship.

Ronnie ends his engagement to Adela, and she returns to Britain. Sometime later Fielding visits Kashmir. Aziz and Godbole have both moved there. Fielding and Aziz meet and are reconciled. Aziz writes to Adela and forgives her, praising the strength and courage it took to tell the truth in court.

We are never shown what actually occurred in the cave, so we can't objectively decide whether anything actually happened. It appears nothing did, but both Forster and Lean left it ambiguous. A great piece of cinematography and character development.

Awards: *Academy Award Wins*: Best Supporting Actress (Peggy Ashcroft) and Best Original Score. *Academy Award Nominations*: Best Picture, Best Director, Best Actress (Judy Davis), Best Adapted Screenplay, Best Art Direction, Best Cinematography, Best Costume Design, Best Film Editing, and Best Sound. *Golden Globe Wins*: Best Foreign Film, Best Performance by an Actress in a Supporting Role in a Motion Picture (Ashcroft), Best Original Score–Motion Picture, Best Director–Motion Picture, and Best Screenplay–Motion Picture

Alternate Film: *Big Fish*

4

NINETEEN EIGHTY-FOUR

Year: 1984

Genre: Drama

Run Time: 1 hour 53 minutes

Date Revealed in Film: 10:34

Availability: DVD (Metro-Goldwyn-Mayer), VHS (USA Home Video)

Director: Michael Radford; **Screenplay**: Michael Radford, based on the novel by George Orwell

Cast: John Hurt (Winston Smith), Richard Burton (O'Brien), Suzanna Hamilton (Julia), Cyril Cusack (Mr. Charrington), James Walker (Syme), Gregor Fisher (Parsons), Andrew Wilde (Tillotson), Corina Seddon (Mrs. Smith), John Boswall (Emmanuel Goldstein)

Winston Smith lives in an alternate dystopian Britain where the Communists seized power long ago. Britain is part of Oceania along with the Americas and is eternally at war with either Eurasia or Eastasia. The repressive government, run by "the Party," controls speech and thought, and monitors everyone while shaping the language so rebellious speech is impossible. Winston's job is to rewrite old news stories, "correcting" them to be in line with current policy statements. At a mass meeting to express loyalty to "Big Brother," the mysterious leader of Oceania, and hatred of Goldstein, former ousted party leader, Winston spots Julia, a girl who appears to be more orthodox than most.

Although Winston appears orthodox, he hates the Party, and on April 4, 1984, starts an illegal private diary (00:20 to 11:04). Winston, a member of the Outer Party, is better off than the prols, the ordinary mass of people who live in poverty and are worked to death to support the eternal war. Julia slips him a note that says, "I love you." They meet in the country, where they can't be observed, and have sex, in part as a protest. Winston rents an unmonitored room from Charrington for their sexual trysts. O'Brien, an elite Inner Party member, gives Winston a copy of the new Newspeak dictionary, but concealed within is a copy of a forbidden book by Goldstein, which Winston reads. The book says that the war is perpetual, never meant to be won, and used by the leaders of the three superstates to keep their populations poor, disheartened, and under control. Winston and Julia discover that their meeting room is being monitored and they are arrested and subjected to their worst nightmares.

A depressing but fascinating film. It may be seen as a warning about many trends in modern society, such as the decline of the nuclear family and the rise of government monitoring and propaganda, along with the danger of political apathy.
Alternate Film: *Timeline*

5

RAY

Year: 2004
Genre: Biography
Run Time: 2 hours 32 minutes
Availability: Blu-ray and DVD (Universal Studios)
Director: Taylor Hackford; **Screenplay**: James L. White
Cast: Jamie Foxx (Ray Charles), Sharon Warren (Aretha Williams), Kerry
  Washington (Della Bea Robinson), Regina King (Margie Hendricks), Re-
  nee Wilson (Pat Lyle), Larenz Tate (Quincy Jones), Harry J. Lennixas (Joe
  Adams), Clifton Powell (Jeff Brown)
In 1948 blind Ray Robinson, aka Ray Charles, leaves Florida for Seattle, where he starts playing piano in a jazz bar. Later he begins to tour. In flashbacks we learn that his mother was a very strong woman who worked hard and made Ray promise never to become a cripple after he went blind at age seven. Ray's contract is sold to Atlantic Records, where he has his first hit.

Ray meets Della and marries her on April 5, 1955 (57:53 to 58:33). His wife finds out he is a heroin addict. Ray goes back on tour, where he uses drugs and has affairs. Ray refuses to play segregated facilities, causing problems in the South. He is arrested for drug possession, but the case is dropped and he goes on a very successful world tour. Some changes he makes, however, cause tension with some of his longtime band members. When he is again arrested for possession, his wife leaves, but he enters rehab. "Georgia on My Mind" is named the state song of that state.

A nitty-gritty biopic that shows the man, "warts and all." Your respect for the man has to increase when you learn that he was heavily involved in making this movie, as the picture it paints is not completely flattering. And of course you get to hear a lot of the great music!
Awards: *Academy Award Wins*: Best Actor (Jamie Foxx) and Best Sound
  Mixing. *Academy Award Nominations*: Best Picture, Best Director, Best

Editing, and Best Costume Design. *Golden Globe Win*: Best Performance by an Actor in a Motion Picture–Comedy or Musical (Foxx). *Golden Globe Nomination*: Best Motion Picture–Comedy or Musical
Source: Lydon, Michael. *Ray Charles: Man and Music*. New York: Riverhead Books, 1998. This book at page 119 gives his wedding date.
Alternate Film: *The Lords of Discipline*

6

TESS

Year: 1979
Genre: Period Drama
Run Time: 3 hours 6 minutes
Availability: Blu-ray (Criterion), DVD (Columbia/TriStar)
Director: Roman Polanski; **Screenplay**: Gerard Brach, John Brownjohn, and Roman Polanski, based on the Thomas Hardy novel *Tess of the d'Urbervilles*
Cast: Nastassja Kinski (Tess Durbeyfield), Peter Firth (Angel Clare), Leigh Lawson (Alec Stokes-d'Urberville), John Collin (John Durbeyfield), Rosemary Martin (Mrs. Durbeyfield), Carolyn Pickles (Miriam), Richard Pearson (Vicar of Marlott)

Pastor Tringham tells poor John Durbeyfield that he's a descendant of the formerly rich d'Urberville family. His wife gets the idea that they should send their eldest daughter, Tess, to see wealthy Mrs. d'Urbeville to "claim kin." Tess goes and meets Alex d'Urberville, who's attracted to her. Mrs. d'Urberville hires Tess to take care of her poultry. Tess learns that Alex's surname is actually Stokes. Tess attracts the jealousy of Alex's former female interest, and after a fight with her Tess and Alex ride off together. Alex rapes Tess. They are lovers for a while, but eventually Tess leaves and goes home. She has a child, who dies.

Tess then goes to work at Mr. Crick's dairy. Tess meets and falls for Angel, a parson's son who wants to become a farmer. Angel proposes, but Tess is reluctant, as she's ashamed of her past. She writes him a letter telling her story and slides it under his door, but she later learns it got caught under the carpet and he never read it. Eventually they get married. On their wedding night Angel confesses a brief affair with an older woman, but when Tess tells him her story, he is shocked. After a few days they separate. Her father dies and they are evicted.

Tess and her family go to Kingbere, where the d'Urberville family crypt is located, arriving on April 6, 1891 (2:11:50 to 2:17:08). Angel returns and finds Tess very unhappily ensconced as Alex's mistress, but she tells Angel to go away. Tess later kills Alex and follows Angel. They travel around together for a while until Tess is arrested. She's later hanged for murder.

A sad and tragic tale. Mr. Tingham's discussion with John Durbeyfield affects many lives and none for the better. Angel's hypocritical sanctimoniousness regarding Tess's affair, which only began after she was raped, points to the differences between men's and women's societal norms.

Awards: *Academy Award Wins*: Best Set Decoration, Best Cinematography, and Best Costume Design. *Academy Award Nominations*: Best Director, Best Picture, and Best Original Score. *Golden Globe Wins*: Best Foreign Film and New Star of the Year in a Motion Picture–Female (Nastassja Kinski). *Golden Globe Nominations*: Best Director–Motion Picture and Best Motion Picture Actress Drama (Kinski)

Source: Hardy, Thomas. *Tess of the d'Urbervilles: A Pure Woman Faithfully Presented*. New York: Barnes & Noble Classics, 2005. This book at page 419 gives the date they arrive in Kingsbere.

Alternate Film: *East of Eden* (1956)

7

HOW THE WEST WAS WON

Year: 1962
Genre: Western
Run Time: 2 hours 44 minutes
Availability: Blu-ray and DVD (Warner Home Video)
Directors: John Ford, Henry Hathaway, and George Marshall; **Screenplay**: James R. Webb
Cast: Carroll Baker (Eve Prescott Rawlings), Henry Fonda (Jethro Stuart), Carolyn Jones (Julie Rawlings), Gregory Peck (Cleve Van Valen), George Peppard (Zeb Rawlings), Robert Preston (Roger Morgan), Debbie Reynolds (Lilith "Lily" Prescott), James Stewart (Linus Rawlings)

The Prescott family, Ma, Pa, and daughters Eve and Lilith, are moving west, and when they reach the Ohio River they build a raft to float downstream. They meet Linus Rawlings, a trapper. Eve is attracted to him, but he leaves. Rawlings avoids being killed by river pirates and also saves the Prescotts.

When Ma and Pa are killed, Rawlings marries Eve and they start a farm. Lily goes to St. Louis and becomes a singer and dancer. When she inherits a gold claim in California, she joins a wagon train. Gambler Cleve Van Valen talks his way into traveling with them. Lily rejects the marriage proposals of both Van Valen and Morgan, the wagon train master. They are attacked by the Cheyenne and Morgan saves her, but she is more concerned when Van Valen is missing, and relieved when he returns. Her claim is a bust, and when she meets Van Valen again she accepts his proposal.

The Civil War begins and Linus Rawlings and his son Zeb join the U.S. Army. At the first day of the battle of Shiloh, Linus is killed. Shortly after midnight the next day, April 7, 1862, Zeb stops a Southern deserter from killing General Grant (1:37:10 to 1:45:06.) After the war Zeb's parents are dead so he joins the cavalry. The Union Pacific changes its route and causes strife with the Arapaho, but Capt. Zeb Rawlings manages to secure peace. Rawlings becomes a marshal and gets married. Lily's husband dies and she is almost bankrupt. She moves to her Arizona ranch and asks her nephew Zeb to come run it for her. He arrives, but Gant, a criminal from his past has followed him. Zeb catches Gant robbing a train and kills him.

The plot is melodramatic and predictable, but it has some fantastic action sequences. There are several great cinematographic aerial shots, too.

Awards: *Academy Award Wins*: Best Screenplay, Best Film Editing, and Best Sound. *Academy Award Nominations*: Best Picture, Best Art Direction, Best Cinematography, Best Costume Design–Color, and Best Music

Source: Keegan, John. *The American Civil War: A Military History*. New York: Alfred A. Knopf, 2009. This book at page 132 gives the date of the battle.

Alternate Film: *Lean on Me*

8

SHE'S OUT OF MY LEAGUE
Year: 2010
Genre: Romantic Comedy
Run Time: 1 hour 44 minutes
Availability: Blu-ray (Warner Home Video) and DVD (DreamWorks)
Director: Jim Field Smith; **Screenplay**: Sean Anders and John Morris

Cast: Jay Baruchel (Kirk Kettner), Alice Eve (Molly McCleish), Krysten Ritter (Patty), T. J. Miller (Stainer), Nate Torrence (Devon), Mike Vogel (Jack), Lindsay Sloane (Marnie), Kim Shaw (Katie McCleish), Jasika Nicole (Wendy), Hayes MacArthur (Ron)

Kirk Kettner is an awkward twenty-something guy who works for the TSA at the Pittsburgh airport until one day he meets super-attractive Molly McCleish when she leaves her cell phone behind. When he returns the phone and saves Molly's sister from getting fired, she gives him two tickets to a pro hockey game. On April 8, 2010 (22:45 to 35:44), Kirk and his friend Stainer along with Molly and her friend Patty attend a Penguins-Islanders game. Kirk and Molly start dating, but Stainer tells Kirk the relationship is doomed since Molly is a 10 and Kirk is a 5, and Patty thinks Molly is dating Kirk because he's "safe." Molly's attraction toward Kirk increases after he is honest about an embarrassing situation. Kirk and Molly break up because of their insecurities. Kirk goes back to his old girlfriend, but when he and his family are preparing for a vacation to Branson, Stainer has a revelation and decides to take action, leading to the movie's satisfying climax.

A different romantic comedy. Reverses the usual story of where the plain girl is revealed to be beautiful and gets the guy. Interesting that Alice Eve's real-life parents, both of whom are actors, play Molly's parents.

Source: Buker, Rick. *Total Penguins*. Chicago: Triumph Books, 2010. This book at page 591 gives the date of this game.

Alternate Film: *Silver Streak*

9
THE GOOD, THE BAD AND THE UGLY

Year: 1966

Genre: Western/Action

Run Time: 2 hours 41 minutes (theatrical release), 2 hours 57 minutes (director's cut)

Availability: Blu-ray and DVD (Metro-Goldwyn-Mayer Home Entertainment)

Director: Sergio Leone; **Screenplay**: Agenorre Incrocci, Furio Scarpelli, Luciano Vincenzoni, and Sergio Leone

Cast: Clint Eastwood (Blondie "The Good"), Lee Van Cleef (Angel Eyes "The Bad"), Eli Wallach (Tuco "The Ugly"), Aldo Giuffrè (the Captain), Mario

Brega (Corporal Wallace), Luigi Pistilli (Father Pablo Ramirez), Al Mulock (One-Armed Bounty Hunter)
The notorious gunslinger known as "Angel Eyes" is looking for Bill Carson, who knows the location of stolen Confederate gold. The mysterious, lightning-fast gunslinger called "Blondie" teams up with the outlaw Tuco. Blondie turns Tuco over for the reward and then frees him just before Tuco is to be hanged. Blondie tires of Tuco's complaints and abandons him in the desert. Tuco survives and tracks Blondie to Albuquerque, New Mexico, as the Confederate Army retreats through the town. On April 8, 1862 (38:11 to 45:54), as Tuco is about to hang Blondie, a well-timed cannon ball saves him. Tuco finally captures Blondie and marches him through the desert. They find a dying Bill Carson, who tells Tuco the name of a cemetery and Blondie the name on the grave where $200,000 (about $4.78 million today) in gold is buried. Blondie and Tuco become reluctant partners. They disguise themselves as Confederates, but are captured. Tuco gives his name as "Bill Carson," and Angel Eyes, a guard in the camp, tortures Tuco for the name of the cemetery, but offers Blondie half in return for the name on the grave. They ride off, but after Tuco escapes Blondie reforms his alliance with Tuco. They head for the cemetery and an action-packed suspenseful climax.

One of the outstanding spaghetti westerns of the 1960s. A classic of plot, cinematography, and score. A must-see film.

Source: Josephy, Alvin M. Jr. *The Civil War in the American West*. New York: Alfred A. Knopf, 1991. This book at page 86 gives the dates when the Yankees shelled Albuquerque.

Alternate Film: *Munich*

10

CHAPLIN

Year: 1992
Genre: Biography
Run Time: 2 hours 23 minutes
Availability: Blu-ray and DVD (Lionsgate Films)
Director: Richard Attenborough; **Screenplay**: William Boyd, Bryan Forbes, and William Goldman, based on *My Autobiography* by Charlie Chaplin and *Chaplin: His Life and Art* by David Robinson

Cast: Robert Downey Jr. (Charlie Chaplin), Geraldine Chaplin (Hannah Chaplin), Moira Kelly (Hetty Kelly/Oona O'Neill), Anthony Hopkins (George Hayden), Dan Aykroyd (Mack Sennett), Marisa Tomei (Mabel Normand)
In 1894 Charlie Chaplin's mother is a dance hall singer, but when she is booed off the stage Charlie saves the day by singing her song. Her children are later sent to a work house, and she goes insane. Charlie gets a job in vaudeville and goes to America on tour. He makes movies at the Mack Sennett studios, where he develops the character "The Little Tramp" and becomes famous. He has an affair with Mabel Normand and then marries Mildred Harris. Charlie comes to the attention of J. Edgar Hoover of the FBI for his support of liberal causes. After his divorce from his second wife, Lita Grey, he has a lengthy affair with Paulette Goddard, whom he later marries. Charlie is resistant to introducing sound into his movies, but finally does in "The Great Dictator." His affair with Joan Barry ends with Charlie having to pay support for a child that was not his. Charlie marries Oona O'Neill. He travels to London to attend the premiere of *Limelight* in 1952, but learns that he will be denied readmittance to the United States, so he stays in Europe. He only returns to the States to receive a special Oscar on April 10, 1972 (2:08:08 to 2:16:27).

An engaging film, but more glossy than intense. You never really get inside Chaplin's character. Skims over some aspects to concentrate on others. Still, it is highly watchable, and it's interesting in that Geraldine Chaplin portrays her own grandmother.
Awards: *Academy Award Nominations*: Best Actor (Robert Downey Jr.), Best Original Score, and Best Set Direction. *Golden Globe Nominations*: Best Performance by an Actor in a Motion Picture–Drama (Robert Downey Jr.), Best Performance by an Actor in a Motion Picture–Drama (Geraldine Chaplin), and Best Original Score–Motion Picture
Source: Vance, Jeffrey. *Chaplin: Genius of the Cinema*. New York: Harry N. Abrams, 2003. This book at page 355 gives the ceremony date.
Alternate Film: *Viva Zapata!*

11
THE ELEPHANT MAN
Year: 1980
Genre: Biography
Run Time: 2 hours 4 minutes
Availability: Blu-ray (Universal), DVD (Paramount Pictures)
Director: David Lynch; **Screenplay:** Christopher De Vore, Eric Bergren, and David Lynch, based on Frederick Treves's book *The Elephant Man and Other Reminiscences* and Ashley Montagu's book *The Elephant Man: A Study in Human Dignity*
Cast: Anthony Hopkins (Frederick Treves), John Hurt (John Merrick), Freddie Jones (Bytes), Wendy Hiller (Mrs. Mothershead), John Gielgud (Carr Gomm), Lesley Dunlop (Nurse Nora), Hannah Gordon (Ann Treves), Anne Bancroft (Madge Kendal)

In Victorian London, Dr. Frederick Treves finds John Merrick in a freak show "managed" by Bytes. Treves presents Merrick to his colleagues as an interesting specimen and later removes him to the hospital. Treves finds out that Merrick is very intelligent and literate. He acted dumb to try and protect himself from abuse. Treves later wonders whether he has actually helped Merrick or not. Bytes kidnaps Merrick and takes him to Europe, where he is again displayed as a freak. He escapes, but after an incident where he confronts a mob with the exclamation, "I AM A MAN," he collapses. He returns to the hospital, but on April 11, 1890, he lies down, a move that, due to his medical condition, he knows will kill him (1:47:02 to 1:59:30).

A moving story of disability and superficiality. Merrick's intelligence and character show him to be a superior person. The hope of the story is that while many cannot get past his appearance, a few are able to see and care for the man inside.

Awards: *Academy Award Nominations:* Best Picture, Best Actor (John Hurt), Best Art Direction, Best Costume Design, Best Director, Best Film Editing, Best Original Music Score, and Best Adapted Screenplay. *Golden Globe Nominations:* Best Motion Picture–Drama, Best Director–Motion Picture, Best Motion Picture Actor–Drama (Hurt), and Best Screenplay–Motion Picture

Source: Montagu, Ashley. *The Elephant Man: A Study in Human Dignity.*
New York: Outerbridge and Dienstfrey, 1971. This book at page 123 gives
his death date.
Alternate Film: *The Life and Times of Judge Roy Bean*

12
RAIN MAN
Year: 1988
Genre: Drama
Run Time: 2 hours 13 minutes
Date Revealed in Film: 26:34–44 and 45:18
Availability: Blu-ray and DVD (Metro-Goldwyn-Mayer)
Director: Barry Levinson; **Screenplay**: Ronald Bass and Barry Morrow
Cast: Dustin Hoffman (Ray Babbitt), Tom Cruise (Charlie Babbitt), Valeria
   Golino (Susanna), Gerald R. Molen (Dr. Bruner), Jack Murdock (John
   Mooney), Michael D. Roberts (Vern), Bonnie Hunt (Sally Dibbs), Ralph
   Seymour (Lenny)
Charlie Babbitt's car import business is in trouble, as some cars he has just
bought don't meet EPA standards and can't enter the country. His estranged
father dies and after the funeral in Cincinnati, he learns all his father has left
him is a 1949 Buick Roadmaster and some rose bushes. Three million dol-
lars went into a trust fund controlled by someone at Walbrook, an upscale
mental home. He finds out the money is being used to support Ray, the older
autistic savant brother that Charlie didn't know existed. Ray's behavior is very
unusual. Charlie is incensed about getting nothing and "kidnaps" Ray, with
the idea of trading Ray back to the trustee for $1.5 million. Ray has a fit when
Charlie tries to put him on an airplane on April 12, 1988, so they drive to Los
Angeles (37:44 to 51:30). However, their cross-country odyssey does not end
the way Charlie anticipated.

   A good movie about love as the springboard for transformation. Charlie's
real legacy from his father was the chance to change from someone who
cared only about himself into someone who cared about others. Charlie may
be monetarily poorer at the end of the movie, but he's definitely emotionally
and spiritually richer.
Awards: *Academy Award Wins*: Best Picture, Best Actor (Dustin Hoffman),
   Best Director, and Best Original Screenplay. *Academy Award Nomina-*

tions: Best Set Direction, Best Cinematography, Best Film Editing, and Best Original Score. *Golden Globe Wins*: Best Motion Picture–Drama and Best Performance by an Actor in a Motion Picture–Drama (Hoffman). *Golden Globe Nominations*: Best Director–Motion Picture and Best Screenplay–Motion Picture

Alternate Film: *The Great Locomotive Chase*

13
LEGENDS OF THE FALL

Year: 1994
Genre: Period Drama
Run Time: 2 hours 13 minutes
Date Revealed in Film: 5:41
Availability: Blu-ray and DVD (Sony Pictures)
Director: Edward Zwick; **Screenplay**: Susan Shilliday and William Wittliff, based on the novella by Jim Harrison
Cast: Anthony Hopkins (William Ludlow), Brad Pitt (Tristan Ludlow), Aidan Quinn (Alfred Ludlow), Julia Ormond (Susannah Ludlow), Henry Thomas (Samuel Ludlow), Karina Lombard (Isabel Decker Ludlow), Christina Pickles (Isabel Ludlow)

Col. William Ludlow retires to Montana and builds a ranch, but his wife leaves him with three sons: Alfred, responsible; Tristan, wild; and Samuel, naive. Col. Ludlow writes a letter to his wife on April 13, 1913, saying he was not equipped to raise sons (6:41 to 7:05). Samuel returns from Harvard with his fiancée, Susannah, who finds she is attracted to Tristan. At the start of World War I, all three sons join the same battalion of the Canadian army. Alfred, an officer, is injured. Samuel volunteers for a dangerous reconnaissance mission and is killed. Tristan is devastated and launches his own private raids that lead to his discharge. After rejecting Alfred's proposal, Susannah starts a relationship with Tristan. Alfred eventually becomes a congressman and gets involved with the O'Bannons, who are bootleggers and crooks.

Susannah and Alfred are married. Tristan gets married, but his wife is killed by one of the O'Bannons. While he is in jail for assaulting the killer, Tristan rejects Susannah's advances and she commits suicide. Tristan kills those responsible for his wife's death, but when their associates come for Tristan, Alfred and his father kill them. Tristan takes the blame for these deaths and disappears. Years later, visiting the graves of his family, he is attacked and killed by a grizzly.

A complicated story of love, hate, and forgiveness. The character of each of the brothers drives their actions. The film has breathtaking shots of the western terrain.

Awards: *Academy Award Win*: Best Cinematography. *Academy Award Nominations*: Best Set Direction and Best Sound. *Golden Globe Nominations*: Best Motion Picture–Drama, Best Director–Motion Picture, Best Original Score–Motion Picture, and Best Performance by an Actor in a Motion Picture–Drama (Brad Pitt)

Alternate Film: *Bat*21*

14

APOLLO 13

Year: 1995

Genre: Action/Drama

Run Time: 2 hours 20 minutes

Availability: Blu-ray and DVD (Universal Studios)

Director: Ron Howard; **Screenplay**: William Broyles Jr. and Al Reinert, based on the book *Lost Moon* by Jim Lovell and Jeffrey Kluger

Cast: Tom Hanks (Jim Lovell), Kevin Bacon (Jack Swigert), Bill Paxton (Fred Haise), Gary Sinise (Ken Mattingly), Ed Harris (Gene Kranz), Kathleen Quinlan (Marilyn Lovell), Loren Dean (John Aaron), Chris Ellis (Deke Slayton)

The film opens with flashbacks to the *Apollo 1* fire and *Apollo 11* moon landings. Jim Lovell, Fred Haise, and Ken Mattingly are switched from *Apollo 14* to *Apollo 13*. Marilyn Lovell has unexplained fears for her husband's fourth space flight. Shortly before launch it is discovered that Ken Mattingly has been exposed to measles. Lovell is given the option of replacing Mattingly with Swigert or switching the whole crew back to *Apollo 14*. He chooses to bump Mattingly.

The launch takes place as usual, with only a slight hiccup. The networks do not show their broadcast to Earth because moon missions have become ordinary. When Swigert per routine stirs the oxygen tanks there is an explosion. The other tanks are shut down, ending all hope of a moon landing. The crew has to turn off the command module and move into the lunar module as a lifeboat. They fly around the moon, crossing the far side on April 14, 1970 (1:09:16 to 1:22:14).

The techs at NASA devise ways to keep the lunar module functioning and Mattingly plays a key role in figuring out how to restart the command module for reentry. There is fear that the explosion damaged the heat shield, but in the end after some agonizing moments, the crew makes it safely back to Earth.

Very good almost docudrama account of the mission. Shows the real tensions among the crew and not the heroic mode often common in such films. Highlights the behind-the-scenes work that helped save the crew and bring them home.

Awards: *Academy Award Wins*: Best Film Editing and Best Sound. *Academy Award Nominations*: Best Supporting Actor (Ed Harris), Best Supporting Actress (Kathleen Quinlan), Best Art Direction, Best Original Music Score, Best Picture, Best Visual Effects, and Best Adapted Screenplay. *Golden Globe Nominations*: Best Motion Picture–Drama, Best Director–Motion Picture, Best Performance by an Actress in a Supporting Role in a Motion Picture (Quinlan), and Best Performance by an Actor in a Supporting Role in a Motion Picture (Harris)

Source: Lovell, Jim, and Kluger, Jeffrey. *Lost Moon*. New York: Houghton Mifflin Co., 1994. This book at pages 214 and 238 gives the date they round the moon.

Alternate Film: *Charlie Wilson's War*

15

TITANIC

Year: 1997
Genre: Period Drama
Run Time: 3 hours 14 minutes
Availability: Blu-ray and DVD (Paramount Pictures)
Director: James Cameron; **Screenplay**: James Cameron
Cast: Kate Winslet (Rose DeWitt Bukater), Leonardo DiCaprio (Jack Dawson), Billy Zane ("Cal" Hockley), Frances Fisher (Ruth DeWitt Bukater), David Warner (Spicer Lovejoy), Bill Paxton (Brock Lovett), Gloria Stuart (Rose Dawson Calvert), Suzy Amis (Lizzy Calvert), Kathy Bates (Margaret "Molly" Brown), Bernard Hill (Captain Smith)

In 1996 Brock Lovett is searching the wreck of the *Titanic* for a diamond, "the Heart of the Ocean," but finds only a sketch of a nude woman wearing the diamond dated the day the ship sank. Elderly Rose Dawson sees this and travels to Lovett's expedition revealing she is the woman in the sketch, Rose Bukater, who was believed to have died in the wreck.

We then flash back to seventeen-year-old Rose and her mother boarding the *Titanic*, along with her wealthy fiancé, Cal Hockley. The engagement was arranged by her mother to get cash to pay their debts. Rose tries to kill herself, but is stopped by a drifter, Jack Dawson, who won a steerage ticket in a card game. Jack sketches her wearing nothing but the necklace, and then Rose and Jack make love in a car in the cargo hold. They witness the collision with the iceberg. Cal finds the sketch and has Lovejoy frame Jack for the theft of the necklace by planting it in Jack's pocket.

Jack is arrested and almost dies, but Rose rescues him. They reach the boat deck, where both Cal and Jack persuade her to enter a lifeboat, with Cal slipping the necklace in Rose's pocket. Rose realizes she can't abandon Jack and returns to the ship. Cal chases them but then uses an abandoned child as cover to slip into a lifeboat.

Rose and Jack stay on the ship until the stern slips under the surface of the frigid North Atlantic early in the morning of April 15, 1912. Rose climbs on a door, but Jack stays in the water, telling Rose she will have a long, happy life before he dies. Rose considers staying there to die with him, but in the end saves herself. She gives her name as Rose Dawson and doesn't contact her mother or Cal (1:48:47 to 3:00:43). Rose still has one secret that is only revealed to the audience.

A big-budget exploration of this tragic event with a somewhat typical "rich girl/poor boy" plot. The special effects are spectacular, as if the film were shot on the *Titanic*.

Awards: *Academy Award Wins*: Best Picture, Best Director, Best Cinematography, Best Costume Design, Best Visual Effects, Best Sound Mixing, Best Sound Editing, Best Original Score, Best Film Editing, Best Original Song, and Best Art Direction. *Academy Award Nominations*: Best Actress (Kate Winslet), Best Supporting Actress (Gloria Stuart), and Best Makeup. *Golden Globe Wins*: Best Director–Motion Picture, Best Original Score–Motion Picture, Best Original Song–Motion Picture, Best Motion Picture–Drama. *Golden Globe Nominations*: Best Performance by an Actress in a Motion Picture–Drama (Winslet), Best Performance by an Actor in a Motion Picture–Drama (Leonardo DiCaprio), Best Performance by an Actress in a Supporting Role in a Motion Picture–Drama (Stuart), and Best Screenplay–Motion Picture

Alternate Film: *Anastasia* (1956)

16
GONE WITH THE WIND

Year: 1939
Genre: Period Drama
Run Time: 3 hours 58 minutes
Availability: Blu-ray and DVD (Warner Home Video)
Director: Victor Fleming; **Screenplay**: Sidney Howard, based on Margaret Mitchell's novel
Cast: Clark Gable (Rhett Butler), Vivien Leigh (Scarlett O'Hara), Leslie Howard (Ashley Wilkes), Olivia de Havilland (Melanie Hamilton), Thomas Mitchell (Gerald O'Hara), Barbara O'Neil (Ellen O'Hara), Ann Rutherford (Carreen O'Hara), George Reeves (Stuart Tarleton), Hattie McDaniel (Mammy), Oscar Polk (Pork), Butterfly McQueen (Prissy)

Scarlett O'Hara lives on her family's plantation, Tara, in Georgia and attends a barbeque on the neighboring plantation of Twelve Oaks on April 16, 1861 (15:26 to 34:49), held to announce the engagement of the man she thinks she loves, Ashley Wilkes, to his cousin Melanie Hamilton. Scarlett confronts him, but he rejects her. They are overheard by a visitor from Charleston, Rhett Butler. The men rush off to enlist in the Confederate Army. Scarlett impulsively marries Melanie Hamilton's brother, Charles, but he dies after a few months.

Scarlett's mother sends her to Atlanta to cheer her up, and she again meets Rhett Butler. At Christmas 1863 Scarlet tries to seduce Ashley Wilkes, but fails. Eight months later, the Yankees are nearing Atlanta. Scarlet is a nurse at a military hospital and has to deliver Melanie's premature baby. Rhett Butler appears and gets them out of the city, but after kissing Scarlett he leaves to join the Confederate Army.

Sherman has burned Twelve Oaks, but Tara has been spared. Her mother is dead and her father has lost his mind. Scarlett takes over running the plantation. She attempts to get the money to pay the taxes on Tara from Rhett

Butler, but fails. She solves the problem by stealing her sister's prosperous beaux, Frank Kennedy. After she is attacked by ruffians, her husband is killed in a vigilante skirmish. Rhett Butler, through his contacts in the Union occupying forces, saves Ashley Wilkes from being arrested.

Rhett proposes to the once-again-widowed Scarlett, who accepts, and they are happy for a while. After the birth of their daughter, Bonnie, Scarlett doesn't like the changes to her figure the pregnancy caused, and she turns Rhett away from the marriage bed, leading to an estrangement. She and Ashley are spied in a compromising position, but Rhett forces her to attend Ashley's birthday party scheduled that same day. Scarlett later miscarries in a tragic accident.

Bonnie is killed in an accident, resulting in an even deeper estrangement. Then Melanie Hamilton dies, and Scarlett realizes that she never meant anything to Ashley Wilkes. Scarlett rushes home, only to find Rhett leaving. When she asks what she will do or where she will go, he responds with the famous line, "Frankly, my dear, I don't give a damn." Scarlett returns to Tara and vows to win him back.

What can you say? Arguably the greatest film ever made. The story is compelling, the acting good, and the cinematography excellent. Hasn't faded in over seventy years.

Awards: *Academy Award Wins*: Best Picture, Best Director, Best Actress (Vivien Leigh), Best Screenplay, Best Supporting Actress (Hattie McDaniel), Best Cinematography, Best Film Editing, and Best Interior Decoration. *Academy Award Nominations*: Best Actor (Clark Gable), Best Supporting Actress (Olivia de Havilland), Best Special Effects, and Best Original Score

Source: Mitchell, Margaret. *Gone with the Wind*. New York: Scribners, 1936. At page 5 one of the Tarleton twins says, "General Beauregard shelled them out of Fort Sumter day before yesterday." Fraser, Walter J. Jr. *Charleston! Charleston! The History of a Southern City*. Columbia: University of South Carolina Press, 1989. This book at page 251 says that Fort Sumter surrendered on April 13. Thus their front porch discussion with Scarlett is on April 15, with the barbeque the next day.

Alternate Film: *Pirates of Silicon Valley*

17
THE KILLING FIELDS

Year: 1984
Genre: Drama
Run Time: 2 hours 21 minutes
Availability: Blu-ray and DVD (Warner Home Video)
Director: Roland Joffe; **Screenplay**: Bruce Robinson
Cast: Sam Waterston (Sydney Schanberg), Haing S. Ngor (Dith Pran), Julian Sands (John Swain), John Malkovich (Al Rockoff), Craig T. Nelson (Military Attache), Spalding Gray (U.S. Consul), Bill Paterson (Dr. MacEntire), Graham Kennedy (Dougal)

In 1973 Sydney Schanberg, a *New York Times* reporter, arrives in Cambodia. With the help of his interpreter, Dith Pran, he covers the bombing of Neak Leung. Two years pass and foreigners are evacuated to escape the Khmer Rouge. Dith Pran's family is removed, but he stays behind. The Khmer Rouge enter Phnom Penh on April 17, 1975, and Schanberg and Pran go to the French embassy to await evacuation (46:08 to 58:39). The Khmer Rouge demand the surrender of all Cambodians, and after an attempt to create a false British passport for Pran fails he leaves the embassy. Schanberg returns to the United States, where he tries to get Pran out. Pran meanwhile is engaged in forced labor, but he escapes and discovers the Khmer Rouge's "killing fields." In a new camp Pran is assigned to care for the son of the commandant. When Vietnam attacks Cambodia in 1979, Pran and three other prisoners take the boy and try to escape after the boy's father is killed. On the way, a landmine unfortunately kills the boy, but Pran makes it to Thailand and is reunited with Schanberg and his family.

A very moving film. You really feel the friendship between Schanberg and Pran and what both of them went through. There are several very tense scenes in this film: when the Khmer Rouge take the city, when they try to create a false passport for Pran, and when Pran temporarily escapes.

Awards: *Academy Award Wins*: Best Supporting Actor (Haing S. Ngor), Best Editing, and Best Cinematography. *Academy Award Nominations*: Best Picture, Best Director, Best Actor (Sam Waterston), and Best Adapted Screenplay

Source: Deas, Wilfred P. *The Road to the Killing Fields*. College Station: Texas A&M University Press, 1997. This book at pages 222–23 gives the date of the fall of Phnom Penh.

Alternate Film: *Pork Chop Hill*

18

THIRTY SECONDS OVER TOKYO

Year: 1944

Genre: War

Run Time: 2 hours 18 minutes

Availability: DVD (Warner Home Video), VHS (MGM/UA Home Video)

Director: Mervyn LeRoy; **Screenplay**: Dalton Trumbo, based on the book by Ted Lawson and Robert Considine

Cast: Van Johnson (Lt. Ted W. Lawson), Robert Walker (Cpl. David Thatcher), Don DeFore (Lt. Charles McClure), Robert Mitchum (Lt. Bob Gray), Spencer Tracy (Lt. Col. Jimmy Doolittle), Phyllis Thaxter (Ellen Lawson)

After Pearl Harbor the U.S. Army Air Force plans to bomb Tokyo by flying bombers off an aircraft carrier. Lt. Col. Jimmy Doolittle is selected to lead the raid, and Lt. Ted Lawson is selected as one of the pilots. The B25s train in Florida to take off on a very short runway. The task force leaves California in secret. However, a Japanese fishing boat spots them twelve hours before their scheduled launch, so they take off at once on April 18, 1942. The planes bomb their targets, but the earlier takeoff means they no longer have the fuel to reach their target bases in China. Most of the planes, including Lawson's, crash in occupied China (1:07:49 to 1:38:10) Chinese guerillas smuggle them out. Lawson loses a leg due to his injuries, but eventually returns home to his wife.

A good action film. Does a good job of character development, as you actually care about what happens to Lawson and his crew. Actually sticks to the facts.

Awards: *Academy Award Win*: Best Sound Effects. *Academy Award Nomination*: Best Cinematography–Black-and-White

Source: Dupuy, R. Ernest, and Dupuy, Trevor N. *The Encyclopedia of Military History from 3500 B.C. to the Present*. New York: Harper & Row, 1977. This book at page 1145 gives the attack date.

Alternate Film: *Al's Lads*

19
MADAME CURIE
Year: 1943
Genre: Biographical Drama
Run Time: 2 hours 4 minutes
Date Revealed in Film: 1:42:32–33
Availability: DVD (Warner Home Video), VHS (MGM/UA Home Video)
Director: Mervyn LeRoy; **Screenplay**: Paul Osborn, Hans Rameau, based on Eve Curie's book
Cast: Greer Garson (Marie Curie), Albert Bassermann (Prof. Jean Perot), Walter Pidgeon (Pierre Curie), Dame May Whitty (Madame Eugene Curie), Henry Travers (Eugene Curie), Margaret O'Brien (Irene Curie at age five)

Marie, a poor Polish refugee in Paris, studies physics and math so intensely that she sometimes forgets to eat and passes out in class. Her professor introduces her to Pierre Curie and convinces him to let her use his lab for her experiments. Pierre considers women a distraction to scientists, but he gradually falls for Marie and they get married. Marie starts working on the source of X-rays in pitchblende. She becomes stumped when the only two radioactive elements in pitchblende don't give off enough radiation individually to account for the radiation pitchblende emits. They figure out there must be an unknown radioactive element in pitchblende and set out to extract it. After 458 failed attempts, they give up for a time, but they finally extract the new element, radium. They become world famous. On April 19, 1906, when they are to be honored for their discovery Pierre goes to buy earrings for Marie, but is run over by a wagon and killed (1:42:07 to 1:52:16). Marie goes into a deep funk. She finally recovers and is honored on the twenty-fifth anniversary of radium's discovery.

One of the better "Hollywoodized" biopics. Garson and Pidgeon play Marie and Pierre as likeable, sympathetic characters. Entertaining, if fluffy. The film manages to explain the science so a layman can understand the problem and the triumph of solution.

Awards: *Academy Award Nominations*: Best Actor (Walter Pidgeon), Best Actress (Greer Garson), Best Art Direction, Best Black-and-White Cinematography, Best Original Music Score, Best Picture, and Best Sound
Alternate Film: *The Man Who Never Was*

20
DOWNFALL

Year: 2004
Genre: Biography
Run Time: 2 hours 36 minutes
Date Revealed in Film: 6:55
Availability: DVD (Sony Pictures)
Director: Oliver Hirschbiegel; **Screenplay:** Bernd Eichinger, based on *Until the Final Hour* by Traudl Junge and Melissa Muller, and *Inside Hitler's Bunker* by Joachim Fest
Cast: Bruno Ganz (Adolf Hitler), Alexandra Maria Lara (Traudl Junge), Ulrich Matthes (Joseph Goebbels), Corinna Harfouch (Magda Goebbels), Juliane Köhler (Eva Braun), Thomas Kretschmann (Hermann Fegelein), Heino Ferch (Albert Speer)

Traudl Junge is selected as Hitler's secretary. Later on April 20, 1945 (6:45–30:10), the Soviets start shelling Berlin. Hitler refuses to accept the reality that the war is lost and awards the Iron Cross to young boys who having been fighting Soviet tanks in the streets of Berlin. Eva Braun throws a party. The next day General Weidling, instead of being shot, is put in charge of Berlin's defenses. Street battles rage in Berlin and Hitler is outraged when he learns an assault by General Steiner that he ordered never occurred. Wounded troops are brought into the bunker and Hitler learns Goering has betrayed him. Speer confesses he has not followed Hitler's orders to destroy Germany's infrastructure and Hitler has Eva Braun's brother-in-law shot for desertion. Hitler dictates his political last will to Traudl, and then marries Eva Braun. Hitler says goodbye to those who remain, then he and Eva kill themselves. Their bodies are burned. Goebbels tries to negotiate with the Soviets, then he and his wife kill their six children, then themselves. Traudl leaves the bunker and escapes.

A fascinating account of the last desperate days of Hitler's Germany. This film shows the Nazi hierarchy as human beings.

Awards: *Academy Award Nomination*: Best Foreign Language Film of the Year
Alternate Film: *Dawn Anna*

21

SCOTT PILGRIM VS. THE WORLD

Year: 2010
Genre: Fantasy
Run Time: 1 hour 52 minutes
Date Revealed in Film: 1:20:00
Availability: Blu-ray and DVD (Universal Studios)
Director: Edgar Wright; **Screenplay:** Michael Bacall and Edgar Wright, based on the *Scott Pilgram* graphic novel series by Bryan Lee O'Malley
Cast: Michael Cera (Scott Pilgrim), Mary Elizabeth Winstead (Ramona Flowers), Kieran Culkin (Wallace Wells), Ellen Wong (Knives Chau), Brie Larson (Natalie "Envy" Adams), Brandon Routh (Todd Ingram), Jason Schwartzman (Gideon Gordon Graves)

Scott Pilgrim is a twenty-two-year-old bassist in a rock band, Sex Bob-omb, who begins dating a high school student, Knives Chau, and then he meets a girl he has dreamed about, Ramona Flowers, and they go on a date. Scott learns that in order to date Ramona, he must defeat her seven evil exes. Even though Scott seems to be at a disadvantage in these battles, with a mixture of psychology and trickery he beats the first four evil exes.

On April 21, 2011 (1:19:56 to 1:28:22), Sex Bob-omb faces off against the Katayanagi Twins, who are Ramona's fifth and sixth evil exes, in an amp versus amp Battle of the Bands. Scott is victorious and wins an extra "life." However, Ramona leaves with Gideon Gordon Graves, her seventh evil ex and record producer, who signs Sex Bob-omb. Scott quits the band, but gets a call from Gideon inviting him to the opening of his new club, where Sex Bob-omb is playing.

Scott goes, and even though he wins the Power of Love Sword, Gideon kills him. In Limbo Scott remembers he has an extra life and uses it to return to before he went to the club. This time, he gets the Power of Self-Respect sword and knocks Gideon down. Then, with the help of Knives, he beats Gideon. Knives tells Scott to go after Ramona and they begin their relationship.

An unusual film. It breaks the fourth wall almost continuously and is presented almost like a video game in concept. Very quirky and self-referential throughout. However, it is a truly funny film. You will either love this film or hate it; there's no in between.
Alternate Film: *The Red Baron*

22

CIMARRON

Year: 1960
Genre: Western
Run Time: 2 hours 27 minutes
Availability: DVD and VHS (Warner Home Video)
Director: Anthony Mann; **Screenplay:** Arnold Schulman, based on Edna Ferber's novel
Cast: Glenn Ford (Yancey Cravat), Maria Schell (Sabra Cravat), Anne Baxter (Dixie Lee), Harry Morgan (Jessie Rickey), Russ Tamblyn (The Cherokee Kid), Lili Darvas (Felicia Venable), Arthur O'Connell (Tom Wyatt), Mercedes McCambridge (Mrs. Wyatt)

Yancey and Sabra Cravat travel to the Kansas-Oklahoma border, meeting the poor Wyatt family. They meet several of Yancey's friends, including "The Cherokee Kid," two of his pals, and Dixie, with whom Yancey obviously has some history. He helps Sam Pegler, a newspaper publisher, save an Indian from being lynched.

Yancey participates in the land rush on April 22, 1889, but loses the land he wanted to Dixie, who picks it to spite him (28:37 to 43:26). When Sam Pegler is killed Yancey takes over running his newspaper, "The Oklahoma Wigwam." When the Indian he had helped earlier is lynched, Yancey kills the ringleader and is absent when his son is born. Yancey saves kids who are being held hostage by the Cherokee Kid after his bank robbery goes wrong, but declines the reward. Yancey and his wife, who is from a well-off family, start to drift apart as she feels he is a romantic and not practical.

Yancey participates in the Cherokee Strip land rush and afterward they separate, with Sabra running the newspaper. Yancey participates in the Yukon gold rush and the Spanish-American War. Sabra even visits Dixie in the hope of finding out Yancey's whereabouts. Yancey finally returns. Oil is found on Mr. Wyatt's land and he becomes wealthy. When oil is located on an Indian reservation, Yancey is convinced Wyatt will swindle the Indians out of the money and publishes editorials to that effect. Wyatt and his pals attempt to buy Yancey off by having Yancey appointed territorial governor, but he turns the job down. The Cravats' son marries the daughter of the Indian killed those many years ago, upsetting his mother.

On the twenty-fifth anniversary of Oklahoma's becoming a state civic leaders suggest Sabra as the subject of a statue to celebrate the spirit of the state. She suggests her husband, Yancey, instead. Yancey enlists in the British army and is killed in the first year of World War I.

Yancey is the Forrest Gump of his time. The film is enjoyable, but don't expect a timeless classic. It is better than the 1931 version, which won the Best Picture Oscar.

Awards: *Academy Award Nominations*: Best Art Direction and Best Sound
Source: Franks, Kenny A., and Lambert, Paul F. *Oklahoma.* Helena, MT: American & World Geographic Publishing, 1994. This book at page 54 and in film at 2:10 give the date of the land run.
Alternate Film: *War of the Buttons*

23
THE MADNESS OF KING GEORGE
Year: 1994
Genre: Period Drama
Run Time: 1 hour 47 minutes
Availability: DVD (Metro-Goldwyn-Mayer), VHS (Hallmark Home Entertainment)
Director: Nicholas Hytner; **Screenplay**: Alan Bennett, based on his play
Cast: Nigel Hawthorne (King George III), Helen Mirren (Queen Charlotte), Ian Holm (Francis Willis), Rupert Graves (Robert Fulke Greville), Amanda Donohoe (Lady Pembroke), Rupert Everett (The Prince of Wales), Julian Wadham (William Pitt)

King George III of Great Britain gives the speech from the throne at the opening of Parliament in 1788. A woman tries to stab him, but he is not harmed. The king and queen don't get along with the Prince of Wales, who has a secret Catholic wife. The king and Prime Minister Pitt disagree about relations with the United States.

The king has an attack and begins to act strangely. He awakens at 4 AM, runs about the countryside in his nightclothes, and tries to assault Lady Pembroke. At a concert he attacks the prince and makes lewd remarks about Lady Pembroke. Later in the middle of the night he believes a flood is coming and carries his grandchildren to the roof. He spits on the queen and accuses her of incest with their son.

The prince orders the king separated from the queen. The doctors disagree on diagnosis and treatment. Dr. Willis is brought in and he restrains the king, but the other doctors attack Willis for not being a real doctor. Pressure increases for a regency. Lady Pembroke seduces Capt. Greville, the king's equerry, so he will let the queen see the king and tell him about the regency bill.

The king recovers suddenly and goes to Parliament, and the Regency Bill is withdrawn. The Capt. Greville is sacked. The royals attend a service of thanksgiving for the king's recovery on April 23, 1789, at St. Paul's Cathedral (1:43:35 to 1:46:21).

A good period piece. Magnificent costumes and sets. Well written and acted.

Awards: *Academy Award Win*: Best Art Direction. *Academy Award Nominations*: Best Actor (Nigel Hawthorne), Best Supporting Actress (Helen Mirren), and Best Adapted Screenplay

Source: Hibbert, Christopher. *George III: A Personal History*. New York: Basic Books, 1998. This book at page 300 gives date of the service.

Alternate Film: *The Diving Bell and the Butterfly*

24

NOTORIOUS

Year: 1946

Genre: Thriller/Drama

Run Time: 1 hour 41 minutes

Date Reveled in Film: 1:25

Availability: Blu-ray and DVD (Metro- Goldwyn-Mayer)

Director: Alfred Hitchcock; **Screenplay**: Ben Hecht

Cast: Cary Grant (T. R. Devlin), Ingrid Bergman (Alicia Huberman), Claude Rains (Alexander Sebastian), Leopoldine Konstantin (Anna Sebastian), Louis Calhern (Paul Prescott), Moroni Olsen (Walter Beardsley), Ricardo Costa (Dr. Julio Barbosa)

On April 24, 1946 (1:27 to 10:42), John Huberman is sentenced to twenty years in jail for treason. His daughter, Alicia Huberman, is introduced to T. R. Devlin, who recruits her to infiltrate a neo-Nazi group in Brazil for the U.S. government. They travel there and Devlin and Alicia begin a relationship. Devlin learns her assignment is to seduce Alexander Sebastian, a former associate of her father, so she can learn what he's up to. When Devlin says nothing to try and dissuade her from taking the job, Alicia feels he was just faking his affection for her and decides to do it. He thinks she cares nothing for him since she took the assignment.

A "chance" meeting is arranged with Sebastian, and after some time Sebastian proposes to Alicia. When Devlin says nothing against the idea, she accepts. After their honeymoon, Alicia discovers that the wine cellar is locked, with Sebastian having the only key. Devlin persuades her to hold a party and invite him so he can search the wine cellar, where he suspects something is hidden.

The night of the party, Alicia secretly gets the key. Alicia and Devlin find a bottle full of black sand in the wine cellar. Sebastian discovers that they searched the cellar and now must get rid of Alicia without letting his cohorts know that he made a blunder in marrying her. He poisons Alicia. We learn the black sand is uranium. Alicia becomes ill, but manages to learn where the uranium came from. Devlin goes to Sebastian's house, sneaks into Alicia's room, professes his love for her, and takes her out of the house. Sebastian begs Devlin to take him with them, but he refuses. Sebastian walks back inside to face his comrades.

One of Hitchcock's best efforts. Great romance, fantastic suspense, and great cinematography. Famous for a shot where the camera zooms in from over the balcony down into the foyer for a tight shot of Bergman's hand holding the wine cellar key.

Awards: *Academy Award Nominations*: Best Original Screenplay and Best Supporting Actor (Claude Rains)

Alternate Film: *Shackleton*

25

EXCALIBUR

Year: 1981
Genre: Fantasy/Drama
Run Time: 2 hours 20 minutes
Date Revealed in Film: 25:13
Availability: Blu-ray and DVD (Warner Home Video)
Director: John Boorman; **Screenplay**: Rospo Pallenberg and John Boorman
Cast: Nigel Terry (King Arthur), Helen Mirren (Morgana Le Fay), Nicol Williamson (Merlin), Paul Geoffrey (Percival), Nicholas Clay (Lancelot),

Cherie Lunghi (Guenevere), Patrick Stewart (King Leondegrance), Gabriel Byrne (Uther Pendragon)

In Dark Age Britain, Merlin gives Uther Pendragon the magical sword Excalibur. However, Uther uses Merlin's talent to enable him to impregnate Igrayne, the wife of Gorlais, Duke of Cornwall. Nine months later Uther learns he is the father of Igrayne's son, whom Uther hands over to Merlin. Uther is killed by supporters of Gorlais. Dying, Uther thrusts Excalibur into a stone. Merlin says that whoever pulls the sword from the stone shall be king! Years later, on Easter day, April 25, 482, knights gather to fight for the right to try and pull Excalibur out. However, the deed is done by Arthur, younger adopted son of Sir Ector, who tells him he is really Uther's son (23:04 to 32:12). This sparks a civil war, but Arthur's bravery wins over his opponent and he becomes king, marrying Guenevere and accepting Lancelot as one of the Knights of the Round Table after beating the Saxons and restoring peace. However, Lancelot falls in love with Guenevere, leading to civil strife. Morgana, Merlin's apprentice and Arthur's half-sister, takes the form of Guenevere and seduces Arthur, conceiving a son, Mordred, whose birth places a curse on the land. Arthur sends his knights on a quest to find the Holy Grail, and Percival at last succeeds. When Arthur drinks from it he is revitalized. He and his knights go to attack Mordred. With the help of Excalibur and the spirit of Merlin, they defeat Mordred.

A fantastic fantasy film. Great action and morality tale. Wonderful cinematography. The fall comes due to lack of self-control. Since Guenevere and Lancelot decide to do the wrong thing, everybody suffers in the end.

Awards: *Academy Award Nomination*: Best Cinematography

Alternate Film: *Mrs. Brown*

26

THE BLIND SIDE

Year: 2009
Genre: Biography
Run Time: 2 hours 9 minutes
Availability: Blu-ray and DVD (Warner Home Video)
Director: John Lee Hancock; **Screenplay**: John Lee Hancock
Cast: Quinton Aaron (Michael Oher), Sandra Bullock (Leigh Anne Tuohy), Tim McGraw (Sean Tuohy), Kathy Bates (Miss Sue), Lily Collins (Collins

Tuohy), Jae Head (Sean S. J. Tuohy Jr.), Ray McKinnon (Coach Cotton), Kim Dickens (Mrs. Boswell)

Lawrence Taylor's career-ending hit on Joe Theisman changed football by making left tackles the second-highest-paid players on NFL teams, as they protect the highest-paid player, the quarterback. Michael Oher, a large African American kid from the poor side of Memphis, gets into the all-white Wingate Christian School. He doesn't fit in there academically or socially.

He's taken in by a white family, the Tuohys. Leigh Anne Tuohy learns that Michael tested in the ninety-eighth percentile in protective instincts. Michael's grades improve as he improves at being a football tackle after Leigh Anne directs his protective instincts toward his teammates. Many colleges recruit him, but he needs a 2.5 GPA to get a scholarship. The Tuohys hire a tutor for Michael, and he decides to go to their alma mater, Ole Miss. He graduates with a 2.52 GPA. The NCAA investigates because they think the Tuohys only took him in to "funnel" him to Ole Miss. Michael convinces them that it was his own idea to go there. On April 26, 2008, Michael Oher is drafted by the Baltimore Ravens to play in the NFL (2:02:59 to 2:03:39).

A great story about strength of character. Michael seized an opportunity that was presented and succeeded. Leigh Anne Tuohy learned to be really thankful for what she had and not take it for granted. As is pointed out in the film, both the school and the Tuohys took Michael in, not because they wanted to get something out of it, but because it was the right thing to do.

Awards: *Academy Award Win*: Best Actress (Sandra Bullock). *Academy Award Nomination*: Best Picture. *Golden Globe Win*: Best Performance by an Actress in a Motion Picture–Drama (Sandra Bullock)

Source: Oher, Michael. *I Beat The Odds*. New York: Gotham Books, 2011. This book at page 184 gives the date of the draft.

Alternate Film: *Hearts in Atlantis*

27

DANCES WITH WOLVES

Year: 1990

Genre: Action/Western

Run Time: 3 hours 1 minute

Availability: Blu-ray and DVD (Metro-Goldwyn-Mayer)

Director: Kevin Costner; **Screenplay**: Michael Blake, based on his novel

Cast: Kevin Costner (Lt. John J. Dunbar/Dances with Wolves), Mary Mc-
Donnell (Stands with a Fist), Graham Greene (Kicking Bird), Rodney A.
Grant (Wind In His Hair), Floyd Red Crow Westerman (Chief Ten Bears),
Tantoo Cardinal (Black Shawl)

Wounded Union soldier John Dunbar wins a battle. He gets a decoration and
choice of posting. He requests a transfer to the West, but finds his post at Fort
Sedgwick deserted. The deaths of the wagon driver who delivered him to the
fort and the officer who sent him there means no one knows he's there by
himself. On April 27, 1863 (37:51 to 40:53), Dunbar meets the Sioux after they
try to steal his horse. He goes to try and talk with them and on the way meets
Stands with a Fist, the white adopted daughter of Kicking Bird, the tribe's
medicine man. He spends more time with the Sioux, adopting their culture,
and eventually marries Stands with a Fist. When the tribe prepares to move
to its winter camp, Dunbar returns to the fort to get his journal, but an unpleasant surprise awaits him there that leads to the end of his idyllic existence.

An unusual western. The opposite of most earlier westerns, it is slanted
toward the Native American point of view. Beautiful cinematography.

Awards: *Academy Award Wins*: Best Picture, Best Director, Best Adapted
Screenplay, Best Cinematography, Best Sound, Best Film Editing, and Best
Original Score. *Academy Award Nominations*: Best Actor (Kevin Costner),
Best Supporting Actor (Graham Greene), Best Supporting Actress (Mary
McDonnell), Best Art Direction–Set Direction, and Best Costume Design.
Golden Globe Wins: Best Director–Motion Picture, Best Screenplay–Mo-
tion Picture, and Best Motion Picture–Drama. *Golden Globe Nominations*:
Best Performance by an Actor in a Motion Picture–Drama (Costner), Best
Performance by an Actress in a Supporting Role in a Motion Picture (Mc-
Donnell) and Best Original Score–Motion Picture

Source: Blake, Michael. *Dances with Wolves*. New York: Fawcett Gold Medal,
1988. This book at page 56 gives the date of the meeting.

Alternative Film: *The Bridge*

28

EUROPA EUROPA

Year: 1990
Genre: Biography
Run Time: 1 hour 52 minutes

Date Revealed in Film: 1:13
Availability: DVD (Metro-Goldwyn-Mayer), VHS (Orion Home Video)
Director: Agnieszka Holland; **Screenplay**: Agnieszka Holland and Paul Hengge, based on Solomon Perel's memoir
Cast: Marco Hofschneider (Solomon Perel), Julie Delpy (Leni), René Hofschneider (Isaak), Ashley Wanninger (Gerd), Halina Łabonarska (Leni's Mother), Klaus Abramowsky (Solomon's Dad), Michèle Gleizer (Solomon's Mother)

Solomon Perel is circumcised on April 8, 1925 (2:28 to 4:06). His Jewish family lives in Germany until the Nazis begin their persecution of the Jews and then move to Poland. When the Germans invade Poland, Solomon and his brother Isaak head for the USSR, but are separated. Solomon is placed in a Soviet orphanage, where he displays a great talent for saying what he needs to say to stay alive and joins the Komsomol, the Soviet youth organization. When the Nazis invade the Soviet Union, he is captured by the German Army. However, after he assists in capturing the son of Stalin the Germans accept his story of being a German. He stays with the army as a translator and eventually his bravery results in him being sent to an elite Hitler Youth School in Germany. There his attempt to woo the blonde beauty Leni ends in failure when Solomon's best friend at the school impregnates her. Solomon confesses to Leni's mother that he is a Jew, but she does not betray him. Solomon survives several close calls where his identity is almost exposed. At war's end, he is captured by the Soviets, who think he is traitor and turn him over to some concentration camp survivors to dispose of. But then someone from his past steps forward.

A very interesting and amazingly true story.

Awards: *Academy Award Nomination*: Best Adapted Screenplay
Alternate Film: *Bose: The Forgotten Hero*

29

127 HOURS

Year: 2010
Genre: Biographical Drama
Run Time: 1 hour 33 minutes
Date Revealed in Film: 4:14–17, 56:02
Availability: Blu-ray and DVD (Fox Home Video)

Director: Danny Boyle; **Screenplay**: Danny Boyle and Simon Beaufoy

Cast: James Franco (Aron Ralston), Kate Mara (Kristi Moore), Amber Tamblyn (Megan McBride), Clémence Poésy (Rana), Lizzy Caplan (Sonja Ralston), Kate Burton (Donna Ralston), Treat Williams (Larry Ralston)

Aron Ralston goes on a hiking trip to Utah's Canyonlands National Park. He meets two girls, Kristi and Megan, and they spend some time together diving into an underground pool. After they part, Aron travels through Blue John Canyon, but he slips and a rock falls, crushing his arm and trapping him. As he suffers from thirst and loss of blood, he begins to hallucinate about his family, the two girls he just met, and a former girlfriend. On April 29, 2003 (56:02 to 1:02:26), Aron spends another day trapped in the canyon. Two days later he sees a vision of a little blond boy, whom he thinks is his future son. This gives him the strength to do what he has to do to escape.

A very intense film.

Awards: *Academy Award Nominations*: Best Picture, Best Actor (James Franco), Best Adapted Screenplay, Best Film Editing, Best Original Score, and Best Original Song. *Golden Globe Nominations*: Best Performance by an Actor in a Motion Picture–Drama (Franco), Best Screenplay–Motion Picture, and Best Original Score–Motion Picture

Alternate Film: *Master of the World*

30
GREAT EXPECTATIONS

Year: 1946
Genre: Period Drama
Run Time: 1 hour 58 minutes
Date Revealed in Film: 1:50:35
Availability: DVD (Criterion), VHS (Paramount Pictures)

Director: David Lean; **Screenplay**: Anthony Havelock-Allan, Cecil McGivern, and Ronald Neame, based on the Charles Dickens novel

Cast: John Mills (Pip), Jean Simmons (Estella Havisham as a girl), Valerie Hobson (Estella), Martita Hunt (Miss Havisham), Finlay Currie (Magwitch), Francis L. Sullivan (Mr. Jaggers), Bernard Miles (Joe Gargery), Alec Guinness (Herbert Pocket), Anthony Wager (Pip as a boy)

In nineteenth-century England, young Pip is visiting his parents' graves when he meets escaped prisoner Magwitch, who coerces him to get a file from the blacksmith shop of Pip's brother-in-law Joe Gargery. Magwitch manages to remove his chains, but is caught. A year later Miss Havisham, a local upper-class lady, asks Pip to visit her in her decrepit house. Pip falls in love with Estella, Miss Havisham's adopted daughter, despite her insults. He then meets the Pockets, Miss Havisham's heirs, and fights and beats a boy who is at the house. Pip stops visiting Miss Havisham when he starts his apprenticeship as a blacksmith with Joe.

Six years later Mr. Jaggers, an attorney, visits and tells Pip an undisclosed person wants to make him a gentleman. Pip goes to London and rooms with Herbert Pocket, the boy he beat up years ago. Pip learns that Miss Havisham had once been jilted and that she changed nothing in her house since that day. Miss Havisham had adopted Estella to raise in order to get her revenge on men. Estella is there and tells Pip that she has no heart.

Magwitch visits Pip and tells him he was exiled to Australia, where he became wealthy. He discloses that he is Pip's benefactor. Magwitch has risked hanging by returning to England, and Pip decides to smuggle Magwitch out of the country. Pip visits Miss Havisham and tells Estella he loves her, but she rejects him and says she is going to marry Bentley Drummle, a society rake. Miss Havisham is killed in an apparent accident. Magwitch's escape goes wrong, and he is arrested and sentenced to death. Pip learns that Estella is the child of Magwitch and Jaggers's servant. Pip becomes ill and wakes up on April 30 to find he's been cared for by Joe Gargery (1:50:00 to 1:51:35). Pip goes to Miss Havisham's house for a final confrontation with Estella.

This film started Alec Guinness and David Lean on the road to fame. A good rendering of Dickens's story. Uses some interesting cinematographic techniques, such as several fades to black and the sequence depicting Pip getting sick.

Awards: *Academy Award Wins*: Best Set Direction–Black-and-White and Best Cinematography–Black-and-White. *Academy Award Nominations*: Best Director, Best Picture, and Best Screenplay

Alternate Film: *Meet Me in St. Louis*

May

1

FOUR WEDDINGS AND A FUNERAL

Year: 1994
Genre: Romantic Comedy
Run Time: 1 hour 57 minutes
Date Revealed in Film: 5:02
Availability: Blu-ray and DVD (Metro-Goldwyn-Mayer)
Director: Mike Newell; **Screenplay**: Richard Curtis
Cast: Hugh Grant (Charles), Andie MacDowell (Carrie), Kristin Scott
   Thomas (Fiona), Simon Callow (Gareth), James Fleet (Tom), Rowan At-
   kinson (Father Gerald), John Hannah (Matthew), David Bower (David),
   Anna Chancellor (Henrietta/"Duckface")

Charles is late to the wedding of his friends Angus and Laura on May 1,
1993, and forgets the ring. At the reception, Charles meets Carrie, an attractive American, and they have a one-night stand. She teases him about
getting married (00:50 to 33:35). Bernard and Lydia meet at this wedding. At
their nuptials Charles learns that Carrie is engaged. Charles is seated at the
reception with his ex-girlfriend, Henrietta. Charles meets Carrie again and
they sleep together (in spite of her being engaged). Charles gets invited to
Carrie's wedding and while shopping for a wedding present meets her and
awkwardly confesses that he loves her. Charles attends Carrie's wedding in a

very depressed mood. Gareth dies at Carrie's reception and after his funeral, Charles wonders if true love is a hopeless prospect. Charles becomes engaged to Henrietta, but their wedding doesn't go quite as planned.

A funny romantic comedy. Hugh Grant's mannerisms make this film, as he is outstanding as the classic indecisive protagonist. You do hope it will come out all right for him in the end.

Awards: *Academy Award Nominations*: Best Picture and Best Original Screenplay. *Golden Globe Win*: Best Performance by an Actor in a Motion Picture–Comedy/Musical (Hugh Grant). *Golden Globe Nominations*: Best Performance by an Actress in a Motion Picture–Comedy/Musical (Andie MacDowell) and Best Screenplay–Motion Picture

Alternate Film: *A Civil Action*

2
YOUNG FRANKENSTEIN
Year: 1974
Genre: Comedy
Run Time: 1 hour 46 minutes
Date Revealed in Film: 1:43:28
Availability: Blu-ray and DVD (Twentieth Century Fox)
Director: Mel Brooks; **Screenplay**: Mel Brooks and Gene Wilder
Cast: Gene Wilder (Dr. Frederick Frankenstein), Marty Feldman (Igor), Peter Boyle (the Monster), Teri Garr (Inga), Cloris Leachman (Frau Blücher), Madeline Kahn (Elizabeth), Kenneth Mars (Inspector Kemp), Richard Haydn (Herr Falkstein)

Dr. Frederick Frankenstein is a medical school teacher who is engaged to the uptight Elizabeth. He rejects any connection to his infamous grandfather, the "mad scientist" Dr. Victor Frankenstein. Then he inherits Castle Frankenstein in Transylvania. Frederick goes there and meets his assistant, Inga; housekeeper, Frau Blücher; and Igor. Frederick finds his grandfather's secret lab and decides to continue his reanimation experiments. Frederick and Igor steal the oversized body of a convicted criminal. However, at the local brain depository Igor accidentally destroys the selected brain of a scientist and instead picks one labeled abnormal.

The monster Frederick brings to life is wild and violent. The local police visit, but Frederick reassures them he is not continuing his grandfather's experiments. The monster escapes. He is recaptured and calmed sufficiently by Frederick so that the creature is exhibited at a lecture, but a small fire terrifies the creature and results in the monster being locked up. The monster escapes and ravishes a not-too-unwilling visiting Elizabeth. The creature is lured to the castle, where Frederick transfers some of his intellect into the creature, who is now able to calm the mob that was attacking the castle. On May 2, 1974, Fredrick marries Inga, while the creature and Elizabeth have become a couple (1:41:43 to 1:45:30).

One of the funniest movies ever. Too many hilarious scenes to list here. You have to see it for yourself. Be prepared to laugh!

Awards: *Academy Award Nominations*: Best Sound and Best Adapted Screenplay. *Golden Globe Nominations*: Best Motion Picture Actress–Musical/Comedy (Cloris Leachman) and Best Supporting Actress–Motion Picture (Madeline Kahn)

Alternate Film: *Sugarland Express*

3

A MATTER OF LIFE AND DEATH

Year: 1946
Genre: Fantasy/Romance
Run Time: 1 hour 44 minutes
Date Revealed in Film: 4:13
Availability: DVD (Sony Pictures), VHS (Luminous Films and Video Works)
Directors: Michael Powell and Emeric Pressburger; **Screenplay**: Michael Powell and Emeric Pressburger
Cast: David Niven (Peter David Carter), Kim Hunter (June), Roger Livesey (Dr. Frank Reeves), Richard Attenborough (an English Pilot), Joan Maude (Chief Recorder), Marius Goring (Conductor 71), Raymond Massey (Abraham Farlan), Abraham Sofaer (Judge)

Returning from a bombing mission over Germany, British squadron leader Peter Carter talks on the radio to June, an American WAC, before he bails out of his crippled Lancaster bomber without a parachute into a fog thicker than pea soup. Peter wakes up on a beach, where he sees June, and it's love at first sight. In heaven, it is discovered that Peter has not yet arrived. Conductor 71, who missed Peter in the fog, is sent to Earth to persuade him to come to heaven. Peter refuses, saying he has fallen in love with June and demands an appeal. The next day, May 3, 1945 (32:15 to 44:13), Peter meets Dr. Reeves, who thinks Peter has a neurological condition. Conductor 71 returns with news that Peter will be allowed an appeal. As Dr. Reeves arranges for an operation, Peter and Conductor 71 try to decide who will be his counsel. Dr. Reeves is killed in a tragic accident, but Peter's operation and trial begin at the same time. With an Anglophobe prosecutor and jury things look bleak. Dr. Reeves, who takes the job as Peter's counsel, gets the jury replaced with an American jury. When the jury and judge travel to Earth, June is called as a witness and has to make a difficult decision if Peter is to win his case.

An interesting drama in the style of *The Sixth Sense* and *Field of Dreams*. **Alternate Film**: *The Conspirator*

4

THE MESSENGER: THE STORY OF JOAN OF ARC
Year: 1999
Genre: Biography
Run Time: 2 hours 28 minutes
Availability: Blu-ray and DVD (Sony Pictures)
Director: Luc Besson; **Screenplay**: Andrew Birken and Luc Besson
Cast: Milla Jovovich (Joan of Arc), Dustin Hoffman (The Conscience), Faye
    Dunaway (Yolande of Aragon), John Malkovich (Charles VII of France),
    Tchéky Karyo (Jean de Dunois), Vincent Cassel (Gilles de Rais), Richard
    Ridings (La Hire)
Joan is a happy child who often confesses in church. The English attack her village, and her sister is raped and killed. Years later, the Dauphin Charles considers messages from Joan, telling him that God has sent her. He tests her to see if she can pick him out of a group of courtiers. She succeeds and is given command of an army to relieve the besieged city of Orleans. Joan suggests an attack at Tourelles, but the next day, May 4, 1429, the army attacks St. Loup without her and is in retreat when Joan appears and turns them around. She leads the capture of St. Loup, but is shot by an arrow in an attack on Tourelles (1:03:02 to 1:08:10). She recovers and captures Tourelles. Joan

rides out alone and begs the English to retreat, and they do, allowing Orleans to be recaptured. Charles is taken to Rheims and crowned King of France, but Joan's attack on Paris fails. Charles tries the diplomatic approach with the English and lets the Burgundians capture Joan to get her out of the way. She is handed over to Bishop Cauchon, who convenes a church court to try her for heresy. The court eventually condemns Joan, who is persuaded to sign a renunciation upon the promise of being confessed and allowed to attend mass. Her "conscience" persuades her that she has renounced God by this act and she renounces her renunciation. The English burn her at the stake. She is canonized in 1920, 489 years after her death.

This movie leaves you wondering if Joan was insane. Both the action and vision sequences have beautiful cinematography.

Source: De Vries, Kelly. *Joan of Arc: A Military Leader*. Stroud, UK: Sutton
    Publishing, 1999. This book at page 80 gives this date for the attack.
Alternate Film: *A World Apart*

5
THE RIGHT STUFF

Year: 1983
Genre: Drama
Run Time: 3 hours 13 minutes
Date Revealed in Film: 1:46:32
Availability: Blu-ray and DVD (Warner Home Video)
Director: Phillip Kaufman; **Screenplay**: Phillip Kaufman, based on Tom
    Wolfe's book
Cast: Sam Shepard (Chuck Yeager), Scott Glenn (Alan Shepard), Ed Harris
    (John Glenn), Dennis Quaid (Gordon Cooper), Fred Ward (Gus Grissom),
    Barbara Hershey (Glennis Yeager), Kim Stanley (Pancho Barnes), Levon
    Helm (Jack Ridley/Narrator)

Chuck Yeager injures himself in an accident, but still flies the *X-1* faster than sound. In 1953, testing of new aircraft continues at Edwards Air Force Base to the dismay of the test pilots' wives. The launch of *Sputnik* by the Soviet Union throws America into a panic. The Mercury program is developed to put an American into space. Yeager is somewhat contemptuous of astronauts, as he considers them passengers, not pilots. He sets a new altitude record, but almost dies. Alan Shepard is launched into space on May 5, 1961 (1:46:30 to 1:56:54). Grissom and Glenn follow him. Yeager comes to have some respect for the astronauts for their willingness to face known danger. Vice President Lyndon Johnson positions himself as a mentor to the space program so he can reap the political benefits. John Glenn has to shield his shy wife from the press during his successful three-orbit mission.

An interesting film that highlights the danger, thrills, and politics of the space race.

Awards: *Academy Award Wins*: Best Sound Effects Editing, Best Film Editing, Best Music–Original Score, and Best Sound. *Academy Award Nominations*: Best Actor in a Supporting Role (Sam Shepard), Best Art Direction, Best Cinematography, and Best Picture. *Golden Globe Nomination*: Best Motion Picture–Drama

Alternate Film: *My Big Fat Greek Wedding*

6

WALL STREET

Year: 1987
Genre: Drama
Run Time: 2 hours 6 minutes
Date Revealed in Film: 13:51
Availability: Blu-ray and DVD (Twentieth Century Fox)
Director: Oliver Stone; **Screenplay**: Stanley Weiser and Oliver Stone
Cast: Michael Douglas (Gordon Gekko), Charlie Sheen (Bud Fox), Daryl Hannah (Darien Taylor), Martin Sheen (Carl Fox), John C. McGinley (Marvin), Terence Stamp (Sir Larry Wildman), Hal Holbrook (Lou Mannheim), Sean Young (Kate Gekko)

Bud Fox is a junior stockbroker who wants to get rich quick, like his hero, super trader Gordon Gekko, whose motto is "Greed is good." This leads him into conflict with his father, a union rep who works at Bluestar Airlines. Bud sees Gekko on his birthday, May 6, 1985, but Gekko won't talk to him until he gives Gekko insider info that he picked up about Bluestar from his dad. (13:25 to 23:27). Based on this success Gekko gives him $1 million to invest. The stock picks Bud makes by regular research all lose money. Bud's spying on Sir Larry Wildman, a British corporate raider, enables Gekko to put Wildman over a barrel. Bud buys a cleaning and maintenance company so he can sneak into offices and get insider information to feed to Gekko.

Bud gets rich and promoted because his commissions are now huge and he moves in with former Gekko girlfriend, Darien Taylor. Bud talks Gekko into buying Bluestar and making money by getting wage concessions from the union. The SEC starts investigating Gekko and Bud. Bud learns Gekko plans to liquidate Bluestar, fire everyone, and take the $75 million pension fund. This causes Bud's father to have a heart attack. Bud turns on Gekko and dumps Darien. Bud manipulates Bluestar stock downward and when it's cheap, Sir Larry Wildman buys the company. Wildman gets revenge on Gekko, and saves the company and Fox senior's job. Then the bottom falls out for Bud and he has to make a tough choice.

A story of greed, greed, and more greed. Bud is lured by the cash and ends up in trouble. Contrary to what Gekko says, greed is not good.

Awards: *Academy Award Win*: Best Actor (Michael Douglas). *Golden Globe Win*: Best Performance by an Actor in a Motion Picture–Drama (Douglas)

Alternate Film: *The Hindenberg*

7

IMMORTAL BELOVED

Year: 1994
Genre: Biography
Run Time: 2 hours 1 minute
Availability: Blu-ray and DVD (Sony Pictures)
Director: Bernard Rose; **Screenplay**: Bernard Rose
Cast: Gary Oldman (Ludwig van Beethoven), Jeroen Krabbé (Anton Felix Schindler), Isabella Rossellini (Anna-Marie Erdödy), Johanna ter Steege (Johanna van Beethoven), Christopher Fulford (Kaspar van Beethoven), Marco Hofschneider (Karl van Beethoven)

After Beethoven's funeral, his executor, Schindler, finds a will leaving everything to the "Immortal Beloved" and a letter addressed to her at an inn in Karlsbad. At the inn he finds that she was there years ago but left just before Beethoven arrived. Schindler visits a former student of Beethoven. Beethoven had proposed to her, and her father said they could marry if Beethoven could still play music. But when it came out that Beethoven was deaf, he refused permission, and she wed someone else. Schindler learns that Beethoven's brother Kaspar married Johanna Reiss, whom Ludwig labeled as a whore; he tried to have them arrested for fornication. Schindler then visits Countess Anna-Marie Erdödy, who lived with Beethoven for a happy year. Schindler remembers how he met Beethoven and became his secretary. Schindler learns that Beethoven did not reach the inn at Karlsbad to meet the "Immortal Beloved" in time due to a carriage breakdown, so he sent a letter. After his brother Kaspar died, Beethoven was made guardian to Kaspar's son, Karl. Beethoven tries to make Karl a piano virtuoso, but the pressure leads to quarrels and Karl's suicide attempt. Schindler visits Johanna van Beethoven, who finally tells him what happened. She was the Immortal Beloved, but she never got the letter and left thinking Beethoven had abandoned her. They were lovers and Karl was Beethoven's son. Out of spite she married his brother. Her attitude toward him improved after she attended the premiere of the Ninth Symphony on May 7, 1824, which greatly moved her (1:35:35 to 1:43:27).

A good biopic. Of course the plot is mainly fiction, but it does give a lot of insight into Beethoven. And of course the music is outstanding!

Source: Lockwood, Lewis. *Beethoven: The Music and the Life.* New York: W.W. Norton and Company, 2003. This book at pages 352–53 gives this date for the premiere.

Alternate Film: *Men in Black*

8
MISTER ROBERTS

Year: 1955
Genre: Comedy/Drama
Run Time: 2 hours 3 minutes
Date Revealed in Film: 1:21:57, 1:32:05
Availability: DVD and VHS (Warner Home Video)
Directors: John Ford and Mervyn LeRoy; **Screenplay**: Frank S. Nugent and Joshua Logan, based on Thomas Heggen and Joshua Logan's play and Thomas Heggen's novel
Cast: Henry Fonda (Lt. J. G. "Doug" Roberts), James Cagney (Captain Morton), William Powell (Lt. "Doc"), Jack Lemmon (Ens. Frank Thurlowe Pulver), Betsy Palmer (Lt. Ann Girard), Ward Bond (Chief Boatswain's Mate Dowdy), Philip Carey (Mannion)

On the USS *Reluctant*, a navy cargo ship in the Pacific during World War II, first officer Doug Roberts wants to be transferred to a combat unit. The crew has had no liberty for over a year and is becoming violent malingerers. The ship reaches Elysium, a liberty port, but the captain only grants liberty after blackmailing Roberts into agreeing to obey his orders. Doug keeps his end of the deal and the crew starts to resent him. On May 8, 1945, the war in Europe ends, but Doug throws the captain's prized palm tree overboard. The crew learns of Doug's deal with the captain and this restores him to their good graces (1:21:48 to 1:43:11). Doug gets a transfer to a destroyer after the crew sent in a transfer request and forged the captain's signature approving it. With Roberts gone, Pulver becomes the captain's pet. Then Pulver gets two letters that force him to take action.

A bittersweet comedy. Excellent character development. Even has some good sight gags.

Awards: *Academy Award Win*: Best Supporting Actor (Jack Lemon). *Academy Award Nominations*: Best Picture and Best Sound Recording

Source: Heggen, Thomas. *Mr. Roberts*. Boston: Houghton Mifflin Co., 1946. This book at page 214 gives the date the letter was received.

Alternate Film: *1776*

9

NIXON

Year: 1995
Genre: Biography
Run Time: 3 hours 12 minutes
Date Revealed in Film: 1:46:10
Availability: Blu-ray and DVD (Disney/Buena Vista)
Director: Oliver Stone; **Screenplay**: Stephen J. Rivele, Christopher Wilkinson, and Oliver Stone
Cast: Anthony Hopkins (Richard Nixon), Joan Allen (Pat Nixon), Annabeth Gish (Julie Nixon Eisenhower), Marley Shelton (Tricia Nixon Cox), James Woods (H. R. Haldeman), Powers Boothe (Alexander Haig), Ed Harris (E. Howard Hunt)

In December 1972 Al Haig brings tapes to the White House. While Nixon reviews them he flashes back. Nixon's father thought his sons Harold and Dick were lazy and his mother tried to get him to always tell the truth. Nixon goes to Whittier College, and while he never gets on the football team, his determination impresses some. The death of his mother's brother allows him to go to Duke Law School. He is elected to Congress and is rocketed to fame with the Alger Hiss case. He marries Pat and is selected in 1952 as Eisenhower's vice president, saving his candidacy with the "Checkers" speech.

Nixon loses the 1960 presidential election. Pat wants him to give up politics, and after he loses the 1962 California governor's race, she tells him she wants a divorce. He gets her to stay by promising not to run again. However, he's persuaded by a group of extreme right-wingers to run for president in 1968 and he talks Pat into agreeing. As president he orders the bombing of Cambodia and is stunned by the public response and even visits the Lincoln Memorial at 4 AM on May 9, 1970, to talk to student protestors (1:46:01 to 1:52:22). When the *Pentagon Papers* are published he authorizes a break-in at the office of Daniel Ellsberg's psychiatrist. In spite of great foreign policy successes in ending the war in Vietnam and visiting China Nixon still feels underrated.

Nixon becomes involved in a cover-up of the Watergate break-in, even though as he knows from the Alger Hiss case it wasn't the act that got him in trouble, but the cover-up. He agrees to pay hush money to the burglars. When an investigation is launched by Congress and the existence of his taping system is exposed he fights releasing this information. In "the Saturday Night Massacre" he fires the special prosecutor, but even this does not stop the investigation. He is eventually forced to hand over transcripts of the tapes. This leads to his impeachment and resignation.

Not Stone's best. If you aren't already familiar with Richard Nixon's story you will have a hard time following this movie. Hopkins may not look that much like Nixon, but he has his paranoid personality down pat.

Awards: *Academy Award Nominations*: Best Actor (Anthony Hopkins), Best Original Score, Best Original Screenplay, and Best Supporting Actress (Joan Allen). *Golden Globe Nomination*: Best Performance by an Actor in a Motion Picture–Drama (Hopkins)

Alternate Film: *And Starring Pancho Villa as Himself*

10
DEEP IMPACT

Year: 1998
Genre: Science Fiction/Disaster
Run Time: 2 hours
Date Revealed in Film: 4:00
Availability: Blu-ray and DVD (Paramount Pictures)
Director: Mimi Leder; **Screenplay**: Bruce Joel Rubin and Michael Tolkin
Cast: Robert Duvall (Capt. Spurgeon "Fish" Tanner), Téa Leoni (Jenny Lerner), Elijah Wood (Leo Beiderman), Morgan Freeman (President Tom Beck), Vanessa Redgrave (Robin Lerner), Maximilian Schell (Jason Lerner), Leelee Sobieski (Sarah Hotchner)

On May 10, 1998 (00:40 to 2:35), amateur astronomer Leo Beiderman discovers a comet. His teacher tells astronomer Marcus Wolf, who realizes the comet is on a collision course with Earth. But Wolf is killed before he can make this news public. A year later TV reporter Jenny Lerner is investigating the resignation of the treasury secretary and stumbles upon a cover-up. This forces the president to reveal the existence of the comet and the construction of a spaceship called the *Messiah* to deal with it. However, the *Messiah*'s mission only results in the comet being split into two unequal parts and the apparent destruction of the spacecraft. The government has built underground shelters for one million people. Leo marries his girlfriend, Sarah, to save her and her family, but when they are not evacuated with Leo, she stays behind. An effort to destroy the comet using ballistic missiles also fails. Leo gets Sarah to high ground in time, but Jenny gives up her place on an evac helicopter to a friend with a small child. Jenny and Sarah's parents, along with millions of others, are killed when the smaller piece of the comet lands in the Atlantic and destroys much of the United States, Europe, and Africa. However, with just hours left until the impact of the larger fragment, the *Messiah* reappears with a proposal that could save the day.

A poignant film. Does a good job of presenting a scientifically accurate disaster story. Concentrates on the characters instead of the gadgets.

Alternate Film: *Gods and Generals*

11
(500) DAYS OF SUMMER

Year: 2009
Genre: Romantic Drama
Run Time: 1 hour 35 minutes
Date Revealed in Film: 1:54, 1:21:18
Availability: Blu-ray and DVD (Fox Home Video)
Director: Marc Webb; **Screenplay**: Scott Neustadter and Michael H. Weber
Cast: Joseph Gordon-Levitt (Tom Hansen), Zooey Deschanel (Summer Finn), Chloë Grace Moretz (Rachel Hansen), Geoffrey Arend (McKenzie), Matthew Gray Gubler (Paul), Clark Gregg (Vance), Rachel Boston (Alison)

Tom Hansen, who studied to be an architect but works at a greeting card company, meets Summer Finn, his boss's assistant. Tom believes in true love, but she does not. Tom chats Summer up at an office party and is intrigued by her. After karaoke night at a local bar, where Summer says she doesn't want to be anybody's girlfriend, Tom's friend McKenzie blurts out that Tom likes Summer. She proposes they be friends, but then kisses him in the copy room. They start a "casual" relationship, as Summer puts it. Tom is soon head over heels in love with her and walking on cloud nine. Tom shows her his favorite spot in the city in a park. One night at a bar a guy comes on to Summer and Tom ends up getting belted. Summer is mad at Tom and they have a fight. On day 290 they breakup after watching *The Graduate*. Tom takes the breakup hard, and his friends McKenzie and Paul call in Tom's sister Rachel to help. Summer quits her job, and Tom's boss moves him to writing consolation cards. Tom and Summer attend a wedding and dance together. Summer invites him to a party at her apartment. He attends with a split screen showing his expectations of what's going to happen—getting back together with Summer—versus the reality of what does happen—Tom leaves when he notices she's wearing an engagement ring. Tom goes into a deep funk, quits his job, but starts looking for architecture jobs. On May 11, 2010, Tom is at the park when Summer comes to talk to him. He expresses his bewilderment at her behavior while she tells him she found love, just with someone else (1:21:20 to 1:27:02). Later while waiting for a job interview, he meets a fellow candidate and asks her out on a date. Her name is Autumn.

A quirky and refreshing film, different from the usual romance film because it has a happy ending for only one of the main characters. It uses unusual film choices, such as Tom's fantasy flash mob and the split-screen view of the party.

Awards: *Golden Globe Nominations*: Best Motion Picture–Comedy or Musical and Best Performance by an Actor in a Motion Picture–Comedy or Musical (Joseph Gordon-Levitt)

Alternate Film: *Dunkirk*

12

THE TERMINATOR

Year: 1984

Genre: Science Fiction

Run Time: 1 hour 47 minutes

Date Revealed in Film: 3:46 and 8:45–47

Availability: Blu-ray and DVD (Metro-Goldwyn-Mayer)

Director: James Cameron; **Screenplay**: James Cameron and Gale Ann Hurd

Cast: Arnold Schwarzenegger (The Terminator), Michael Biehn (Kyle Reese), Linda Hamilton (Sarah Connor), Earl Boen (Dr. Silberman), Paul Winfield (Ed Traxler), Lance Henriksen (Hal Vukovich), Bess Motta (Ginger Ventura)

On May 12, 1984, two men suddenly appear out of thin air in Los Angeles (3:24 to 50:29). One is actually a cyborg from the future with the mission of killing Sarah Connor, who will give birth to John Connor, leader of the resistance to the killing machines of the future. The other, Reese, has been sent back to protect her. The cyborg follows the simple expedient of killing all women in Los Angeles named Sarah Connor. The cyborg tries to kill the protagonist, but Reese rescues her. She has trouble believing Reese's story of being from a future where computers started a nuclear war and then created machines to try and kill off humanity.

The cyborg attacks the police station where they are being held, killing many officers, and Sarah flees with Reese. They have a romantic interlude. She makes a mistake and calls her mother, leading to a climactic battle to the death with the cyborg.

A disturbing and violent film with an interesting sci-fi premise that is well developed by Cameron. Noted for two lines, the cyborg's "I'll be back" and the most effective pickup line ever (delivered by Reese to Sarah Connor), "Come with me if you want to live." Who could refuse?

Alternate Film: *J. Edgar*

13
BRIDGE ON THE RIVER KWAI

Year: 1957

Genre: War

Run Time: 2 hours 41 minutes

Date Revealed in Film: 21:29–30, 1:46:09–1:46:18, and 2:07:10

Availability: Blu-ray (Sony Pictures), DVD (Columbia Pictures)

Director: David Lean; **Screenplay**: Carl Foreman and Michael Wilson, based on the novel by Pierre Boulle

Cast: William Holden (Commander Shears), Alec Guinness (Colonel Nicholson), Jack Hawkins (Major Warden), Sessue Hayakawa (Colonel Saito), James Donald (Major Clipton), Geoffrey Horne (Lieutenant Joyce), André Morell (Colonel Green)

A contingent of British POWs, led by Col. Nicholson, march into their camp. They find Allied POWs already there, including American Commander Shears. The Japanese Commandant Col. Saito tells the British that all of them will work to build the eponymous bridge, but Nicholson says officers will not, even when Saito threatens to have them shot. They are put into punishment cells. The other ranks work on the bridge, sabotaging their own efforts. Saito is finally forced to release the officers to get the work moving. Nicholson has the men work on the bridge to restore morale and he becomes obsessed with it, to the point of having officers work on the bridge. Shears escapes and makes it to Ceylon, where he is revealed as an ordinary sailor who assumed an officer's identity in hopes of better treatment. He is forced to return with a British commando team to blow up the bridge rather than face a court-martial. The commandos arrive and wire the completed bridge with explosives. The next morning, May 13, 1943, the water level of the river has dropped and Col. Nicholson spots the explosives, and he and Col. Saito trace the wires, leading to a final confrontation with Shears (2:24:23 to 2:40:24).

This is more than your average war film. It is in large part a battle of wills between two determined men. Good character development throughout.

Awards: *Academy Award Wins*: Best Picture, Best Director, Best Actor (Alec Guinness), Best Adapted Screenplay, Best Score, Best Film Editing, and Best Cinematography. *Academy Award Nomination*: Best Actor in a Supporting Role (Sessue Hayakawa). *Golden Globe Wins*: Best Motion Picture–Drama, Best Motion Picture Actor–Drama (Guinness), Best Motion Picture Director. *Golden Globe Nomination*: Best Supporting Actor (Hayakawa)
Alternate Film: *To Hell and Back*

14
BEYOND THE SEA

Year: 2004
Genre: Biography
Run Time: 1 hour 58 minutes
Availability: DVD and VHS (Lionsgate Home Entertainment)
Director: Kevin Spacey; **Screenplay**: Lewis Colick and Kevin Spacey
Cast: Kevin Spacey (Bobby Darin), Kate Bosworth (Sandra Dee), Bob Hoskins (Charlie Cassotto Maffia), John Goodman (Steve "Boom Boom" Blauner), Brenda Blethyn (Polly Cassotto), Caroline Aaron (Nina Cassotto Maffia), Greta Scacchi (Mary Douvan)

Bobby Darin is starring in a biopic about himself and annoying everyone with obsessive perfectionism. After a talk with the boy playing him as a child he flashes back. Walden Robert Cassotto lived with his mom, sister Nina, and brother-in-law Charlie. He has rheumatic fever, but his mom introduces him to music, and he celebrates his tenth birthday on May 14, 1946 (13:37 to 13:42). Later he sings at nightclubs and changes his name to Bobby Darin. He appears on TV and has a hit with "Splish Splash." He makes a movie with Sandra Dee and they get married. When Bobby plays at the Copacabana Club, he refuses to replace his African American comedy opening act. The couple has a son while continuing to act in movies and he continues to sing to the point that Sandra thinks they don't spend enough time together. Nina reveals that she's his mother, not his sister, and he goes into depression. He moves into a camper on the coast. He performs folk-style songs and is booed off the stage. He returns to play Las Vegas in triumph, but gets sick and dies.

An interesting biopic. Often breaks the fourth wall by breaking into big musical productions featuring Darin's songs. Commendable for being objective and not a paean to a celebrity.

Awards: *Golden Globe Nomination*: Best Performance by an Actor in a Motion Picture–Comedy or Musical (Kevin Spacey)

Source: Starr, Michael S. *Bobby Darin: A Life*. New York: Taylor Trade Publishing, 2004. This book at page 3 gives his birth date.

Alternate Film: *Master and Commander: The Far Side of the World*

15

SEVEN DAYS IN MAY

Year: 1964

Genre: Drama/Thriller

Run Time: 1 hour 58 minutes

Date Revealed in Film: 56:52

Availability: DVD and VHS (Warner Home Video)

Director: John Frankenheimer; **Screenplay**: Rod Serling, based on the novel by Fletcher Knebel and Charles W. Bailey II

Cast: Burt Lancaster (General Scott), Kirk Douglas (Colonel Jiggs Casey), Fredric March (President Jordan Lyman), Ava Gardner (Eleanor Holbrook), Edmond O'Brien (Senator Ray Clark), Martin Balsam (Paul Girard)

A nuclear disarmament treaty signed with the Soviet Union raises political tensions between those who see it as the way out and those who see it as a sell-out. Among the latter is General James Scott, chairman of the Joint Chiefs of Staff. Col. "Jiggs" Casey, director of the Joint Chiefs, learns that a friend of his, Col. "Mutt" Henderson, is executive officer of ECOMCON, a unit he's never heard of. Later Jiggs discovers Senator Prentice has learned of a top-secret military test alert. He observes a secret meeting between Scott and Prentice, but Scott lies to Jiggs and denies meeting Prentice. Casey meets President Lyman and tells him he thinks a coup may be in the works.

The next day, May 15, Lyman tells Scott he's not participating in the alert and going fishing in Maine (56:44 to 1:21:51). Ray Clark, a senator and Lyman's best friend, flies to El Paso and locates the top secret ECOMCON base, but is held incommunicado. Presidential aide Paul Girard meets with Admiral Barnswell and gets a signed statement about the plot. Jiggs gets documents from Eleanor Holbrook, Scott's former mistress, that reveal Scott's affair with her. Scott sends men to scout the president's fishing hole with an eye to kidnapping him. Paul Girard's plane crashes. Clark talks Col. Henderson, the base commander, into returning to Washington with him, but when they arrive Henderson is picked up by MPs. Scott won't quit and Lyman won't use Holbrook's letters to force his resignation. At a press conference, Lyman gets Girard's notes and the three joint chiefs allied with Scott resign. Scott decides to abandon the coup.

A taut political thriller. Keeps you on the edge of your seat for two hours. One of the best political movies, as it discusses patriotism as well as war and peace.

Awards: *Academy Award Nominations*: Best Actor in a Supporting Role (Edmond O'Brien) and Best Art Direction–Set Decoration–Black-and-White. *Golden Globe Win*: Best Supporting Actor (O'Brien). *Golden Globe Nominations*: Best Motion Picture Director, Best Motion Picture Actor–Drama (Fredric March), and Best Original Score

Alternate Film: *Cast a Giant Shadow*

16
FIELD OF DREAMS
Year: 1989
Genre: Fantasy
Run Time: 1 hour 47 minutes
Date Revealed in Film: 54:28, 54:40
Availability: Blu-ray and DVD (Universal Studios)
Director: Phil Alden Robinson; **Screenplay**: Phil Alden Robinson, based on the novel *Shoeless Joe* by W. P. Kinsella
Cast: Kevin Costner (Ray Kinsella), Amy Madigan (Annie Kinsella), Gaby Hoffman (Karin Kinsella), James Earl Jones (Terrance Mann), Burt Lancaster ("Moonlight" Graham), Ray Liotta ("Shoeless Joe" Jackson), Timothy Busfield (Mark)

Ray Kinsella, unsuccessful farmer and baseball fan, lives in Iowa. Out in the cornfields he has a vision of a baseball diamond and a voice saying, "If you build it, he will come." Ray builds the diamond and a year passes. One day he spots what appears to be the ghost of Shoeless Joe Jackson on the field, who later returns with the rest of the (dead) 1919 Chicago Black Sox. Ray hears the voice say, "Ease his pain," and decides the "he" is Terrance Mann, 1960s author and activist now living as a recluse in Boston.

Ray travels to Boston, where he persuades Mann to attend a Red Sox game at Fenway Park on May 16, 1988, where they are the only ones to hear the voice say, "Go the distance," and the jumbotron reveals the stats on "Moonlight" Graham's one time at bat in the major leagues (44:21 to 57:27). They travel to Minnesota where Graham worked as a doctor and are startled to find he died sixteen years ago. One night, while walking, Ray is transported back in time to meet Doc Graham. Graham confesses he still wants to play baseball, but does not regret his decision to leave the game for a medical practice.

Ray returns to the present, but on the way home to Iowa, he and Mann pick up a young version of Doc Archie Graham. He joins the spectral players in their games. In a scuffle Ray's daughter falls to the ground. The young Archie Graham walks off the field, becoming the "old" Doc Graham and saves her life. He cannot revert to his younger self and brushes aside Ray's apologies, but accepting the praise of his spectral teammates departs into the cornrows of the outfield. Shoeless Joe invites Terrance Mann to return with them. Ray is upset that he is not allowed to go, but then he learns the real meaning of the first message.

A quirky film about the power of dreams. It effectively blurs the line between fantasy and reality.

Awards: *Academy Award Nominations*: Best Picture, Best Original Score, and Best Adapted Screenplay

Alternate Film: *The Dam Busters*

17

MEMPHIS BELLE

Year: 1990
Genre: War
Run Time: 1 hour 47 minutes
Date Revealed in Film: 1:39:57
Availability: Blu-ray (Warner Home Video)
Director: Michael Caton-Jones; **Screenplay**: Monte Merrick

Cast: Matthew Modine (Capt. Dennis Dearborn), Eric Stoltz (Sgt. Danny Dale), Tate Donovan (First Lt. Luke Sinclair), D. B. Sweeney (Lt. Phil Lowenthal), Billy Zane (Lt. Val Kozlowski), Sean Astin (Sgt. Richard Moore), Harry Connick Jr. (Sgt. Clay Busby), John Lithgow (Lt. Col. Bruce Derringer), David Stathairn (Col. Craig Harriman)

The *Memphis Belle* is the first plane to reach twenty-four successful bombing missions over Europe in World War II, with one more to go before the crew is rotated home. The Army Air Corps sends Lt. Col. Derringer to tell the crew that they are to tour the States to help raise morale. The crew watches the crash of the last plane in a returning mission. They pilfer items from the kit of the crew of the crashed plane and then head to a dance held in their honor.

The next morning, May 17, 1943, the crew prepares for a mission to bomb an aircraft factory in Bremen. While the mission is under way, Harriman and Derringer argue, with Derringer accusing Harriman, the base commander, of being cold-hearted. In reply Harriman shows him letters from the families of dead fliers that he has had to answer. When two other planes are knocked out *Memphis Belle* becomes the squadron's lead plane. The carefree copilot, Sinclair, leaves the cockpit and shoots down a German fighter with the tail gun, but is horrified when that plane hits another B-17, making it crash. Their perfectionist pilot makes the squadron abort their first run and circle, as they can't see the target due to smoke. On their second attempt they hit the target. On the way back to England the plane is hit and damaged. Dale is injured. They are the last plane to return to the base and the celebration prepared for them (23:27 to 1:40:39).

Good character development as well as exciting action scenes.

Alternate Film: *King Solomon's Mines* (1950)

18
A FEW GOOD MEN

Year: 1992
Genre: Courtroom Drama
Run Time: 2 hours 18 minutes
Date Revealed in Film: 16:07
Availability: Blu-ray and DVD (Sony Pictures)
Director: Rob Reiner; **Screenplay**: Aaron Sorkin, based on his play

Cast: Tom Cruise (Daniel Kaffee), Jack Nicholson (Col. Nathan R. Jessup), Demi Moore (Lt. Cdr. JoAnne Galloway), Kevin Pollak (Lt. Sam Weinburg), Kevin Bacon (Capt. Jack Ross), Kiefer Sutherland (Lt. Jonathan Kendrick), Cuba Gooding Jr. (Cpl. Carl Hammaker)

At the naval base at Guantanamo Bay, Cuba, two Marines, Cpl. Dawson and Pvt. Downey, enter the room of Pvt. Santiago and tie him up. Santiago later dies from this. In Washington Lt. Cdr. JoAnne Galloway wants to represent Dawson and Downey, but Lts. Kaffee and Weinberg are appointed instead. A flashback shows Santiago was not a very good Marine and on May 18, 1992, he was pushed down a hill by Lt. Kendrick and ended up in the hospital (15:47 to 16:23). Santiago wanted off the base and in a letter offered to trade, in exchange for a transfer, information about an incident where Dawson illegally fired a weapon into Cuba. Dawson and Downey say they did "Code Red" on Santiago, which is unofficial punishment of a Marine. The prosecutor, Capt. Jack Ross, says that the platoon commander, Lt. Kendrick, specifically told everyone to leave Santiago alone. Kaffee, Galloway, and Weinberg fly to Cuba. The base commander, Col. Jessup, says he had planned to transfer Santiago off the base, with him leaving on the first flight the next day at 6 AM, but Santiago was killed first. Dawson and Downey tell Kaffee that Kendrick ordered them to do a "Code Red" on Santiago. Ross implies this case is a plot to get Jessup and offers a deal, which Dawson and Downey reject. Kaffee suspects he got the file because someone didn't want the case to go to trial. The base executive officer, Markinson, disappears. The trial begins. Markinson contacts Kaffee and says Jessup lied about getting Santiago off the base. Records of an earlier available flight out of Gitmo disappear. Markinson commits suicide. On the stand Jessup testifies the 6 AM flight was the first available for Santiago. After Kaffee catches Jessup in a contradiction, Jessup snaps. He rants about his importance to national security, saying, "You can't handle the truth," and confesses to ordering "Code Red." Jessup is arrested, while Dawson and Downey are acquitted of murder, but dishonorably discharged.

An intense drama. This movie lays out the plot very carefully, giving out just enough facts a little at a time to keep you on the edge of your seat. Excellent performances by the cast.

Awards: *Academy Award Nominations*: Best Picture, Best Supporting Actor (Jack Nicholson), Best Film Editing, and Best Sound. *Golden Globe Nominations*: Best Motion Picture–Drama, Best Director–Motion Picture, Best

Performance by an Actor in a Motion Picture–Drama (Tom Cruise), Best
Performance by an Actor in a Supporting Role in a Motion Picture–Drama
(Nicholson), and Best Screenplay–Motion Picture
Alternate Film: *Voyage of the Damned*

19
AVATAR

Year: 2009
Genre: Science Fiction
Run Time: 2 hours 42 minutes
Date Revealed in Film: 9:48
Availability: Blu-ray and DVD (Twentieth Century Fox)
Director: James Cameron; **Screenplay:** James Cameron
Cast: Sam Worthington (Corporal Jake Sully), Stephen Lang (Colonel Miles
  Quaritch), Sigourney Weaver (Dr. Grace Augustine), Giovanni Ribisi
  (Parker Selfridge), Joel David Moore (Dr. Norm Spellman), Zoe Saldana
  (Neytiri), C. C. H. Pounder (Mo'at)
The RDA Company is mining unobtainium on Pandora, a moon in the Al-
pha Centauri system inhabited by the Na'vi, twelve-foot-tall, blue-skinned
sapient humanoids. The company uses avatars, human–Na'vi hybrid bodies
controlled by a genetically compatible human, to interact with the Na'vi.
Jake Sully, a quadriplegic Marine veteran, decides to replace his murdered
twin brother on a mission to Pandora. After a six-year trip Jake arrives on
Pandora. Jake documents his experiences in a video log, with an initial entry
on May 19, 2154 (3:17 to 10:18). Jake and two scientists, Grace and Norm, go
to collect specimens as avatars. Jake is attacked by a predator and has to flee.
Neytiri, a female Na'vi, saves him, and after Jake becomes involved with the
Na'vi, Col. Quaritch, head of RDA security, tells Jake he will get the surgery
needed to restore the use of his legs if Jake spies on the Na'vi. Hometree is
situated over the richest unobtainium deposit for two hundred kilometers.
Jake is imitated as a Na'vi and chooses Neytiri as his mate. Selfridge orders
mining to begin. This forces Jake to choose which side he is going to fight for.
  Creates a fully realized world. The CGI work is fantastic to look at. The
plot is somewhat clichéd. Still, this movie keeps you interested enough to
watch until the end.

Awards: *Academy Award Wins*: Best Art Direction, Best Cinematography, and Best Visual Effects. *Academy Award Nominations*: Best Picture, Best Director, Best Film Editing, Best Original Score, Best Sound Editing, and Best Sound. *Golden Globe Wins*: Best Director–Motion Picture and Best Motion Picture–Drama. *Golden Globe Nominations*: Best Original Score–Motion Picture and Best Original Song–Motion Picture
Alternate Film: *Matewan*

20
HAMBURGER HILL
Year: 1987
Genre: War
Run Time: 1 hour 50 minutes
Date Revealed in Film: 1:31:37
Availability: Blu-ray (Lionsgate Films), VHS (Avid Home Entertainment)
Director: John Irvin; **Screenplay**: James Carabastos
Cast: Dylan McDermott (Sgt. Adam Frantz), Steven Weber (Sfc. Dennis Worcester), Courtney B. Vance (Spc. [Medic] Abraham Johnson), Don Cheadle (Pvt. Johnny Washburn), Michael Boatman (Pvt. Ray Motown), Anthony Barrile (Vincent Languilli)
During the Vietnam War, a squad comes off the front line and gets replacements, but even in rear areas there are Viet Cong attacks. They return to the jungle and are attacked almost at once. They are ambushed and rain makes life miserable. They continue to try and take the hill from a mostly unseen enemy who retreat into bunkers when they are bombed to emerge when the planes and choppers leave. The squad is hit by friendly fire from a chopper. They continue their uphill fight against heavy opposition. A TV crew appears and the men don't react too well. They fight uphill through rain and mud. On May 20, 1969, the sun returns as they finally reach the top of the hill (1:31:20 to 1:45:00).

Shows just the guts of war. The men are fighting for a hill with no strategic value. There's no glory here.
Alternate Film: *The Odd Couple*

21
THE SPIRIT OF ST. LOUIS
Year: 1957
Genre: Biography
Run Time: 2 hours 15 minutes
Availability: DVD and VHS (Warner Home Video)
Director: Billy Wilder; **Screenplay**: Charles Lederer, Wendall Mayes, and Billy Wilder, based on the book by Charles Lindbergh
Cast: James Stewart (Charles Lindbergh), Murray Hamilton (Harlan A. "Bud" Gurney), Patricia Smith (Mirror Girl), Bartlett Robinson (Benjamin Frank Mahoney), Marc Connelly (Father Hussman), Arthur Space (Donald A. Hall)

Charles Lindbergh trades his motorcycle for an airplane and becomes a barnstormer. He joins the Army Air Force and becomes an airmail pilot. He gets some businessmen in St. Louis to buy a plane that he will fly nonstop from New York to Paris in order to win the Ortiz prize of $25,000. Ryan Aircraft in San Diego builds the plane in sixty-three days. Lindbergh flies to New York but has to wait a week due to heavy rain. He barely manages to take off on a muddy field. Lindbergh encounters many problems, including clouds, ice, and lack of sleep. On the evening of May 21, 1927, Lindbergh lands at Le Bourget field in Paris to a tumultuous welcome (1:48:31 to 2:14:21).

Jimmy Stewart does a good job portraying Col. Lindbergh. It's a good story of a brave effort. Told with a touch of humor throughout.
Awards: *Academy Award Nomination*: Best Effects
Source: Hardesty, Van. *Lindbergh.* New York: Harcourt, Inc., 2002. This book at page 90 gives the date of the flight.
Alternate Film: *The Duchess*

22
THE AFFAIR OF THE NECKLACE
Year: 2001
Genre: Period Drama
Run Time: 1 hour 58 minutes
Date Revealed in Film: 1:29:28–31
Availability: DVD and VHS (Warner Home Video)

Director: Charles Shyer; **Screenplay**: John Sweet

Cast: Hilary Swank (Jeanne de Valois), Jonathan Pryce (Cardinal de Rohan), Christopher Walken (Count Cagliostro), Simon Baker (Rétaux de Villette), Adrien Brody (Nicholas de Lamotte), Joely Richardson (Marie Antoinette), Hayden Panettiere (Young Jeanne)

Jeanne de Valois's father is killed by the ancien regime in France and his property seized. Jeanne tries to get the queen, Marie Antoinette, to notice her so she can present a petition for the return of her property. Jeanne then uses some of the queen's stolen notepaper to engineer a plot where Cardinal Rohan unknowingly helps Jeanne and her lover steal a valuable necklace. On the feast of the Assumption, when the king summons him, Rohan thinks he is to be made chief minister, so he burns the letters from the queen. Instead, he is arrested for using the queen's name to get the necklace for free. He blames Jeanne of course, who is also arrested. The queen wants a full public trial to establish it is Rohan, not Jeanne, who is lying about these events. People gather at the gates of the court on May 22, 1786, when the trial begins (1:29:28 to 1:30:10). Even though offered a deal, Jeanne is so annoyed at the queen for ignoring her that she refuses to implicate Rohan. Her lover is convicted and banished, while Rohan is acquitted. Jeanne is convicted. She is jailed, flogged, and branded. She later escapes to England.

It's hard to believe this is a true story, but it is. The affair was yet another incident that led to the French revolution. Beautiful, accurate costumes and scenery.

Awards: *Academy Award Nomination*: Best Costume Design

Alternate Film: *The Late Shift*

23

CLOSE ENCOUNTERS OF THE THIRD KIND

Year: 1977

Genre: Science Fiction

Run Time: 2 hours 17 minutes

Date Revealed in Film: 34:43

Availability: Blu-ray and DVD (Sony Pictures)

Director: Steven Spielberg; **Screenplay**: Steven Spielberg

Cast: Richard Dreyfuss (Roy Neary), François Truffaut (Claude Lacombe), Melinda Dillon (Jillian Guiler), Cary Guffey (Barry Guiler), Teri Garr (Ronnie Neary), Bob Balaban (David Laughlin), Josef Sommer (Larry Butler)

In the Mexican desert a group of Navy planes missing since 1945 are found. On May 23, 1977, over Muncie, Indiana, an airliner almost collides with a UFO. That night, three-year-old Barry Guiler sees an alien, runs outside, and is pursued by his mother, Jillian (7:37 to 23:59). Roy Neary, an electrical lineman trying to deal with an unexplainable blackout, has an encounter with a UFO. Along with the police, he follows four UFOs and watches them fly off and then ascend into the clouds. Later, he encounters Jillian and Barry. Roy and Jillian both become obsessed with a melody and an image of a flat-topped mountain they can't get out of their heads. The UFO returns and removes a not-very-reluctant Barry from his house. Roy's wife leaves him because of his UFO obsession. Other witnesses report hearing the UFO's five-tone melody. When played back into space the tones produce a reply pinpointing a spot near Devil's Tower, Wyoming. The government creates a cover story about an accidental nerve gas release to clear the area. A broadcast about this that shows Devil's Tower stuns Roy and Jillian as they realize this is the mountain they have been obsessing about. They travel there and, avoiding capture, reach the area where scientists are trying to communicate with a large UFO that appears. It lands and releases many humans who had been abducted over the years, including Barry. Roy is drafted to join the human team that is taken aboard the mother ship.

One of the better sci-fi films. Presents the story in a no-nonsense factual manner. The special effects are very good for 1977.

Awards: *Academy Award Win*: Best Cinematography. *Academy Award Nominations*: Best Director, Best Supporting Actress (Melinda Dillon), Best Visual Effects, Best Art Direction, Best Original Score, Best Film Editing, and Best Sound. *Golden Globe Nominations*: Best Motion Picture–Drama, Best Director–Motion Picture, Best Screenplay–Motion Picture, and Best Original Score–Motion Picture

Alternate Film: *Cloverfield*

24

CHICAGO

Year: 2002
Genre: Musical
Run Time: 1 hour 53 minutes
Availability: Blu-ray and DVD (Miramax)
Director: Rob Marshall; **Screenplay**: Bill Condon, based on the musical play
by Bob Fosse and Fred Ebb and the play by Maurine Dallas Watkins
Cast: Renée Zellweger (Roxie Hart), Catherine Zeta-Jones (Velma Kelly),
Richard Gere (Billy Flynn), Queen Latifah (Mama Morton), John C. Reilly
(Amos Hart), Christine Baranski (Mary Sunshine), Lucy Liu (Kitty Bax-
ter), Dominic West (Fred Casely)

Roxie Hart, who wants to be a vaudeville star, leaves a club with Fred Casely
for a romantic interlude. When Roxie finds out Fred lied about getting her
a club singing date, she shoots him. Her husband starts to take the rap for
her when she says a stranger tried to rape her, but when he finds out it was
Fred, he tells the truth and Roxie is arrested. She meets her idol, singer Velma
Kelly, in jail. Velma shot her sister and her husband for fooling around with
each other. "Big Mama," the warden, suggests Roxie get Billy Flynn to represent her. Flynn's typical approach is to launch a publicity campaign to create
sympathy, which he does for Roxie, making her a star in the tabloids. During
the trial Velma is called as a rebuttal witness and reads some very damaging
stuff from Roxie's diary. Flynn creates the impression that Velma is lying and
that Mama Morton created the diary. On May 24, 1925, Roxie is found innocent. We learn Roxie's pregnancy was fake, and she dumps her loyal husband
(1:33:31 to 1:37:26). Roxie and Velma go on stage.

This is no "sweetness and light" romantic musical. *Chicago* is all hard-
boiled and cynical. The musical numbers are very good and as well staged as
any from the golden age of Hollywood.

Awards: *Academy Award Wins*: Best Picture, Best Supporting Actress (Cath-
erine Zeta-Jones), Best Art Direction, Best Costume Design, Best Film
Editing, and Best Sound Mixing. *Academy Award Nominations*: Best
Actress (Renée Zellweger), Best Supporting Actor (John C. Reilly), Best
Supporting Actress (Queen Latifah), Best Director, Best Adapted Screen-
play, Best Cinematography, and Best Original Song. *Golden Globe Wins*:
Best Performance by an Actress in a Motion Picture–Comedy or Musical

(Zellweger), Best Performance by an Actor in a Motion Picture–Comedy or Musical (Richard Gere), and Best Motion Picture–Comedy or Musical. *Golden Globe Nominations*: Best Performance by an Actress in a Motion Picture–Comedy or Musical (Zeta-Jones), Best Performance by an Actress in a Supporting Role in a Motion Picture–Comedy or Musical (Latifah), Best Performance by an Actor in a Supporting Role in a Motion Picture–Comedy or Musical (Reilly), Best Director–Motion Picture, and Best Screenplay–Motion Picture

Alternate Film: *In Which We Serve*

25

WILDE

Year: 1997
Genre: Biography
Run Time: 1 hour 58 minutes
Availability: DVD (Sony Pictures), VHS (Columbia/TriStar Home Video)
Director: Brian Gilbert; **Screenplay**: Julian Mitchell, based on Richard Ellman's biography *Oscar Wilde*
Cast: Stephen Fry (Oscar Wilde), Jude Law (Lord Alfred "Bosie" Douglas), Tom Wilkinson (John Douglas, Ninth Marquess of Queensberry), Jennifer Ehle (Constance Lloyd Wilde), Michael Sheen (Robbie Ross), Vanessa Redgrave (Jane Wilde)

After his tour of America, Oscar Wilde returns to England and gets married, but soon begins a homosexual affair with Robbie Ross. Wilde's play *Lady Windermere's Fan* is a big hit. Wilde is introduced to "Bosie" Douglas, son of the Marquess of Queensbery, and they begin an affair. They separate for a while, but reunite, while the Marquess tries to break them up. Wilde's play *The Importance of Being Earnest* is a big success. The Marquess sends Wilde an insulting card and Wilde, against Robbie's advice, sues the Marquess for slander. Wilde loses, and a warrant for his arrest for gross indecency is sworn out, but he refuses to leave the country. Wilde is tried and convicted and on May 25, 1895, sentenced to two years of hard labor (1:35:26 to 1:36:56). After his release Wilde is a broken man.

A very sad story. Wilde allowed his sense of self-importance to overrule his judgment. His friends warned him not to pursue the case, but he wouldn't listen.

Source: Parini, Jay. *British Writers Retrospective: Supplement VII*. New York: Charles Scribner's Sons, 2002. This book at page 371 gives the date of Wilde's sentencing.

Awards: *Golden Globe Nomination*: Best Performance by an Actor in a Motion Picture–Drama (Stephen Fry)

Alternate Film: *Thunderball*

26

DESPICABLE ME

Year: 2010

Genre: Comedy/Crime

Run Time: 1 hour 35 minutes

Date Revealed in Film: 1:00:24

Availability: Blu-ray and DVD (Universal Studios)

Directors: Pierre Coffin and Chris Renaud; Screenplay: Ken Daurio and Cinco Paul

Voice Cast: Steve Carell (Gru), Jason Segel (Vector), Russell Brand (Dr. Nefario), Julie Andrews (Gru's mother, Marlena), Will Arnett (Mr. Perkins), Kristen Wiig (Miss Hattie), Miranda Cosgrove (Margo), Danny R. McBride (Gru's next door neighbor)

After he's one-upped by the nerdy villain Vector, super-villain Gru decides to steal the Moon by shrinking it. He tries to get a loan from the Bank of Evil, but Perkins, the president, refuses until he produces the shrink ray. Gru steals the shrink ray, but it is stolen from him in turn by Vector. Gru adopts three cookie-selling orphans as part of a plan to enter Vector's lair to steal it back. Gru gradually becomes attached to the girls. The Bank of Evil still won't fund Gru, but the girls and the yellow minions take up a collection. Gru soon faces a choice: the Moon will be in prime position on the day of the girls' ballet recital. Dr. Nefario, Gru's assistant, has the girls returned to the orphanage. Gru goes to the Moon and shrinks it on May 26, 2007. He comes to regret what he did to the girls and rushes to the recital. It is over, but he finds a note saying Vector has kidnapped the girls and wants the Moon as ransom. Gru agrees, but Vector reneges. Gru storms Vector's lair, but Vector leaves in an escape pod with the shrunken Moon and the girls. Gru goes after the girls, but in the end they have to decide if they can ever trust Gru again (1:09:10 to 1:25:02).

A very funny movie. Functions on both the adult and child levels. Kids will see it as an adventure, while parents can get the message about what's really important in life.

Awards: *Golden Globe Nomination*: Best Animated Film
Alternate Film: *13 Going on 30*

27

MRS. MINIVER

Year: 1942
Genre: Drama
Run Time: 2 hours 14 minutes
Availability: Blu-ray and DVD (Warner Home Video)
Director: William Wyler; **Screenplay**: George Froeschel, James Hilton, Claudine West, and Arthur Wimperis, based on the novel by Jan Struther
Cast: Greer Garson (Mrs. Kay Miniver), Walter Pidgeon (Clem Miniver), Teresa Wright (Carol Beldon), Dame May Whitty (Lady Beldon), Reginald Owen (Foley), Henry Travers (Mr. Ballard), Richard Ney (Vin Miniver)

The Minivers are an upper-class British family living near London at the start of World War II. Their older son, Vin, meets and marries Carol, the niece of the local aristocrat, Lady Belden, before he joins the RAF. The family endures the Blitz. Vin is called to duty on May 27, 1940 (48:25 to 59:47). The next day, Mr. Miniver takes his boat to assist in the evacuation at Dunkirk. While he is gone Mrs. Miniver manages to capture a German pilot who had been shot down. After the local flower show in which the stationmaster's rose, named "The Mrs. Miniver," beats Lady Beldon's entry, Mrs. Miniver and Carol drive Vin to his base. Then unexpected tragedy strikes.

The film presents a sanitized version of life in Britain during the period of the Blitz. It is a classic melodrama, but still very good. Modern audiences can still relate to these characters and their problems.

Awards: *Academy Award Wins*: Best Picture, Best Director, Best Actress (Greer Garson), Best Adapted Screenplay, Best Supporting Actress (Teresa Wright), and Best Black-and-White Cinematography. *Academy Award Nominations*: Best Actor (Walter Pidgeon), Best Supporting Actor (Henry Travers), Best Supporting Actress, Best Special Effects, Best Film Editing, and Best Sound Recording

Source: Seboq-Montifiore, Hugh. *Dunkirk: Fight to the Last Man*. Cambridge, MA: Harvard University Press, 2006. This book at pages 378–79 gives the date the boats gathered to go to Dunkirk as May 28.

Alternate Film: *Operation Daybreak*

28

DAZED AND CONFUSED

Year: 1993
Genre: Comedy/Drama
Run Time: 1 hour 42 minutes
Date Revealed in Film: 2:35
Availability: Blu-ray and DVD (Universal Studios)
Director: Richard Linklater; **Screenplay**: Richard Linklater
Cast: Jason London (Randall "Pink" Floyd), Wiley Wiggins (Mitch Kramer), Rory Cochrane (Ron Slater), Matthew McConaughey (David Wooderson), Sasha Jenson (Don Dawson), Ben Affleck (Fred O'Bannion), Renée Zellweger (Nesi)

On May 28, 1976 (00:56 to 1:07:44), it is the last day of school in Austin, Texas. The seniors haze the incoming freshman class, while the football team is asked to sign a pledge not to take drugs. But quarterback "Pink" Floyd is unsure about this, believing it violates his individuality. Mitch Kramer initially escapes the hazing by the seniors, but is later caught and paddled by Fred O'Bannion. Pink takes Mitch home, and later takes him to a local pool hall. Mitch meets Julie Simms, and he and his friends get revenge on O'Bannion by dumping paint on him. Three "smart kids"—Cynthia, Mike, and Tony—decide to attend a midnight keg party. Mike Newhouse is pushed around by tough guy Clint, but later attacks him and is beaten up. Cynthia Dunn meets David Wooderson, a twenty-year-old who hangs around with the high school students. Pink later tells the coach while he might play football, he is not going to sign the pledge and leaves with his pals to get Aerosmith concert tickets. When Mitch gets home at dawn, his mother tells him this is his one time to stay out all night without punishment.

A funny teen comedy.

Alternate Film: *Anger Management*

29
THE FBI STORY
Year: 1959
Genre: Drama
Run Time: 2 hours 29 minutes
Date Revealed in Film: 16:56–57
Availability: DVD (Warner Home Video)
Director: Mervyn LeRoy; **Screenplay**: Richard L. Breen and John Twist,
   based on the book *The FBI Story: A Report to the People* by Don Whitehead
Cast: James Stewart ("Chip" Hardesty), Vera Miles (Lucy Ann Hardesty),
   Joyce Taylor (Anne Hardesty), Murray Hamilton (Sam Crandall), Larry
   Pennell (George Crandall), Nick Adams (Jack Graham), Diane Jergens
   (Jennie Hardesty), Jean Willes (Anna Sage)

Agent "Chip" Hardesty tells how the FBI cracked an airline bombing case.
He then flashes back to when he worked in the Knoxville field office in 1924,
where he met Lucy Ballard, who agrees to marry him on the condition that
he leave the FBI. After a meeting with the new chief, J. Edgar Hoover, on May
29, 1924, he convinces Lucy to let him stay with the bureau, and she tells him
she's pregnant (27:03 to 32:47). Hardesty is sent to the South to investigate
the KKK, and then to Oklahoma to investigate the deaths of several Native
Americans in a plot to steal oil leases. The FBI is authorized to carry firearms
to combat the gangsters. Chip is involved in a shootout with "Baby Face" Nelson, who kills his pal, Sam Crandall. During attempted arrests, John Dillinger,
Baby Face Nelson, and "Pretty Boy" Floyd are killed. Lucy leaves Chip for a
while, but eventually comes back. "Ma" Barker is killed and "Machine Gun"
Kelly arrested. George Crandall, Sam's son, joins the FBI, but Mike Hardesty,
Chip's son, joins the Marines during World War II. Hardesty is sent to South
America to extract several undercover FBI agents. One of them is George
Crandall, who returns to marry Hardesty's daughter Anne. Mike is killed at
Iwo Jima. Hardesty succeeds in breaking up a Soviet spy ring in New York.

More of a paean to the FBI than the real story. It's a good movie, but gives
the story the way an FBI press agent would. Steers clear of any negative facts
about the bureau.

Alternate Film: *Gods and Monsters*

30
AMAZING GRACE
Year: 2006
Genre: Biography
Run Time: 1 hour 58 minutes
Availability: DVD (Twentieth Century Fox)
Director: Michael Apted; **Screenplay**: Steven Knight
Cast: Ioan Gruffudd (William Wilberforce), Romola Garai (Barbara Spooner), Benedict Cumberbatch (William Pitt the Younger), Albert Finney (John Newton), Michael Gambon (Charles James Fox), Rufus Sewell (Thomas Clarkson)

William Wilberforce, MP, is ill, so he visits his cousin Henry in Bath, where he meets Barbara Spooner. We flash back fifteen years to when Wilberforce aroused the enmity of some by speaking in favor of peace in the American War of Independence. Wilberforce comes to feel God has found him. John Newton, Wilberforce's boyhood pastor, advises him to work against slavery. The first presentation of a bill to end the slave trade is easily defeated. Wilberforce tries to whip up public opinion against the slave trade, but without much success. Back in the present, Wilberforce and Barbara Spooner find all their opinions are identical, and they are wed on May 30, 1797 (1:22:04 to 1:25:52). Prime Minister William Pitt and Wilberforce are reconciled. A bill passes that effectively ends the slave trade, and Wilberforce is praised in Parliament for his efforts.

A great movie about a great man. As a character says, those who are called great are mainly men of war and we rarely recognize the great men of peace. Well worth watching.

Source: Hague, William. *William Wilberforce: The Life of the Great Anti-Slave Trade Campaigner*. New York: Harcourt, 2007. This book at page 280 gives the date of the wedding.
Alternate Film: *The President's Lady*

31
JOURNEY TO THE CENTER OF THE EARTH
Year: 1959
Genre: Adventure
Run Time: 2 hours 9 minutes

Date Revealed in Film: 18:46

Availability: DVD and VHS (Twentieth Century Fox)

Director: Henry Levin; **Screenplay**: Walter Reisch and Charles Brackett, based on the Jules Verne novel

Cast: James Mason (Sir Oliver Lindenbrook), Pat Boone (Alec McKuen), Arlene Dahl (Carla Goetabaug), Peter Ronson (Hans Belker), Thayer David (Count Saknussemm), Robert Adler (Groom), Alan Napier (Dean), Diane Baker (Jenny)

Alec McKuen gives Professor Lindenbrook a strange rock as a present. Inside is a plumb bob inscribed with a message from Arni Saknussemm, a famous geologist who vanished in Iceland, that Lindenbrook believes points to how to reach the center of the Earth. He contacts Professor Goetabaug in Stockholm for corroboration, but learns Goetebaug has headed for Iceland to steal all the glory for himself. Lindenbrook and McKuen head for Iceland, where they find Goetabaug has bought up all the equipment they need for the expedition. They discover that Count Saknussemm, a descendant of Arni, has murdered Goetabaug. Carla, Goetabaug's widow, arrives and teams up with Lindenbrook, allowing use of the equipment if she can go along. On May 31, 1880, Carla, Lindenbrook, and McKuen enter the volcano, followed secretly by Count Saknussemm and a servant (45:46 to 57:15). They are almost drowned in a flood. Saknussemm tries to capture them but is overpowered. Saknussemm is brought along when none of them can bring themselves to execute him. They find natural sources of light and food and reach a subterranean ocean with a whirlpool at its center, the Earth's core. Saknussemm is killed. They find the ruins of Atlantis and Arni Saknussemm's body, which points to a way out. They use gunpowder in Saknussemm's backpack to make a bomb to remove a rock blocking their route to the surface. It causes an eruption and they ride an altar stone to the surface. They all return to Edinburgh.

Primitive special effects by today's standards. However, it's still amusing to watch.

Awards: *Academy Award Nominations*: Best Art Direction–Set Decoration, Best Special Effects, and Best Sound

Alternate Film: *Cold Turkey*

June

1

ATONEMENT

Year: 2007

Genre: Period Drama

Run Time: 2 hours 3 minutes

Date Revealed in Film: 1:50:06

Availability: Blu-ray and DVD (Universal Studios)

Director: Joe Wright; **Screenplay**: Christopher Hampton, based on Ian Mc-
Ewan's novel

Cast: Keira Knightley (Cecilia Tallis), James McAvoy (Robbie Turner),
Saoirse Ronan (Briony Tallis, age thirteen), Romola Garai (Briony Tallis,
age eighteen), Vanessa Redgrave (Briony Tallis, age seventy-seven), Juno
Temple (Lola Quincey), Benedict Cumberbatch (Paul Marshall)

In 1935 England Briony Tallis witnesses a sexually charged moment between
her older sister, Cecilia, and Robbie Turner. Robbie writes several notes to
Cecilia, including one very erotic one, which he accidentally gives to Briony
to deliver for him. Briony reads the note and later thinks Robbie is forcing her
sister into a sexual encounter. Briony later encounters a man running away
from having raped her cousin Lola. Lola says she can't identify her attacker.
Briony says it is Robbie, and everyone believes her after she shows them the
note. Robbie goes to jail. In 1939 Robbie and Cecilia are reunited. After Rob-

bie is evacuated from Dunkirk, Briony goes to see Cecilia to apologize. Robbie demands she tell the truth. Briony reveals the rapist was actually Lola's present husband. We switch to decades later and learn Briony has become a novelist and that the story we have just seen was from her novel. Actually Robbie died on June 1, 1940, at Dunkirk (1:49:57 to 1:50:32). Her sister died soon after in the Blitz. Briony never went to see Cecelia. She wrote the novel to "unite" them, as they deserved.

A very unusual "breaking the fourth wall" kind of film, a fiction written by one of the characters. She wrote it as "atonement" for her actions, thus the title.

Awards: *Academy Award Win*: Best Original Score. *Academy Award Nominations*: Best Art Direction, Best Cinematography, Best Costume Design, Best Picture, Best Actress in a Supporting Role (Saoirse Ronan), and Best Adapted Screenplay. *Golden Globe Wins*: Best Motion Picture–Drama and Best Original Score–Motion Picture. *Golden Globe Nominations*: Best Performance by an Actress in a Motion Picture–Drama (Keira Knightley), Best Performance by an Actor in a Motion Picture–Drama (James McAvoy), Best Performance by an Actress in a Supporting Role in a Motion Picture–Drama (Ronan), Best Director–Motion Picture, and Best Screenplay–Motion Picture

Alternate Film: *The Pelican Brief*

2

BUTCH CASSIDY AND THE SUNDANCE KID

Year: 1969
Genre: Western
Run Time: 1 hour 52 minutes
Availability: Blu-ray (Twentieth Century Fox)
Director: George Roy Hill; **Screenplay**: William Goldman
Cast: Paul Newman (Butch Cassidy), Robert Redford (the Sundance Kid), Katherine Ross (Etta Place), Strother Martin (Percy Garris), Cloris Leachman (Agnes), Ted Cassidy (Harvey Logan), Kenneth Mars (Marshal), George Furth (Woodcock)

"Butch" Cassidy and his partner, the "Sundance Kid," return to the base of the Hole in the Wall Gang, who decide to rob the *Union Pacific Flyer* twice. The first robbery on June 2, 1899, goes well (15:37 to 26:10). Butch and Sundance enjoy themselves in town, and visit Sundance's mistress, Etta Place. The second robbery goes horribly wrong. A second train arrives, carrying a special posse sent by the railroad to hunt them down. This posse is relentless, and the two only escape by jumping off a cliff into a river. They travel to Bolivia with Etta, and resume their career of bank robbery. They are spotted and cornered in a small town and surrounded by the army. They refuse to surrender and charge out, dying in a hail of bullets.

One of the first antihero movies, it presents the "bad guys" as the protagonists. Noted for its use of humor and music, something usually not found in westerns.

Source: Hatch, Thom. *The Last Outlaws: The Lives and Legends of Butch Cassidy and the Sundance Kid.* New York: New American Library, 2013. This book at page 184 gives the date of the robbery.

Awards: *Academy Award Wins*: Best Cinematography, Best Original Score, Best Song, and Best Original Screenplay. *Academy Award Nominations*: Best Director, Best Picture, and Best Sound

Alternate Film: *The Queen's Sister*

3
JANE EYRE

Year: 2011
Genre: Period Drama
Run Time: 2 hours
Availability: Blu-ray and DVD (Universal Studios)
Director: Cary Fukunaga; **Screenplay**: Moira Buffini, based on Charlotte Brontë's novel
Cast: Mia Wasikowska (Jane Eyre), Michael Fassbender (Edward Rochester), Jamie Bell (St. John Rivers), Judi Dench (Mrs. Fairfax), Sally Hawkins (Mrs. Reed), Tamzin Merchant (Mary Rivers), Imogen Poots (Blanche Ingram), Sophie Ward (Lady Ingram)

Orphan Jane Eyre lives with her aunt, Mrs. Reed, who physically and emotionally abuses her. Jane is sent to Lowood Girls School, where the director, Mr. Brocklehurst, abuses her. Jane's best friend, Helen, dies of "consumption." Eight years later Jane leaves the school to be a governess at Thornfield

Hall for Adele Varens. One day out walking she encounters a horseman whom she later learns is Mr. Rochester, owner of Thornfield. One night Mr. Rochester's bed catches on fire, and it would have killed him if Jane had not raised the alarm. A house party arrives including the woman Mr. Rochester is supposedly interested in marrying. Mr. Mason arrives, but is stabbed by an unknown person. Jane gets a letter saying her aunt is dying. She goes to see her and learns that her uncle wanted to adopt her, but her aunt told him Jane was dead. Mr. Rochester proposes to Jane. However, the wedding is stopped by the sudden appearance of the recovered Mr. Mason, who reveals that Mr. Rochester is already married to Mason's now insane sister, who is locked up in a room at Thornfield. Mr. Rochester asks Jane to be his mistress, but she refuses and leaves. Jane ends up at the home of the Rivers. Jane learns that her uncle, John Eyre, has left her his entire fortune. Mr. Rivers proposes to her, but she refuses. On June 3, 1847, she travels back to Thornfield, which is a ruin. She learns the first Mrs. Rochester died in a fire she set. Mr. Rochester was partially blinded in the fire. Jane goes to him, convinces him that she still loves him, and they become engaged (1:47:18 to 1:54:10).

One of the classic novels. A great dramatic romance. This version is well paced and has good cinematography.

Awards: *Academy Award Nomination*: Best Costume Design

Source: Brontë, Charlotte. *Jane Eyre*. New York: Barnes & Noble Classics, 2003. This book at pages 487–98 establishes that Jane became engaged on this date.

Alternate Film: *I Shot Andy Warhol*

4

THE MAN WHO KNEW TOO MUCH

Year: 1956

Genre: Suspense/Drama

Run Time: 2 hours

Date Revealed in Film: 24:26, 1:05:57, and 1:29:15

Availability: Blu-ray and DVD (Universal Studios)

Director: Alfred Hitchcock; **Screenplay**: John Michael Hayes, based on a story by Charles Bennett and D. B. Wyndham-Lewis

Cast: James Stewart (Dr. Benjamin "Ben" McKenna), Doris Day (Josephine Conway "Jo" McKenna), Christopher Olsen (Henry "Hank" McKenna),

Brenda De Banzie (Lucy Drayton), Bernard Miles (Edward Drayton), Daniel Gélin (Louis Bernard)

On June 4, 1955, Dr. Ben McKenna; his wife, Jo; and their son, Hank, are on a bus to Marrakech and meet Louis Bernard, a mysterious Frenchman, and later an English couple, the Draytons (2:49 to 25:06). The next day in the marketplace, a dying Louis Bernard, disguised as an Arab, whispers a message to Dr. McKenna. Dr. McKenna gets a message threatening harm to Hank, who has been kidnapped by the Draytons, if he reveals the message to the police. Ben and Jo fly to London the next day to find Hank. Ben goes to see Ambrose Chappell, a name given to him by Bernard, but it's a wild goose chase. Jo realizes Bernard meant Ambrose Chapel, a place, and she and Ben go there. The Draytons are holding Hank there, and they and another man plan to kill a foreign prime minister at a concert at the Royal Albert Hall. Jo and Ben end up at the Royal Albert Hall during the concert. The assassin spots Jo and she realizes he's there to kill someone. Ben tries to stop him. The suspense builds until Jo sees the gunman take aim. Her scream makes him miss and only wound his target. The gunman tries to escape, but falls to his death. That country's ambassador to England had plotted with the Draytons to kill his prime minister, and he now wants Hank dead. This upsets Mrs. Drayton. The McKennas learn Hank is at the embassy and go there, ostensibly so the prime minister can thank Jo. However, the McKennas really plan to rescue Hank from the murderous clutches of his captors.

One of the outstanding suspense-filled films directed by Hitchcock. This is another story of ordinary people getting caught up in fantastic events. A great film.

Awards: *Academy Award Win*: Best Original Song
Alternate Film: *24 Hour Party People*

5
MY LEFT FOOT: THE STORY OF CHRISTY BROWN

Year: 1989
Genre: Biographical Drama
Run Time: 1 hour 43 minutes
Availability: DVD (Lionsgate Films), VHS (HBO Video)
Director: Jim Sheridan; **Screenplay**: Jim Sheridan and Shane Connaughton, based on Christy Brown's autobiography, *My Left Foot*

Cast: Daniel Day-Lewis (Christy Brown), Brenda Fricker (Bridget Brown), Ray McAnally (Paddy Brown), Fiona Shaw (Dr. Eileen Cole), Kirsten Sheridan (Sharon Brown), Alison Whelan (Sheila Brown), Hugh O'Conor (young Christy Brown)

Christy Brown was born handicapped on June 5, 1932 (6:56 to 8:57). He could not walk or talk, but was loved and supported by most of his family. The family celebrates his seventeenth birthday (28:47 to 30:08). Christy starts painting, using his left foot (the only part of his body he can control). A girl he likes rebuffs him and things get tough when his father loses his job and his favorite sister gets married and moves out. Christy meets Dr. Eileen Cole, who persuades a friend of hers to hold an exhibition of Christy's art. Afterward he learns she is engaged to be married and he considers suicide, as he had developed a crush on her. He builds his own private studio, but his father soon thereafter dies of a stroke. Christy starts writing his autobiography, *My Left Foot*. Dr. Cole returns and they resume their friendship.

A very uplifting film. Anyone feeling depressed would probably be thankful for how small their problems really are after watching this film. Daniel Day-Lewis certainly deserved his Oscar for bringing out Christy Brown's personality without using words.

Awards: *Academy Award Wins*: Best Actor (Daniel Day-Lewis) and Best Supporting Actress (Brenda Fricker). *Academy Award Nominations*: Best Picture, Best Director, and Best Adapted Screenplay. *Golden Globe Nominations*: Best Performance by an Actor in a Motion Picture–Drama (Day-Lewis), Best Performance by an Actress in a Supporting Role in a Motion Picture–Drama (Fricker)

Source: Hambleton, Georgina Louise. *Christy Brown: The Life That Inspired My Left Foot*. London: Mainstream Publishing, 2007. This book at page 20 gives his birth date.

Alternate Film: *'68*

6

THE LONGEST DAY
Year: 1962
Genre: War
Run Time: 2 hours 58 minutes
Availability: Blu-ray and DVD (Twentieth Century Fox)

Directors: Ken Annakin, Andrew Marton, and Bernhard Wicki; **Screenplay**: Cornelius Ryan, based on his book

Cast: John Wayne (Lt. Col. Benjamin Vandervoort), Henry Fonda (Brigadier General Theodore Roosevelt Jr.), Robert Mitchum (Brigadier General Norman Cota), Curt Jurgens (Gen Blumentritt), Eddie Albert (Colonel Thompson), Fabian (U.S. Army Ranger)

The Allies and Germans prepare for the invasion of Europe. German intelligence intercepts part one of a two-part message to the French resistance, with part two signaling the invasion within twenty-four hours, but the German commander General Rommel refuses to order an alert based on this and travels to Germany for his wife's birthday. Eisenhower decides the invasion must go on in spite of poor weather. Part two of the message is broadcast and German troops are put on alert in the Pas-de-Calais, but not Normandy, which is the target of the invasion. In the early morning hours of June 6, 1944, British glider troops seize the strategic Orne river bridge and American paratroopers are dropped with the mission of capturing the village of St. Marie-Eglise, but they are scattered. The French resistance blows up the transport and communication systems. Many German officers are away at a war game and efforts to get the tank reserve force released are thwarted when Hitler takes a sleeping pill and gives orders "not to be disturbed." Troops land on Utah and Omaha beaches, at the latter facing heavy opposition. The British and Canadians do better at Gold, Sword, and Juno. The Orne river bridge force is relieved and troops on Omaha beach blow up obstructions and finally get off the beach (50:03 to 2:54:22).

A great ensemble war film. Almost a documentary, as it's totally factual. Good combat sequences.

Awards: *Academy Award Wins*: Best Cinematography and Best Special Effects. *Academy Award Nominations*: Best Art Direction, Best Editing, and Best Picture. *Golden Globe Win*: Best Black-and-White Cinematography. *Golden Globe Nomination*: Best Motion Picture–Drama

Alternate Film: *The Americanization of Emily*

7

FORREST GUMP

Year: 1994

Genre: Drama

Run Time: 2 hours 22 minutes

Date Revealed in Film: 1:27:08
Availability: Blu-ray and DVD (Warner Home Video)
Director: Robert Zemekis; **Screenplay**: Eric Roth, based on Winston Groom's novel
Cast: Tom Hanks (Forrest Gump), Michael Conner Humphreys (young Forrest Gump), Robin Wright (Jenny Curran), Hanna R. Hall (young Jenny Curran), Gary Sinise (Dan Taylor), Mykelti Williamson (Buford "Bubba" Blue), Sally Field (Mrs. Gump)

Forrest Gump was born disabled and mentally deficient. On the first day of school he met Jenny, who defended him. After he lost his leg braces, his ability to run fast got him a football scholarship to Alabama. Later he joined the army, serving in Vietnam, becoming friends with an African American nicknamed "Bubba," who worked on a shrimp boat, and they agree to become partners after the war. In an ambush, Bubba is killed on June 7, 1967, but Forrest wins the Medal of Honor for his actions (48:42 to 56:21). He is resented by his commander, Lt. Dan, who would rather have died a hero than live as a cripple. Forrest joins the U.S. table tennis team and takes part in "Ping-Pong" diplomacy. At an antiwar rally he meets Jenny. He endorses a Ping-Pong paddle company and earns enough to buy a shrimp boat, with Capt. Dan becoming his first mate. Forrest returns home to care for his dying mother, and later Jenny comes to live with him. Although she refuses his marriage proposal they make love before she leaves. Despondent, Forrest runs cross-country several times. Forrest travels to meet Jenny and their son, named Forrest. They return to Alabama, where Jenny soon dies of AIDS. The movie ends with Forrest waiting with his son for the bus on the first day of school.

A quirky film. Forrest's straightforward naiveté disarms the more cynical people around him. Interesting special effects insert Forrest into historical footage.

Awards: *Academy Award Wins*: Best Picture, Best Actor (Tom Hanks), Best Director, Best Film Editing, Best Visual Effects, and Best Adapted Screenplay. *Academy Award Nominations*: Best Supporting Actor (Gary Sinise), Best Art Direction, Best Makeup, Best Cinematography, Best Original Score, Best Sound Mixing, and Best Sound Editing. *Golden Globe Wins*: Best Director–Motion Picture, Best Performance by an Actor in a Motion Picture–Drama (Hanks), and Best Motion Picture–Drama. *Golden Globe Nominations*: Best Performance by an Actress in a Supporting Role in a

Motion Picture–Drama (Robin Wright), Best Performance by an Actor in a Supporting Role in a Motion Picture–Drama (Sinise), Best Screenplay–Motion Picture, and Best Original Score–Motion Picture

Alternate Film: *Harlow*

8

PERCY JACKSON AND THE OLYMPIANS: THE LIGHTNING THIEF

Year: 2010

Genre: Fantasy

Run Time: 1 hour 58 minutes

Date Revealed in Film: 4:00

Availability: Blu-ray and DVD (Twentieth Century Fox)

Director: Chris Columbus; **Screenplay**: Craig Titley, based on Rick Riordan's novel *The Lightning Thief*

Cast: Logan Lerman (Percy Jackson), Brandon T. Jackson (Grover Underwood), Alexandra Daddario (Annabeth Chase), Jake Abel (Luke Castellan), Sean Bean (Zeus), Kevin McKidd (Poseidon), Steve Coogan (Hades), Melina Kanakaredes (Athena)

Zeus warns Poseidon that unless Poseidon's demi-god son Percy Jackson return's his master thunderbolt, a war will break out. The next day, June 8, 2010 (4:46 to 9:45), Percy holds his breath underwater for seven minutes. Percy is attacked by a fury seeking the bolt, and learns that his friend Grover is really a satyr and that he's the son of Poseidon. He goes to a camp for demigods, but his mother is apparently killed. Hades offers to trade the bolt for Percy's mom, whom he is holding captive. Percy, Grover, and Annabeth, the daughter of Athena, set out to rescue his mom. They locate and seize three of Persephone's pearls, which will allow them to escape from the Underworld. The gateway to the Underworld is in Hollywood, where they get Charon to ferry them to Hades's palace. Hades prepares to kill them all, but his wife, Persephone, does not want a war, so she takes the bolt from Hades and gives it to Percy. However, Percy must face an attack from an unexpected quarter before he can return the bolt and stop the war.

One of the better teen action adventures. Has a plot that makes sense. The special effects are very good. The actors playing the main trio give very good performances, while the supporting cast does a good job.

Alternate Film: *The Assassination of Jesse James by the Coward Robert Ford*

9
SAVING PRIVATE RYAN
Year: 1998
Genre: War
Run Time: 2 hours 49 minutes
Date Revealed in Film: 36:13
Availability: Blu-ray (Paramount Pictures), DVD (DreamWorks)
Director: Steven Spielberg; **Screenplay:** Robert Rodat
Cast: Tom Hanks (Captain John H. Miller), Matt Damon (PFC James Francis
    Ryan), Tom Sizemore (Tech Sergeant "Mike" Horvath), Edward Burns
    (PFC Richard Reiben), Vin Diesel (PFC Adrian Caparzo), Ted Danson
    (Captain Fred Hamill)

An old man visits a military cemetery in Normandy. In a flashback, Capt.
Miller and the rangers land on Omaha beach on D-Day. Back in the United
States General Marshall learns that three of the four sons of the Ryan fam-
ily have all been killed within days of each other, leaving only Pvt. James
Francis Ryan alive. On June 9, 1944, Miller is ordered to find Ryan and get
him home. He assembles a squad to do this (36:09 to 1:13:41). They travel to
Neuville, where they find a Pvt. Ryan, but not the correct one. They travel on
to Ramalle, where they are told Ryan is located. The squad releases the only
German survivor of an attack on a machine gun nest. When they reach the
town, Ryan refuses to leave his fellow paratroopers. Miller leads the defense
against a German counterattack.

   This film touches on fate, duty, honor, and friendship. A warning though:
the combat footage in this film is graphic and not for kids or the faint-hearted.
Awards: *Academy Award Wins*: Best Director, Best Cinematography, Best
    Film Editing, Best Sound Editing, and Best Sound. *Academy Award Nomi-
    nations*: Best Picture, Best Actor (Tom Hanks), Best Original Screenplay,
    Best Art Direction, Best Makeup, and Best Original Score. *Golden Globe
    Wins*: Best Motion Picture–Drama and Best Director–Motion Picture.
    Golden Globe Nominations: Best Performance by an Actor in a Motion Pic-
    ture–Drama (Hanks), Best Screenplay–Motion Picture and Best Original
    Score–Motion Picture
Alternate Film: *Duel*

10

INVICTUS

Year: 2009

Genre: Drama

Run Time: 2 hours 14 minutes

Availability: Blu-ray and DVD (Warner Home Video)

Director: Clint Eastwood; **Screenplay**: Anthony Peckham

Cast: Morgan Freeman (Nelson Mandela), Matt Damon (Francois Pienaar), Adjoa Andoh (Brenda Mazikubo), Tony Kgoroge (Jason Tshabalala), Julian Lewis Jones (Etienne Feyder), Patrick Mofokeng (Linga Moonsamy), Matt Stern (Hendrik Booyens)

Nelson Mandela is released from prison after tweny-seven years and elected president of South Africa. The Springboks, the national rugby team, plays England and loses badly, much to the disgust of their captain, Francois Pienaar. The now African-controlled National Sports Council votes to eliminate the Springbok emblem and colors, but Mandela convinces them to reverse the vote as a gesture of goodwill toward the white minority. There is tension in the presidential security corps between holdover white agents and the new ones. Mandela meets with Pienaar and tells him he supports the team. The day before the World Cup begins Mandela helicopters into the team's practice to show his support. The Springboks beat Australia and then visit Robben Island, where Mandela had been imprisoned. On June 10, 1995, the Springboks beat Western Samoa (1:22:20 to 1:24:02). They beat France in the rain and the team and the president watch the "All Blacks" from New Zealand beat England. South Africans of all races pull for the Springboks in the thrilling final game of the Rugby World Cup.

An uplifting film. Promotes the idea that everyone must do more than they may want to in order to achieve reconciliation. Good, sharp performances by Freeman and Damon.

Awards: *Academy Award Nominations*: Best Actor (Morgan Freeman) and Best Supporting Actor (Matt Damon). *Golden Globe Nominations*: Best Performance by an Actor in a Motion Picture–Drama (Freeman), Best Performance by an Actor in Supporting Role in a Motion Picture–Drama (Damon), and Best Director–Motion Picture

Source: Davies, Gerald. *The History of the World Rugby Cup*. London: Sanctuary Publishing, Ltd., 2003. This book at page 319 gives the date of the match with Western Samoa.
Alternate Film: *From Russia with Love*

11
THE WHOLE WIDE WORLD
Year: 1996
Genre: Drama
Run Time: 1 hour 51 minutes
Date Revealed in Film: 1:35:34
Availability: Blu-ray (Sony Pictures), VHS (Columbia/TriStar Home Video)
Director: Dan Ireland; **Screenplay**: Michael Scott Myers, based on Novalyne Price Ellis's books *One Who Walked Alone* and *Days of the Stranger: Further Memories of Robert E. Howard*
Cast: Vincent D'Onofrio (Robert E. "Bob" Howard), Renée Zellweger (Novalyne Price), Ann Wedgeworth (Mrs. Howard), Harve Presnell (Dr. Howard), Benjamin Mouton (Clyde Smith), Michael Corbett (Booth Adams)
In rural 1930s Texas, schoolteacher Novalyne Price is introduced to pulp writer Bob Howard. They hit it off, as both are interested in writing, even though they have totally different writing styles. He writes about a fantasy world, while she wants to write about ordinary people. The first problems appear when Bob refuses to go to a Christmas party with Novalyne, and he gives her a copy of the salacious works of Pierre Louys in order to shock her. Novalyne gets accepted into the master's program at LSU and meets Truett Vinson. Bob happens to see Novalyne and Truett at the movies. Bob accuses her of hiding her friendship with Truett. Bob is very attached to his mother, who suffers from a debilitating disease. Bob and Novalyne's rocky relationship continues for some time. Novalyne goes to LSU, but on June 11, 1936, she gets a telegram telling her that Bob Howard committed suicide (1:33:56 to 1:35:37).

A bittersweet love story. Novalyne and Bob are totally different, but they still love each other. Unfortunately, he is not able to overcome some inner demons that plague him.
Alternate Film: *Elizabeth*

12

THE HELP

Year: 2011

Genre: Drama

Run Time: 2 hours 26 minutes

Availability: Blu-ray and DVD (Disney/Buena Vista)

Director: Tate Taylor; **Screenplay**: Tate Taylor, based on Kathryn Stockett's novel

Cast: Emma Stone ("Skeeter" Phelan), Viola Davis (Aibileen Clark), Bryce Dallas Howard (Hilly Holbrook), Octavia Spencer (Minny Jackson), Jessica Chastain (Celia Foote), Sissy Spacek (Mrs. Walters), Mary Steenburgen (Elaine Stein)

Aibileen Clark and Minny Jackson are black maids in 1963 Jackson, Mississippi. Skeeter Phelan is a young white woman who has moved back home after college and wants to be a writer. Skeeter is uncomfortable with the racist attitudes her friends have toward their maids and she decides to write a book so the maids can tell their story. The maids are reluctant to talk, fearing retaliation. Aibileen is the first to share, and Minny follows after being fired by Skeeter's acquaintance, Hilly. Skeeter's editor says her draft needs more than Minny's and Aibileen's stories. Medgar Evers is assassinated in Jackson on June 12, 1963, and Hilly has her new maid arrested on a trumped-up charge. The maids realize Skeeter's book will let them tell their story (1:20:34 to 1:24:01). The book is published and is a success, to the delight of Skeeter and the maids, with whom she shares her royalties. When Skeeter tells her boyfriend about the book and her new job with a publishing house, he dumps her. Hilly gets her revenge on Aibileen by getting her fired on a false accusation of theft. Aibileen denounces Hilly as a godless woman and she leaves to start her own life.

A very good film. Has great characters. The story is compelling and exposes the ridiculousness of segregation.

Awards: *Academy Award Wins*: Best Supporting Actress (Octavia Spencer). *Academy Award Nominations*: Best Picture, Best Actress (Viola Davis), and Best Supporting Actress (Jessica Chastain). *Golden Globe Win*: Best Performance by an Actress in a Supporting Role in a Motion Picture (Octavia Spencer). *Golden Globe Nominations*: Best Performance by an Actress in a Motion Picture–Drama (Davis), Best Performance by an

Actress in a Supporting Role in a Motion Picture (Chastain), Best Original Song–Motion Picture, and Best Motion Picture–Drama
Source: Evers-Williams, Myrlie, and Marable, Manning. *The Autobiography of Medgar Evers*. New York: Basic Books, 2005. At page 293 this book gives Evers's death date.
Alternate Film: *Escape from Alcatraz*

13
MIDWAY
Year: 1976
Genre: War
Run Time: 2 hours 12 minutes
Availability: Blu-ray and DVD (Universal Studios)
Director: Jack Smight; **Screenplay**: Donald S. Sanford
Cast: Henry Fonda (Adm. Chester Nimitz), Glenn Ford (R. Adm. Raymond A. Spruance), Edward Albert (Ensign Thomas Garth), James Coburn (Capt. Vinton Maddox), Charlton Heston (Capt. Matthew Garth), Hal Holbrook (Cmdr. Joseph Rochefort)

Captain Garth meets with Commander Rochefort about his intelligence estimate that the Japanese are planning a new campaign. His son, Ensign Tom Garth, arrives in Hawaii and wants to marry a Japanese American girl. Meanwhile, Admiral Yamamoto presents a plan to use an attack on Midway to lure the American carriers into a final battle. The Americans confirm the Japanese target is Midway. Washington does not block Nimitz's plan to sortie and try and surprise the Japanese. The Japanese fleet sails. Spruance replaces Admiral Halsey. Hiruko tries to break up with Tom, but cannot tell him that she does not love him. Captain Garth asks that they be released. The Japanese fleet does not know that the American carriers are not at Pearl Harbor. The Aleutian Islands are attacked, PBY Catalinas spot the Japanese fleet, and Midway is bombed. The *Enterprise, Hornet*, and *Yorktown* launch their planes. Waldron's torpedo squadron attacks and is destroyed, but this pulls the Japanese air patrol down to sea level, so when McClusky's dive-bombers appear, they face no fighter opposition. They sink three Japanese carriers. Tom Garth is injured in a crash landing on his carrier. The *Yorktown* is bombed twice and later sinks. Captain Garth sinks the last Japanese carrier, the *Hiryu*, but is killed trying to land his damaged plane on the *Enterprise*. The *Enterprise* and *Hornet* arrive at Pearl Harbor on June 13, 1942, where Hiruko meets the injured Tom (2:07:50 to 2:11:10).

A pretty good movie. It mainly sticks to the facts as far as the battle goes. The melodramatic romance of Tom and Hiruko doesn't do much for the plot.

Source: Lord, Walter. *Incredible Victory*. New York: Harper & Row, 1967.

This book at page 287 gives the date the carriers returned to Pearl Harbor.

Alternate Film: *Quiz Show*

14

THE SAND PEBBLES

Year: 1966
Genre: Drama
Run Time: 3 hours 16 minutes
Date Revealed in Film: 32:14
Availability: Blu-ray and DVD (Twentieth Century Fox)
Director: Robert Wise; **Screenplay**: Robert Woodruff Anderson
Cast: Steve McQueen (Jake Holman), Richard Attenborough (Frenchy Bur-
    goyne), Richard Crenna (Lieutenant Collins), Candice Bergen (Shirley
    Eckert), Emmanuelle Arsan (Maily), Mako (Po-han), Joe Turkel (Bron-
    son), Gavin MacLeod (Crosley)

Jake Holman is on the way to take up a post on the USS *San Pablo* far up the Yangtze River and meets Mr. Jamison, a missionary, and Shirley Eckert, a teacher, on their way to the China Light Mission. Holman is disturbed by the ship's "coolie" system, where the crew gets the Chinese to do all the work. On June 14, 1926, the ship begins a "show-the-flag" cruise (32:14 to 33:14). After a coolie is killed, Holman is ordered to train a new coolie. At a brothel, Holman's friend Frenchy is attracted to the new Maylie, whose price is $200, a huge sum. Holman trains Po-han as the new engine coolie. After riots, the ship is sent to rescue the Americans at China Light, who are taken to Changsa. On the way, Po-han is killed by Holman to keep him from being tortured to death when he is caught in a riot. At Changsa the crew returns to the ship after being pelted with garbage by Chinese civilians. At the brothel Maily is spirited away by Frenchy, and they start a common-law marriage, as no one will marry them. Shirley suggests Holman return to China Light with her and he considers it. The coolies leave and the ship is blockaded. Shirley and Mr. Jamison return to China Light. With no coolies, the crew has to actually work. Frenchy sneaks ashore to be with Maylie, but he dies suddenly. When Maylie is killed, the Chinese blame the visiting Holman and want him handed over. The crew agrees, but the captain refuses. The Nationalists capture Nanking, resulting in widespread rioting. The captain, without orders, takes the ship to rescue those at China Light in an action-packed conclusion.

An interesting film about a little-explored era. It speaks of fate and destiny. Forces beyond their control shape the fates of the characters here.

Awards: *Academy Award Nominations*: Best Picture, Best Actor (Steve McQueen), Best Supporting Actor (Mako), Best Color Set Decoration, Best Color Cinematography, Best Film Editing, Best Sound, and Best Original Score. *Golden Globe Win*: Best Supporting Actor (Richard Attenborough). *Golden Globe Nominations*: Best Motion Picture–Drama, Best Motion Picture Director, Best Motion Picture Actor (Steve McQueen), Best Supporting Actor (Mako), Most Promising Newcomer (Candice Bergen), Best Screenplay, and Best Original Score

Alternate Film: *Roman Holiday*

15

BARRY LYNDON

Year: 1975
Genre: Period Drama
Run Time: 3 hours 4 minutes
Date Revealed in Film: 1:43:04–08
Availability: Blu-ray and DVD (Warner Home Video)
Director: Stanley Kubrick; **Screenplay**: Stanley Kubrick, based on William Thackeray's novel *The Luck of Barry Lyndon*
Cast: Ryan O'Neal (Redmond Barry/Barry Lyndon), Marisa Berenson (Lady Lyndon), Patrick Magee (The Chevalier de Balibari), Hardy Krüger (Capt. Potzdorf), Gay Hamilton (Nora Brady), Leon Vitali (Lord Bullingdon), Michael Hordern (Narrator)

In eighteenth-century Ireland, Redmond Barry appears to kill Captain Quinn in a duel over his cousin Nora, and flees. Highwaymen rob Redmond, and he has to join the army. He learns Nora's family faked the duel to get rid of

him and force Quinn to propose. Redmond's regiment is sent to Germany
for the Seven Years War. He deserts by impersonating a courier. He meets
the Prussian Captain Potzdorf, who realizes Redmond is a fake and arrests
him. Redmond joins the Prussian Army instead of being handed back to the
British as a deserter. He saves Potzdorf's life, and after the war he is recruited
to spy on Chevalier de Balibari by posing as his valet. Redmond realizes Balibari is a fellow Irishman and tells all. They become allies, Redmond helping
Balibari to cheat at cards, and Redmond submits innocent reports. Redmond
and Balibari tour Europe as professional gamblers. Redmond decides to better himself by marriage and on June 15, 1773, he marries Lady Lyndon after
her elderly husband dies (1:42:46 to 1:44:29). Her son, Lord Bullingdon, hates
Redmond. At Lady Lyndon's birthday party, Lord Bullingdon says he hates
Redmond, who tries to thrash him. Redmond dotes on his own son, Brian,
and when the boy is killed in an accident, Redmond turns to drink. Lady
Lyndon retreats into religion and finally attempts suicide. Lord Bullingdon
challenges Redmond to a duel. This leads to Barry's downfall, even though
for once he does the right thing.

Beautiful cinematography combined with an interesting story. The characters are very intriguing. This film is an overlooked classic and a must see.

Awards: *Academy Award Wins*: Best Set Decoration, Best Cinematography,
Best Costume Design, and Best Music. *Academy Award Nominations*: Best
Picture, Best Director, and Best Adapted Screenplay. *Golden Globe Nomi-
nations*: Best Motion Picture–Drama and Best Director–Motion Picture
Alternate Film: *Manhattan Melodrama*

16
WINDTALKERS
Year: 2002
Genre: War
Run Time: 2 hours 14 minutes
Date Revealed in Film: 34:00
Availability: Blu-ray and DVD (Metro-Goldwyn-Mayer)
Director: John Woo; **Screenplay**: John Rice and Joe Batteer
Cast: Nicolas Cage (Sgt. Joe Enders), Adam Beach (Pvt. Ben Yahzee), Roger
Willie (Pvt. Charlie Whitehorse), Peter Stormare (Gy. Sgt. Hjelmstad),

Noah Emmerich (Pvt. Chick), Mark Ruffalo (Cpl. Pappas), Christian Slater (Sgt. Pete "Ox" Anderson)

Cpl. Enders's squad is wiped out on Guadalcanal and Enders is left deaf in one ear, but he finds a way around the hearing test and returns to combat. Navajos Ben Yahzee and Charlie Whitehorse join the Marines to be "codetalkers" passing radio messages in a code based on the Navajo language. Enders and his pal Anderson are assigned to either protect the codetalkers or kill them to ensure they are not captured. They land on Saipan on June 16, 1944 (33:52 to 49:20). Enders recklessly attacks the Japanese. Enders and Yazhee penetrate Japanese lines to stop a friendly-fire bombardment. In a Japanese counterattack, Anderson is killed and Enders is forced to kill Whitehorse to prevent his capture. Yahzee learns of this and almost kills Enders. However, in the last battle on the island Yazhee learns how Enders really feels about him.

I liked this movie better than the critics did. None of the characters here act like you expect them to. Both the combat sequences and "behind the lines" shots were good.

Alternate Film: *Hollywoodland*

17

A DRY WHITE SEASON

Year: 1989
Genre: Drama
Run Time: 1 hour 37 minutes
Date Revealed in Film: 19:38
Availability: DVD (Metro-Goldwyn-Mayer), VHS (CBS Fox Video)
Director: Euzhan Palcy; **Screenplay**: Colin Welland and Euzhan Palcy
Cast: Donald Sutherland (Ben du Toit), Janet Suzman (Susan du Toit), Jürgen Prochnow (Captain Stolz), Marlon Brando (Ian McKenzie), Susannah Harker (Suzette du Toit), Zakes Mokae (Stanley Makhaya), Susan Sarandon (Melanie Bruwer)

In apartheid-era South Africa, Jonathan, the son of teacher Ben du Toit's gardener, Gordon, is arrested and dies in police custody. On June 17, 1976, Mr. du Toit reads about the subsequent riots and is upset (19:37 to 20:49). Then Gordon is arrested and also dies in police custody. After seeing the body, du Toit is convinced Gordon was murdered, but Captain Stolz perjures himself at the inquest to cover up what really happened. Du Toit starts to work with Melanie Bruwer, a reporter. He starts to feel pressure at work and has problems with his wife. The police search his house. Du Toit's son gets roughed up, but he tells his father not to stop. Du Toit gets fired and he and his wife separate. Melanie Bruwer is deported. Then a family betrayal leads to a final, deadly confrontation.

A brutally honest depiction of apartheid in South Africa. Du Toit finally learns that "evil flourishes when good men do nothing." He finally does something.

Awards: *Academy Award Nomination*: Best Supporting Actor (Marlon Brando). *Golden Globe Nomination*: Best Performance by an Actor in a Supporting Role in a Motion Picture (Brando)

Alternate Film: *Tom and Huck*

18
DISCLOSURE

Year: 1994

Genre: Drama

Run Time: 2 hours 9 minutes

Availability: Blu-ray and DVD (Warner Home Video)

Director: Barry Levinson; **Screenplay**: Paul Attanasio, based on Michael Crichton's novel

Cast: Michael Douglas (Tom Sanders), Demi Moore (Meredith Johnson), Donald Sutherland (Bob Garvin), Caroline Goodall (Susan Hendler), Roma Maffia (Catherine Alvarez), Dylan Baker (Philip Blackburn), Rosemary Forsyth (Stephanie Kaplan)

Tom Sanders goes to work at DigiCom, where he's head of manufacturing their CD-ROM drive, expecting a promotion since this is the day the company's merger with Conley-White is revealed. But instead it goes to Meredith White, his former lover. That evening during a meeting with Meredith, while she takes a call from the boss, Tom calls a subordinate of his and leaves a message. Meredith then comes on to him in a sexual manner. Tom pushes her away, but Meredith is upset and threatens him. Tom gets blamed at a meeting, since he doesn't know why there are problems at the Malaysian factory, and learns Meredith has made sexual harassment claims against him. Tom gets e-mails, most attacking him, but one, from "A Friend" leads him to an attorney who handles sexual harassment cases, Catherine Alvarez. She tries to talk him out of doing anything, but Tom files a claim anyway. The company agrees to arbitrate. Tom figures out that he hit the wrong button on speed dial and so his encounter with Meredith was recorded on his friend's answering machine. The next day, June 18, 1992, when this tape is played the company gives in and agrees to keep him on, but "A Friend" (whom Tom has learned is a college professor who's out of the country) sends more warning e-mails, and he figures out they're planning to legally fire him for incompetence over the manufacturing problems (1:30:56 to 1:52:05). Meredith made changes in the guidelines Tom set up, causing problems. Meredith deletes this information, but Tom has one more card up his sleeve to save his day.

Another good one by Michael Crichton. Informative and exciting. Keeps it realistic while making it interesting.

Source: Crichton, Michael. *Disclosure*. New York: Alfred A. Knopf, 1994.

This book at page 6 gives Monday's date as June 15.

Alternate Film: *Talk Radio*

19

TOTAL RECALL

Year: 1990
Genre: Science Fiction
Run Time: 1 hour 53 minutes
Date Revealed in Film: 44:52
Availability: Blu-ray (Lionsgate Films), DVD (Artisan Entertainment)
Director: Paul Verhoeven; **Screenplay**: Ronald Shusett, Dan O'Bannon, and Gary Goldman, based on Philip K. Dicks's short story *We Can Remember It for You Wholesale*
Cast: Arnold Schwarzenegger (Douglas Quaid/Hauser), Sharon Stone (Lori Quaid), Ronny Cox (Vilos Cohaagen), Michael Ironside (Richter), Rachel Ticotin (Melina), Marshall Bell (George/Kuato), Mel Johnson Jr. (Benny), Roy Brocksmith (Dr. Edgemar)

Construction worker Doug Quaid has a recurrent dream of a brunette on Mars, but he's married to the blonde Lori. The Pyramid Mine on Mars that supplies turbinium has been shut down; rumor says because alien artifacts were found, but Governor Cohaagen blames it on independence-minded rebels. Quaid goes to Rekall to buy a "secret agent on Mars" vacation, which is implanted in his memory. This leads to Quaid discovering his memory has been erased and that's he's really Hauser, who had helped Cohaagen against the rebels until he switched sides, whereupon Cohaagen had Hauser's memory erased. On June 19, 2084, Quaid arrives on Mars to stop Cohaagen (43:10 to 1:15:20). Quaid meets Melina, the girl in his dream, but she is angry and refuses to believe his story. After killing an agent of Cohaagen, he is attacked by the police, but Melina rescues him, believing him now that she has seen that Cohaagen is trying to kill him. Quaid meets Kuato, a psychic mutant, who helps him remember what he's forgotten—that there is an alien atmosphere-making machine in the Pyramid Mine that could end Cohaagen's power. A cab driver, Benny, who had attached himself to Quaid, turns out to be a mole, and he shoots Kuato. Quaid and Melina are captured by Cohaagen. Cohaagen explains that Hauser's memory was purposely erased to become Quaid so that he could pass Kuato's psychic test. He orders Hauser's original personality re-implanted. Quaid doesn't believe him. He and Melina escape before their memories can be programmed, which leads to a violent final battle with Cohaagen.

An interesting science-fiction film. It tries to blur the line between dreams and reality. There are several great action sequences in the film.

Awards: *Academy Award Win*: Best Visual Effects. *Academy Award Nominations*: Best Sound and Best Sound Editing

Alternate Film: *That Thing You Do!*

20

MARTY

Year: 1955
Genre: Romantic Comedy
Run Time: 1 hour 30 minutes
Date Revealed in Film: 38:10, 1:26:02
Availability: Blu-ray (Metro-Goldwyn-Mayer), VHS (MGM/UA Home Video)
Director: Delbert Mann; **Screenplay**: Paddy Chayefsky
Cast: Ernest Borgnine (Marty Piletti), Betsy Blair (Clara), Joe Mantell (Angie), Esther Mincotti (Mrs. Piletti), Augusta Ciolli (Aunt Catherine), Karen Steele (Virginia), Jerry Paris (Tommy)

Marty Piletti is a shy "nice guy" butcher in New York City who lives with his mother and goes with his friend Angie to the Stardust Ballroom, where he meets the equally shy Clara. They realize they have a lot in common, and Marty tells Clara about his fears and dreams. Just after midnight on June 20, 1954 (47:18 to 1:28:29), they start walking back to Marty's house, where he awkwardly tells Clara he likes her and tries for a kiss. They kiss, just as his mother returns. Marty takes Clara home, and tells her he will call at 2:30 tomorrow. The next day after his family and friends belittle Clara, Marty realizes he has a choice to make.

This film reminds me of *Sleepless in Seattle*. In both what is thought of as the "real" romance story occurs after the film ends. Two people reject cynicism for love.

Awards: *Academy Award Wins*: Best Picture, Best Director, Best Actor (Ernest Borgnine), and Best Adapted Screenplay. *Academy Award Nominations*: Best Supporting Actor (Joe Mantell), Best Supporting Actress (Betsy Blair), Best Art Direction–Set Direction–Black-and-White, and Best Black-and-White Cinematography. *Golden Globe Win*: Best Motion Picture Actor–Drama (Borgnine)
Alternate Film: *Bugsy*

21
MISSISSIPPI BURNING
Year: 1998
Genre: Mystery/Drama
Run Time: 2 hours 8 minutes
Availability: DVD (Metro-Goldwyn-Mayer), VHS (Orion Home Video)
Director: Alan Parker; **Screenplay**: Chris Gerolmo and Frederick Zollo
Cast: Gene Hackman (Rupert Anderson), Willem Dafoe (Alan Ward), Brad Dourif (Clinton Pell), Frances McDormand (Mrs. Pell), Gailard Sartain (Sheriff Ray Stuckey), R. Lee Ermey (Mayor Tilman), Stephen Tobolowsky (Clayton Townley)
On June 21, 1964, after three civil rights activists are released from jail, they are abducted by the Klan and vanish (3:09 to 8:09). Two FBI agents, Anderson and Ward, with totally different styles, arrive to investigate. The Klan tries to intimidate them and potential witnesses. The activists' car is found in

a swamp, and the Klan starts burning African American churches. The FBI investigates Deputy Pell, who refuses to talk. Four people are convicted of the attacks on the churches, but their sentences are suspended. This causes a riot in the African American community. After Deputy Pell's wife talks, the bodies of the civil rights workers are found, but Pell beats her. Anderson finally talks Ward into letting him do things his way. He has the mayor kidnapped and intimidates him into talking. With this information they pressure the conspirators. One man finally talks, and they arrest the killers.

A powerful film about a sad time in America's past. Good performances by all the actors. Well worth watching.

Awards: *Academy Award Win*: Best Cinematography. *Academy Award Nominations*: Best Actor (Gene Hackman), Best Supporting Actress (Frances McDormand), Best Director, Best Film Editing, Best Picture, and Best Sound. *Golden Globe Nominations*: Best Motion Picture–Drama, Best Director–Motion Picture, Best Performance by an Actor in a Motion Picture–Drama (Gene Hackman), and Best Screenplay–Motion Picture
Alternate Film: *A Connecticut Yankee in King Arthur's Court*

22
HEAVENLY CREATURES

Year: 1994
Genre: Drama
Run Time: 1 hour 39 minutes
Date Revealed in Film: 36:51
Availability: Blu-ray (Lionsgate Films), DVD (Miramax)
Director: Peter Jackson; **Screenplay**: Fran Walsh and Peter Jackson
Cast: Melanie Lynskey (Pauline Parker), Kate Winslet (Juliet Hulme), Sarah Peirse (Honora Parker), Diana Kent (Hilda Hulme), Clive Merrison (Dr. Henry Hulme), Simon O'Connor (Herbert Rieper), Peter Elliott (Bill Perry), Gilbert Goldie (Dr. Bennett)

In Christchurch, New Zealand, in the 1950s poor girl Pauline Parker becomes friends with rich girl Juliet Hulme. They develop an imaginary kingdom named Borovnia through playacting and writing and develop a quasi-religion based on the "Fourth World." Juliet starts coughing up blood and learns she has tuberculosis. Juliet is sent to a clinic, and when she returns home her friendship with Pauline has become so intense it worries Juliet's father. He goes to Pauline's parents with his concerns. Juliet's dad discovers his wife's extramarital affair and they plan to divorce, with Juliet to be sent to South Africa to live. The girls plan to run away together. They perceive Pauline's mother as the main impediment, so Pauline cold-bloodily decides to take action on June 22, 1954 (1:33:25 to 1:49:15).

A horrifying story. However, you just can't tear yourself away. These girls have a great friendship, but somewhere it makes a wrong turn.

Awards: *Academy Award Nomination*: Best Original Screenplay
Alternate Film: *Houdini*

23
THE ENGLISHMAN WHO WENT UP A HILL AND CAME DOWN A MOUNTAIN

Year: 1995
Genre: Romantic Comedy
Run Time: 1 hour 39 minutes
Date Revealed in Film: 34:17, 1:06:57–1:07:07
Availability: DVD and VHS (Miramax Home Entertainment)
Director: Christopher Monger; **Screenplay:** Christopher Monger
Cast: Hugh Grant (Reginald Anson), Ian McNeice (George Garrad), Tara FitzGerald (Betty), Colm Meaney (Morgan the Goat), Ian Hart (Johnny Shellshocked), Robert Pugh (Williams the Petroleum), Kenneth Griffith (Rev. Jones), Ieuan Rhys (Sgt. Thomas)

During World War I two English cartographers, the pompous Garrad and his assistant Anson, come to the Welsh village of Ffynnon Garw to measure the height of what the locals call "the first mountain in Wales." They tell the locals that a mountain must be more than one thousand feet high and their announcement that the hill is only 984 feet is met with consternation. A plan is devised to haul enough dirt from the valley to make up the difference. Morgan the Goat, reprobate owner of the inn where the Englishmen are staying, sabotages their car to keep them in the village. Even schoolchildren help with the plan to add dirt to their hill to make it a mountain. Morgan recruits Betty to charm Garrad and keep him there through a rainy spell over two days, including June 23, 1917 (1:07:05 to 1:07:21). However, she falls for

Anson instead. Rev. Jones, to the surprise of Morgan, takes as his sermon text Psalm 99:9, "Exalt the Lord our God and worship at his holy hill," and tells everyone he is going to haul dirt and that he expects them to do so also. The villagers haul dirt the entire day until Rev. Jones has a stroke and dies. His burial means the work is not complete until it is too late for Anson to take his measurements. However, Betty has a plan.

This is a low-key film with appealing dry humor. I like it, especially since my ancestry is part Welsh. The poor English are no match for the slyness and determination of the Welsh. *Hir yn byw Cymru!*

Alternate Film: *The Jokers*

24

EMMA

Year: 1996
Genre: Period Drama
Run Time: 2 hours 1 minute
Availability: DVD and VHS (Miramax Home Entertainment)
Director: Douglas McGrath; **Screenplay**: Douglas McGrath, based on Jane Austen's novel
Cast: Gwyneth Paltrow (Emma Woodhouse), Jeremy Northam (George Knightly), Toni Collette (Harriet Smith), Ewan McGregor (Frank Churchill), James Cosmo (Mr. Weston), Alan Cumming (Mr. Elton), Sophie Thompson (Miss Bates), Polly Walker (Jane Fairfax)

After matching her former governess, Miss Taylor, to the older Mr. Weston, Emma Woodhouse tries to match the minister Mr. Elton and poor, illegitimate Miss Harriet Smith. Emma persuades Harriet to say no when Robert Martin proposes. After the Weston's Christmas party Mr. Elton shocks Emma by proposing to her, and she learns he never had any interest in Harriet. He is firmly rejected. Jane Fairfax arrives, and the just-arrived Frank Churchill, Mr. Weston's son from his first marriage, rescues Emma. Emma gets the mistaken idea that Frank Churchill likes Harriet. A ball is held, where newly married Mr. Elton refuses to dance with Harriet, but George Knightly, Emma's brother-in-law, does. Emma and Harriet are accosted by gypsies, but saved by Frank Churchill. At a picnic held on June 24, Harriet confesses she likes her rescuer. Emma thinks she means Mr. Churchill. Emma belittles

Miss Bates, and George Knightly scolds Emma (1:26:51 to 1:33:08). Frank Churchill and Jane Fairfax are secretly engaged. When Emma tells this to Harriet, she learns that Harriet likes George Knightly, who "rescued" her at the dance. This forces Emma into some self-analysis that leads to the romantic climax.

A delightful romantic comedy. Of course when Jane Austen writes your script, you can hardly go wrong. A classic book makes a classic movie.

Awards: *Academy Award Win*: Best Original Score. *Academy Award Nomination*: Best Costume Design

Alternate Film: *Kit Carson*

25

RAGTIME

Year: 1981

Genre: Period Drama

Run Time: 2 hours 35 minutes

Availability: Blu-ray and VHS (Paramount Pictures)

Director: Miloš Forman; **Screenplay**: Michael Weller, based on E. L. Doctorow's novel

Cast: Debbie Allen (Sarah), James Cagney (Rhinelander Waldo), Jeff Daniels (P. C. O'Donnell), Fran Drescher (Mameh), Brad Dourif (Younger Brother), Elizabeth McGovern (Evelyn Nesbitt), Howard E. Rollins Jr. (Coalhouse Walker Jr.), James Olson (Father), Mary Steenburgen (Mother)

An upper-class family in New Rochelle finds an African American baby in their garden. The Mother insists on taking the baby and its mom in. Harry K. Thaw murders Stanford White on June 25, 1906, over a nude statute he thinks was modeled on his wife, Evelyn Nesbitt, White's former mistress (16:20 to 20:36). Evelyn testifies in favor of Harry after his family offers to pay her $1 million. Evelyn meets Tateh, who makes flipbooks. Harry Thaw is found not guilty, but committed. Evelyn Nesbitt agrees to take only $25,000, as she's committed adultery with Younger Brother. Musician Coalhouse Walker Jr., the father of Sarah's baby, agrees to marry her. On the way back to New York, his car is stopped and vandalized by the racist members of a volunteer fire department, but he ends up getting arrested. The Father bails him out. Coalhouse tries various legal means of getting redress. Sarah runs away and tries to approach the vice president with this issue, but she is injured and dies. The racist fire company are killed by Walker's "gang," except for Conklin, the chief. Younger Brother joins Coalhouse's gang and they take over the Morgan Library in New York, threatening to blow it up unless they get Coalhouse's car and Conklin. Booker T. Washington tries to talk Coalhouse out, but fails. The Father goes to talk to Coalhouse, who says if the car is delivered and his men can leave in it, he will then come out. Father stays in the library as a hostage. The car is brought and the men make their escape. Coalhouse comes out and is shot. Mother leaves with Tateh. Harry K. Thaw is released from jail.

A rich, multilayered drama about America at the turn of the last century, with an interesting blending of the factual and the fictional. A compelling story line and good performances make this film an overlooked classic.

Awards: *Academy Award Nominations*: Best Supporting Actor (Howard E. Rollins Jr.), Best Supporting Actress (Elizabeth McGovern), Best Art Direction, Best Costume Design, Best Cinematography, Best Original Score, Best Original Song, and Best Adapted Screenplay. *Golden Globe Nominations*: Best Motion Picture–Drama, Best Director–Motion Picture, Best Motion Picture Actress in a Supporting Role (Mary Steenburgen), Best Motion Picture Actor in a Supporting Role (Rollins), New Star of the Year in a Motion Picture (McGovern), New Star of the Year in a Motion Picture (Rollins), and Best Original Song–Motion Picture

Source: Baker, Paul R. *Stanney*. New York: The Free Press, 1989. This book at pages 371–73 gives Stanford White's death date.

Alternate Film: *They Died with Their Boots On*

26

WILSON

Year: 1944
Genre: Biography
Run Time: 2 hours 34 minutes
Availability: DVD and VHS (Twentieth Century Fox)
Director: Henry King; **Screenplay**: Lamar Trotti
Cast: Alexander Knox (Woodrow Wilson), Charles Coburn (Doctor Henry Holmes), Geraldine Fitzgerald (Edith Bolling Galt), Thomas Mitchell (Jo-

seph Tumulty), Cedric Hardwicke (Henry Cabot Lodge), Vincent Price (William Gibbs McAdoo)

Woodrow Wilson, president of Princeton University, is recruited by Senator "Big Ed" Jones to run for governor of New Jersey on June 26, 1910 (6:58 to 14:13). Wilson gets Jones to promise not to run for senator again. He is nominated for governor and elected. Jones puts his name in for the Senate seat, but Wilson stops his reelection. Wilson is nominated for president as a compromise candidate after a deadlocked convention. He is elected and passes a series of progressive legislative acts. His wife gets sick and dies. The *Lusitania* is sunk, but Wilson refuses to rush into war. He gets Germany to promise to stop submarine warfare. Wilson meets Edith Galt and proposes to her and they are wed. He is reelected with slogan "He kept us out of war." The Germans resume unrestricted submarine warfare and Wilson asks for and gets a declaration of war. Wilson makes his "Fourteen Points" speech, setting out a program for the peace. The war ends and he goes to the Versailles conference, where the League of Nations is made a part of the treaty. Congress refuses the treaty so Wilson tours the country. He has a stroke and leaves the White House.

A decent movie about a great president. Somewhat melodramatic, but still worth watching.

Awards: *Academy Award Wins*: Best Art Direction, Best Cinematography, Best Film Editing, Best Sound–Recording, and Best Original Screenplay. *Academy Award Nominations*: Best Actor (Alexander Knox), Best Director, Best Special Effects, and Best Music. *Golden Globe Win*: Best Motion Picture Actor (Knox)

Source: Link, Arthur S., ed. *The Papers of Woodrow Wilson, Vol. 20*. Princeton, NJ: Princeton University Press, 1971. This book at pages 543–45 gives the date Wilson was asked to run for governor.

Alternate Film: *Veronica Guerin*

27
OPERATION THUNDERBOLT

Year: 1978
Genre: Action
Run Time: 2 hours 4 minutes
Availability: DVD (Globus Group), VHS (MGM/UA Home Video)

Director: Menahem Golan; **Screenplay**: Ken Globus, Menahem Golan, and Clarke Reynolds

Cast: Yehoram Gaon (Col. Yonatan Netanyahu), Gila Almagor (Nurit Aviv), Assi Dayan (Shuki), Klaus Kinski (Wilfried Bose), Sybil Danning (Halima), Arik Lavie (Gen. Dan Shomron), Mark Heath (Idi Amin Dada), Henry Czarniak (Michel Bacos)

On June 27, 1976 (3:02 to 39:06), Air France Flight 139 leaves Tel Aviv for Athens. After it takes off for Paris, Germans and Palestinians hijack the plane, which is flown to Benghazi and on to Uganda. Negotiations begin for the passengers to be released, and the Israeli army develops a plan to free them. Jewish passengers are segregated, and the rest are flown back to Paris, but the crew volunteers to stay. Idi Amin, the Ugandan president, visits the hostages and talks about trading them for imprisoned terrorists. The Israeli government says it will negotiate and gets an extension until July 4. The army's rescue team gets the go ahead. The commandos land, kill the terrorists, and free the hostages, except for two. They return to Israel amid great joy.

A great action/suspense story based on real events. The director keeps the tension high, even though you know how it comes out. Watch this one instead of the Hollywood version, *Victory at Entebbe*.

Awards: *Academy Award Nomination*: Best Foreign Film

Source: Ben-Porat, Benjamin, Haber, Eitan, and Schiff, Zeev. *Entebbe Rescue*. New York: Delacorte Press, 1976. This book at pages 9 and 20–21 gives the date of the hijack.

Alternate Film: *Kidnapped* (1971)

28

SOMEWHERE IN TIME

Year: 1980

Genre: Romantic Fantasy

Run Time: 1 hour 43 minutes

Date Revealed in Film: 1:00:57

Availability: Blu-ray and DVD (Universal Studios)

Director: Jeannot Szwarc; **Screenplay**: Richard Matheson, based on his novel

Cast: Christopher Reeve (Richard Collier), Jane Seymour (Elise McKenna), Christopher Plummer (William Fawcett Robinson), Teresa Wright (Laura

Roberts), Bill Erwin (Arthur Biehl), Susan French (Older Elise), Jiri Voskovec (Dr. Gerard Finney)
In May 1972, at the debut of a play he has written, Richard Collier is ap-
proached by an elderly woman, who pushes a pocket watch into his hand,
saying, "Come back to me." Eight years later, suffering from writer's block
he goes to the Grand Hotel and becomes obsessed with a photo of Elise Mc-
Kenna, an actress who performed at the hotel in 1912. He learns she was the
woman who gave him the watch and died that same night. Richard learns she
read a book on time travel written by one of his old professors and had become a recluse after 1912. Richard decides to try the book's idea of time travel
by hypnosis. He dresses in period clothes and tries to "will" himself back, and
he succeeds after finding an old hotel register with his signature. He awakens
in 1912 and finds Elise, who asks if he is "the one." Her manager, Robinson,
has warned her that she will meet a man who will change her life. Elise and
Richard dine and dance that evening. The next day, June 28, 1912 (54:58 to
1:23:07), the two spend the day together as their attraction for each other
grows. Richard attends her play and watches her pose for the photo that will
captivate him sixty-eight years later. Robinson has Richard tied up and left
in the stables, planning to take Elise on to their next stop. But Richard wakes
up the next morning and finds Elise has not left. They make love and discuss
marriage. Then unexpected tragedy strikes.

An interesting film that is more a romance than a sci-fi film. Reeve and
Seymour give natural performances that make the picture.

Awards: *Academy Award Nomination*: Best Costume Design. *Golden Globe*
   Nomination: Best Original Score–Motion Picture

Alternate Film: *Ned Kelly*

29

WHERE THE HEART IS

Year: 2000
Genre: Drama
Run Time: 2 hours
Date Revealed in Film: 20:19
Availability: DVD (Twentieth Century Fox)

Director: Matt Williams; **Screenplay**: Lowell Ganz and Babaloo Mandel, based on Billie Letts's novel

Cast: Natalie Portman (Novalee Nation), Ashley Judd (Lexie Coop), Stockard Channing (Sister Husband), James Frain (Forney Hull), Dylan Bruno (Willy Jack Pickens), Keith David (Moses Whitecotton), Sally Field (Mama Lill)

Pregnant Novalee Nation and her boyfriend, Willy Jack Pickens, leave Tennessee for California, but he abandons her at the Wal-Mart in Sequoyah, Oklahoma. Novalee meets Sister Husband, who gives her a buckeye tree in a can. Novalee is accidentally locked in the Wal-Mart when it closes and starts living in the store.

On June 29, 1995 (19:34 to 22:52), Novalee visits the Sequoyah Public Library to learn about her tree and meets Forney, the librarian. Novalee reconnects with Sister, and Forney follows her back to the Wal-Mart. When Novalee goes into labor, he breaks into the store and delivers her baby. The birth of the child, named Americus, in a Wal-Mart sets off a media frenzy. People send her money and Wal-Mart gives her a job. Sister Husband takes in Novalee and Americus. Novalee becomes friends with Lexie, who was Americus's nurse. Novalee learns that Forney takes care of his alcoholic sister at the expense of his dream to become a history teacher. Novalee becomes interested in photography. Americus is kidnapped, but returned safely.

Novalee makes money with her photography, but a tornado hits the town, killing Sister Husband. Novalee wins a photography award and almost meets Willy Jack again. Lexie's new boyfriend abuses her kids and beats her up, so she moves in with Novalee. Forney's sister dies, and when he does not show up at the funeral, Novalee tracks him down and they have a romantic interlude. Novalee, who has secretly never thought she was good enough for the college-educated Forney, lies and says no when he asks if she loves him. Forney returns to Maine. When Willy Jack enters her life again, Novalee is forced to confront her true feelings.

Rather than a sickeningly sweet romantic comedy where no one has any doubts or problems, these feel like real people that you might actually know or know of. Novalee grows up a lot in this film, with the support of her friends.

Alternate Film: *Auto Focus*

30
WE BOUGHT A ZOO
Year: 2011
Genre: Comedy/Drama
Run Time: 2 hours 4 minutes
Date Revealed in Film: 1:42:26
Availability: Blu-ray and DVD (Twentieth Century Fox Home Entertainment)
Director: Cameron Crowe; **Screenplay:** Aline Brosh McKenna and Cameron Crowe, based on Benjamin Mee's book
Cast: Matt Damon (Benjamin Mee), Scarlett Johansson (Kelly Foster), Thomas Haden Church (Duncan Mee), Colin Ford (Dylan Mee), Maggie Elizabeth Jones (Rosie Mee), Angus Macfadyen (Peter MacCreedy), Elle Fanning (Lily Miska)

Although both his brother, Duncan, and son, Dylan, think he's crazy, widower Benjamin Mee buys a house in the country with a dilapidated, run-down zoo attached, in part because his daughter, Rosie, loves it. Under the guidance of the zookeeper, Kelly Foster, they start work on restoring the zoo in order to reopen it to the public. An inspection reveals the zoo needs $100,000 worth of repairs to be reopened. Benjamin decides to use a large legacy from his deceased wife to make the repairs. As they work on the zoo, Benjamin becomes closer to Kelly, while Dylan, reluctantly at first, becomes attached to Lily, Kelly's younger cousin. Finally, on June 30, 2011 (1:37:06 to 1:44:43), the zoo passes inspection. A week of rain threatens their grand reopening. The day of the opening contains some happy surprises for everyone at the zoo.

Good family entertainment. This film has something for everyone from kids to adults. Has good dramatic and comedic moments.
Alternate Film: *The Break-Up*

July

1

SUPERMAN

Year: 1978
Genre: Fantasy/Action
Run Time: 2 hours 23 minutes
Date Revealed in Film: 1:34:15
Availability: Blu-ray and DVD (Warner Home Video)
Director: Richard Donner; **Screenplay**: Mario Puzo, David Newman, Leslie
    Newman, and Robert Benton
Cast: Marlon Brando (Jor-El), Gene Hackman (Lex Luthor), Christopher
    Reeve (Clark Kent/Superman), Ned Beatty (Otis), Jackie Cooper (Perry
    White), Glenn Ford (Jonathan Kent), Margot Kidder (Lois Lane), Valerie
    Perrine (Eve Teschmacher)

On the planet Krypton, the scientist Jor-El is unable to convince other leaders
that Krypton will explode, but he sends his infant son, Kal-El, in an automated
spacecraft to Earth. The ship crashes in the American Midwest in the 1930s.
Kal-El is found by the Kents, who raise him as their son, Clark, but hide his
superhuman abilities. When Clark is eighteen his adoptive father dies and he
"hears" a call to go to the Arctic, where a glowing green crystal from his ship
builds "the Fortress of Solitude," a Kryptonian structure, out of ice. An image
of Jor-El tells Clark who he really is and spends twelve years teaching him.

Clark goes to Metropolis and becomes a reporter for *The Daily Planet*. He meets Lois Lane and is attracted to her, but she thinks Clark Kent is a dork. After Clark, in his Kryptonian outfit, saves Lois Lane and *Air Force One* and captures criminals, the city is mystified. Clark, in his costume, visits Lois Lane on July 1, 1978, and she dubs him Superman (1:18:53 to 1:34:08). She falls for him and continues to ignore Clark. Criminal mastermind Lex Luthor buys up worthless desert on the east side of the San Andreas fault line and plans to use a hijacked nuclear bomb to set off an earthquake, which will cause everything west of the fault to slide into the ocean, leaving his land as the new (and now extremely valuable) West Coast.

Luthor reprograms a missile to land on the fault and another in Hackensack, New Jersey. Luthor uses a piece of Kryptonite (a fragment of the planet) to weaken Superman, and taunts him by revealing the missiles' destinations, saying Superman could not stop both in time, even if he had his powers. This horrifies Miss Teschmacher, Luthor's mistress, as her mother lives in Hackensack. Luthor doesn't care, but she frees Superman on his promise to stop the Jersey-bound missile first. He does, but the other hits and causes a massive earthquake in California. Superman physically forces the plates back into place. Lois Lane, who was investigating the purchase of tracts of worthless desert, is killed in an aftershock. Superman is so upset that he flies around the Earth at such speed as to reverse the flow of time enough to save her. He then delivers Luthor to the authorities.

Has some humor, but it doesn't go over the top and devolve into camp. Some humor references the comics and earlier TV show.

Awards: *Academy Award Nominations*: Best Editing, Best Original Score, and Best Sound. *Golden Globe Nomination*: Best Original Score–Motion Picture

Alternate Film: *Jaws*

2

INDEPENDENCE DAY

Year: 1996
Genre: Science Fiction
Run Time: 2 hours 24 minutes
Date Revealed in Film: 00:40
Availability: Blu-ray and DVD (Twentieth Century Fox)

Director: Ronald Emmerich; **Screenplay**: Dean Devlin and Roland Emmerich

Cast: Will Smith (Capt. Steven Hiller), Bill Pullman (President Thomas J. Whitmore), Jeff Goldblum (David Levinson), Mary McDonnell (Marilyn Whitmore), Judd Hirsch (Julius Levinson), Robert Loggia (Gen. William Grey), Randy Quaid (Russell Casse)

On July 2, 1996, a huge alien craft releases several dozen huge saucer-shaped crafts that position themselves over major cities (00:45 to 54:19). In New York David Levinson finds broadcasts that he thinks are the countdown to an attack. He warns the president, who orders cities evacuated, but the attack occurs first. An attack on the craft by the Air Force is defeated, but Capt. Steve Hiller manages to capture a wounded alien. Hiller and the wounded alien are taken to Area 51, where the president is bunkered.

It is revealed that the Roswell Incident was real and scientists have been examining a captured craft since 1947. The wounded alien regains consciousness long enough to try to psychically attack the president, and is killed. Nuclear attacks on the ships prove futile. Levinson and Hiller come up with a plan to save the day.

An action film with some too convenient plot devices. For example, David Levinson's ex-wife just happens to work in the White House, so he can use her as a conduit to the president. And how could a laptop interface with an alien spacecraft?

Awards: *Academy Award Win*: Best Visual Effects. *Academy Award Nomination*: Best Sound

Alternate Film: *Sphere*

3

GETTYSBURG

Year: 1993

Genre: War

Run Time: 4 hours 31 minutes

Date Revealed in Film: 2:55:31

Availability: Blu-ray and DVD (Warner Home Video)

Director: Ronald F. Maxwell; **Screenplay**: Ronald F. Maxwell, based on Michael Shaara's novel *The Killer Angels*

Cast: Tom Berenger (Lt. Gen. James Longstreet), Jeff Daniels (Col. Joshua Chamberlain), Martin Sheen (Gen. Robert E. Lee), Kevin Conway (Sgt. "Buster" Kilrain), C. Thomas Howell (Lt. Thomas Chamberlain)

The Confederate Army has invaded the North, while Jeb Stuart has ridden off on his own glory-seeking mission. A Southern spy, Harrison, finds the Union forces and reports back to Gen. Longstreet. Col. Chamberlain has taken over the Twentieth Maine and has been sent 120 men who want out of the army, but he convinces them to stay. Buford's cavalry rides into Gettysburg. Heth's Southern division attacks. Reynolds's Union division comes up, but after he is shot the Union forces retreat to Cemetery and Culp's Hills, south of town. Gen. Ewell fails to take the hills. The next day, Gen. Hood's CSA division attacks Little Round Top and is barely repelled by the Twentieth Maine. Stuart returns and is chastised by Lee. The next day, July 3, 1863, Gen. Pickett leads a charge directly at the Federal lines, but in spite of great bravery by the attackers it is repulsed (2:38:20 to 4:02:46). The Army of Northern Virginia retreats to the South.

Magnificent cinematography. Interesting in that it was filmed on the actual battlefield. Good use of dialogue to create a feel for the characters.

Alternate Film: *The Doors*

4

SHANE

Year: 1953

Genre: Western/Drama

Run Time: 1 hour 58 minutes

Date Revealed in Film: 1:01:32–33

Availability: Blu-ray (Warner Home Video), DVD (Paramount Pictures)

Director: George Stevens; **Screenplay**: A. B. Guthrie Jr., based on Jack Schaefer's novel

Cast: Alan Ladd (Shane), Jean Arthur (Marian Starrett), Van Heflin (Joe Starrett), Brandon De Wilde (Joey Starrett), Jack Palance (Jack Wilson), Ben Johnson (Chris Calloway), Edgar Buchanan (Fred Lewis), Emile Meyer (Rufus Ryker)

The gunfighter Shane arrives at the Starretts' farm, home to Joe, Marian, and little Joey. The Starretts and Shane come into conflict with a local rancher,

Ryker, who wants to run all the homesteaders off the open range. On Independence Day, July 4, a gunfighter hired by Ryker, Jack Wilson, rides in and is taunted by a farmer, Joe Torrey. The farmers have a celebration (1:00:26 to 1:11:31). Ryker tries to buy Starrett away from the farmers, but he refuses. When Torrey next rides into town, Wilson kills him. Ryker sends word he wants to meet with Starrett and Shane has to beat him up to keep him from going. Shane rides to town for a final showdown with Wilson.

One of the classic westerns. Straightforward good guy Shane versus Wilson, Starrett versus Ryker. All presented in a low-key manner.

Awards: *Academy Award Win*: Best Cinematography (Color). *Academy Award Nominations*: Best Supporting Actor (Brandon De Wilde and Jack Palance), Best Director, Best Picture, and Best Screenplay

Alternate Film: *My Girl*

5

COOL HAND LUKE

Year: 1967
Genre: Comedy/Drama
Run Time: 2 hours 6 minutes
Date Revealed in Film: 1:14:04
Availability: Blu-ray and DVD (Warner Home Video)
Director: Stuart Rosenberg; **Screenplay:** Donn Pearce and Frank Pierson, based on Donn Pearce's novel
Cast: Paul Newman (Luke Jackson), George Kennedy (Dragline), J. D. Cannon (Society Red), Lou Antonio (Koko), Robert Drivas (Loudmouth Steve), Strother Martin (Captain), Jo Van Fleet (Arletta), Clifton James (Carr), Morgan Woodward (Boss Godfrey)

Luke Jackson is arrested and sent to a Florida prison camp. Luke ignores the pecking order among the prisoners but is eventually accepted because of his unquenchable good spirits and never-say-die attitude. When he wins a poker game on a bluff, the prisoner's leader, Dragline, gives him the nickname "Cool Hand Luke." Luke escapes during an Independence Day celebration and spends July 5 in the hot sun on the run (1:17:48 to 1:21:36). He is recaptured and fitted with leg irons. The captain delivers a warning speech to the other inmates, beginning with a famous line: "What we've got here is failure to communicate." Luke manages to escape again for a short time. The captain thinks he has finally broken Luke, but when a chance comes to steal the guard's truck, he and Dragline make a desperate bid for freedom.

A great film. Full of comedy and drama and many now classic scenes, such as the egg-eating contest.

Awards: *Academy Award Win*: Best Supporting Actor (George Kennedy). *Academy Award Nominations*: Best Actor (Paul Newman), Best Original Score, and Best Adapted Screenplay. *Golden Globe Nominations*: Best Motion Picture Actor–Drama (Newman) and Best Supporting Actor (Kennedy)

Alternate Film: *The Quiet Earth*

6

A MAN FOR ALL SEASONS

Year: 1966

Genre: Period Drama

Run Time: 2 hours

Availability: DVD (Sony Pictures), VHS (RCA/Columbia Pictures Home Video)

Director: Fred Zinnemann; **Screenplay**: Robert Bolt, based on his play

Cast: Paul Scofield (Sir Thomas More), Wendy Hiller (Alice More), Leo McKern (Thomas Cromwell), Robert Shaw (Henry VIII of England), Orson Welles (Thomas Cardinal Wolsey), Susannah York (Margaret More), John Hurt (Richard Rich)

Cardinal Wolsey, chancellor for Henry VIII of England, chastises Sir Thomas More for opposing the king's desire for a divorce, and More is scandalized when Wolsey suggests applying pressure to get it. More also refuses his daughter's request to marry Roper, a Protestant. Wolsey is banished, and More is made lord chancellor. More argues with the king about divorce. The king declares himself "Head of the Church" and More quits. He is ordered to attend Henry VIII's wedding to Anne Boleyn, but he refuses. The king orders that all must take a new oath, as he suspects Catholics are trying to depose him. More refuses and is put on trial for treason. He is convicted, based on perjured testimony. More is executed on July 6, 1535 (1:57:49 to 1:59:03).

A wonderful drama. It depicts the manipulation Henry VIII used to secure his divorce. More remains loyal to the king, but refuses to change his beliefs to suit him.

Awards: *Academy Award Wins*: Best Picture, Best Actor (Paul Scofield), Best Color Cinematography, Best Color Costume Design, Best Director, Best Adapted Screenplay. *Academy Award Nominations*: Best Supporting Actor (Robert Shaw) and Best Supporting Actress (Wendy Hiller). *Golden Globe Wins*: Best Motion Picture–Drama, Best Motion Picture Director, Best Motion Picture Actor–Drama (Scofield), and Best Screenplay. *Golden Globe Nomination*: Best Supporting Actor (Shaw)

Source: Weir, Alison. *Henry VIII: The King and His Court.* New York: Ballantine Books, 2001. This book at page 357 gives the date of More's execution.

Alternate Film: *The Audrey Hepburn Story*

7

THE AVIATOR

Year: 2004

Genre: Biography

Run Time: 2 hours 50 minutes

Date Revealed in Film: 1:41:15

Availability: Blu-ray and DVD (Warner Home Video)

Director: Martin Scorsese; **Screenplay**: John Logan

Cast: Leonardo DiCaprio (Howard Hughes), Cate Blanchett (Katharine Hepburn), Kate Beckinsale (Ava Gardner), John C. Reilly (Noah Dietrich), Alec Baldwin (Juan Trippe), Alan Alda (Owen Brewster), Ian Holm (Professor Fitz), Gwen Stefani (Jean Harlow)

In 1927 Hollywood Howard Hughes is a wealthy movie producer who becomes obsessed with his movie *Hells Angels*. After it is completed the introduction of sound makes the film obsolete, so he reshoots with sound. Hughes is romantically linked with Katharine Hepburn, and she helps him keep his obsessive-compulsive disorder under control. Hughes buys control of Trans World Airlines and runs afoul of Senator Brewster and Juan Trippe, who only want Pan Am to fly overseas routes. He breaks up with Hepburn, fights film censors over *The Outlaw*, and gets U.S. Army contracts for a spy plane and an oversized transport, the *Spruce Goose*. On July 7, 1946, he takes the spy plane for a test flight and crashes (1:41:09 to 1:48:54). The FBI starts investigating whether he embezzled government funds in the plane contracts. Hughes is pressured to sell TWA to Pan Am and the investigation will go away. However, Hughes shows up at a Senate hearing and embarrasses his accusers. After he flies the *Spruce Goose*, he has another obsessive-compulsive attack.

A very good bio. DiCaprio does a good job showing both the genius and nuttiness that was Hughes. The well-written script lets you follow the story even if you're not familiar with Hughes.

Awards: *Academy Award Wins*: Best Supporting Actress (Cate Blanchett), Best Art Direction, Best Costume Design, Best Cinematography, and Best Film Editing. *Academy Award Nominations*: Best Actor (Leonardo DiCaprio), Best Supporting Actor (Alan Alda), Best Director, Best Original Screenplay, Best Picture, and Best Sound Mixing. *Golden Globe Wins*: Best Performance by an Actor in a Motion Picture–Drama (DiCaprio), Best Original Score–Motion Picture, and Best Motion Picture–Drama. *Golden Globe Nominations*: Best Performance by an Actress in a Supporting Role (Blanchett), Best Director–Motion Picture, and Best Screenplay–Motion Picture

Alternate Film: *Chitty Chitty Bang Bang*

8

IN LOVE AND WAR

Year: 1997

Genre: Drama

Run Time: 1 hour 53 minutes

Date Revealed in Film: 46:37–40

Availability: DVD and VHS (New Line Home Video)

Director: Richard Attenborough; **Screenplay**: Allan Scott, Clancy Sigal, and Anna Hamilton Phelan, based on Henry Villard and James Nagel's book *Hemingway in Love and War*

Cast: Mackenzie Astin (Henry Villard), Chris O'Donnell (Ernest Hemingway), Sandra Bullock (Agnes von Kurowsky), Ingrid Lacey (Elsie MacDonald), Emilio Bonucci (Dr. Domenico Caracciolo), Alan Bennett (Porter)

Agnes von Kurowsky and Ernest Hemingway go to Italy in 1918 as part of the U.S. medical corps. He travels to the front and is wounded carrying an injured man to safety on July 8, 1918 (11:19 to 17:22). He is sent to Agnes's hospital and immediately asks her to marry him. Agnes persuades Dr. Caracciolo not to amputate Hemingway's leg. The doctor is also attracted to Agnes. Hemingway recovers, and Agnes starts to return his interest. Hemingway gets a medal for his exploit. Agnes, Hemingway, and Harry Villard go on an outing that ends with Agnes slapping Ernest after he, in a fit of jealousy, lies and tells Harry that he and Agnes have slept together. Agnes later forgives Ernest. Agnes and Dr. Caracciolo are sent closer to the front. Ernest visits her there and they have sex. Ernest is sent back to the States and the war ends. Dr. Caracciolo asks Agnes to marry him, and she agrees, setting up the tragic climax.

A bittersweet romance. Agnes and Ernest do love each other. Unfortunately, they don't love each other at the same time. An excellent film that follows the growth and death of their relationship.

Alternate Film: *The Party*

9

THE BIG RED ONE

Year: 1980
Genre: War
Run Time: 1 hour 53 minutes
Availability: Blu-ray and DVD (Warner Home Video)
Director: Samuel Fuller; **Screenplay**: Samuel Fuller
Cast: Lee Marvin (The Sergeant), Mark Hamill (Pvt. Griff), Robert Carradine (Pvt. Zab), Bobby Di Cicco (Pvt. Vinci), Kelly Ward (Pvt. Johnson), Siegfried Rauch (Schroeder)

On the last day of World War I the Sergeant kills a German who's trying to surrender, but the war was already over. In 1942 the Sergeant leads a rifle squad ashore in North Africa, where Griff freezes in action. At Kasserine Pass, General Rommel's Afrika Corps overruns them and the Sergeant is captured but later released when the Allies capture Tunis. The squad gets replacements and they engage in a rough bull session with them on July 9, 1943, the night before the invasion of Sicily (39:32 to 41:05). They battle snipers and tanks in Sicily. On D-Day in Normandy, Griff puts a Bangalore torpedo in place that blows up the barrier blocking their route off the beach. In France they are almost wiped out in a German trap. They fight in the Battle of the Bulge and advance across Germany. A few hours after the war has ended the Sergeant stabs a German officer who is trying to surrender. This time they give him medical care and save him.

A gritty war film. An interesting concept is the German officer who seems to "shadow" the squad from North Africa to the end. Definitely worth watching.

Source: Atkinson, Rick. *The Day of Battle: The War in Sicily and Italy 1943–1944.* New York: Henry Holt and Company, 2007. At page 79 this book gives the invasion date.

Alternate Film: *Flushed Away*

10

THE GREEN MILE

Year: 1999
Genre: Fantasy
Run Time: 3 hours 9 minutes
Date Revealed in Film: 25:06
Availability: Blu-ray and DVD (Warner Home Video)
Director: Frank Darabont; **Screenplay**: Frank Darabont, based on Stephen King's novel
Cast: Tom Hanks (Paul Edgecomb), Michael Clarke Duncan (John Coffey), Bonnie Hunt (Jan Edgecomb), David Morse ("Brutal" Howell), Doug Hutchison (Percy Wetmore), Sam Rockwell ("Wild Bill" Wharton), James Cromwell (Warden Hal Moores)

Elderly Paul Edgecomb tells his story to fellow nursing home resident Ellie. In 1935 he was a guard on death row in Louisiana. A big African American, John Coffey, arrives on death row. After observing him, Paul finds it hard to believe that Coffey committed the crime attributed to him. On July 10, 1935, a prisoner, Bitterbuck, is executed (41:49 to 47:49). Percy, the governor's sadistic nephew, who is a guard, tells Paul that if he will let him work an execution, Percy will transfer to Briar Ridge Mental Asylum. A new vicious death row inmate, William Wharton, arrives. Coffey cures Paul of his urinary tract infection by grasping his hand, with Coffey saying that he "took it back." Paul talks to Coffey's attorney, who says Coffey is guilty. Percy purposely steps on "Mr. Jingles," a prisoner's pet rat, but when Coffey holds the body it revives.

Percy deliberately fails to put a wet sponge between Delacroix's head and the electrode at his execution, causing Delacroix to die in agony. Paul persuades the other guards to illegally take Coffey to cure the warden's wife of cancer. On their return Percy fatally shoots Wharton. Paul takes Coffey's hand and "sees" that Wharton killed the two girls that Coffey was accused of killing, as Coffey learned this when Wharton grabbed him earlier. Coffey found them dead. He said he tried to "take it back, but it was too late." Percy goes to Briar Ridge, but as a patient, not a guard. Coffey tells Paul he wants to die and, as his last request, he watches *Top Hat*. Coffey is put to death. Back in the present, Paul tells Ellie he's 108 and that Mr. Jingles is still alive.

Another mystical magical tale from Stephen King. Most people are all too ready to believe that the very large Coffey is guilty of murder, but Paul sees something else. A tragedy in that Coffey can't save himself, and Paul outlives everyone he's known.

Awards: *Academy Award Nominations*: Best Supporting Actor (Michael Clarke Duncan), Best Picture, Best Sound Mixing, and Best Adapted Screenplay. *Golden Globe Nomination*: Best Performance by an Actor in a Supporting Role in a Motion Picture (Duncan)

Alternate Film: *The Lake House*

11
CHARIOTS OF FIRE

Year: 1981
Genre: Drama
Run Time: 2 hours 4 minutes
Availability: Blu-ray and DVD (Warner Home Video)
Director: Hugh Hudson; **Screenplay**: Colin Welland
Cast: Ben Cross (Harold Abrahams), Ian Charleson (Eric Liddell), Nicholas Farrell (Aubrey Montague), Nigel Havers (Lord Andrew Lindsay), Cheryl Campbell (Jennie Liddell), Alice Krige (Sybil Gordon), Ian Holm (Sam Mussabini)

The film opens in a double flashback. Starting at Harold Abrahams's memorial service, it flashes back to Aubrey Montague writing a letter to his parents just before the 1924 Summer Olympics, and then flashes back to 1919 as he recalls arriving at Cambridge and meeting Harold Abrahams. Abrahams, a

Jew, is forced to deal with the subtle and not-so-subtle anti-Semitism of the times, but he decides to "take them on . . . and run them off their feet." He is a runner, and wins the "college dash," the first man in seven centuries to do so. Meanwhile, Eric Liddell, the son of Scottish missionaries, also runs as a way to honor God and attract attention for the church. Abrahams goes to watch Liddell run in a meet for Scotland against France and is shocked when Liddell wins even after being knocked down. Abrahams meets Sam Mussabini, who agrees to coach him after Liddell beats Abrahams in their first meeting. Abrahams meets and falls in love with Sybil Gordon, an actress. Liddell faces opposition to his running from his family. Liddell and Abrahams are both picked for the 1924 British Olympic team. A problem arises when Liddell refuses to run in the 100-meter heats because they are to be held on a Sunday. He trades events with a team member and wins a gold medal in the 200 meters on July 11, 1924 (1:52:04 to 1:56:43). Abrahams wins the 100-meter gold, but doesn't get a rematch with Liddell. Abrahams goes on to become an icon in British sport, while Liddell dies in occupied China in 1944.

The film is rare in presenting a positive image of people of faith in detailing the determination of Eric Liddell not to violate his beliefs. The theme by Vangelis became a hit. A very good film of true events, even though some artistic liberties are taken with the facts.

Awards: *Academy Award Wins*: Best Picture, Best Original Music Score, Best Writing–Original Screenplay, and Best Costume Design. *Academy Award Nominations*: Best Supporting Actor (Ian Holm), Best Director, and Best Film Editing. *Golden Globe Win*: Best Foreign Film

Source: Wallechinsky, David, and Loucky, Jaime. *The Complete Book of the Olympics*. London: Aurum Press, 2012. This book at page 79 gives the day Liddell won the medal.

Alternate Film: *El Cid*

12

BOBBY JONES: STROKE OF GENIUS

Year: 2004
Genre: Biography
Run Time: 2 hours
Availability: DVD (Sony Pictures), VHS (Columbia/TriStar Home Entertainment)

Director: Rowdy Herrington; **Screenplay**: Rowdy Herrington, Bill Pryor, and
Tony DePaul
Cast: James Caviezel (Bobby Jones), Devon Gearhart (young Bobby Jones),
Claire Forlani (Mary Malone Jones), Jeremy Northam (Walter Hagen),
Malcolm McDowell (O. B. Keeler), Aidan Quinn (Harry Vardon), John
Shepherd (Bob Woodruff)
Famous golfer Bobby Jones visits St. Andrews in Scotland on his way to the
1936 Summer Olympics in Berlin and receives a heartfelt welcome from the en-
tire town. Bobby started playing golf as a little boy, even though he was a sickly
child, and improved by rigorous practice. He is noticed by Grantland Rice and
O. B. Keeler, well-known sports reporters. During World War I, Bobby plays
in charity tournaments, including one where he loses to the flamboyant pro,
Walter Hagen. Bobby goes to Georgia Tech, where he meets Mary Malone. He
keeps playing golf, finishing second in four tournaments in a row. He is a well-
known figure, which causes problems in his relationship with Mary, who cares
nothing for fame. Bobby goes to St. Andrews to play in the 1921 British Open
against his idol Harry Vardon. Bobby walks off the course after making a bad
shot, but Vardon encourages him to continue playing golf. Bobby graduates
from Georgia Tech and Harvard, sells real estate, and later becomes a lawyer.
He gets married and has a family. He wins the U.S. and British Opens. Bobby
decides he wants to win all four major championships in one year. At St. Andrews, Bobby wins the British Amateur and the British Open, beating Walter
Hagen with a miraculous shot out of the bunker. On the opening day of the
U.S. Open, Hagen tries to "fake him out," but fails. On July 12, 1930, Bobby
Jones wins the U.S. Open and his pal O. B. Keeler decks a reporter who questions the truth of Jones's amateur status (1:49:18 to 1:51:18). Although Bobby
suffers from stomach pains and cramps during the entire grand slam quest, he
wins the U.S. Amateur Open. Bobby retires from tournament golf and goes on
to supervise the construction of the Masters course in Augusta.

A great biopic about a "true amateur and a gentleman." Some people
found this movie dull. I guess it's because Bobby had none of the vices that
usually make up athletic bios, like alcohol, drugs, or infidelity.
Source: Frost, Mark. *The Grand Slam: Bobby Jones, America and the Story of
Golf*. New York: Hyperion Books, 2004. This book at page 400 gives the
date Bobby won the 1930 U.S. Open.
Alternate Film: *Battle at Apache Pass*

13

GANGS OF NEW YORK

Year: 2002
Genre: Period Drama
Run Time: 2 hours 47 minutes
Availability: Blu-ray (Disney/Buena Vista), DVD (Miramax)
Director: Martin Scorsese; **Screenplay**: Jay Cocks, Steven Zaillian, and Kenneth Lonergan
Cast: Leonardo DiCaprio (Amsterdam Vallon), Daniel Day-Lewis (Bill "The Butcher" Cutting), Cameron Diaz (Jenny Everdeane), Liam Neeson ("Priest" Vallon), Jim Broadbent ("Boss" Tweed), Brendan Gleeson ("Monk" McGinn)

In 1846 in New York's Five Points district, the "Natives," led by William "Bill the Butcher" Cutter, square off in Paradise Square against the "Dead Rabbits," Irish immigrants led by "Priest" Vallon. The Natives win and Vallon is killed, but his son, Amsterdam, is sent to an orphanage. Sixteen years later Amsterdam returns and finagles an introduction to Butcher. Amsterdam goes to work for Butcher with the idea of eventually killing him. Amsterdam meets Jenny Everdeane and saves Butcher from getting killed. Jenny nurses Butcher, but ends up making love with Amsterdam. On the evening of the annual ceremony held to commemorate the defeat of the Dead Rabbits, Butcher learns who Amsterdam really is and taunts him by cutting Jenny. This causes Amsterdam to throw a knife at Butcher. He deflects it and then stabs Amsterdam. Jenny nurses Amsterdam back to health and wants them to flee to San Francisco. Amsterdam leaves the skin of a dead rabbit in Paradise Square as a sign that the Dead Rabbits are back. Boss Tweed and Amsterdam make a deal for the Irish to support Tammany Hall if an Irishman, McGinn, is elected sheriff. McGinn wins, but Butcher kills him. During his funeral, Amsterdam challenges Butcher to a gang brawl, which he accepts. On July 13, 1863, the New York City draft riots break out. As the two gangs converge on Paradise Square for the showdown, the U.S. Navy opens up with cannon fire. Amsterdam and Butcher try to fight in the dust thrown up by the cannon fire, but Butcher is killed by a piece of shrapnel (2:29:16 to 2:22:47). Butcher is buried beside Vallon.

An interesting period piece about a little-explored era of American history. It evokes the power of loyalty and the thirst for revenge.

Awards: *Academy Award Nominations*: Best Picture, Best Director, Best Art Direction, Best Original Song, Best Actor (Daniel Day-Lewis), Best Cinematography, Best Costume Design, Best Editing, Best Sound, and Best Original Screenplay. *Golden Globe Wins*: Best Director–Motion Picture and Best Original Song–Motion Picture. *Golden Globe Nominations*: Best Motion Picture–Drama, Best Performance by an Actor in a Motion Picture–Drama (Day-Lewis), and Best Performance by an Actress in a Supporting Role in a Motion Picture (Cameron Diaz)

Alternate Film: *O Brother, Where Art Thou?*

14

FAIR GAME

Year: 2010
Genre: Biographical Drama
Run Time: 1 hour 48 minutes
Date Revealed in Film: 1:00:07
Availability: Blu-ray and DVD (Summit Entertainment)
Director: Doug Liman; **Screenplay**: Jez Butterworth and John-Henry Butterworth, based on Valerie Plame's memoir
Cast: Naomi Watts (Valerie Plame), Sean Penn (Joseph Wilson), Noah Emmerich (Bill), Ty Burrell (Fred), Sam Shepard (Sam Plame), Bruce McGill (James Pavitt)

Valerie Plame is an energy analyst who also works undercover as a CIA agent on nuclear non-proliferation. Her husband, Joe Wilson, a former U.S. diplomat, has personal knowledge of and contacts in the African country of Niger. Wilson, at the CIA's request, goes to Niger and determines that a report that Iraq is trying to buy five hundred tons of yellowcake uranium is false. Plame learns that aluminum tubes purchased by Iraq are not the kind needed for use in nuclear reactors. Plame also makes contact with scientists who used to work in the Iraqi nuclear program. Both the national security advisor and the vice president lie on TV about the yellowcake and the tubes, saying the exact opposite of what the CIA reported. Plame complains that the Bush White House is cherry-picking data to support its foreign policy agenda. The third Gulf War begins with "shock and awe." Joe Wilson writes an op-ed for the

New York Times exposing the administration's misstatements, and Scooter Libby, Vice President Cheney's chief of staff, violates the law and leaks Valerie Plame's CIA connection. A news article naming her as a CIA agent appears on July 14, 2003 (1:00:01 to 1:06:49). The fallout from this affects Plame, her marriage, her husband, and the Iraqi scientists as she has to decide whether to fight back or not.

Both Watts and Penn bring a rare intensity to their roles. A movie revealing recent true events that continue to impact the world.

Alternate Film: *Washington Square*

15

ROMEO AND JULIET

Year: 1968

Genre: Period Drama

Run Time: 2 hours 18 minutes

Availability: DVD (Warner Home Video), VHS (Paramount Home Video)

Director: Franco Zeffirelli; **Screenplay**: Franco Brusati, Masolino D'Amico, and Franco Zeffirelli, based on William Shakespeare's play

Cast: Leonard Whiting (Romeo Montague), Olivia Hussey (Juliet Capulet), John McEnery (Mercutio), Milo O'Shea (Friar Lawrence), Pat Heywood (The Nurse), Robert Stephens (Prince Escalus), Michael York (Tybalt), Bruce Robinson (Benvolio)

On July 15, the servants of the Montagues and Capulets fight in the marketplace of Verona, but the prince's men break it up. Paris asks to marry Juliet, but her father thinks she's too young, as she's only thirteen. Capulet gives a masked ball and Romeo sneaks in. When he and Juliet see each other, it's love at first sight. They discover each other's identities. Romeo sneaks into Capulet's garden, where he and Juliet declare their love and agree to marry (00:01 to 50:40). Friar Lawrence marries them, as he thinks this will restore peace between their families. Romeo meets Juliet's kinsman, Tybalt, and through no fault of his own a fight ensues, where he kills Tybalt and is declared an outlaw. Romeo and Juliet spend their wedding night together, but he then flees to Mantua. Her parents tell Juliet that she is to marry Paris. Juliet goes to see Friar Lawrence, who devises a plan. He gives Juliet a potion to simulate death for two days. After she's buried, Juliet can be taken out of the tomb and join Romeo. She drinks the potion, is found apparently dead, and is buried.

Balthazar races to tell Romeo she's dead and passes the messenger Friar Lawrence sent to tell Romeo of the plan. Romeo returns to Verona and goes to the Capulet family tomb. Seeing Juliet apparently dead, he commits suicide by drinking poison. Juliet awakens, sees Romeo's dead body and stabs herself to death. Their deaths bring about a reconciliation of the two families.

An immortal tale by the Bard. A story of great love and the cost of mindless hatred. This version was filmed on location and has fantastic costumes and sets. Rare in that it used actors for the leads who were close to the ages indicated in the play.

Awards: *Academy Award Wins*: Best Cinematography and Best Costume Design. *Academy Award Nominations*: Best Picture and Best Director. *Golden Globe Wins*: Best English Language Foreign Film, Most Promising Newcomer–Female (Olivia Hussey), and Most Promising Newcomer–Male (Leonard Whiting). *Golden Globe Nominations*: Best Motion Picture Director and Best Original Score

Alternate Film: *One Day*

16

SARAH'S KEY

Year: 2010
Genre: Drama
Run Time: 1 hour 51 minutes
Date Revealed in Film: 2:55
Availability: Blu-ray (Starz/Anchor Bay), DVD (Weinstein Company)
Director: Gilles Paquet-Brenner; **Screenplay**: Serge Joncour and Gilles Paquet-Brenner, based on Tatiana de Rosnay's novel
Cast: Kristin Scott Thomas (Julia Jarmond), Frédéric Pierrot (Bertrand Tezac), Michel Duchaussoy (Édouard Tezac), Gisèle Casadesus (Bertrand's grandmother), Xavier Béja (Bertrand's grandfather), Mélusine Mayance (young Sarah Starzynski)

On July 16, 1942, the Paris police arrest many of the cities Jews, including the Starzynski family, consisting of Mother, Father, son Michel, and daughter Sarah. Sarah locks Michel in a hidden cupboard and tells him to stay until she returns (00:57 to 6:21). In 2009 Paris, Julia Jarmond, an American journalist with a French magazine, is writing an article about the 1942 deportations. She learns that her husband's family moved into the Starzynskis' apartment in August 1942. In 1942 the Starzynskis are sent to the Vel d'Hiv Velodrome, and Sarah is upset when an opportunity is missed to free Michel (10:47 to 18:05). In 2009, Bertrand, Julia's husband, is not happy that she is pregnant and wants her to get an abortion. In a new camp when Sarah wakes up after three days of fever, only children are there. She escapes with the help of a policeman and finds refuge at the Dufaure farm. Julia confronts her father-in-law about the apartment, and he says that on the second day that they were there, the Dufaures arrived with Sarah. They find Michel's dead body in the cupboard. Julia learns that her husband's grandfather sent the Dufaures money to support Sarah. Julia decides not to get an abortion and visits the Dufaure's granddaughter, who says Sarah moved to America in the 1950s. Julia tracks down Sarah's son, William, who knows nothing of his mother's Jewish heritage or story. Sarah had killed herself over guilt about Michel. Two years later, William and Julia meet again in New York. Julia and Bertrand have separated. William is very touched when he learns Julia has named her little girl Sarah.

A moving story. Julia's respect for life increases, as William learns the truth about his mother.

Alternate Film: *Someone Like You*

17

THE FLYING SCOTSMAN

Year: 2006
Genre: Biography
Run Time: 1 hour 36 minutes
Date Revealed in Film: 53:05
Availability: Blu-ray (Metro-Goldwyn-Mayer)
Director: Douglas Mackinnon; **Screenplay**: John Brown, Declan Hughes, and Simon Rose
Cast: Jonny Lee Miller (Graeme Obree), Laura Fraser (Anne Obree), Billy Boyd (Malky McGovern), Brian Cox (Douglas Baxter), Morven Christie (Katie), Ron Donachie (Scobie)

Graeme Obree is bullied as a child, but later uses his bike to escape. When he grows up he works as a courier, marries, then opens a bike shop. He befriends Malky McGovern and builds a bike to try for the one-hour distance record.

McGovern finds a sponsor, while Obree battles depression. He goes to Norway to break the record, but fails. The next day, July 17, 1993, he tries again and sets the record (46:54 to 53:46). He also wins the 1993 World Bicycle Championship and sets a new record. Then the World Cycling Federation bans his racing style, and when he changes his bike to comply, they change the rules, and this happens a second time. The bullies of his past resurface and taunt Obree again, and he tries to hang himself but later goes into therapy. Finally he devises a new, legal racing style and wins the one-hour record again in Bogotá.

A tough, gritty bio. Not your usual paean to a superhero, but shows a real person with real problems. A feel-good story of overcoming the past.
Alternate Film: *Cobb*

18
QUO VADIS
Year: 1951
Genre: Period Drama
Run Time: 2 hours 51 minutes
Availability: Blu-ray and DVD (Warner Home Video)
Director: Mervyn LeRoy; **Screenplay**: S. N. Behrman, Sonya Levien, and John
   Lee Mahin, based on Henryk Sienkiewicz's novel
Cast: Robert Taylor (Marcus Vinicius), Deborah Kerr (Lygia), Leo Genn
   (Petronius), Peter Ustinov (Nero), Patricia Laffan (Poppaea), Finlay Currie (Saint Peter), Abraham Sofaer (Paul of Tarsus), Marina Berti (Eunice),
   Buddy Baer (Ursus)
Roman general Marcus Vinicius returns from the wars and falls in love with Lygia, a Christian who is a hostage of Rome being raised as the adoptive daughter of a Roman general. Vinicius persuades Emperor Nero to assign Lygia's custody to him. She rejects him and is hidden by the Christians of Rome. Nero sets fire to Rome in the early morning hours of July 18, 64 AD, to make an artistic statement (1:26:57 to 1:56:00). Vinicius rescues Lygia and her family. Nero blames Christians for the fire and arrests them and any sympathizers, including Vinicius. St. Peter tries to flee Rome, but has a vision of Christ on the road saying he is going to Rome to be killed in Peter's place. In jail Lygia and Vinicius are married by St. Peter. Poppaea, who desires Vinicius

and was rejected by him, gets her revenge. She has Lygia tied up in the arena with her bodyguard, the giant Ursus, who must try to kill a wild bull let loose therein with his bare hands. Vinicius is forced to watch. While Ursus wrestles with the bull, Vinicius, who was not a Christian, cries out, "Christ, give him strength." Ursus suddenly finds the strength to kill the bull. The crowd wants to save them, but Nero refuses. Vinicius breaks free and with the help of troops loyal to him frees Ursus and Lygia. He announces that General Galba is marching on Rome. The populace revolts. Nero flees to his palace and kills Poppaea, but is unable to commit suicide until a slave who loved him kills him just before the mob reaches him. Lygia and Vinicius live happily ever after.

A good film with some great action sequences, including the fire and the arena scenes. However, some of the acting seems a little bit stilted. See if you can spot Sophia Loren as an extra in the banquet scene.

Awards: *Academy Award Nominations*: Best Supporting Actor (Leo Genn and Peter Ustinov), Best Art Direction, Best Cinematography, Best Costume Design, Best Film Editing, Best Original Music Score, and Best Picture. *Golden Globe Wins*: Best Supporting Actor (Peter Ustinov) and Best Cinematography–Color. *Golden Globe Nomination*: Best Motion Picture–Drama

Source: Hibbert, Christopher. *Rome: The Biography of a City*. New York: W.W. Norton, 1985. This book at page 40 gives the date of the fire.

Alternate Film: *Glory*

19

LADY JANE

Year: 1986
Genre: Biography
Run Time: 2 hours 22 minutes
Availability: DVD and VHS (Paramount Home Video)
Director: Trevor Nunn; **Screenplay**: David Edgar
Cast: Helena Bonham Carter (Lady Jane Grey), Cary Elwes (Lord Guilford Dudley), Jane Lapotaire (Queen Mary), Patrick Stewart (Henry Grey, 1st Duke of Suffolk), Sara Kestelman (Lady Frances Brandon), Warren Saire (Edward VI)

The death of Henry VIII of England causes problems, as the new king, Edward VI, is under age and ill. John Dudley plots to put Edward's cousin Jane on the throne to keep his Catholic half-sister Mary off of it. He forces a marriage of Jane to his son. They resist at first but soon fall in love. When the king dies, Jane is proclaimed queen. However, she refuses to be a puppet and supports reformist ideas. The council abandons her and she is deposed on July 19, 1553 (1:40:59 to 1:48:11). A revolt is later raised against Mary, and Jane, her husband, and father are executed.

A feminist rewriting of history. Jane was not a reformist and she and her husband never got along. Still, it is entertaining.

Source: Porter, Linda. *The First Queen of England: The Myth of Bloody Mary*. New York: St. Martin's Press, 2007. This book at page 214 gives the date of her deposition.

Alternate Film: *The Lady*

20

VALKYRIE

Year: 2008
Genre: Suspense
Run Time: 2 hours 1 minute
Date Revealed in Film: 1:02:02
Availability: Blu-ray and DVD (Metro-Goldwyn-Mayer)
Director: Bryan Singer; **Screenplay**: Christopher McQuarrie and Nathan Alexander
Cast: Tom Cruise (Col. Claus von Stauffenberg), Kenneth Branagh (Maj. Gen. Henning von Tresckow), Bill Nighy (Gen. Friedrich Olbricht), Terence Stamp (Col. Gen. Ludwig Beck), Tom Wilkinson (Col. Gen. Friedrich Fromm), David Bamber (Adolf Hitler)

Colonel von Stauffenberg is disgusted with the Nazis for various reasons and is invited to join an anti-Hitler conspiracy, but he is reluctant because he doesn't think it can succeed. Later he changes his mind and proposes they use Plan Valkyrie, which uses the reserve army to put down any attempted coup by the SS if Hitler should die. But he suggests using the plan to arrest the SS and launch an actual coup. Gen. Fromm, head of the reserve army, says he's on Hitler's side, as long as Hitler lives, which the conspirators take to mean he will join them once Hitler is dead. Stauffenberg gets Hitler to sign new orders for the reserve army to seize Berlin in the event of trouble. On July 20, 1944, he goes to the Wolf's Lair and sets off a bomb. A conspirator cuts the phone lines and Stauffenberg flies back to Berlin. As the conspirators could not confirm Hitler was dead, Plan Valkyrie isn't activated until Stauffenberg arrives back in Berlin. The plan is going well until Hitler gets in contact with the reserve army troops (1:01:57 to 1:45:33). They crush the coup and all the plotters are executed.

A good thriller. Tells the story of a brave man who deserves to be remembered. The suspense keeps you on the edge of your seat throughout.

Alternate Film: *Robinson Crusoe on Mars*

21
AROUND THE WORLD IN EIGHTY DAYS

Year: 1956
Genre: Adventure
Run Time: 2 hours 55 minutes
Availability: DVD and VHS (Warner Home Video)
Director: Michael Anderson; **Screenplay**: James Poe, John Farrow, and S. J. Perelman, based on Jules Verne's novel
Cast: David Niven (Phileas Fogg), Cantinflas (Passepartout), Shirley MacLaine (Princess Aouda), Robert Newton (Mr. Fix), John Gielgud (Foster), John Carradine (Col. Proctor)

Hyper-meticulous Phileas Fogg hires the Frenchman Passepartout as his valet. Fogg bets other members of the Reform Club £20,000 that he can travel around the world in eighty days. He and Passepartout leave on the journey and reach Suez, where Passepartout meets Mr. Fix, who befriends him. He is a detective and thinks Fogg is the man who stole £55,000 from the Bank of England. They reach Bombay on July 21, 1872, and Passepartout gets in trouble over a sacred cow (1:05:40 to 1:14:00). They take a train across India, but the line is not finished and Fogg buys an elephant to travel on. Fogg helps save a young widow, Aouda, from being burned alive. She becomes their traveling companion. They sail from Calcutta to Hong Kong. Due to the machinations of Fix, Passepartout ends up alone in Japan with no money, while Fogg has to hire a ship to get him to that country and is only miraculously reunited with his valet. They all set sail for San Francisco. There Fogg trades insults with Colonel Proctor and gets on the train for New York. Fogg learns Colonel Proctor is on the train and they are set to fight a duel, but then Indians attack the train. Fogg leads a group of army volunteers and rescues the captured Passepartout. They use a sail-powered rail car to reach Omaha. From there they race to New York, but miss the boat to Liverpool. Fogg sails on the *Henrietta* and bribes the crew to redirect it to Liverpool. Fogg reaches Liverpool on the morning of the eightieth day, but is arrested by Fix. He is released hours later when it is learned the real robber was already arrested, but this delay is enough to put Fogg in London too late. However, a happy twist of fate is still ahead for our hero.

A star-studded Hollywood epic. This is a piece of mindless fun from Hollywood's golden age. Niven does a great job of portraying the imperturbable Mr. Fogg.

Awards: *Academy Award Wins*: Best Picture, Best Cinematography, Best Film Editing, Best Original Music Score, and Best Adapted Screenplay. *Academy Award Nominations*: Best Art Direction, Best Costume Design–Color, and Best Director. *Golden Globe Wins*: Best Motion Picture–Drama and Best Motion Picture Actor–Comedy/Musical (Cantinflas). *Golden Globe Nomination*: Best Motion Picture Director

Source: Verne, Jules. *Around the World in Eighty Days*. New York: Lancer Books, 1968. At page 56 the travelers reach Bombay. Also see the film at 20:02.

Alternate Film: *Inherit the Wind*

22

EXODUS

Year: 1960
Genre: Drama
Run Time: 3 hours 28 minutes
Availability: DVD (Metro-Goldwyn-Mayer), VHS (MGM/UA Home Video)
Director: Otto Preminger; **Screenplay**: Dalton Trumbo, based on Leon Uris's novel
Cast: Paul Newman (Ari Ben Canaan), Eva Marie Saint (Kitty Fremont), Ralph Richardson (Gen. Sutherland), Peter Lawford (Maj. Caldwell), Lee J.

Cobb (Barak Ben Canaan), Sal Mineo (Dov Landau), Jill Haworth (Karen Hanson)

Ari Ben Canaan, a Haganah operative, sneaks into Cyprus by boat. Kitty, a nurse and widow of a journalist killed in Palestine, goes to Carados Jewish refugee camp and meets Karen and Dov, two teenagers. Kitty offers to take Karen to America. Using fake orders, Ari requisitions trucks from the British and uses them to take Jewish refugees to a ship, but the harbor entrance is blocked before they can leave. They rename the ship *Exodus* and threaten to blow it up if the British board. Karen refuses to leave the ship with Kitty. The passengers start a hunger strike, which attracts international attention, and the British finally give in and let the ship go to Palestine. Karen goes to a kibbutz, Gan Dafna, and Dov joins the Irgun, a hard-line Jewish underground group. Kitty meets Ari again and they become romantically involved. On July 22, 1946, Dov blows up the King David Hotel for the Irgun (2:05:12 to 2:15:55). Akiva, Ari's uncle and leader of the Irgun, is arrested and sentenced to death. Dov and Ari get him out, but Akiva is killed during the escape and Ari wounded. He gradually recovers and the UN votes to partition Palestine. Kitty and Ari's relationship has blossomed. However, an attack by the Arabs on Gan Dafna leads to a tragic conclusion.

A so-so adaptation of a great book. It cuts out a lot of subplots and some characters. On the whole it's still worth watching.

Awards: *Academy Award Win*: Best Original Score. *Academy Award Nominations*: Best Supporting Actor (Sal Mineo) and Best Cinematography. *Golden Globe Win*: Best Supporting Actor (Mineo). *Golden Globe Nomination*: Best Original Score

Alternate Film: *Life as We Know It*

23

PATTON

Year: 1970
Genre: Biography
Run Time: 2 hours 52 minutes
Availability: Blu-ray and DVD (Twentieth Century Fox)

Director: Franklin J. Schaffner; **Screenplay**: Francis Ford Coppola and Edmund H. North, based on Ladislaus Farago's biography *Patton: Ordeal and Triumph* and Omar Bradley's memoir *A Soldier's Story*

Cast: George C. Scott (Gen. George S. Patton), Karl Malden (Gen. Omar Bradley), Stephen Young (Capt. Chester B. Hansen), Michael Strong (Brig. Gen. Hobart Carver), Michael Bates (Gen. Bernard Law Montgomery), Siegfried Rauch (Captain Steiger)

The film opens with Patton's über-patriotic speech. The scene shifts to Gen. Omar Bradley touring the Kasserine Pass battlefield. Patton is appointed to command the II Corps and moves to restore discipline, while we learn about Patton's belief in his past incarnations. After driving the Germans out of Africa, Patton meets and develops an intense dislike for the British general Montgomery. When he feels like Monty is getting the easy tasks in Sicily, Patton leads his army to capture Palermo on July 23, 1943 (1:10:23 to 1:12:25). Patton still beats the British to capture Messina. Patton gets in trouble when he slaps a soldier who is suffering from battle fatigue. The Germans are more impressed with his abilities than his own commanders, so he is relegated to commanding a nonexistent force to decoy the Germans away from Normandy. Eventually he is restored to an army command and fights across France and into Germany, saving the 101st airborne division at Bastogne along the way. He gets into trouble again for disparaging the Russians and employing ex-Nazis.

A different kind of biopic. Scott became Patton, giving an excellent and Oscar-worthy portrayal of the egotistic general. Famous for its often-parodied opening scene.

Awards: *Academy Award Wins*: Best Actor (George C. Scott), Best Picture, Best Director, Best Film Editing, Best Original Screenplay, Best Sound, and Best Art Direction. *Academy Award Nominations*: Best Cinematography, Best Visual Effects, and Best Original Score. *Golden Globe Win*: Best Motion Picture Actor–Drama (Scott). *Golden Globe Nominations*: Best Motion Picture–Drama and Best Motion Picture Director

Source: Blumenson, Merlin, ed. *The Patton Papers, Vol. 2*. New York: Houghton Mifflin, 1974. This book at page 207 gives the date of his arrival at Palermo.

Alternate Film: *The Music Man*

24

BONNIE AND CLYDE

Year: 1967

Genre: Biography

Run Time: 1 hour 51 minutes

Availability: Blu-ray and DVD (Warner Home Video)

Director: Arthur Penn; **Screenplay:** David Newman and Robert Benton

Cast: Warren Beatty (Clyde Barrow), Faye Dunaway (Bonnie Parker), Michael J. Pollard (C. W. Moss), Gene Hackman (Buck Barrow), Estelle Parsons (Blanche Barrow), Denver Pyle (Frank Hamer), Dub Taylor (Ivan Moss), Gene Wilder (Eugene Grizzard)

In Depression-era Texas small-time hood Clyde Barrow meets bored waitress Bonnie Parker and they join up, committing robberies along the way. They add C. W. Moss and Clyde's brother Buck and sister-in-law Blanche into the "Barrow Gang." They commit bank robberies and killings across the Midwest and become popular icons. After a shootout on July 24, 1933, Buck and Blanche are captured (1:24:30 to 1:28:33). The police promise C. W. Moss's father leniency for his son if he helps get Bonnie and Clyde. The police set a trap for the famous duo on a rural road.

Interesting study of these two misfit sociopaths. The film may have tried to make them heroes, but all the impartial observer is left with is the mindless violence. Both Bonnie and Clyde and the police kill with little or no compunction.

Awards: *Academy Award Wins*: Best Supporting Actress (Estelle Parsons) and Best Cinematography. *Academy Award Nominations*: Best Picture, Best Director, Best Writing–Story and Screenplay, Best Actor (Warren Beatty), Best Actress (Faye Dunaway), Best Supporting Actor (Michael J. Pollard), Best Supporting Actor (Gene Hackman), and Best Costume Design. *Golden Globe Nominations*: Best Motion Picture–Drama, Best Motion Picture Director, Best Motion Picture Actress–Drama (Dunaway), Best Motion Picture Actor–Drama (Beatty), Best Supporting Actor and Most Promising Newcomer–Male (Pollard), and Best Screenplay

Source: Guinn, Jeff. *Go Down Together*. New York: Simon and Schuster, 2009. This book at page 224 gives the date of Buck's capture.

Alternate Film: *Suburban Madness*

25

MATA HARI

Year: 1931

Genre: Biography

Run Time: 1 hour 29 minutes

Availability: DVD (Warner Home Video), VHS (MGM/UA Home Video)

Director: George Fitzmaurice; **Screenplay**: Benjamin Glazer, Leo Birinski, Doris Anderson, and Gilbert Emery

Cast: Greta Garbo (Mata Hari), Ramon Novarro (Lt. Alexis Rosanoff), Lionel Barrymore (Gen. Serge Shubin), Lewis Stone (Andriani), C. Henry Gordon (Dubois), Karen Morley (Carlotta), Alec B. Francis (Maj. Caron), Blanche Federici (Sister Angelica)

Mata Hari, an exotic dancer in Paris in the Great War, is suspected by Dubois, the head of French counterintelligence, of being a spy, but he can't get any evidence against her. Mata Hari is surrounded by a coterie of officers, diplomats, and government officials. At a rendezvous with Shubin, a Russian general, she learns that important dispatches have come from Russia and that Ronsoff, a Russian pilot who is attracted to her, has them. She lures Ronsoff into an amorous interlude. Her compatriots use Ronsoff's inattention to his job to steal and photograph the dispatches. Dubois tells Shubin that Mata Hari is in love with Rosanhoff, and, out of jealousy, Shubin calls to turn her in, but Mata Hari shoots him, making it look like suicide. Mata Hari's controller plans to send her to Holland, but she learns Rosanoff is injured in a crash and stays to be with him. Mata Hari is arrested and at the trial, trying to save Rosanoff, implicates herself and is found guilty. On July 25, 1917, she is sentenced to death (1:18:22 to 1:18:53). Mata Hari is shot as a spy.

This is the oldest film on this list and it shows. The action doesn't move as smoothly as in later films, and everything seems kind of overacted and heavy-handed. However, we do get to see that famous film icon Greta Garbo in one of her classic roles.

Source: Shipman, Pat. *Femme Fatale: Love, Lies and the Unknown Life of Mata Hari*. New York: William Morrow, 2007. This book at page 355 gives the date of her sentencing.

Alternate Film: *Henry of Navarre*

26
EVITA
Year: 1996
Genre: Musical/Drama
Run Time: 2 hours 15 minutes
Availability: Blu-ray and DVD (Disney/Buena Vista)
Director: Alan Parker; Screenplay: Alan Parker, Oliver Stone, and Tim Rice
Cast: Madonna (Evita Perón), Antonio Banderas (Che), Jonathan Pryce (Juan
    Perón), Jimmy Nail (Agustin Magaldi)

It is announced that Evita ("Eva") Perón has died (2:08 to 4:28). We then flash back to when Evita Duarte was born out of wedlock and she and her mother are not allowed to attend her father's funeral. Eva has an affair with Magaldi, a tango singer, and persuades him to take her to Buenos Aires. She becomes the mistress of increasingly powerful men. She is a model, an actress, and becomes a popular radio personality. Then she meets Col. Juan Perón at a benefit he organized for the victims of an earthquake. She uses her radio show to promote him, even using her crowd appeal to get him released from jail. Peron becomes president and Eva tries to aid the poor, while the political elite despise her common roots. She becomes ill and dies on July 26, 1952, prompting an outpouring of grief (2:02:33 to 2:05:46).

An interesting story of a very interesting character. Who was the real Evita? Was it the poor girl thrust into prominence or a rich radio star who played on her poor roots to gain wealth and power? We'll never really know. Unusual film in that there are probably only fifty words of spoken dialogue in the whole film. The rest is the great songs of Tim Rice and Andrew Lloyd Weber.

Awards: *Academy Award Win*: Best Song. *Academy Award Nominations*: Best Art Direction, Best Cinematography, Best Film Editing, and Best Sound. *Golden Globe Wins*: Best Motion Picture–Comedy/Musical, Best Performance by an Actress in a Motion Picture–Comedy/Musical (Madonna), and Best Original Song–Motion Picture. *Golden Globe Nominations*: Best Director–Motion Picture and Best Performance by an Actor in a Motion Picture–Comedy/Musical (Banderas)

Source: de Elia, Tomas, and Queiroz, Juan Pablo. *Evita: An Intimate Portrait of Eva Perón*. New York: Rizzoli, 1997. This book at page 166 gives her death date.

Alternate Film: *Guadalcanal Diary*

27

HIGH NOON

Year: 1952
Genre: Western
Run Time: 1 hour 25 minutes
Date Revealed in Film: 5:16, 7:11, and 54:35
Availability: Blu-ray and DVD (Olive Films)
Director: Fred Zinnemann; **Screenplay**: Carl Foreman, based on John W. Cunningham's magazine story "The Tin Star"
Cast: Gary Cooper (Marshal Will Kane), Grace Kelly (Amy Kane), Lloyd Bridges (Deputy Sheriff Harvey Pell), Katy Jurado (Helen Ramirez), Ian MacDonald (Frank Miller), Sheb Wooley (Ben Miller), Lee Van Cleef (Jack Colby)

At 10:35 AM, Sunday July 27, 1873, three gunmen ride through Hadleyville to the train depot, passing by the Justice of the Peace's office, where the town marshal, Will Kane, is marrying Quaker Amy Fowler. At the depot the three gunmen settle in to wait for the noon train. Kane reluctantly turns in his badge, as the new marshal will not arrive until tomorrow. They learn that Frank Miller, whom Kane had sent to jail, has been released and is coming on the noon train to get revenge on Kane, together with the three gunmen waiting at the depot. Kane leaves at his wife's request, but changes his mind and returns to the town. Amy tells Kane if he doesn't leave right now she will be on the noon train without him and heads for the station when he refuses. Deputy Pell, who thinks Kane sabotaged Pell's efforts to replace him, refuses to aid Kane unless he gets the marshal's job. Kane refuses and Pell quits. Kane visits Helen, a former flame of his to tell her Frank Miller is back, as she used to also be Frank's girlfriend, but she already knows. Kane can't get anyone in the town to become deputies. Pell tries to get Kane to leave town and after he refuses they fight, with Pell being knocked out. When the whistle of the noon train is heard, Kane comes out to stand in the empty street in time to see Helen and Amy riding to the depot together. The noon train arrives, and Frank Miller gets off and Amy and Helen get on. The four gunmen walk to town, beginning a classic cinematic gunfight that ends with Kane and Miller facing each other down. (The entire film takes place on July 27, 1873.)

A classic western film. It is a story about the courage to do the right thing even when you are afraid and alone. Kane faces up to evil alone, as all of the townspeople prefer to take the easy route and do nothing.

Awards: *Academy Award Wins*: Best Actor (Gary Cooper), Best Film Editing, Best Original Music Score, and Best Song. *Academy Award Nominations*: Best Director, Best Picture, and Best Adapted Screenplay. *Golden Globe Wins*: Best Motion Picture Actor–Drama (Cooper), Best Supporting Actress (Katy Jurado), Best Motion Picture Score, and Best Cinematography–Black-and-White. *Golden Globe Nominations*: Best Motion Picture Drama, Most Promising Newcomer–Female (Jurado), and Best Screenplay

Alternate Film: *Who Is Clark Rockefeller?*

28

WITHOUT LIMITS

Year: 1998
Genre: Biography
Run Time: 1 hour 57 minutes
Date Revealed in Film: 53:58
Availability: DVD and VHS (Warner Home Video)
Director: Robert Towne; **Screenplay**: Robert Towne and Kenny Moore
Cast: Billy Crudup (Steve Prefontaine), Donald Sutherland (Bill Bowerman), Monica Potter (Mary Marckx), Jeremy Sisto (Frank Shorter), Judith Ivey (Barbara Bowerman), Dean Norris (Dellinger), Billy Burke (Kenny Moore), Frank Shorter (Fred Long)

We start at the 1972 Olympics in Munich, the 5,000-meter race, then flash back. Steve Prefontaine is recruited by many colleges for their track program, but he's finally persuaded to go to Oregon by Coach Bill Bowerman. The first day at Oregon Steve sees and falls instantly in love with Mary Marckx. Steve ignores the rule about no racing during workouts as well as the coach's advice that he not start a race in the lead, but Steve goes on to beat Stanford anyway. Steve dates Mary, but she says he's not her type. Bowerman warns that leading from the start of a race costs time by wearing out too fast, but Steve says he wants to run "flat out" and not "steal" the race at the end. At the 1970 NCAA championships, Steve is injured during an amorous encounter, but runs and wins the next day anyway. He persuades Mary to give him a chance and they start a relationship. At the AAU meet in Oulu, Finland, on July 28, 1971, Colin Ponder, head of the American AAU, does not allow Steve to run, so Steve attacks him (53:57 to 56:15). Back at Oregon the coach gives him a plan to win and in the Olympic trials he sets a new record in the 5,000 meters. When Steve finishes fourth in the 5,000-meter Olympic race he goes into a deep funk. He turns down $200,000 to turn pro and reconnects with Mary. Then tragedy strikes.

An interesting sports biopic. Prefontaine and Bowerman have totally different "theories" of running. Steve wants to run flat out all the time, while Bowerman favors any strategy that will result in a win.

Awards: *Golden Globe Nomination*: Best Performance by an Actor in a Supporting Role in a Motion Picture (Donald Sutherland)

Alternate Film: *Bridesmaids*

29
WHAT'S UP, DOC?

Year: 1972
Genre: Romantic Comedy
Run Time: 1 hour 34 minutes
Date Revealed in Film: 1:16:23–25, 1:23:19–20
Availability: Blu-ray and DVD (Warner Home Video)
Director: Peter Bogdanovich; **Screenplay**: Peter Bogdanovich, Buck Henry, David Newman, and Robert Benton
Cast: Barbra Streisand (Judy Maxwell), Ryan O'Neal (Howard Bannister), Madeline Kahn (Eunice Burns), Kenneth Mars (Hugh Simon), Austin Pendleton (Frederick Larrabee), Sorrell Booke (Harry), Randy Quaid (Professor Hosquith)

A group of travelers with identical plaid traveling cases packed with top-secret documents, jewelry, rocks, clothes, and lingerie arrive in San Francisco on July 29, 1972 (3:11 to 47:58). The rocks belong to absent-minded music professor Howard Bannister, who with his domineering fiancée, Eunice Burns, has come to the Congress of American Musicologists convention, where he hopes to win the $20,000 Larrabee grant for a paper on prehistoric man's musical igneous rocks. Howard goes to get aspirin and meets free spirit Judy Maxwell, who flirts with him. At the banquet Judy impersonates Eunice as "Burnsie" and impresses Larrabee, so that when Eunice does show up, Howard says he doesn't know her. Through a series of break-ins the bags get mixed up and moved around. Howard returns to his room, finds Judy in the tub, and chaos ensues. The next morning Howard meets Judy in the hotel's unfinished penthouse, and they have an amorous interlude. Howard wins the grant and is invited to a reception at Larrabee's house. Everyone eventually realizes they have the wrong case, and they race to Larrabee's house, where a riot occurs. Howard and Judy take all the bags and drive off on a stolen bicycle. The others follow in a classic comedy chase scene. They are all arrested and hauled into court, where the judge turns out to be Judy's father. Howard is about to lose the grant until Judy remembers a significant fact that changes the course of events.

A hilarious slapstick comedy with many laugh-out-loud lines. O'Neal's deadpan delivery and Madeline Kahn's over-the-top performance make this one of the all-time classics of comedy. As hard as it is to believe today, the film was not nominated for even one Academy Award.

Awards: *Golden Globe Nomination*: Most Promising Newcomer–Female (Madeline Kahn)

Alternate Film: *The Winslow Boy*

30
COLD MOUNTAIN
Year: 2003
Genre: Period Drama
Run Time: 2 hours 34 minutes
Availability: Blu-ray (Lionsgate Films), DVD (Miramax)
Director: Anthony Minghella; **Screenplay**: Anthony Minghella, based on Charles Frazier's novel
Cast: Jude Law (W. P. Inman), Nicole Kidman (Ada Monroe), Renée Zellweger (Ruby Thewes), Brendan Gleeson (Stobrod Thewes), Philip Seymour Hoffman (Reverend Veasey), Natalie Portman (Sara), Donald Sutherland (Reverend Monroe)

On July 30, 1864 (1:10 to 5:19), the Yankees detonate a bomb under the Confederate lines at Petersburg. We flash back to when Ada Monroe and her minister father arrive in Cold Mountain, North Carolina, from Charleston and she meets W. P. Inman. In the Battle of the Crater, Inman is wounded (9:12 to 16:53 and 22:38 to 24:18). Ada and Inman's developing relationship is interrupted by the start of the Civil War. Inman joins the Confederate Army, but Ada says she will wait for him. Things become difficult for Ada after her father dies. Deserters are made subject to the death penalty. Ada has a vision of Inman returning to her. Ruby Thewes shows up to help Ada run her farm. Inman has deserted and is walking back home. He runs into an immoral minister named Veasey, is arrested as a deserter, and is wounded. Teague, the leader of the Cold Mountain home guard who has his eye on Ada, kills neighbors of Ada. Stobrod Thewes, Ruby's estranged father and a deserter, and his two pals Pangle and Georgia show up at Cold Mountain. Teague and the Home Guard track down Stobrod's group. Pangle is killed and Stobrod is injured. Ruby nurses her father back to health and they are reconciled. Inman arrives at Cold Mountain and he and Ada have one night together. However, Teague is on Inman's trail and this leads to a final confrontation.

A very good romantic drama. Both Inman and Ada are admirable for being faithful to each other even though they both go through difficult circumstances.

Awards: *Academy Award Win*: Best Supporting Actress (Renée Zellweger). *Academy Award Nominations*: Best Actor (Jude Law), Best Cinematography, Best Editing, Best Original Score, and Best Original Song

Source: Weigley, Russell. *A Great Civil War*. Bloomington: Indiana University Press, 2000. This book at page 340 gives the date of the blast.

Alternate Film: *The Caine Mutiny*

31

THE LAST EMPEROR

Year: 1987
Genre: Biography
Run Time: 2 hours 43 minutes
Availability: Blu-ray and DVD (Criterion)
Director: Bernardo Bertolucci; **Screenplay**: Mark Peploe and Bernardo Bertolucci, based on Henry Pu Yi's autobiography, *The Last Manchu*
Cast: John Lone (Pu Yi as adult), Joan Chen (Wanrong), Peter O'Toole (Reginald Johnston), Ying Ruocheng (Detention Centre Governor), Victor

Wong (Chen Baochen), Dennis Dun (Big Li), Ryuichi Sakamoto (Amakasu Masahiko), Maggie Han (Eastern Jewel)

Little Pu Yi is taken to the Forbidden City to meet the dowager empress, and later he becomes emperor. He lives in the Forbidden City in splendid isolation. Eventually he learns he has been deposed. In 1919 Reginald Johnston, a Scot, becomes his tutor. Pu Yi's mother dies and he tries to leave the Forbidden City to see her body, but this is not allowed. Pu Yi is married to Wan Jang and Wen Xiu. His attempt to take charge results in a fire that destroys the royal storerooms and the expulsion of the royal eunuchs. In 1924 Pu Yi is forced out of the Forbidden City. He lives in Tientsin as a rich playboy, financed by the Japanese. His second wife leaves him and he goes to Manchuria. In 1935 he is crowned emperor of Manchuria, which causes conflict with his wife, as she recognizes he is just a puppet of the Japanese. After a visit to Japan Pu Yi too learns he has no real power. The Soviets invade, capture Pu Yi, and imprison him for five years. He is turned over to the Chinese on July 31, 1950 (2:08 to 6:32, 20:05 to 21:52). The Chinese subject him to reeducation and interrogate him many times to get him to confess. He is freed in 1959. During the Cultural Revolution he tries to save his former jailer.

An interesting film. The shots actually filmed in the Forbidden City are spectacular. It glosses over some of the more unpleasant events of his imprisonment.

Awards: *Academy Award Wins*: Best Picture, Best Art Direction, Best Cinematography, Best Costume Design, Best Director, Best Film Editing, Best Music–Original Score, Best Sound, and Best Adapted Screenplay. *Golden Globe Wins*: Best Director–Motion Picture, Best Screenplay–Motion Picture, Best Original Score–Motion Picture, and Best Motion Picture–Drama. *Golden Globe Nomination*: Best Performance by an Actor in a Motion Picture–Drama (John Lone)

Source: Pu Yi, Henry. *The Last Manchu*. New York: G. P. Putnam's Sons, 1967. This book at page 279 gives the date of his return.

Alternate Film: *Run Silent, Run Deep*

August

THE PIANIST

Year: 2002
Genre: Historical Drama
Run Time: 2 hours 30 minutes
Date Revealed in Film: 1:43:46
Availability: DVD and VHS (Universal)
Director: Roman Polanski; **Screenplay**: Ronald Harwood, based on Wladyslaw Szpilman's memoir
Cast: Adrien Brody (Wladyslaw Szpilman), Thomas Kretschmann (Captain Wilm Hosenfeld), Frank Finlay (Father Szpilman), Maureen Lipman (Mother Szpilman), Ronan Vibert (Andrzej Bogucki), Ruth Platt (Janina Bogucki), Emilia Fox (Dorota)

Wladyslaw Szpilman is a pianist caught up in the German invasion of Poland at the start of World War II. He and his family are forced into the ghetto, since they are Jewish, and then all of his family but Wladyslaw are sent to Treblinka. One day Wladyslaw sees Janina Bogucki, a friend from prewar days. He contacts her and is hidden in an apartment and Janina's brother brings him food. Then Andrzej Bogucki is arrested, but Wladyslaw continues to hide until he runs out of food. He leaves and makes contact with Dorota, a girl he knew in the early days of the war, who gets him a new apartment in a German sector of the city. His main enemy here is boredom. On August 1, 1944 (1:43:44 to 1:45:42), the Warsaw uprising begins. When the Germans begin shelling his building he has to leave and start scrounging in the ruins, where a German officer, Captain Wilm Hosenfeld, discovers him. He lets Wladyslaw hide in the attic and brings him food. Eventually the Soviets capture the city. Then Wladyslaw gets a request for help that tests the limits of his humanity.

A moving film. Wladyslaw endures a lot, but he has an eternally optimistic nature that helps him get through the tough times. Showcases the brave people who, at the risk of their own lives, helped him survive.

Awards: *Academy Award Wins*: Best Actor (Adrien Brody), Best Director, and Best Adapted Screenplay. *Academy Award Nominations*: Best Picture, Best Film Editing, Best Cinematography, and Best Costume Design. *Golden Globe Nominations*: Best Motion Picture–Drama and Best Performance by an Actor in a Motion Picture–Drama (Brody)

Alternate Film: *Rush* (2013)

2

WILD BILL

Year: 1995

Genre: Western

Run Time: 1 hour 38 minutes

Availability: DVD and VHS (MGM Home Entertainment)

Director: Walter Hill; **Screenplay**: Walter Hill, based on Pete Dexter's book *Deadwood* and Thomas Babe's play *Fathers and Sons*

Cast: Jeff Bridges (Wild Bill Hickok), Ellen Barkin (Calamity Jane), John Hurt (Charley Prince), Diane Lane (Susannah Moore), Keith Carradine (Buffalo Bill), David Arquette (Jack McCall), Christina Applegate (Lurline Newcomb), Bruce Dern (Will Plummer)

Wild Bill Hickok is a hard-drinking, card-playing, fast-shooting western legend who drifts from town to town, finally ending up in Deadwood, Dakota Territory. There he meets an old lover, Calamity Jane, but he rejects her offer to renew their relationship. He also meets Jack McCall, who says he is going to kill Wild Bill for seducing and then abandoning his mother. Hickok's feelings for Susannah Moore, McCall's mother, leads him to not kill McCall outright. After an unsuccessful attempt to kill Hickok, McCall hires a gang to help him do the job. While practically the entire population of Deadwood has left to scout out a new gold strike, McCall and his gang find Hickok in a compromising position with Calamity Jane. However, after toying with Hickok for hours in a saloon, McCall says he can't kill Hickok and lets him go. On August 2, 1876, Hickok kills all the gang members and returns to the saloon. McCall finally works up the nerve and shoots Hickok in the back of the head while Wild Bill is holding "the dead man's hand," two black aces and two black eights (1:21:08 to 1:31:55).

A somewhat fanciful, but interesting biopic.

Source: Nash, Jay Robert. *Encyclopedia of Western Lawmen and Outlaws*. New York: Paragon House, 1992. This book at page 158 gives Hickok's death date.

Alternate Film: *Hannibal* (2006)

3
THE LAST OF THE MOHICANS

Year: 1992
Genre: Action/Adventure
Run Time: 1 hour 57 minutes
Availability: Blu-ray and DVD (Twentieth Century Fox)
Director: Michael Mann; **Screenplay**: Michael Mann and Christopher Crowe, based on James Fenimore Cooper's novel
Cast: Daniel Day-Lewis (Hawkeye), Madeleine Stowe (Cora Munro), Russell Means (Chingachgook), Eric Schweig (Uncas), Jodhi May (Alice Munro), Steven Waddington (Maj. Duncan Heyward), Wes Studi (Magua), Maurice Roëves (Col. Edmund Munro)

In 1757 in upstate New York Capt. Heyward and a native guide, Magua, are escorting Cora and Alice Munro, daughters of Col. Munro, the commander to Fort William Henry. Magua is a traitor and they are attacked by the Hurons, but saved by Hawkeye and his adoptive Native American father, Chingachgook, and brother, Uncas. They escort them to the fort, arriving the day the French siege begins, August 3, 1757 (34:05 to 47:15). With Hawkeye's help a runner is sent to get help. The militia wants to leave to defend their homes, as they were promised. Col. Munro refuses, so Hawkeye helps them desert and is sentenced to hang. The French commander offers generous terms: the garrison can go to Albany if they pledge not to fight again. Since no help is coming, Col. Munro agrees. The British march out, but are attacked by Hurons led by Magua, who has an implacable hatred for Col. Munro. Hawkeye, Chingachgook, Uncas, Cora, Alice, and Heyward escape and reach a cave behind a waterfall. With wet powder they can't shoot, so to avoid a fight that might get the women killed, Hawkeye and the two natives leap into the river and escape, after Hawkeye promises to retrieve Cora. The sisters and Heyward are captured. Negotiations with the Hurons result in Heyward being killed, Cora released, and Alice taken by Magua. After a duel between Uncas and Magua, Alice makes a shocking decision.

An interesting, if violent, film. Lots of action and smoldering romance. More historical soap opera than real history, but very watchable nonetheless.

Awards: *Academy Award Win*: Best Sound. *Golden Globe Nomination*: Best Original Score–Motion Picture

Sources: Fowler, William M. Jr. *Empires at War*. New York: Walker & Co., 2005. This book at pages 122–23 gives the siege's start date. Cooper, James F. *The Last of the Mohicans*. New York: Charles Scribner's Sons, 1947. This book at page 150 says they arrived on the first day of the siege.

Alternate Film: *The Wedding Singer*

4

THE DIARY OF ANNE FRANK

Year: 1959

Genre: Drama

Run Time: 3 hours

Date Revealed in Film: 2:39:16–17

Availability: Blu-ray and DVD (Twentieth Century Fox)

Director: George Stevens; **Screenplay**: Frances Goodrich and Albert Hackett, based on Anne Frank's memoir, *The Diary of a Young Girl*

Cast: Millie Perkins (Anne Frank), Joseph Schildkraut (Otto Frank), Shelley Winters (Petronella van Daan), Richard Beymer (Peter van Daan), Gusti Huber (Edith Frank), Lou Jacobi (Hans van Daan), Diane Baker (Margot Frank), Ed Wynn (Albert Dussell)

In 1942 in occupied Holland, the Jewish Frank family goes into hiding from the Nazis in the Secret Annex. Anne receives a diary. The van Daans and Dr. Dussell move in later. The tight quarters are tough on everyone and a lot of petty arguments erupt. Anne and Peter van Daan argue, but later share their first kiss. Burglars break into the building at least twice, and the residents are terrified a police investigation will find them. The group also has to deal with air raids and starvation rations. The arrest of the grocer who had unknowingly been supplying their food leads to their discovery and arrest on August 4, 1944 (2:37:03 to 2:50:48).

A moving story of tragedy and hope. If you can feel the loss of Anne Frank and multiply it by eleven million you can come close to comprehending what the Nazis did to the world. One of those rare films whose message is much more than mere entertainment.

Awards: *Academy Award Wins*: Best Supporting Actress (Shelley Winters), Best Cinematography, and Best Art Direction. *Academy Award Nominations*: Best Picture, Best Supporting Actor (Ed Wynn), Best Costume Design, Best Director, and Best Original Score. *Golden Globe Win*: Best Film Promoting International Understanding. *Golden Globe Nominations*: Best Motion Picture–Drama, Best Motion Picture Director, Best Motion Picture Actor–Drama (Joseph Schildkraut), and Best Supporting Actress (Winters)

Alternate Film: *Liz and Dick*

5

BRAVEHEART

Year: 1995
Genre: Drama
Run Time: 2 hours 57 minutes
Availability: Blu-ray (Warne Home Video), DVD (Paramount Pictures)
Director: Mel Gibson; **Screenplay**: Randall Wallace
Cast: Mel Gibson (William Wallace), Patrick McGoohan (King Edward I), Angus Macfadyen (Robert the Bruce), Brendan Gleeson (Hamish Campbell), Sophie Marceau (Princess Isabelle), Peter Hanly (Prince Edward), Ian Bannen (Robert de Brus)

Edward I of England has occupied Scotland and this leads to the deaths of William Wallace's father and brothers. Wallace is raised abroad, but returns and marries his childhood sweetheart Murron in secret to avoid the droit de seigneur. English soldiers attempt to rape her, but after they are beaten off she is executed for assaulting them. Wallace and some companions kill some English officials. Scotland rises in revolt. Wallace's army defeats the English on several occasions and contacts Robert the Bruce, chief contender for the throne. Bruce's father wants to secure the throne for his son by collaboration with the English. Wallace is almost captured at the Battle of Falkirk, but goes underground to lead a guerilla war. He meets the English princess Isabelle and they have a tryst, leading to her pregnancy. The English finally capture Wallace on August 5, 1305 (2:27:08 to 2:30:05) and he pays the price.

A rousing adventure. The complete lack of historical accuracy lessened my liking of this movie. Facts are created or discarded for this entertaining but inaccurate film

Awards: *Academy Award Wins*: Best Cinematography, Best Director, Best Makeup, Best Picture, and Best Sound Editing. *Academy Award Nominations*: Best Costume Design, Best Film Editing, Best Original Dramatic Score, Best Sound, and Best Original Screenplay. *Golden Globe Win*: Best Director–Motion Picture. *Golden Globe Nominations*: Best Motion Picture–Drama, Best Screenplay–Motion Picture, and Best Original Score–Motion Picture

Source: Bruce, Duncan A. *The Scottish 100: Portraits of History's Most Influential Scots*. New York: Carroll and Graf Publishers, 2000. This book at page 208 gives the date of Wallace's arrest.

Alternate Film: *The Omega Man*

6

ABOVE AND BEYOND

Year: 1952 (Metro-Goldwyn-Mayer)

Genre: Drama

Run Time: 2 hours 2 minutes

Availability: VHS (Turner Entertainment Company)

Director: Melvin Frank and Norman Panama; **Screenplay**: Beirne Lay Jr., Melvin Frank, and Norman Panama

Cast: Robert Taylor (Col. Paul W. Tibbets), Eleanor Parker (Lucey Tibbets), James Whitmore (Maj. William Uanna), Larry Keating (Maj. Gen. Vernon C. Brent), Larry Gates (Capt. William Sterling Parsons), Marilyn Erskine (Marge Bratton)

Lt. Col. Paul W. Tibbets is plucked from flying bombing missions in North Africa to become chief test pilot for the new B-29 bomber. He accepts the assignment even though it means continued separation from his wife. When the B-29 is pronounced ready for combat, he's selected to head Operation Silverplate, the preparation of a unit to deliver the atomic bomb to the target. Tibbets's wife feels lonely and alienated, especially when she has her second child without her husband by her side. Tibbets had planned not to bring his wife since he would not be able to confide in her, but reluctantly agrees to let his wife move to the base when she learns the other wives are there. Friction develops between the Tibbets, as she thinks he's acting like a self-important, perfectionist marionette, while he thinks she's continually doing and saying things she shouldn't. As the project nears its conclusion, he sends her away. The squadron flies to the Pacific and on August 6, 1945, drops the atom bomb on Hiroshima (1:40:35 to 1:58:50). This has a dramatic effect on the Tibbets's marriage.

More of what I would call a soap opera film than a war movie. Still, the characters are well developed and the story holds your interest.

Awards: *Academy Award Nominations*: Best Screenplay and Best Original Score

Source: Dupuy, R. Ernest, and Dupuy, Trevor N. *The Encyclopedia of Military History from 3500 B.C. to the Present*. New York: Harper & Row, 1977. This book at page 1,197 gives the date of the bombing.

Alternate Film: *Blow*

7

GALLIPOLI

Year: 1981
Genre: Adventure
Run Time: 1 hour 50 minutes
Date Revealed in Film: 1:45:46
Availability: DVD and VHS (Paramount Home Video)
Director: Peter Weir; **Screenplay**: David Williamson

Cast: Mark Lee (Archy Hamilton), Mel Gibson (Frank Dunne), Bill Hunter (Maj. Barton)

In western Australia in May 1915 word of the Gallipoli landings have reached Archie Hamilton, an eighteen-year-old stockman and runner, who even wins a race against a man on horseback. Frank Dunne, an unemployed rail worker enters a race in hopes of winning a prize, but loses to Archie and they strike up a friendship. As he is underage, Archie travels to Perth, where he is unknown, to enlist in the Tenth Light Horse, and Frank joins the infantry. Both are shipped to Egypt for training. Frank transfers to the Light Horse and the unit is sent to Gallipoli. On the morning of August 7, 1915, Major Barton tells Archie that he is to be the "runner" for the regimental commander, but he declines so Frank will be picked instead. After two charges against the Turkish trenches are wiped out, Barton sends a message to General Robinson at brigade HQ for the third charge to be canceled, but Robinson insists the attack continue. Frank suggests going over Robinson's head to General Gardiner, but as the phone lines are out Frank has to run there. Gardiner cancels the attack, and as Frank races back to the trenches with the order canceling the scheduled attack it becomes a race between life and death (1:33:47 to 1:48:03).

One of the best antiwar films ever made. If after watching this film you don't think war is to be the very last option instead of the first, then you are totally without any morals at all. Just think of the lost potential represented by Archie and multiply it by the sixteen million soldiers killed in World War I alone and it makes you want to cry.

Awards: *Golden Globe Nomination*: Best Foreign Film
Alternate Film: *Is Paris Burning?*

8

BUSTER

Year: 1988
Genre: Biography
Run Time: 1 hour 42 minutes
Availability: DVD (Metro-Goldwyn-Mayer), VHS (HBO Video)
Director: David Green; **Screenplay**: Colin Shindler
Cast: Phil Collins (Buster Edwards), Julie Walters (June Edwards), Larry Lamb (Bruce Reynolds), Stephanie Lawrence (Franny Reynolds), Ellie

Beaven (Nicky Edwards), Ralph Brown (Ronald Biggs); Martin Jarvis (Inspector Jack Mitchell)

Small-time English hood "Buster" gets involved with and participates in the "Great Train Robbery" on August 8, 1963, resulting in the largest robbery to date in Great Britain (17:13 to 27:11). He and his family live underground for a while, but finally make it to Mexico, where they have trouble adjusting. His wife returns to Britain and "Buster" eventually follows her back, knowing he faces certain arrest. He's picked up and does fifteen years. He runs a flower stand for twelve years.

An interesting film about a quirky character. Phil Collins and Julie Walters are very good. Breaks the fourth wall at the end to address the audience directly.

Awards: *Academy Award Nomination*: Best Original Song. *Golden Globe Win*: Best Original Song–Motion Picture

Source: Yapp, Nick. *True Crime*. Bath, UK: Parragon Publishing, 2006. This book at page 42 gives the date of the robbery.

Alternative Film: *Casualties of War*

9

EMPIRE OF THE SUN

Year: 1987

Genre: Drama

Run Time: 2 hours 32 minutes

Availability: Blu-ray and DVD (Warner Home Video)

Director: Steven Spielberg; **Screenplay**: Tom Stoppard, based on J. G. Ballard's novel

Cast: Christian Bale (Jim Graham), John Malkovich (Basie), Miranda Richardson (Mrs. Victor), Nigel Havers (Dr. Rawlins)

Jim Graham lives a privileged life with his family in the European Settlement in Shanghai. When the Japanese attack after Pearl Harbor, Jim is separated from his family. He avoids capture for a while, hiding out in the abandoned European quarter, but is eventually captured and interned. Basie, an American POW, befriends him. Jim becomes a trader in the camp and idolizes the camp doctor, Rawlins. Basie has Jim set traps for game outside the wire to see if the area is mined. The camp is mistakenly attacked by U.S. Mustang fighters and evacuated by the Japanese. Basie escapes alone, breaking his promise to Jim to take him with him. During the march Jim observes in the distance the flash of the Nagasaki atomic bombing on August 9, 1945 (2:09:02 to 2:10:18). After Japan's surrender Jim returns to the camp nearly dead from hunger. He meets a Japanese pilot whom he had befriended earlier and who offers Jim some food. Basie arrives with armed survivors to loot air-dropped Red Cross packages. They kill the Japanese pilot, upsetting Jim. He is finally reunited with his parents.

This edgy film is based on a true story. Combines the war and coming-of-age genres. Jim grows up too fast in this film.

Awards: *Academy Award Nominations*: Best Art Direction, Best Cinematography, Best Editing, Best Music Score, Best Costume Design, and Best Sound. *Golden Globe Nominations*: Best Motion Picture–Drama and Best Original Score–Motion Picture

Source: Dupuy, R. Ernest, and Dupuy, Trevor N. *The Encyclopedia of Military History from 3500 B.C. to the Present*. New York: Harper & Row, 1977. This book at page 1,197 gives the date of the bombing.

Alternate Film: *What Ever Happened to Baby Jane?*

10

BEYOND RANGOON

Year: 1995
Genre: Drama
Run Time: 1 hour 40 minutes
Availability: DVD (Warner Home Video)
Director: John Boorman; **Screenplay**: Alex Lasker and Bill Rubenstein
Cast: Patricia Arquette (Laura Bowman), Frances McDormand (Andy Bowman), U Aung Ko (U Aung Ko), Johnny Cheah (Min Han), Adelle Lutz (Aung San Suu Kyi), Spalding Gray (Jeremy Watt), Tiara Jacquelina (San San), Victor Slezak (Mr. Scott)

Laura Bowman takes a trip to Burma after her husband and son are killed in a home invasion. One night, Laura leaves her hotel in Rangoon, and at an antigovernment protest she sees the bravery of Aung San Suu Kyi. Laura has to stay in Burma because she lost her passport. She meets U Aung Ko, who takes Laura sightseeing. Their car breaks down, but they reach the house of

Ko's former students. Ko used to be a college professor who was banned from teaching. Laura has a breakdown and tells Ko what happened to her family. The 8888 revolt has begun. Ko takes Laura to get a train to Rangoon, but when Ko is beaten by troops, she gets him in the car and drives off. Ko is shot and wounded, but they escape and get on a raft to Rangoon. There Laura, who is a doctor, operates on Ko. The next day on August 10, 1988 (53:43 to 1:04:44), the raft stops at a village. Laura goes to find drugs for Ko, and takes a pistol with her. Laura finds the drugs she needs, but has to shoot a soldier to keep from being raped. When they arrive in Rangoon, the city is in the throes of a full-scale revolt, and Laura can't get to the U.S. embassy. Laura and Ko go to the border and try a daring escape to Thailand.

This is a very good film with a spiritual message. An overlooked true classic.

Source: Steinberg, David. *Burma/Myanmar: What Everyone Needs to Know.* New York: Oxford University Press, 2010. This book at page 78 gives the start date of the 8888 riots and this is two days after that. The film at 1:15 says it is August 1988.

Alternate Film: *Sunrise at Campobello*

11
JULIE AND JULIA
Year: 2009
Genre: Biography
Run Time: 2 hours 3 minutes
Date Revealed in Film: 18:20
Availability: Blu-ray and DVD (Sony Pictures)
Director: Nora Ephron; **Screenplay**: Nora Ephron, based on Julie Powell's book and Julia Childs and Alex Prud'homme's biography *My Life in France*
Cast: Meryl Streep (Julia Child), Amy Adams (Julie Powell), Stanley Tucci (Paul Child), Chris Messina (Eric Powell), Linda Emond (Simone Beck), Helen Carey (Louisette Bertholle), Jane Lynch (Dorothy McWilliams Dean), Mary Lynn Rajskub (Sarah)

Julie Powell works for the Lower Manhattan Development Corporation answering phone calls from the families of 9/11 victims and the public and feels she's not accomplishing anything with her life. On August 11, 2002, she starts a blog, indicating her intent to prepare all 524 recipes in Julia Child's *Mastering the Art of French Cooking* in one year (18:00 to 18:49). Her mother thinks this is a crazy idea, but makes the first comment on her blog. Soon many people are commenting. Eventually she gets a call from Judith Jones, who originally edited Child's cookbook, and Julie invites her to dinner. However, Jones doesn't show. This leads to a fight with her husband, who leaves for a while, but returns. An article appears in the *New York Times* about her blog. This leads to other interviews and a book offer. She learns Julia Child "hates" her. Julie and her husband go to see the exhibit of Julia's kitchen at the Smithsonian. Julia Child moves to France with her husband, a diplomat, in 1949. She is bored and after she gets a big, fat French cookbook for her birthday, she starts taking cooking lessons at the Cordon Bleu. Julia starts teaching cooking with two French ladies and she starts working on a French cookbook for Americans. Julia's husband is eventually recalled to Washington, where the FBI investigates him because he was in China during the war. The Childs move back to the United States and Alfred A. Knopf decides to publish her cookbook.

A quirky but entertaining film. It serves as a kind of dual biography. In the movie there is constant switching back and forth between the two stories.

Awards: *Academy Award Nomination*: Best Actress (Meryl Streep). *Golden Globe Win*: Best Performance by an Actress in a Motion Picture–Comedy or Musical (Streep). *Golden Globe Nomination*: Best Motion Picture–Comedy or Musical

Alternate Film: *District 9*

12

CLEOPATRA

Year: 1963

Genre: Period Drama

Run Time: 3 hours 12 minutes (theatrical release), 4 hours 6 minutes (video release)

Availability: Blu-ray and DVD (Twentieth Century Fox)

Director: Joseph L. Mankiewicz; **Screenplay**: Carlo Maria Franzero, Sidney Buchman, Ben Hecht, Ranald MacDougall, and Joseph L. Mankiewicz, based on Carlo Mario Franzero's book *The Life and Times of Cleopatra*

Cast: Elizabeth Taylor (Cleopatra), Richard Burton (Marc Antony), Rex Harrison (Julius Caesar), Carroll O'Connor (Servilius Casca), Roddy McDowall (Octavian), Martin Landau (Rufio), Hume Cronyn (Sosigenes), Andrew Keir (Agrippa)

In the Roman Civil war Julius Caesar travels to Egypt in pursuit of his defeated rival Pompey and meets Cleopatra, one of the co-rulers of the country. Caesar and Cleopatra begin an affair. Cleopatra becomes pregnant and Caesar's wife learns of their affair. Their son Caesarion is born. Caesar returns to Rome and three years pass. Caesar is made dictator for life and Cleopatra goes to Rome. Caesar asks to be made emperor and the Senate offers him kingship of all territory outside Italy. Caesar is assassinated and Cleopatra leaves for Egypt. Marc Antony and Octavion, Caesar's heirs, track down and defeat the assassins at the Battle of Phillipi. Octavian, Antony, and Lepidus divide the Roman world, but Octavian soon forces Lepidus out. Antony needs the gold and grain of Egypt to control the east. Cleopatra will not come to Antony and he will not come to her. She sails to where he is and they meet on her ship and begin their affair. Octavian and Antony meet and divide the world and Antony marries Octavian's sister. War develops with Antony and Cleopatra against Octavian. At the Battle of Actium, Octavian wins. After Antony kills himself, Cleopatra commits suicide on August 12, 30 BC, when she learns Octavian plans to drag her back to Rome to grace his triumphal parade (3:57:38 to 4:08:16).

An overblown melodrama. The scenery and sets are spectacular, but the plot is formulaic and clichéd. Still any movie that almost bankrupted a major studio is worth seeing. Plus, for men at least, any film where you get to watch Elizabeth Taylor for four hours is time well spent.

Awards: *Academy Award Wins*: Best Cinematography, Best Art Direction, Best Costume Design, and Best Visual Effects. *Academy Award Nominations*: Best Picture, Best Actor (Rex Harrison), Best Film Editing, Best Original Score, and Best Sound Mixing. *Golden Globe Nominations*: Best Motion Picture–Drama, Best Motion Picture Director, Best Motion Picture Actor–Drama (Harrison), and Best Supporting Actor (Roddy McDowell)

Source: Tyldesley, Joyce. *Cleopatra: Last Queen of Egypt*. New York: Basic Books, 2008. This book at page 198 gives her death date.

Alternate Film: *Walking Tall*

13
BATTLE OF BRITAIN
Year: 1969
Genre: War
Run Time: 2 hours 12 minutes
Date Revealed in Film: 34:00
Availability: Blu-ray and DVD (Metro-Goldwyn-Mayer)
Director: Guy Hamilton; **Screenplay**: James Kennaway and William
 Greatorex, based on Derek Dempster and Derek Wood's book, *The Narrow Margin*
Cast: Laurence Olivier (Air Chief Marshal Sir Hugh Dowding), Trevor Howard (Air Vice-Marshal Sir Keith Park), Christopher Plummer (Colin Harvey), Michael Caine (Squadron Leader Canfield), Robert Shaw ("Skipper"), Susannah York (Maggie Harvey)

An RAF squadron has to evacuate its French airfield in a hurry to keep from being overrun by the Nazi blitz. Air Marshal Dowding advises that no more planes be sent to the continent. The British Army is evacuated from France in the Dunkirk evacuation. The Germans propose to end the war by settlement. The RAF waits for the Germans to attack. August 13, 1940, British radar allows them to spot the Germans before they reach England and alert their fighters (33:57 to 54:44). The Germans attack the radar stations and the British have to rely on the observer corps. The Germans attack the airbases and Harvey's squadron has to take off while under attack. The Germans launch a diversionary attack from Norway to northern England to draw off planes, but it is defeated. The British have a shortage of planes and pilots and have to move to auxiliary airfields due to German bombing. The Germans start bombing London, so the RAF launches a raid on Berlin. Hitler orders London razed, which allows the RAF to repair its airfields and train new pilots. Hitler cancels the invasion.

A somewhat melodramatic film. It does have some great aerial combat sequences, but these are offset by the plodding romantic subplot involving the Harveys. Not the greatest war film, but it is entertaining enough.
Alternate Film: *Mary Shelley's Frankenstein*

14
55 DAYS AT PEKING
Year: 1963
Genre: Period Drama
Run Time: 2 hours 34 minutes
Date Revealed in Film: 2:35:43
Availability: Blu-ray (Anchor Bay), DVD (Soul Media)
Director: Nicholas Ray; **Screenplay:** Philip Yordan, Bernard Gordan, Robert Hamer, and Ben Barzman
Cast: Charlton Heston (Maj. Matt Lewis), Ava Gardner (Baroness Natalie Ivanoff), David Niven (Sir Arthur Robinson), Flora Robson (Dowager Empress Cixi), John Ireland (Sergeant Harry), Leo Genn (Gen. Jung-Lu), Harry Andrews (Father de Bearn)

In 1900 Peking (Beijing) Dowager Empress Cixi decides to use the Boxer rebels to try to toss the foreigners out of China. Major Lewis of the U.S. Marines arrives in Peking to take over security at the American Embassy. He meets Baroness Natalie Ivanoff and begins a romantic relationship. After the Boxers kill the German ambassador, the Dowager Empress tells all foreigners to leave Peking, but they vote to stay and barricade the compound. The Boxers scale the walls, but an almost suicidal counterattack drives them off. The relief force is stopped when Chinese army troops join the Boxers. The Chinese start bombarding the compound with heavy guns. While the Chinese are celebrating, the Europeans send out a commando force and blow up a Chinese arsenal. An attempt to contact the relief force fails. The Baroness trades her jewelry for food and drugs, but is shot while bringing it back and later dies. The Chinese launch a night attack with fire rockets, but a counterattack destroys the launchers. The Chinese launch one last desperate attack, on August 14, 1900, just before the relief force arrives (2:24:29 to 2:31:12).

A moderately good action film. Avoids being too melodramatic. However, the love scenes between Heston and Gardner seem somewhat stilted.

Awards: *Academy Award Nominations*: Best Song and Best Original Score
Alternate Film: *Star 80*

15

VICTORY

Year: 1981
Genre: Adventure
Run Time: 1 hour 56 minutes
Date Revealed in Film: 22:14
Availability: DVD and VHS (Warner Home Video)
Director: John Huston; **Screenplay:** Evan Jones and Yabo Yablonsky
Cast: Michael Caine (Capt. John Colby), Sylvester Stallone (Capt. Robert
  Hatch), Max Von Sydow (Maj. Kurt Von Steiner), Tim Piggott-Smith
  (Rose), Daniel Massey (Col. Waldron), Clive Merrison (the forger), Carole
  Laure (Rene), Anton Diffring (announcer)

During World War II, German Major Kurt Von Steiner proposes to British
Captain John Colby that a team of Allied POWs play a soccer match against a
German team. Colby agrees if his players get extra rations. The senior British
officers in the camp see the match as a chance for the team to escape, while
the Germans view it as a chance to prove German racial superiority. The Germans decide that an all-star Allied POW team will play an exhibition match
against the German national team in Paris. An American, Captain Robert
Hatch, talks his way onto the team as the trainer. Hatch, following the orders
of the senior British officer, escapes, goes to Paris, and contacts the resistance.
They come up with a plan for the entire team to escape through the sewers
under the stadium. Hatch lets himself be captured and returned to the camp
so he can pass on the escape plan. On August 15, 1943 (1:13:10 to 1:52:35),
the team travels to Paris. In the first half they fall behind 4–1. At halftime the
prisoners decide to stay and win to deny the Germans their propaganda coup.
They manage to play to a 4–4 draw. The crowd storms the field. The prisoners
blend in with the mob as they leave the stadium and escape.

   This is an entertaining film. Of course the story is complete hokum for
several reasons, but it's an enjoyable action film.
Alternate Film: *Buffalo Bill*

16

THE PATRIOT

Year: 2000
Genre: Period Drama

Run Time: 2 hours 45 minutes
Availability: Blu-ray and DVD (Sony Pictures)
Director: Roland Emmerich; **Screenplay**: Robert Rodat
Cast: Mel Gibson (Benjamin Martin), Heath Ledger (Gabriel Martin), Joely Richardson (Charlotte Selton), Jason Isaacs (Col. William Tavington), Chris Cooper (Col. Harry Burwell), René Auberjonois (Rev. Oliver), Tom Wilkinson (Lord Cornwallis)

In 1775 Benjamin Martin is a widower raising seven children on his South Carolina plantation. He wants to stay out of the war, until British forces under Col. Tavington take Benjamin's son Gabriel to be hanged as a spy and his brother Thomas is killed. Benjamin and his two youngest sons ambush the squad, taking Gabriel and freeing him. Benjamin joins the army and with Gabriel witnesses the colonists' defeat at the Battle of Camden on August 16, 1780 (47:43 to 55:31). Martin raises a militia force to battle the British in a guerilla war. When he encounters Tavington again at a prisoner exchange Martin promises to kill him. Tavington burns down the plantation of Benjamin's sister-in-law where his children are staying, but they escape with help from Gabriel. He weds his sweetheart Anne, while Benjamin becomes attached to his widowed sister-in-law, Charlotte. Anne Martin, her family, and others are locked up in a church and burned alive by Tavington's men. Tavington kills Gabriel and Martin is devastated. At Cowpens the British are defeated and Martin kills Tavington. After Yorktown the Martin family returns home to find the militia rebuilding their home.

This is the one film on this list I have a personal connection to. I remember when the film was shot in the area where I live and I am acquainted with several of the local people who were cast as extras in the film. On the whole a good period action piece. The movie ignores slavery and seems to overdo the level of British atrocities, although they did actually perpetrate them in South Carolina. Somewhat melodramatic, but overall well worth watching.

Awards: *Academy Award Wins*: Best Sound, Best Cinematography, and Best Original Music Score
Source: Dupuy, R. Ernest, and Dupuy, Trevor N. *The Encyclopedia of Military History from 3500 B.C. to the Present.* New York: Harper & Row, 1977. This book at page 719 gives the date of the battle.
Alternate Film: *Ed Wood*

17
GUNG HO!
Year: 1943
Genre: War/Drama
Run Time: 1 hour 28 minutes
Availability: DVD (Alpha Video), VHS (Republic Pictures home Video)
Director: Ray Enright; **Screenplay:** W. S. LeFrançois and Lucien Hubbard
Cast: Randolph Scott (Col. Thorwald), Rod Cameron (Rube Tedrow), Alan
   Curtis (Pvt. John Harbison), Noah Beery Jr. (Cpl. Kurt Richter), Sam
   Levene (Sgt. "Transport" Magakian), Robert Mitchum (Pvt. "Pig-Iron"
   Matthews), Grace McDonald (Lt. Kathleen Corrigan), Milburn Stone
   (Cmdr. Blake)

The Marines ask for and get many volunteers for a special combat unit. Tedrow has already killed someone with a knife. Harbison is seminary graduate who wants to help the other men. Frankie is a no-good kid who wants to prove himself. Two half-brothers Ritcher and O'Ryan want to join to show each other up. Pig-Iron wants to join to show he is worth something. The men begin training. Richter and O'Ryan spend an evening with a girl they both love, Kathleen Corrigan. Later Richter meets Kathleen and asks her to wait for him, but O'Ryan interrupts them before he gets an answer. The Marines ship out from San Diego. At Pearl Harbor the 210 Marines in the battalion get on two submarines. They struggle to keep up morale in the subs, even celebrating Gunner's birthday. The men learn they are landing on Makin Island and that as they are defending the Japanese will have a six-to-one advantage. However, all of the Marines' training has been focused on the specifics of this mission. They dive to avoid Japanese planes, but an exhausted Tedrow is left on deck. The sub recovers Tedrow and they get depth charged, but aren't hit. On August 17, 1942 (46:20 to 1:25:35), they land on the island. They take out snipers in the trees. O'Ryan is killed and Frankie races forward and tosses grenades, taking out a machine gun nest. Pig-Iron, who has been shot in the throat and can't yell a warning, saves the doc's life by throwing a knife into the back of a wounded Japanese who revived and tried to shoot the doc. When Japanese aircraft appear, the Marines attack the radio station controlling them, but they are pinned down until a captured steamroller flattens the station. When the Japanese launch a major air raid the Marines appear to be doomed, but a little ingenuity and trickery saves the day.

A decent action film. Made during the war, it sometimes drifts over into propaganda. The combat sequences are well done.

Source: Salmaggi, Cesare, and Pallavisini, Alfredo. *2194 Days of War*. New York: Gallery Books, 1977. This book at page 285 gives the date of the landing.

Alternate Film: *Carlito's Way*

18
TAKING WOODSTOCK
Year: 2009
Genre: Comedy/Drama
Run Time: 2 hours
Availability: Blu-ray and DVD (Universal Studios)
Director: Ang Lee; **Screenplay**: James Schamus, based on Elliot Tiber and Rom Monte's book *Taking Woodstock: A True Story of a Riot, a Concert, and a Life*
Cast: Demetri Martin (Elliot Tiber), Imelda Staunton (Sonia Teichberg), Henry Goodman (Jake Teichberg), Liev Schreiber (Vetty von Vilma), Jonathan Groff (Michael Lang), Eugene Levy (Max Yasgur), Emile Hirsch (Billy), Jeffrey Dean Morgan (Dan)

Elliot Tiber, aspiring interior designer, lives with his Jewish parents in Bethel, New York, at the dilapidated El Monaco Motel. They have until summer's end to pay the mortgage or lose the building. Elliot has a permit to hold a classical music festival at the hotel, but when he learns the promoters of the Woodstock Rock Festival have no permit, he lets them use his. A neighbor allows the use of his farm for the festival. Elliot wins his parents over to the festival by showing them stacks of cash the hotel has made. There is some initial opposition to the festival that fades away as business flows into the area. Elliot visits the festival. On the last day, August 18, 1969, Elliot packs up to leave home (1:47:06 to 1:54:36).

An interesting and somewhat amusing behind-the-scenes look at the "three days of Peace and Love." One disappointment is not getting to hear any of the music from the concert. Elliott and his parents (especially his mother) are a hoot and fun to watch!

Source: *The Sixties Chronicle*. Lincolnwood, IL; Legacy Publishing, 2004. This book at page 428 gives the date of the last day of the concert.

Alternate Film: *The Lost Colony*

19
ANGELA'S ASHES

Year: 1999

Genre: Biography

Run Time: 2 hours 25 minutes

Availability: DVD and VHS (Paramount Pictures)

Director: Alan Parker; **Screenplay**: Laura Jones and Alan Parker, based on
Frank McCourt's memoir

Cast: Emily Watson (Angela McCourt), Robert Carlyle (Malachy McCourt),
Ciaran Owens (middle Frank), Michael Legge (older Frank), Kerry Con-
don (Theresa Carmondy), Pauline McLynn (Aunt Aggie), Susan Fitzgerald
(Sister Rita)

Frank McCourt's father is a storytelling rogue who can't find work because
he's a drunk. McCourt's mother often has to rely on charity to survive. Frankie
has an interesting childhood, even though they live in the slums. Frankie gets
a teacher who recognizes and encourages his writing talent. Frank leaves
home and goes to stay with his uncle Pat. His Aunt Aggie gets him a job as
a telegraph delivery boy. An older girl who has tuberculosis seduces Frank.
Mrs. Finucane, the moneylender, hires him to write threatening letters to
people who owe her. Frank starts saving money so he can go to America. On
his birthday, August 19, 1948, Frank confesses to St. Francis all of his sins and
finds Mrs. Finucane dead of a stroke, so he steals half her money and destroys
her ledgers (2:08:50 to 2:14:30). He later leaves for America.

This is a touching film. It manages to be funny and tragic, almost at the
same time. You are made to really feel for Frank and his problems.

Awards: *Academy Award Nomination*: Best Original Score. *Golden Globe
Nomination*: Best Original Score–Motion Picture

Source: Sharp, Michael D. *Popular Contemporary Writers, Vol. 8*. New York:
Marshall Cavendish, 2006. This book at page 1,013 tells us that Frank Mc-
Court was born on this date, which he references at 2:09:19.

Alternate Film: *The Treasure of the Sierra Madre*

20
THE THREE FACES OF EVE

Year: 1957

Genre: Drama

Run Time: 1 hour 31 minutes
Date Revealed in Film: 3:50–51
Availability: Blu-ray and DVD (Twentieth Century Fox)
Director: Nunnally Johnson; **Screenplay**: Nunnally Johnson, based on Corbett Thigpen and Hervey Cleckley's book
Cast: Joanne Woodward (Eve White, Eve Black, Jane), Lee J. Cobb (Dr. Curtis Luther), Nancy Culp (Mrs. Black), Edwin Jerome (Francis Day), Alistair Cooke (Narrator)

Demure and submissive Eve White is taken to psychiatrist Dr. Luther on August 20, 1951, by her husband because she has headaches and "spells" where she can't remember what happened (3:43 to 7:33). A second personality, Eve Black, who is the opposite of Eve White, emerges. Eve Black is a confident party girl who, according to her, is not married. After Eve Black tries to kill Eve White's child, Eve White is committed. Eve White's husband eventually leaves her and takes their daughter. A third personality, Jane, emerges, but the three personalities exist in largely separate lives. Eve White tries to kill herself, but Eve Black stops her. Eve White recalls that as a little girl her mother forced her to kiss her dead grandmother's face and this traumatic event caused her personality to fracture. Jane is eventually able to recall everything that happened to Eve White and Eve Black. She remarries and gets her daughter back.

An interesting film. A somewhat dated one, as spousal abuse is presented with no condemnation at all. Also her problem is presented in a somewhat simplified way.

Awards: *Academy Award Win*: Best Actress (Joanne Woodward). *Golden Globe Win*: Best Motion Picture Actress–Drama (Woodward)
Alternate Film: *All The Kings Men* (1947)

21

RIDE WITH THE DEVIL
Year: 1999
Genre: War/Drama
Run Time: 2 hours 18 minutes
Availability: Blu-ray (Criterion), DVD (Universal Studios)
Director: Ang Lee; **Screenplay**: James Schamus, based on Daniel Woodrell's book *Woe to Live On*

Cast: Toby Maguire (Jake Roedel), Skeet Ulrich (Jack Bull Chiles), Jewel (Sue Lee Shelley), Jeffrey Wright (Daniel Holt), Simon Baker (George Clyde), Jonathan Rhys Meyers (Pitt Mackeson), Jim Caviezel (Black John Ambrose), Tom Guiry (Riley Crawford)

Jake Roedel and Jack Bull Chiles join the pro-Southern Bushwhackers after Jake's father is murdered by pro-Union Jayhawkers. Jake sends a neighbor of his to Union headquarters with an offer to trade three prisoners of the Bushwhackers for two of the Union's, but this offer is refused, so the three are killed. The band splits up for the winter. Jake, Jack Bull, George Clyde, and George's former slave, Holt, live in a shack on the Evans farm. Jack Bull and the Evans's widowed daughter, Sue Lee Shelly, become romantically involved, but Jack Bull later dies of wounds. In the spring they join Quantrill's forces. On August 21, 1863 (1:31:02 to 1:49:02), Quantrill leads them on a raid on Lawrence, Kansas. When Roedel spares a young boy, he arouses the wrath of Pitt Mackeson, who intentionally shoots Jake in the leg during the retreat. Back in Missouri they learn Sue Lee has had Jack Bull's child, but everyone thinks Jake is the father and he eventually marries her. They leave for California and Holt heads for Texas.

A decent war film. Really more of a character study as this film does not have a lot of combat scenes. This movie explores the Civil War in the West, an area that is rarely touched on.

Source: Goodrich, Thomas. *Black Flag: Guerrilla Warfare on the Western Border, 1861–1865.* Bloomington: Indiana University Press, 1995. This book at pages 71–92 gives the date of the raid.

Alternate Film: *Black August*

22

DOG DAY AFTERNOON
Year: 1975
Genre: Drama
Run Time: 2 hours 5 minutes
Date Revealed in Film: 00:15
Availability: Blu-ray and DVD (Warner Home Video)
Director: Sidney Lumet; **Screenplay:** Frank Pierson, based on P. F. Kluge's magazine article "The Boys in the Bank"

Cast: Al Pacino (Sonny Wortzik), John Cazale (Sal Naturile), Charles Durning (Sgt. Eugene Moretti), James Broderick (Agent Sheldon), Lance Handrickson (Agent Murphy), Chris Sarandon (Leon Shermer)

Sonny and Sal hold up a bank on August 22, 1972, but there's only $1,100 in the branch. Unsure what to do, they remain in the bank, holding the bank employees hostage. The police are alerted and surround the bank. When Sonny steps outside and sees all the police arrayed against him, he shouts, "Attica! Attica!" The onlookers cheer him. They demand a helicopter to take them to the airport so they can fly out of the country. Sonny robbed the bank to get the money to pay for his lover, Leon, to have sex-change surgery. Sonny and Leon talk on the phone and Leon tells Sonny he tried to commit suicide and was in Bellevue when the police came to get him to take him to the scene of the robbery. Sonny's mom tries, unsuccessfully, to talk him into giving up. Sonny, Sal, the remaining hostages, and Agents Sheldon and Murphy leave in a limo for the airport. Sheldon wrests Sal's gun away, allowing Murphy to shoot Sal. Sonny is arrested.

Both a crime drama and a psychological study. Very convincing performances.

Awards: *Academy Award Win*: Best Original Screenplay. *Academy Award Nominations*: Best Picture, Best Director, Best Actor (Al Pacino), Best Supporting Actor (Chris Sarandon), and Best Film Editing. *Golden Globe Nominations*: Best Motion Picture–Drama, Best Supporting Actor–Motion Picture (John Cazale), Best Supporting Actor–Motion Picture (Charles Durning), Best Director–Motion Picture, Best Motion Picture Actor–Drama (Pacino), Best Screenplay–Motion Picture, and Best Acting Debut in a Motion Picture–Male (Chris Sarandon)

Alternate Film: *Michael Collins*

23
THE BOURNE IDENTITY

Year: 2002
Genre: Action
Run Time: 1 hour 59 minutes
Availability: Blu-ray and DVD (Universal Studios)
Director: Doug Liman; **Screenplay**: Tony Gilroy and William Blake Herron, based on Robert Ludlum's novel

Cast: Matt Damon (Jason Bourne), Franka Potente (Marie Helena Kreutz),
Brian Cox (Ward Abbott), Julia Stiles (Nicolette Parsons), Chris Cooper
(Alexander Conklin), Clive Owen (The Professor), Adewale Akinnuoye-
Agbaje (Nykwana Wombosi)

A man floating in the sea near Marseille is found by a fishing boat. He has
two bullets in him and a device that has a Swiss bank account number. The
man has amnesia, but later heads to Zurich. Meanwhile, Wombosi, an exiled
African leader, plans to expose CIA ops in Africa, unless he's restored to
power. A CIA attempt to kill Wombosi fails. At the bank the man finds a
safe deposit box with cash, a gun, and passports in different names, including
Jason Bourne and Michael Kane. He learns he lived in Paris. Cops follow him
from the bank to the U.S. consulate. They try to arrest him, but he escapes
and hires Marie to drive him to Paris. The CIA activates European agents to
kill him. Bourne learns "Michael Kane" is dead. An assassin tries to kill him,
but Bourne kills him instead. Marie stays with Bourne and after a car chase
through Paris they escape and have an amorous interlude. A sniper kills
Wombosi. Bourne learns Wombosi alleged that a CIA hit man tried to kill
him just before Bourne turned up on the boat. Bourne and Marie are tracked
to her half-brother's home, where a CIA killer tries to kill them, but Bourne
kills him. Marie leaves. Bourne finds the CIA safe house. Bourne recalls that
on August 23, 2001, he was going to kill Wombosi, but couldn't do it in front
of his kids (1:42:59 to 1:44:21). He has to fight his way out of the safe house,
but his CIA controller is killed by order of the head of the agency.

A very good action thriller. Unique plot: What does a secret agent do if he
doesn't remember who he is anymore? Great action sequences.

Source: Ludlum, Robert. *The Bourne Identity*. New York: Richard Marek
Publishers, 1980. The book at page 154 gives the date he was pulled from
the water as August 24 (the day after he tried to kill Wombosi).

Alternate Film: *Midnight in the Garden of Good and Evil*

24

WHIP IT

Year: 2009
Genre: Drama
Run Time: 1 hour 51 minutes
Date Revealed in Film: 9:56, 10:35

Availability: Blu-ray and DVD (Fox Home Video)
Director: Drew Barrymore; **Screenplay:** Shauna Cross, based on her novel *Derby Girl*
Cast: Ellen Page (Bliss Cavendar), Alia Shawkat (Pash), Marcia Gay Harden (Brooke Cavendar), Daniel Stern (Earl Cavendar), Landon Pigg (Oliver), Jimmy Fallon ("Hot Tub" Johnny Rocket), Kristen Wiig (Maggie Mayhem), Drew Barrymore (Smashley Simpson)

Bliss Cavender is a seventeen-year-old living in Bodeen, Texas, whose mother enters her in beauty pageants, which Bliss hates. On August 24, 2008 (9:56 to 10:45), Bliss and her friend Pash decide to surreptitiously attend a roller derby match the next day. Bliss later joins the Hurl Scouts, the doormat of the league, telling them she is twenty-two. Her mother pushes Bliss to get ready for the Miss Bluebonnet pageant. The team makes the finals, in part due to Bliss. The league finals and the pageant are scheduled for the same day. After Pash is arrested for underage drinking, Bliss's parents learn what she's been up to. Bliss moves out but can't skate unless a parent gives permission. Bliss later returns home and decides to compete in the Miss Bluebonnet pageant. Her father gives Bliss permission to skate. The finals are a very exciting day for Bliss in more ways than one.

A quirky coming-of-age story. Very refreshing that this is a girl's story, but it is still somewhat clichéd. Of course the finals and the pageant are on the same day! Oh well, this movie's unusual story line and believable characters make it worth watching.
Alternate Film: Inside Daisy Clover

25

THE GODFATHER

Year: 1972
Genre: Drama
Run Time: 2 hours 55 minutes
Availability: Blu-ray and DVD (Paramount Pictures)
Director: Francis Ford Coppola; **Screenplay:** Mario Puzo and Francis Ford Coppola, based on Mario Puzo's novel
Cast: Marlon Brando (Vito Corleone), Al Pacino (Michael Corleone), James Caan (Sonny Corleone), Richard S. Castellano (Peter Clemenza), Robert

Duvall (Tom Hagen), Diane Keaton (Kay Adams), Talia Shire (Connie Corleone)

On Saturday August 25, 1945, the day of his daughter Connie's wedding, crime lord Vito Corleone hears petitions for favors, including one by singer Johnnie Fontaine for help in getting a movie part. Also attending are his sons, Sonny, the eldest; Michael, who wants nothing to do with "the family business" and who has brought his Anglo girlfriend, Kay Adams; and youngest son, Fredo (1:17 to 27:02). Vito Corleone's opposition to his organization becoming involved in drug trafficking leads to an attempt on his life that draws Michael into being a part of the retaliation. Michael has to flee to Sicily, where he weds Appollonia, who is killed by a bomb intended for him. After the eldest son, Sonny, is killed, Michael becomes head of the Corleone family and marries Kay. Michael lures the other Dons into a false sense of security, and then on the day of the baptism of Connie and Carlo's son, for whom Michael will be godfather, Michael takes action.

A powerful and violent film. Gave us the classic movie line "I'll make him an offer he can't refuse."

Awards: *Academy Award Wins*: Best Picture, Best Adapted Screenplay, and Best Actor (Marlon Brando). *Academy Award Nominations*: Best Supporting Actor (Al Pacino, James Caan, and Robert Duvall), Best Director, Best Costume Design, Best Film Editing, and Best Sound Mixing. *Golden Globe Wins*: Best Motion Picture–Drama, Best Motion Picture Actor–Drama (Brando), Best Director–Motion Picture, Best Screenplay, and Best Original Score. *Golden Globe Nominations*: Best Motion Picture Actor–Drama (Pacino) and Best Supporting Actor–Motion Picture (Caan)

Source: Puzo, Mario. *The Godfather*. New York: New American Library, 1969. This book at page 11 gives the date of the wedding.

Alternate Film: *The Age of Innocence*

26

DAY OF THE JACKAL

Year: 1973
Genre: Suspense
Run Time: 2 hours 23 minutes
Availability: DVD (Universal Studios), VHS (MCA Universal Home Video)

Director: Fred Zinnemann; **Screenplay**: Kenneth Ross, based on the Frederick Forsyth novel
Cast: Edward Fox (The Jackal), Michael Lonsdale (Claude Lebel), Alan Badel (The Minister), Derek Jacobi (Caron), Michel Auclair (Colonel Rolland), Cyril Cusack (The Gunsmith), Maurice Denham (General Colbert)
After their failure to kill President Charles de Gaulle, the underground OAS realizes they are so infiltrated by police agents that their only hope lies in hiring a contract killer. They hire an Englishman, codenamed "the Jackal," to do the job. His preparations, including procuring his weapon, and false identities are shown in detail. The French police lure a bodyguard of the OAS leaders to France, torture him, and learn that a hit man has been hired. But without a name or description they can do nothing. Commissioner Claude Lebel is brought in to uncover this information. After contacting his counterparts in several other countries, the British Secret Service comes back with a name and the first false identity the assassin is using. The Jackal enters France and at a hotel has a fling with a married woman. He eludes the police and follows her to her home, where he later is forced to kill her and move on to his second identity. This allows the police to begin a public hunt for the killer. The Jackal allows himself to be picked up by a gay man at a bathhouse, then kills him and hides out in his apartment. Lebel has determined when the Jackal intends to strike. On Liberation Day the Jackal, disguised as a wounded war veteran, infiltrates close enough to take a shot that misses by a miracle. Lebel just in the nick of time tracks down and kills the Jackal, saving de Gaulle. The next day, August 26, 1963, the Jackal is buried in an unmarked grave (2:19:48 to 2:20:35).

One of the classic espionage films. The carefully laid out details and the excellent underplayed portrayals by all the actors create an atmosphere of believable suspense. Even though you know de Gaulle lives, this film keeps you interested until the very end.
Awards: *Academy Award Nomination*: Best Film Editing. *Golden Globe Nominations*: Best Motion Picture–Drama, Best Screenplay–Motion Picture, and Best Director–Motion Picture
Source: Forsyth, Frederick. *The Day of the Jackal*. New York: Viking Press, 1971. This book at pages 379–80 gives the date of the burial.
Alternate Film: *Shine*

27
MONEYBALL
Year: 2011
Genre: Drama
Run Time: 2 hours 13 minutes
Availability: Blu-ray and DVD (Sony Pictures)
Director: Bennett Miller; **Screenplay:** Steven Zaillian and Aaron Sorkin, based on Michael Lewis's book *Moneyball: The Art of Winning an Unfair Game*
Cast: Brad Pitt (Billy Beane), Jonah Hill (Peter Brand), Philip Seymour Hoffman (Art Howe), Chris Pratt (Scott Hatteberg), Casey Bond (Chad Bradford), Stephen Bishop (David Justice), Robin Wright (Sharon)

After the Oakland A's lose to the New York Yankees in the 2001 American League playoffs, Billy Beane, their general manager, is unhappy. He hires Peter Brand, a young Yale economics graduate with a radical idea about how to rate players. Instead of relying on the scouts' experience and intuition, Brand selects players based almost exclusively on their on-base percentage. Brand thus puts together a team of undervalued players with far more potential than the A's poor financial posture would otherwise allow. The A's start the season poorly, leading critics within and outside the team to dismiss the new recruiting method as a failure. Beane convinces the owner to stay the course, and the team improves, winning an unprecedented twenty consecutive games, including the fourteenth straight victory against the Kansas City Royals on August 27, 2002 (1:36:26 to 1:36:30). The A's lose in the first round of the postseason to the Minnesota Twins. Beane is disappointed at this loss, but satisfied that the season has demonstrated the value of his and Brand's methods.

A good baseball film. Shows the unfortunate power of money in baseball. The film also encourages people to "think outside the box."

Awards: *Academy Award Nominations*: Best Picture, Best Actor (Brad Pitt), Best Supporting Actor (Jonah Hill), Best Adapted Screenplay, Best Film Editing, and Best Sound Mixing. *Golden Globe Nominations*: Best Perfor-

mance by an Actor in a Motion Picture–Drama (Brad Pitt), Best Performance by an Actor in a Supporting Role in a Motion Picture (Jonah Hill), Best Screenplay–Motion Picture, and Best Motion Picture–Drama
Source: *The Toronto Star*. August 29, 2002, section E, page 8. "A's 6 Royals 4."
Alternate Film: *Man of a Thousand Faces*

28

ELENI

Year: 1985
Genre: Drama
Run Time: 1 hour 54 minutes
Availability: DVD (Paramount Home Entertainment), VHS (Embassy Home Entertainment)
Director: Peter Yates; **Screenplay**: Steve Tesich, based on Nicholas Gage's memoir
Cast: John Malkovich (Nicholas Gage), Kate Nelligan (Eleni), Linda Hunt (Katrina), Oliver Cotton (Katis), Ronald Pickup (Spiro), Stefan Gryff (Tassos)
Before the outbreak of World War II Eleni's husband went to America to find work, leaving her in Greece with their five children. The end of the war did not end their troubles. They get caught up in a war between the government and communist rebels. Then the communists propose sending the children to communist countries. Eleni has the children smuggled to safety. The rebels arrest Eleni and based on false, coerced testimony she is convicted and sentenced to death. On August 28, 1948, with a cry of "My children!" Eleni is executed (1:37:17 to 1:39:45). In America, her son Nick becomes a reporter for the *New York Times*. He takes the bureau chief post in Athens so he can find and kill those who killed his mother. He tracks down the man who sentenced his mother to death. Nick confronts him, but the sight of the man's grandchild prevents Nick from killing him.

A powerful and moving story of a mother's love for her children. Eleni sacrificed everything for them. Nick wants revenge, but finds he can't become like those who killed his mother.
Source: Gage, Nicholas. *Eleni*. New York: Random House, 1983. This book at page 3 gives her death date.
Alternate Film: *Billy Budd*

29
TERMINATOR 2: JUDGMENT DAY

Year: 1991

Genre: Science Fiction

Run Time: 2 hours 17 minutes

Date Revealed in Film: 1:18–19

Director: James Cameron; **Screenplay**: James Cameron and William Wisher Jr.

Cast: Arnold Schwarzenegger (Terminator), Linda Hamilton (Sarah Connor), Edward Furlong (John Connor), Robert Patrick (the T-1000), Earl Boen (Dr. Silberman), Joe Morton (Dr. Miles Bennett Dyson), S. Epatha Merkerson (Tarissa Dyson)

In 1995 John Connor lives in L.A. with his foster parents. His mother, Sarah Connor, became mentally ill and was committed. Skynet sends a new machine, the T-1000, back in time to kill him. It can replicate the appearance of anything of approximately its body weight. John Connor in the future sends back a reprogrammed T-800 to protect his younger self. Both converge on John at a mall, but John and the T-800 escape. John accepts his help and they rescue Sarah from the mental asylum. Sarah plans to flee to Mexico, but she has a horrific vision of Judgment Day, a nuclear war on August 29, 1997 (00:24 to 00:47; 3:22 to 5:09; 1:16:57 to 1:18:37). Sarah resolves to stop it. They next visit Dr. Dyson, the man responsible for Skynet. After seeing the T-800 he agrees to help and they enter the Cyberdyne factory to destroy the parts of the previous T-800 that are being used to reverse-engineer the technology. Dr. Dyson is killed. The T-1000 pursues them to a steel mill, where it is destroyed in a vat of molten steel. The T-800 destroys itself to prevent any chance of its parts being used to continue the research.

Lots and lots of action. The characters seem somewhat one dimensional, but with this much action you really don't care. The movie never lets you get bored from start to finish.

Awards: *Academy Award Wins*: Best Sound, Best Sound Effects Editing, Best Visual Effects, and Best Makeup. *Academy Award Nominations*: Best Cinematography and Best Film Editing

Alternate Film: *42nd Street*

30

CRAZY HEART

Year: 2009
Genre: Drama
Run Time: 1 hour 52 minutes
Date Revealed in Film: 38:50
Availability: Blu-ray and DVD (Twentieth Century Fox)
Director: Scott Cooper; **Screenplay:** Scott Cooper, based on Thomas Cobb's novel
Cast: Jack Nation (Buddy), Jeff Bridges (Otis "Bad" Blake), Maggie Gyllenhaal (Jean Craddock), Colin Farrell (Tommy Sweet), Robert Duvall (Wayne Kramer), Paul Herman (Jack Greene)

Otis "Bad" Blake is a washed-up, alcoholic former country music star who has been reduced to playing in bowling alleys for peanuts. At a gig in Santa Fe, the bar owner asks him to let his divorced niece, Jean Craddock, who works for a local newspaper, interview him. Blake's agent gets him the job to open at a concert for rising country star Tommy Sweet, who asks Blake to write some songs for him. The next day, August 30, 2009, on the way from the concert to see Jean, Blake falls asleep and flips his truck, breaking his ankle (51:52 to 55:08). Blake moves in with Jean and her four-year-old son, Buddy, to recuperate. After a scary incident involving Buddy, Jean breaks up with Blake. Blake checks himself into rehab and gets sober. He finishes what he thinks is his best song ever and sells it to Tommy. In an epilogue set a year later we learn what has happened to Blake, Jean, and Buddy.

An interesting film about the redeeming power of love. The only thing that could get Blake off his road to self-destruction was his love for Jean. At the end, though, he continues on the right road for himself.

Awards: *Academy Award Wins:* Best Actor (Jeff Bridges) and Best Original Song. *Academy Award Nomination:* Best Supporting Actress (Maggie Gyllenhaal). *Golden Globe Wins:* Best Performance by an Actor in a Motion Picture–Drama (Bridges) and Best Original Song–Motion Picture
Alternate Film: *Judgment in Berlin*

31
THE QUEEN
Year: 2006
Genre: Drama
Run Time: 1 hour 43 minutes
Date Revealed in Film: 11:17
Availability: Blu-ray and DVD (Miramax)
Director: Stephen Frears; **Screenplay**: Peter Morgan
Cast: Helen Mirren (Elizabeth II), Michael Sheen (Tony Blair), James Cromwell (Prince Philip), Helen McCrory (Cherie Blair), Alex Jennings (Charles, Prince of Wales), Sylvia Syms (The Queen Mother), Tim Mc-Mullan (Stephen Lamport)

Elizabeth II selects Tony Blair as British prime minister. On August 31, 1997, Diana, Princess of Wales, is killed in car crash in Paris (12:49 to 32:04). There is an immediate outpouring of grief over this. The queen wants to distance the royal family from this, but Blair and Prince Charles get her to change her mind. She returns to London, makes a televised address, flies the flag at half-staff over Buckingham Palace, and permits a state funeral for Diana. Later she and Blair discuss modernizing the role of the royal family.

An interesting film. Almost has the feel of a documentary sometimes, like a soap opera at others. All the actors are very good and seem to meld right into their roles.

Awards: *Academy Award Win*: Best Actress (Helen Mirren). *Academy Award Nominations*: Best Picture, Best Director, Best Screenplay, Best Original Score, and Best Costume Design. *Golden Globe Wins*: Best Performance by an Actress in a Motion Picture–Drama (Mirren) and Best Screenplay–Motion Picture. *Golden Globe Nominations*: Best Motion Picture–Drama and Best Director–Motion Picture
Alternate Film: *Jack the Ripper*

September

1

MISS PETTIGREW LIVES FOR A DAY

Year: 2008
Genre: Period Comedy/Drama
Run Time: 1 hour 32 minutes
Date Revealed in Film: 41:37, 42:15
Availability: DVD (Universal Studios)
Director: Bharat Nalluri; **Screenplay**: David Magee and Simon Beaufoy, based on Winifred Watson's novel
Cast: Frances McDormand (Guinevere Pettigrew), Amy Adams (Delysia Lafosse), Lee Pace (Michael Pardue), Tom Payne (Phil Goldman), Mark Strong (Nick Calderelli), Shirley Henderson (Edythe Dubarry), Ciarán Hinds (Joe Blomfield)

After Miss Guinevere Pettigrew is fired from her job, she wanders the streets, homeless. The next day she hijacks a job to be a social secretary to singer and actress Delysia Lafosse, who sings at a club owned by Nick Calderelli, with whom she is living. After Guinevere helps to get Phil Goldman out of her bed and the apartment in time not to be seen by Nick, Delysia hires her and gives her a makeover. Michael Pardue, the piano player at Nick's club, is also involved with Delysia and proposes that they get married and go to New York. At a party Delysia hosts, Guinevere meets Joe Blomfield, a lingerie designer, while Phil announces Delysia has gotten the lead in a new musical show he is producing. Later at the club there is an altercation between Michael and Nick. The next morning, September 1, 1939 (1:21:58 to 1:27:15), Michael and Delysia leave to sail to New York on the *Queen Mary*. Guinevere is pleased that Delysia took her advice to seize love over security or fame. She's homeless again, but fate has one more surprise left for her.

A decent romantic comedy. Miss Pettigrew and Delysia are both funny characters in their own way. A snappy film that never drags or has wasted scenes.

Alternate Film: *Hawaii*

2

THE FOUR FEATHERS

Year: 1939
Genre: Adventure
Run Time: 2 hours 9 minutes
Availability: Blu-ray (Criterion), DVD (Metro-Goldwyn-Mayer)
Director: Zoltan Korda; **Screenplay**: R. D. Sherriff, based on A. E. W. Mason's novel
Cast: John Clements (Harry Faversham), Ralph Richardson (Captain John Durrance), C. Aubrey Smith (General Burroughs), June Duprez (Ethne Burroughs), Allan Jeayes (General Faversham), Jack Allen (Lt. Willoughby), Donald Gray (Peter Burroughs)

In the year the Khalifa conquers Sudan, Harry Faversham's father and his Crimean war cronies tell stories of courage and cowardice that deeply affect the sensitive boy. Ten years later Harry, Durrance, Burroughs, and Willoughby are officers in the same regiment. Harry is engaged to Ethne, Burroughs's sister, who rejected Durrance for him. Just before the regiment goes to Sudan, Harry resigns his commission and gets four white feathers symbolizing cowardice from his three friends and Ethne. Harry tells an old acquaintance, Dr. Sutton, that he resigned because he was afraid of "freezing" up in combat. Harry then goes to Egypt, disguises himself as a native, and saves Durrance's life. Still disguised, Harry passes a file to the imprisoned Burroughs and Willoughby, but the guards are suspicious, so he is imprisoned with them at Omdurman. Harry reveals who he is and organizes the prisoners for escape. When, on September 2, 1898, they hear the sound of the battle of Omdurman, they overpower the guards and seize the armory, helping to win the battle (1:34:56 to 1:43:45). Durrance, who has been blinded, returns to England and becomes engaged to Ethne, but ends it after learning who rescued him.

One of a crop of 1930s swashbuckler films. A lot of action. Still watchable.

Awards: *Academy Award Nomination*: Best Cinematography (Color)

Source: Dupuy, R. Ernest, and Dupuy, Trevor N. *The Encyclopedia of Military History from 3500 B.C. to the Present.* New York: Harper & Row, 1977. This book at page 848 gives the date of the battle of Omdurman.

Alternate Film: *Friday Night Lights*

3

THE KING'S SPEECH

Year: 2010

Genre: Drama

Run Time: 1 hour 58 minutes

Availability: Blu-ray (Starz/Anchor Bay), DVD (Weinstein Company)

Director: Tom Hooper; **Screenplay**: David Seidler

Cast: Colin Firth (King George VI), Geoffrey Rush (Lionel Logue), Helena Bonham Carter (Queen Elizabeth), Guy Pearce (King Edward VIII), Michael Gambon (King George V), Timothy Spall (Winston Churchill), Jennifer Ehle (Myrtle Logue)

Albert, Duke of York, gives a speech at the close of the Wembley Exposition and due to his stuttering it's a disaster. After conventional speech therapy fails, the Duchess of York finds Lionel Logue, who after initial resistance by Albert is able to help Albert with his stuttering. George V dies and Edward VIII's involvement with Wallis Simpson causes tension in the royal family, leading to Edward's abdication. Albert becomes King George VI and the pressure causes him to start stuttering again. Logue helps the king get through the coronation service. When the king has to make a radio address on September 3, 1939, when war is declared on Germany, Logue returns and helps the king deliver a successful speech. (1:33:41 to 1:51:25).

A good historical drama. Well played by all the actors and lets you get a glimpse into the character and inner feelings of the main characters. Keeps it light and avoids that heavy-handed ponderousness often seen in historical dramas.

Awards: *Academy Award Wins*: Best Picture, Best Director, Best Actor (Colin Firth), and Best Original Screenplay. *Academy Award Nominations*: Best Cinematography, Best Supporting Actor (Geoffrey Rush), Best Supporting Actress (Helena Bonham Carter), Best Art Direction, and Best Costume Design. *Golden Globe Win*: Best Performance by an Actor in a Motion Picture–Drama (Firth). *Golden Globe Nominations*: Best Motion Picture–Drama, Best Performance by an Actor in a Supporting Role in a Motion Picture (Rush), Best Performance by an Actress in a Supporting Role in a Motion Picture (Carter), Best Direction–Motion Picture, Best Screenplay–Motion Picture, and Best Original Score–Motion Picture

Source: Overy, Richard. *1939: Countdown to War*. New York: Viking, 2009. This book at pages 92–93 gives the date of the speech.

Alternate Film: *Hope and Glory*

4

STAND BY ME

Year: 1986 (Columbia Pictures Corporation, Act III Productions, Act III Communications, The Body)

Genre: Adventure

Run Time: 1 hour 39 minutes

Date Revealed in Film: 1:03, 1:39, and 1:19:14–17

Availability: Blu-ray and DVD (Sony Pictures)

Director: Rob Reiner; **Screenplay**: Bruce A. Evans and Raynold Gideon, based on Stephen King's novel

Cast: Wil Wheaton (Gordie Lachance), River Phoenix (Chris Chambers), Corey Feldman (Teddy Duchamp), Jerry O'Connell (Vern Tessio), Kiefer Sutherland ("Ace" Merrill), Casey Siemaszko (Billy Tessio), Gary Riley (Charlie Hogan)

Gordie Lachance reads in the newspaper of Chris Chambers's death (00:35 to 1:36). This causes him to flash back to when he was twelve. In the flashback Geordie is a dreamer and not loved by his parents as much as his athletic now-dead older brother. Chris Chambers is the son of the town drunk and treated accordingly. Teddy Duchamp's dad abused him so much that he now has to wear a hearing aid. Vern Tessio is fat and bullied. In spite of their differences, the four are friends. On September 4, 1959, Vern overhears his brother talk about finding the body of a missing youth who had been accidentally killed by a train. The four friends set out to find the body and be "heroes" (1:36 to 53:29). They almost get run over by a train and trek through a leech-infested swamp. They finally find the body, preventing a gang of older youths from taking it. They report their find by an anonymous phone call and return home.

Although the story line may seem a little morbid, this is actually a very funny film. The characters of the four friends are fully developed and likeable. There is enough action in the film to keep it exciting.

Awards: *Academy Award Nomination*: Best Adapted Screenplay. *Golden Globe Nominations*: Best Motion Picture–Drama and Best Director–Motion Picture

Alternate Film: *A Place in the Sun*

5

PICNIC

Year: 1955
Genre: Drama
Run Time: 1 hour 55 minutes
Date Revealed in Film: 3:42
Availability: Blu-ray (Twilight Time), DVD (Sony Pictures)
Director: Joshua Logan; **Screenplay**: William Taradash, based on William Inge's play
Cast: William Holden (Hal Carter), Kim Novak (Madge Owens), Cliff Robertson (Alan Benson), Verna Felton (Mrs. Potts), Betty Field (Mrs. Owens), Susan Strasberg (Millie Owens), Rosalind Russell (Rosemary), Arthur O'Connell (Howard Bevans)

On Labor Day, September 5, 1955, Hal Carter, an unemployed former football star and actor, arrives by freight car in a small Kansas town to visit Alan Benson, an old fraternity buddy. Hal meets Madge Owens, Alan's girlfriend, whom Alan's father thinks is beneath him. Alan promises Hal a job and invites him to the Labor Day picnic with Madge's younger sister Millie as his date. Disaster strikes at the picnic. Middle-aged schoolteacher Rosemary came to the dance with storeowner Howard. She causes an altercation that Hal gets blamed for. Madge and Hal drive off in Alan's car. He tells her he is a failure, but she kisses him and they agree to meet the next day. Alan has reported his car stolen, so Hal has to hide out at Howard's house (00:01 to 1:37:43). The next day Hal leaves town the way he arrived, but with hope for the future.

An offbeat romance film. Two disparate characters come together, as each can supply what the other lacks. A time capsule of small-town America of the 1950s.

Awards: *Academy Award Wins*: Best Art Direction and Best Film Editing. *Academy Award Nominations*: Best Supporting Actor (Arthur O'Connell), Best Director, Best Original Music Score, and Best Picture. *Golden Globe Win*: Best Motion Picture Director

Alternate Film: *The Man in the Iron Mask* (1998)

6

THE STING

Year: 1973
Genre: Comedy/Drama
Run Time: 2 hours 9 minutes
Date Revealed in Film: 1:38, 3:22
Availability: Blu-ray and DVD (Universal Studios)
Director: George Roy Hill; **Screenplay**: David S. Ward
Cast: Paul Newman (Henry "Shaw" Gondorff), Robert Redford (Johnny "Kelly" Hooker), Robert Shaw (Doyle Lonnegan), Charles Durning (Lt. William Snyder), Ray Walston (J. J. Singleton), Eileen Brennan (Billie), Harold Gould (Kid Twist)

On September 6, 1936, in Joliet, Illinois, Johnny Hooker and his partner, Luther, manage to con $11,000 off of a guy (1:23 to 24:05). Unfortunately, their victim was carrying money that belonged to Mob boss Lonnegan, who orders a hit put on them. Hooker teams up with Henry Gondorff to pull a fast one on Lonnegan after Lonnegan's men kill Luther. Eventually he proposes to run "the wire" and they recruit other con artists to assist in setting up a supposed betting parlor. Gondorff, using the alias "Shaw," arranges to put Lonnegan in his debt. Hooker, in his disguise as "Kelly," "Shaw's" lieutenant, convinces Lonnegan that he wants to "take down" "Shaw" and can do it with his help by using inside info to wipe out "Shaw" with a big win on a horse race. Hooker convinces Lonnegan the plan will work and Lonnegan agrees to supply $400,000 for a bet. The pair hold their breath on the day they run "the sting" as they have to deal with Lonnegan's suspicions and an FBI agent who threatens to arrest them if they don't cooperate.

A good story and interesting characters. Has a couple of great plot twists. Good music too.

Awards: *Academy Award Wins*: Best Picture, Best Director, Best Original Screenplay, Best Art Direction, Best Costume Design, Best Film Editing, and Best Music. *Academy Award Nominations*: Best Actor (Robert Redford), Best Cinematography, and Best Sound. *Golden Globe Nomination*: Best Screenplay–Motion Picture

Alternate Film: *The Producers* (1967)

7

GENTLEMAN JIM

Year: 1942
Genre: Sports/Biography
Run Time: 1 hour 44 minutes
Availability: DVD (Warner Home Video), VHS (MGM/UA Home Video)
Director: Raoul Walsh; **Screenplay**: Vincent Lawrence and Horace McCoy
Cast: Errol Flynn (James J. Corbett), Alexis Smith (Victoria Ware), Jack Carson (Walter Lowrie), Alan Hale Sr. (Pat Corbett), William Frawley (Bill Delaney), Ward Bond (John L. Sullivan), Madeline LeBeau (Anna Held), Minor Watson (Buck Ware)

In 1887 San Francisco the police raid an illegal prizefight, but Comstock bank employee Jim Corbett uses his quick wits to get himself and bank director Judge Geary released without charges and earns a raise. Corbett finagles his way into the prestigious Olympic club, where he holds his own in a bout with English boxer Watson. Corbett's self-confident attitude wears on Miss Ware, but he wins all the bouts she hopes he will lose. Corbett travels the country engaging in prizefights, winning them all. Corbett meets the world heavyweight champ, John L. Sullivan, and provokes him into agreeing to a $25,000 prize bout. The bout takes place on September 7, 1892, in New Orleans. Corbett finally KO's Sullivan. At Corbett's celebratory dinner, Sullivan shows up and personally hands over the heavyweight title belt to Corbett. Miss Ware finally admits she likes Corbett (1:24:34 to 1:44:07).

An interesting, if Hollywoodized, biopic of the famous boxer who brought the sport out of the bare-knuckles era into the modern age. One of Flynn's best performances, as he plays Corbett as a smooth-talking, self-aggrandizing type. Bond's scene where he hands over the belt makes the movie.

Source: Roberts, James B. *The Boxing Register*. Ithaca, NY: McBooks Press, 1997. This book gives the date of the bout at page 61.

Alternate Film: *The Lost Weekend*

8

SHAKESPEARE IN LOVE

Year: 1998
Genre: Romantic Comedy
Run Time: 2 hours 3 minutes
Date Revealed in Film: 1:55
Availability: Blu-ray (Lionsgate Films), DVD (Miramax)
Director: John Madden; **Screenplay**: Marc Norman and Tom Stoppard
Cast: Joseph Fiennes (William Shakespeare), Gwyneth Paltrow (Viola de Lesseps), Colin Firth (Lord Wessex), Ben Affleck (Ned Alleyn), Geoffrey Rush (Philip Henslowe), Judi Dench (Queen Elizabeth I), Tom Wilkinson (Hugh Fennyman)

On September 8, 1593, Henslowe, manager of the Globe Theatre who is in debt to Fennyman, saves himself by offering Fennyman a partnership in Will Shakespeare's new play, *Romeo and Ethel, the Pirate's Daughter* (00:54 to 15:56). Will has writer's block, however. His girlfriend Rosalind and Richard Burbage, a fellow actor, betray him. He meets Viola de Lesseps, who learns her parents are forcing her to marry Lord Wessex, a penniless nobleman. At their engagement ball Wessex notices Will and Viola's attraction to each other, but Will gives his name as "Christopher Marlowe." Will gets his muse back and Kent (Viola in disguise) gets the part of Romeo. Will learns Viola is Kent. Will and Viola begin an affair. Wessex arrives and takes Viola to meet Queen Elizabeth, with Will in drag as her chaperone. Wessex makes a bet with Viola, to be judged by the queen, that "a play cannot disclose the true nature of love." Wessex has Christopher Marlowe killed, but Viola thinks

Will has been killed. Wessex shows up to kill Will and Viola is exposed as a woman, so the Globe is closed. Burbage allows Will to use his theater, the Curtain, to perform *Romeo and Juliet*. Wessex and Viola are wed that day, but she runs away to the play and ends up playing Romeo's part. The Master of the Revels arrives to arrest everyone for allowing a woman on stage. However, a member of the audience puts things aright.

A delightful film. Its many anachronistic touches are a hoot. Not very factual, but definitely very funny.

Awards: *Academy Award Wins*: Best Picture, Best Actress (Gwyneth Paltrow), Best Supporting Actress (Judi Dench), Best Art Direction, Best Costume Design, Best Original Score, and Best Original Screenplay. *Academy Award Nominations*: Best Director, Best Supporting Actor (Geoffrey Rush), Best Cinematography, Best Film Editing, and Best Makeup. *Golden Globe Wins*: Best Motion Picture–Comedy/Musical, Best Performance by an Actress in a Motion Picture–Comedy/Musical (Paltrow), and Best Screenplay–Motion Picture. *Golden Globe Nominations*: Best Director–Motion Picture, Best Performance by an Actress in a Supporting Role in a Motion Picture (Dench), and Best Performance by an Actor in a Supporting Role in a Motion Picture (Rush)

Alternate Film: *MacArthur*

9

VON RYAN'S EXPRESS

Year: 1965
Genre: Adventure
Run Time: 1 hour 57 minutes
Availability: Blu-ray and DVD (Twentieth Century Fox)
Director: Mark Robson; **Screenplay**: Wendell Mayes and Joseph Landon, based on David Westheimer's novel
Cast: Frank Sinatra (Colonel Joseph L. Ryan), Trevor Howard (Major Eric Fincham), Brad Dexter (Sergeant Bostick), Sergio Fantoni (Captain Oriani), John Leyton (Orde), Edward Mulhare (Captain Costanzo), Wolfgang Preiss (Major Von Klemment)

An American air force pilot, Capt. Joseph Ryan, is shot down over Italy and taken to a mostly British-occupied Italian POW camp run by Major Battaglia.

Ryan becomes the senior Allied officer and by force of will restores discipline and gets better conditions for the prisoners. While Ryan is in the punishment box, Italy's armistice with the Allies is announced and almost all the guards desert. Ryan is released on September 9, 1943, and has to stop the British from trying Battaglia as a war criminal (31:26 to 38:59). Germans show up and capture the POWs, putting them on trains to take them to Germany. Ryan and his officers take over the train, impersonating the guards, and head for Switzerland. They have some tense moments and hair-raising escapes as the film builds toward an exciting climax as the train nears the Swiss border.

A very improbable story, but a good one. Plenty of action and suspense. Also good character studies and contrast of British and American attitudes.

Awards: *Academy Award Nomination*: Best Special Effects

Source: Atkinson, Rick. *The Day of Battle: The War in Sicily and Italy 1943–1944*. New York: Henry Holt and Company, 2007. This book at page 195 gives the time and date Eisenhower announced the Italian surrender as 6:30 PM on September 8, 1943.

Alternate Film: *I Am Legend*

10

300

Year: 2006

Genre: War

Run Time: 1 hour 57 minutes

Availability: Blu-ray and DVD (Warner Home Video)

Director: Zack Snyder; **Screenplay**: Zack Snyder, Kurt Johnstad, and Michael B. Gordon

Cast: Gerard Butler (Leonidas I of Sparta), Lena Headey (Gorgo), Giovani Cimmino (Pleistarchus), Dominic West (Theron), David Wenham (Aristodemus), Tom Wisdom (Astinos), Andrew Tiernan (Ephialtes of Trachis), Rodrigo Santoro (Xerxes I of Persia)

Leonidas is put through the brutal Spartan system to become a warrior and king. Messengers arrive from Persia demanding Sparta's submission, but Leonidas kills them. Leonidas proposes using the narrow pass of Thermopyle to funnel the Persians into a narrow killing field, negating their numerical superiority. Theron, a Persian agent, stops a declaration of war, so Leonidas only has the three hundred men of his "bodyguard." At the pass they build a wall. Leonidas refuses the hunchback Ephialtes's request to fight with the Spartans. The Persians attack, but they are defeated. Ephialtes defects to the Persians and tells them of a path around the Spartans. Leonidas sends Dilios for reinforcements. In Sparta Queen Gorgo allows Theron to have sex with her in return for agreeing to support the decision to send the whole army to support Leonidas. However, Theron says the exact opposite, so she kills Theron, whose treachery is discovered. Back at Thermopyle, the Greeks are attacked from both sides on September 10, 480 BC, and wiped out (1:33:51 to 1:43:15). A year later, Dilios leads a unified Greek army to victory against the Persians.

The action is a lot bloodier than was really needed. Commendable for on the whole sticking to the classical story of this great battle.

Source: Greswell, Edward. *The Origins of the Greek Calendar*. London: E. Doychincki Collin & Co., 1827. This book at page 374 gives the date of the battle.

Alternate Film: *Flight of the Intruder*

11
EXTREMELY LOUD & INCREDIBLY CLOSE
Year: 2011
Genre: Drama
Run Time: 2 hours 9 minutes
Date Revealed in Film: 10:44–45
Availability: Blu-ray and DVD (Warner Home Video)
Director: Stephen Daldry; **Screenplay**: Eric Roth, based on Jonathan Foer's novel
Cast: Thomas Horn (Oskar Schell), Tom Hanks (Thomas Schell), Sandra Bullock (Linda Schell), Max von Sydow (The Renter), Viola Davis (Abby Black), Jeffrey Wright (William Black), John Goodman (Stan the door-man), Zoe Caldwell (Oscar's grandma)

At his father's funeral Oskar Schell, who has Asperger's syndrome, complains that since the coffin is empty, the funeral makes no sense. Thomas and his father engaged in scavenger hunts and puzzles. On September 11, 2001, Oskar is let out of school early and goes home alone because his mother, Linda, is at work. Oskar finds messages on the answering machine from his father saying that he is trapped in the World Trade Center and Oskar hides under his bed (9:44–11:47; 33:40–40:03; 50:44–52:57; 1:22:18–1:22:24; 1:22:40–1:22:59; 1:23:19–1:23:38; 1:24:07–1:24:12; 1:40:57–1:41:37; and 1:42:40–1:42:43). A year later, Oskar enters his father's closet for the first time since he died and breaks a blue vase. This leads him to a puzzle that involves meeting all the people named Black in New York to find out about a key. A man who moves in with his grandmother tells Oskar he is a stranger. Oskar has hidden from his mother the calls his father made on September 11. Oskar visits many Blacks, none of whom knew his father or about the key. Oskar and his mother have a fight because she can't explain to Oskar why his father died. The stranger goes with Oskar and helps him on his quest. Oskar concludes that the stranger is his grandfather. The stranger moves out and tells Oskar not to search anymore. Then Oskar calls a phone number he found on a newspaper clipping his father gave him and this leads him to the conclusion of his search. Oskar makes a scrapbook about the search.

A moving film about a boy's effort to make sense of the inexplicable. We, like Oskar, want everything to have an explanation, but some events have no explanation.

Awards: *Academy Award Nominations*: Best Picture and Best Supporting Actor (Max von Sydow)

Alternate Film: *Brian's Song* (2011)

12

CRY FREEDOM

Year: 1987
Genre: Drama
Run Time: 2 hours 37 minutes
Date Revealed in Film: 1:09:29
Availability: Blu-ray (Universal Studios), VHS (MC Home Video)
Director: Richard Attenborough; **Screenplay**: John Briley, based on Donald Woods's books *Biko* and *Asking for Trouble*
Cast: Denzel Washington (Steve Biko), Kevin Kline (Donald Woods), Penelope Wilton (Wendy Woods), John Thaw (Jimmy Kruger), Robert Jones (Charles Jenkins), John Hargreaves (Bruce Haigh), Josette Simon (Mamphela Ramphele)

After a police raid on Crossroads Township near Capetown, editor Donald Woods writes an article about Steven Biko, calling him "racist." He is challenged on this and he meets with Biko, and this leads to a change in Woods's attitude about race relations. As a result, Woods becomes the object of a police investigation. Biko leaves his banned area and is arrested. He dies in police custody on September 12, 1977 (1:08:27 to 1:09:37). Donald Woods is not allowed to leave the country and his work is banned. An elaborate plan is hatched to get him and his family out of the country.

A good film with likeable, well-developed characters. Doesn't really show the brutality of the apartheid regime. It does show the duplicity of South Africa's white leaders.

Awards: *Academy Award Nomination*: Best Supporting Actor (Denzel Washington). *Golden Globe Nominations*: Best Motion Picture–Drama, Best Director–Motion Picture, Best Performance by an Actor in a Motion Picture–Drama (Washington), and Best Original Score–Motion Picture

Alternate Film: *The Chronicles of Narnia: The Voyage of the Dawn Treader*

13
IN THE HEAT OF THE NIGHT

Year: 1967
Genre: Drama
Run Time: 1 hour 49 minutes
Date Revealed in Film: 14:09, 14:36
Availability: Blu-ray and DVD (Metro-Goldwyn-Mayer)
Director: Norman Jewison; **Screenplay**: Stirling Silliphant, based on John Ball's novel
Cast: Sidney Poitier (Virgil Tibbs), Rod Steiger (Bill Gillespie), Warren Oates (Sam Wood), Lee Grant (Mrs. Leslie Colbert), Larry Gates (Eric Endicott), James Patterson (Lloyd Purdy), William Schallert (Mayor Schubert), Quentin Dean (Delores Purdy)

Police officer Sam Wood is patrolling just after midnight on September 13, 1966, in the small town of Sparta, Mississippi, when he finds the murdered body of Mr. Colbert, who had come to the town to build a much wanted and needed factory. An African American is arrested, but it turns out he's Virgil Tibbs, a police detective from Philadelphia whose chief "volunteers" him to assist on the case. Tibbs and Chief Gillespie do not work together well, but pressure from Colbert's widow, who hints she might move the factory else-where, forces them to work together (00:25 to 1:12:48). They suspect three different people in turn, including Sam Wood. However, Tibbs is convinced Sam is innocent and sets out to clear him and in the process uncovers the real killer and the real reason for Colbert's death.

A powerful indictment of racial prejudice. Excellent performances by all the actors and a great score by Quincy Jones. It also happens to be a pretty good police procedural murder mystery.

Awards: *Academy Award Wins*: Best Picture, Best Actor (Rod Steiger), Best Film Editing, Best Sound, and Best Adapted Screenplay. *Academy Award Nominations*: Best Director and Best Sound Editing. *Golden Globe Wins*: Best Motion Picture–Drama, Best Motion Picture Actor–Drama (Steiger), and Best Screenplay. *Golden Globe Nominations*: Best Motion Picture Director, Best Motion Picture Actor–Drama (Sidney Poitier), Best Supporting Actress (Lee Grant and Quentin Dean).

Alternate Film: *On Her Majesties' Secret Service*

14
ALL THE PRESIDENT'S MEN
Year: 1976
Genre: Drama
Run Time: 2 hours 18 minutes
Availability: Blu-ray and DVD (Warner Home Video)
Director: Alan J. Pakula; **Screenplay**: William Goldman, based on Carl Bernstein and Bob Woodward's book
Cast: Dustin Hoffman (Carl Bernstein), Robert Redford (Bob Woodward), Jack Warden (Harry M. Rosenfeld), Martin Balsam (Howard Simons), Hal Holbrook (Deep Throat), Jason Robards (Ben Bradlee), Jane Alexander (Judy Hoback)

Five men are caught breaking into Democratic Party National Headquarters in the Watergate Hotel in Washington, D.C., in the summer of 1972. Bob Woodward starts an investigation of this and is joined by Carl Bernstein. An FBI contact of Woodward, called "Deep Throat," gives them clues that enable them to trace the money used to pay the burglars to President Nixon's re-election campaign. Through former Nixon campaign treasurer Hugh

Sloan and a bookkeeper at the Committee to Re-Elect the President (CREEP), whom Bernstein interviews on September 14, 1972, they trace a connection to H. R. Haldeman, the White House chief of staff, and former attorney general John Mitchell (1:13:40 to 1:24:57). Although "Deep Throat" warns their lives are in danger; Woodward and Bernstein persist in the investigation, which ultimately leads to the resignation of President Richard Nixon.

An almost documentary story following the early days of the Watergate scandal. Highlights an almost forgotten era in America when reporters actually investigated the facts instead of making them up. Very realistic performances by Redford and Hoffman.

Awards: *Academy Award Wins*: Best Art Direction, Best Adapted Screenplay, Best Sound, and Best Supporting Actor (Jason Robards). *Academy Award Nominations*: Best Director, Best Editing, and Best Supporting Actress (Jane Alexander). *Golden Globes Nominations*: Best Motion Picture–Drama, Best Director–Motion Picture, Best Motion Picture Actor in a Supporting Role (Robards), and Best Screenplay–Motion Picture

Alternate Film: *Missing*

15

THE UNTOUCHABLES

Year: 1987

Genre: Crime Drama

Run Time: 1 hour 59 minutes

Date Revealed in Film: 6:43

Availability: Blu-ray (Warner Home Video), DVD (Paramount Home Video)

Director: Brian De Palma; **Screenplay**: David Mamet, based on Eliot Ness and Oscar Fraley's book

Cast: Kevin Costner (Eliot Ness), Sean Connery (Jim Malone), Robert De Niro (Al Capone), Charles Martin Smith (Oscar Wallace), Andy García (George Stone), Patricia Clarkson (Catherine Ness), Billy Drago (Frank Nitti), Richard Bradford (Mike Dorsett)

Al Capone enforces his control over bootlegging in Chicago by violence. On September 15, 1931, Eliot Ness starts his job in Chicago as a federal treasury agent (6:41 to 15:54). The first tip he gets embarrassingly leads to veggies and not liquor. Oscar Wallace, an accountant, comes from the home office and suggests going after Capone for income tax evasion. Ness convinces Malone, a Chicago cop he's met, to join his task force. They recruit "George Stone" from the police academy. Capone threatens Ness's family, so Ness sends them away. Based on a tip from Malone they stop a big liquor shipment at the border. By shooting a corpse, Malone tricks an arrested Capone flunky into revealing info about Capone's finances. Capone has the talkative flunky and Wallace killed. After personally confronting Capone, Ness almost gives up his quest. He changes his mind and subpoenas Capone's bookkeeper. Capone has Malone killed, but he lives long enough to tell Ness when the bookkeeper is leaving town. In a bloody shootout at Union Station, Ness and Stone kill the guards with the bookkeeper and take him into custody; he agrees to cooperate. Capone is put on trial for income tax evasion. During the trial Ness has to fight both Capone and the courts to get justice.

A good police procedural. Plenty of action and suspense. A lot of on-screen violence. Good performances by all the major players.

Awards: *Academy Award Win*: Best Supporting Actor (Sean Connery). *Academy Award Nominations*: Best Costume Design, Best Set Decoration, and Best Score. *Golden Globe Win*: Best Performance by an Actor in a Supporting Role in a Motion Picture (Connery). *Golden Globe Nomination*: Best Original Score–Motion Picture

Alternate Film: *Sabrina* (1954)

16
THE DAY THE EARTH STOOD STILL
Year: 1951
Genre: Science Fiction
Run Time: 1 hour 32 minutes
Availability: Blu-ray and DVD (Twentieth Century Fox)
Director: Robert Wise; **Screenplay**: Edmund H. North, based on Harry Bates's short story "Farewell to the Master"
Cast: Michael Rennie (Klaatu), Patricia Neal (Helen Benson), Billy Gray (Bobby Benson), Hugh Marlowe (Tom Stevens), Sam Jaffe (Professor Jacob Barnhardt), Frances Bavier (Mrs. Barley), Lock Martin (Gort), Frank Conroy (Mr. Harley)

On September 16, 1951, a flying saucer lands on the Ellipse in Washington, DC. A man emerges, but when he opens a device he is holding a nervous soldier shoots him. A huge robot emerges and destroys all the army's weapons without harming anyone. The man, Klaatu, is treated at a hospital. He says he has a message for the entire world but is told international divisions mean world leaders can't even agree on a place to hear it. Klaatu escapes and checks into a boarding house, calling himself Mr. Carpenter. There he meets Helen Benson, a war widow, and her son, Bobby (00:14 to 17:45). At Klaatu's request, Bobby names scientist Jacob Barnhardt as the greatest man in the world. They visit the professor's house and Klaatu solves a problem he has left on a blackboard. Klaatu returns, meets Dr. Barnhardt, and tells him other planets are concerned due to Earth's discovery of atomic power and that if Klaatu's message is rejected, Earth will be eliminated. Dr. Barnhardt pleads for a demonstration of Klaatu's power and he agrees. The next day Klaatu speaks to Helen while they are stuck in an elevator, as Klaatu has ended electric power all over the Earth for a time. Klaatu tells her who he is and asks for her help. However, Helen's boyfriend has become suspicious of "Mr. Carpenter," and when Klaatu is killed Helen becomes the world's only hope for peace.

One of the classic sci-fi films. Presents its antiwar message without beating you over the head. And of course it gave us the classic phrase "Klaatu barada nikto!"

Awards: *Golden Globe Win*: Best Film Promoting International Understanding. *Golden Globe Nomination*: Best Motion Picture Score

Source: Healy, Raymond J., and McComas, Francis, eds. *Adventures in Time and Space*. New York: Random House, 1946. This book at page 789 gives the date as September 16.

Alternate Film: *Far and Away*

17
A BRIDGE TOO FAR

Year: 1977
Genre: War
Run Time: 2 hours 55 minutes
Availability: Blu-ray and DVD (Metro-Goldwyn-Mayer)

Director: Richard Attenborough; **Screenplay**: William Goldman, based on
the Cornelius Ryan book
Cast: Dirk Bogarde (Gen. Browning), James Caan (Eddie Dohun), Michael
Caine (Col. Vandeleur), Sean Connery (Gen. Urqhart), Edward Fox (Gen.
Horrocks), Elliott Gould (Col. Stout), Gene Hackman (Gen. Sosabowski),
Anthony Hopkins (Col. Frost)

In 1944 after the Normandy breakout and the fall of Paris the Germans
retreat but stiffen their lines along the Dutch-Belgian border. Gen. Montgomery plans "Operation Market-Garden," where paratroops will seize the
Rhine Bridge at Arnhem and others in between it and the Allied lines and
hold until Allied armor can reach them. The planning is rushed. Meanwhile,
the Germans unfortunately decide to rest the II SS Panzer Corps at Arnhem.
The drops go as planned on September 17, 1944 (36:43 to 1:19:44). However,
problems develop. Radios don't work and the Germans capture a complete
set of Allied plans. One bridge is blown up that takes thirty-six hours to repair, slowing the Allied tanks. Then the Allies have to mount an amphibious
operation to capture the big Nijmegan bridge. Meanwhile, at Arnhem the
small British force holding one end of the bridge crumbles under attacks by
two SS divisions. The tanks arrive near Arnhem just in time to evacuate the
survivors of the paratroopers.

The last of the epic World War II battle movies. Ultra realistic and detailed.
Shows the "don't rock the boat" mentality that contributed to failure.
Source: Hastings, Max. *Armageddon: The Battle for Germany 1944–1945.*
New York: Alfred A. Knopf, 2004. This book at page 37 give the date of
the landings.
Alternate Film: *Frida*

18

THE ROOKIE

Year: 2002
Genre: Biography
Run Time: 2 hours 7 minutes
Availability: Blu-ray (Disney/Buena Vista)
Director: John Lee Hancock; **Screenplay**: Mike Rich
Cast: Dennis Quaid (Jim Morris), Rachel Griffiths (Lorri), Brian Cox (Jim
Morris Sr.), Angus T. Jones (Hunter), Angelo Spizzirri (Joel De La Garza),
Jay Hernandez (Joaquin "Wack" Campos), Rick Gonzalez (Rudy Bonilla)

Jim Morris grows up in a military family that moves around a lot with a father who does not support his baseball dreams. Morris had to have shoulder surgery after being drafted by the majors and never played. He ends up teaching science and coaching baseball in Big Lake, Texas. The team is losing, but he bets them that if they win the district championship, he will try out for the major leagues after they clocked his pitching speed at over 90 mph. They win the title and he goes to the tryout and pitches at 98 mph. He gets a second tryout and joins the Orlando AA team. His pitching wins games, and he moves on to the Durham Bulls. He considers quitting the team to be with his family. He gets called up by the Tampa Bay Devil Rays and pitches his first game on September 18, 1999. He reconnects with his dad and the whole town of Big Lake comes to the game to cheer him on (1:45:57 to 2:02:16).

A movie about believing in yourself. This movie keeps the melodrama under control and it turns out pretty good. One movie that the whole family can see.

Source: Morris, Jim, and Engel, Joel. *The Rookie*. New York: Warner Books, 2001. This book at pages 263–70 gives the date of the game.

Alternate Film: *The Way We Were*

19
THE GREATEST GAME EVER PLAYED

Genre: Sports/Biography
Run Time: 2 hours
Date Revealed in Film: 1:14:00
Availability: Blu-ray and DVD (Disney/Buena Vista)
Director: Bill Paxton; **Screenplay**: Mark Frost, based on his book
Cast: Shia LaBeouf (Francis Ouimet), Stephen Dillane (Harry Vardon), Josh Flitter (Eddie Lowery), Peter Firth (Lord Northcliffe), Peyton List (Sarah Wallis), Elias Koteas (Arthur Ouimet), Len Cariou (Stedman Comstock), Stephen Marcus (Ted Ray)

This is the story of caddie Francis Ouimet, who overcomes his father's opposition to play in the Eighteenth U.S. Open. He faces English pro Harry Vardon, a gardener's son who is fighting his own battle to be accepted by the upper-crust English golf establishment. Ouimet plays well enough in the first and second rounds to stay close. The next day he is one stroke back after the rainy third round. Ouimet plays well enough in the afternoon fourth round, September 19, 1913, to force a playoff. Ouimet and Vardon are neck and neck in the playoff until the seventeenth hole, when Vardon's attempt to put him away backfires and Ouimet takes a one-stroke lead, which he maintains on the eighteenth hole to win the round and the tournament (1:08:34 to 1:24:14).

Another great movie about the power of self-confidence. Both Ouimet and Vardon believe in themselves, which makes them unstoppable. Excellent special effects work helps make the shots of play much more interesting. **Alternate Film**: *The Crucible*

20
SENSE AND SENSIBILITY
Year: 1995
Genre: Period Drama
Run Time: 2 hours 16 minutes
Availability: Blu-ray and DVD (Sony Pictures)
Director: Ang Lee; **Screenplay**: Emma Thompson, based on Jane Austen's novel
Cast: Emma Thompson (Elinor Dashwood), Alan Rickman (Col. Christopher Brandon), Kate Winslet (Marianne Dashwood), Hugh Grant (Edward Ferrars), Greg Wise (John Willoughby), Gemma Jones (Mrs. Dashwood), Robert Hardy (Sir John Middleton)

When the elder Mr. Dashwood dies, by law everything goes to his son John, child of his first marriage, leaving nothing for his widow and three daughters, Elinor, Marianne, and Margaret. John allows his wife, Fanny, to talk him out of seriously helping his half-sisters and the couple take over the Dashwood's home, Norland. Fanny's brother, Edward Ferrars, comes to visit and seems to be forming an attachment to Elinor Dashwood, but later leaves. The elder Mrs. Dashwood and her daughters relocate to Barton Cottage in Devon through the charity of her cousin Sir John Middleton. While there, they meet Col. Brandon and John Willoughby. Willoughby carries Marianne home after she is injured on September 20, 1797 (36:27 to 44:55). He calls on her several times. Unfortunately, and unknown to the Dashwoods, Willoughby has seduced Col. Brandon's ward Eliza Williams and his aunt disinherits him, necessitating his removal to London without explanation, leaving Marianne broken hearted. Sir John's mother-in-law Mrs. Jennings invites her daughter, Mrs. Palmer, to the area. She brings with her the impoverished Lucy Steele,

who confides to Elinor that she and Edward Ferrars have been secretly engaged for five years. The Dashwoods travel to London, where they meet Willoughby and learn that he is now engaged to a wealthy woman, devastating
Marianne. Edward Ferrars's secret engagement comes to light and his mother
disinherits him. Col. Brandon gives Edward Ferrars the post of minister at
the parish church on his estate. Returning from London, Elinor, Marianne,
and Col. Brandon stop at the home of the Palmers, where Marianne walks in
a storm to see Willoughby's estate and becomes seriously ill. She develops a
tenderness for Col. Brandon after he carries her back to the house and rides
to bring her mother to her. They return home, where Col. Brandon courts
Marianne. They learn that Lucy Steele has become Mrs. Ferrars and presume
she is wed to Edward until he arrives and tells them that since he was disin-
herited Miss Steele has wed his newly rich younger brother instead. Edward
and Elinor marry in a double ceremony with Col. Brandon and Marianne.

Another classic by Jane Austen. A romance of manners. Great plots twists
keep you guessing on this one until the very end.

Awards: *Academy Award Win*: Best Adapted Screenplay. *Academy Award
Nominations*: Best Picture, Best Actress (Emma Thompson), Best Supporting Actress (Kate Winslet), Best Cinematography, Best Costume Design,
and Best Original Score. *Golden Globe Wins*: Best Screenplay–Motion
Picture and Best Motion Picture–Drama. *Golden Globe Nominations*: Best
Director–Motion Picture, Best Performance by an Actress in a Motion
Picture–Drama (Thompson), Best Performance by an Actress in a Supporting Role in a Motion Picture (Winslet), and Best Original Score–Motion Picture

Source: http://www.jimandellen.org/austen/s&s.calendar.html

Alternate Film: *The Kingdom of Heaven*

21
PLACES IN THE HEART

Year: 1984
Genre: Drama
Run Time: 1 hour 51 minutes
Date Revealed in Film: 1:19:20, 1:23:54
Availability: DVD (Sony Pictures), VHS (CBS/Fox Video)

Director: Robert Benton; **Screenplay**: Robert Benton
Cast: Sally Field (Edna Spalding), Lindsay Crouse (Margaret Lomax), Danny
  Glover (Moze), John Malkovich (Mr. Will), Ed Harris (Wayne Lomax),
  Ray Baker (Sheriff Royce Spalding), Amy Madigan (Viola Kelesey), Yank-
  ton Hatten (Frank Spalding)
In 1935 in Waxahachie, Texas, Sheriff Spalding is accidentally shot by an
African American youth, leaving behind his widow, Edna, and two children,
Frank and "Possum." Of course, the townspeople lynch the youth despite it
being an accident. The bank wonders how Edna is going to pay the mortgage.
Mrs. Spalding's bother-in-law, Wayne, who's married to her sister, Margaret,
is having an affair with Viola, a schoolteacher. An African American man,
Moze, shows up asking for work and tells Edna she could make money by
cotton farming. She sends him away, but later Moze is brought back with sil-
verware he stole from her. Edna covers for him and asks him to stay and help
her grow cotton. The banker brings his blind brother-in-law, Mr. Will, to live
with her and pay room and board. After cotton prices fall, Mrs. Spalding decides the only way to make enough money to pay the mortgage is to have the
first bale of cotton baled in the county, which earns a $100 prize. They have
to hire pickers to get the cotton picked in time and when the itinerant pickers
arrive in the county it becomes a race. They pick through the night and win
the race. On September 21, 1935, Mrs. Spalding takes her cotton to the gin
and even gets an above-market price so the gin can keep the "honor" of gun-
ning the first bale of cotton that year (1:26:32 to 1:31:31). The Spaldings go to
a dance, and while they are gone, the Ku Klux Klan comes after Moze, but Mr.
Will saves him by disclosing that he can identify them by voice. Moze leaves.
Margaret forgives Wayne and we end with the iconic communion service.
    A powerful film. Deals with prejudice, faith, and forgiveness. An over-
looked classic.
Awards: *Academy Award Wins*: Best Actress (Sally Field) and Best Original
  Screenplay. *Academy Award Nominations*: Best Picture, Best Director, Best
  Costume Design, Best Supporting Actress (Lindsay Crouse), and Best Ac-
  tor (John Malkovich). *Golden Globe Win*: Best Performance by an Actress
  in a Motion Picture–Drama (Fields). *Golden Globe Nominations*: Best Motion Picture–Drama and Best Screenplay–Motion Picture
Alternate Film: *Monday Night Mayhem*

22

GOOD MORNING, VIETNAM

Year: 1987
Genre: War/Comedy
Run Time: 2 hours 1 minute
Date Revealed in Film: 1:28:28
Availability: Blu-ray and DVD (Disney/Buena Vista)
Director: Barry Levinson; **Screenplay**: Mitch Markowitz
Cast: Robin Williams (Adrian Cronauer), Forest Whitaker (Pfc. Garlick),
   Tung Thanh Tran (Tuan), Chintara Sukapatana (Trinh), Bruno Kirby
   (Steven Hauk), Robert Wuhl (Staff Sgt. Marty Lee Dreiwitz), J. T. Walsh
   (Sgt. Maj. Phillip Dickerson)
Early in the Vietnam War, Airman Second Class Adrian Cronauer arrives in
Saigon to be a DJ on Armed Forces Radio and his irreverent style, signature
opening yell of "Good Morning, Vietnam!" and introduction of rock-and-roll
music make him wildly popular with the troops in the field. This arouses the
ire of by-the-book Lt. Steven Hauk and Sergeant Major Phillip Dickerson,
but earns the friendship of Pfc. Garlick. Cronauer starts dating Trinh and
becomes friends with her brother Tuan. After violating policy, Adrian is suspended for a time, while Trinh breaks it off with him, saying their relationship
has no future. Dickerson approves Cronauer's plan to record interviews of
soldiers in the field knowing the route to An Lac, where Cronauer is going,
has fallen under the control of the Viet Cong. On September 22, 1965 (1:27:52
to 1:34:48), en route to An Lac, Cronauer and Garlick's jeep hits a mine and
they are forced to hide in the jungle to avoid the Viet Cong. Tuan saves them,
but this changes everything for Adrian, himself, Trinh, and Garlick.

   This is a funny film. The director didn't let Williams go over the top and
kept him under enough control, though much of Williams's banter was un-
scripted. The film also touches on the question of whether enemies can ever
be friends.

Awards: *Academy Award Nomination*: Best Actor (Robin Williams). *Golden
   Globe Win*: Best Performance by an Actor in a Motion Picture–Comedy/
   Musical (Williams)
Alternate Film: *Brighton Beach Memoirs*

23
AIR FORCE ONE
Year: 1997
Genre: Action/Adventure
Run Time: 2 hours 4 minutes
Date Revealed in Film: 1:57:35
Availability: Blu-ray and DVD (Sony Pictures)
Director: Wolfgang Petersen; **Screenplay:** Andrew W. Marlowe
Cast: Harrison Ford (James Marshall), Gary Oldman (Ivan Korshunov), Glenn Close (Kathryn Bennett), Wendy Crewson (Grace Marshall), Liesel Matthews (Alice Marshall), Xander Berkeley (Agent Gibbs), William H. Macy (Maj. Caldwell)

Russian and American forces land in Kazakhstan and capture a Russian, General Radek, who had led a genocidal regime there. Three weeks later, on September 23, 1995, U.S. president Jim Marshall and his wife and daughter are in Moscow. On the way home, men who are loyal to Radek hijack *Air Force One* with the help of a traitor. Marshall does not leave in the escape pod, but stays on board. The hijackers want Radek released. Marshall knocks out a guard and gets a weapon. He finds a satellite phone and calls the White House. Marshall is captured briefly, but escapes. He then frees most of the hostages and enables them to parachute to safety while a midair refueling is taking place. A firefight when the hijackers stop this results in the refueling tanker plane crashing and Marshall being captured. Under duress Marshall calls the Russian president and convinces him to release Radek. Marshall gets untied and defeats the hijackers. Radek is killed just as he is about to reach freedom. However, Marshall's problems are not over as there is not a pilot on *Air Force One*, the plane is almost out of fuel, and a traitor is still on board. (All the scenes in Washington are this date; the scenes on *Air Force One* are the next day.)

A wonderful film with lots of action. Gary Oldman is very good at creating the character of the crazy leader of the hijackers. Keeps you on the edge of your seat, as some of the best action occurs after what you think is the climax. **Awards:** *Academy Award Nominations*: Best Film Editing and Best Sound
Alternate Film: *John Paul Jones*

24

RADIO

Year: 2003
Genre: Biographical Drama
Run Time: 1 hour 49 minutes
Availability: Blu-ray (Sony Pictures), VHS (Columbia/TriStar Home Entertainment)
Director: Mike Tollin; **Screenplay**: Mike Rich
Cast: Cuba Gooding Jr. (James "Radio" Robert Kennedy), Ed Harris (Coach Jones), S. Epatha Merkerson (Mama Kennedy), Alfre Woodard (Principal Daniels), Debra Winger (Linda), Riley Smith (Johnny), Chris Mulkey (Frank), Patrick Breen (Tucker)

Football coach Jones at T. L. Hanna High School in Anderson, South Carolina, gets extremely angry when he discovers his football team has abused a young mentally challenged African American called "Radio" after the item he always has with him. The coach starts letting Radio help during practices. At the games, including the one against Easley on September 24, 1976 (31:09 to 31:33), Radio acts as a cheerleader. Some people in town start complaining about Radio's involvement with the team. Then some jocks at the school decide to get Radio.

A true feel-good story. As the coach says, Radio treats all of us the way we wish we treated each other.

Source: *The Greenville News-Piedmont* (Saturday, September 25, 1976), p. 1.
Alternate Film: *Ghost*

25

PRINCESS CARABOO

Year: 1994
Genre: Period Comedy
Run Time: 1 hour 37 minutes
Date Revealed in Film: 32:50
Availability: DVD and VHS (Columbia/TriStar Home Video)
Director: Michael Austin; **Screenplay**: Michael Austin and John Wells
Cast: Jim Broadbent (Mr. Worrall), Wendy Hughes (Mrs. Worrall), Kevin Kline (Frixos), Phoebe Cates (Princess Caraboo/Mary Baker), John

Lithgow (Professor Wilkinson), Stephen Rea (Gutch), Peter Eyre (Lord Apthorpe)

In Regency England an exotically dressed woman is found speaking a language no one can understand. She ends up at the home of the Worrall family, the local gentry. Their Greek butler, Frixos, thinks the woman is a fraud. Mrs. Worrall agrees to care for her. Mr. Gutch, a local printer and reporter, takes an interest when the woman claims via pantomime to be Princess Caraboo. When the Worralls are out the servants inspect her for a tattoo, which they believe all natives of the South Seas have, and are shocked to find she has one. On September 25, 1817 (32:49 to 34:20), Frixos tells Gutch he thinks she's real. Mr. Worrall uses her to recruit investors for the spice trade that will be facilitated by Princess Caraboo in her native land. Gutch brings in Professor Wilkinson, a linguist who refuses to say she is a fraud. Local society finds Princess Caraboo fascinating and Lady Apthorpe takes Caraboo to a ball for the Prince Regent. Gutch learns Caraboo is actually Mary Baker and Mary is locked up. However, in a surprise twist, that's not the end of Mary's story.

A very interesting movie based on a true story. Cates does an outstanding job of portraying Caraboo and Mary. A lighthearted comedy about the ability of people to believe what they want.

Alternate Film: *Goldfinger*

26

THE EXPRESS

Year: 2008
Genre: Biographical Drama
Run Time: 2 hours 10 minutes
Date Revealed in Film: 44:21
Availability: Blu-ray and DVD (Universal Studios)
Director: Gary Fleder; **Screenplay**: Charles Leavitt, based on Robert C. Gallagher's book *Ernie Davis: The Elmira Express*
Cast: Rob Brown (Ernie Davis), Charles S. Dutton (Willie "Pops" Davis), Dennis Quaid (Ben Schwartzwalder), Darrin Henson (Jim Brown), Omar Benson Miller (Jack Buckley), Nelsan Ellis (Will Davis Jr.), Nicole Beharie (Sarah Ward)

African American Ernie Davis can outrun racist bullies while growing up and plays pee wee football. Jim Brown, football superstar and player for the Cleveland Browns, recruits Ernie to play for Syracuse University. As a freshman, Ernie is so impressive he is put on the varsity squad, even though under NCAA rules at that time he can't play. He starts a romance with Sarah, a co-ed from Colgate. On September 26, 1959 (43:47 to 47:33), Ernie plays in his first game against Kansas. Ernie refuses to get involved in civil rights activism, while the team wins every game. The now number-one-ranked team votes to play number two, Texas, in the Cotton Bowl. In Dallas the three African Americans on the team have to stay in subpar rooms at the segregated hotel. In the Cotton Bowl, the racist behavior of the Texas team almost causes an on-field riot. Ernie makes an interception, and then scores on an eighty-seven-yard catch and run to put the game away. On defense he disrupts Texas's last-second Hail Mary attempt. The team boycotts the trophy presentation when they learn it is to be held at a segregated facility. Two years later, Ernie wins the Heisman trophy and is drafted by the Cleveland Browns. Then tragedy strikes.

An interesting, if Hollywoodized, biopic. This film takes many liberties with the facts. It's a good story, but whether it bears any relation to Ernie Davis's real life is an open question.

Alternate Film: *Machine-Gun Kelly*

27

ZODIAC

Year: 2007
Genre: Crime Drama
Run Time: 2 hours 37 minutes
Date Revealed in Film: 17:49
Availability: Blu-ray and DVD (Paramount Home Video)
Director: David Fincher; **Screenplay**: James Vanderbilt, based on Robert Graysmith's book
Cast: Jake Gyllenhaal (Robert Graysmith), Mark Ruffalo (SFPD Inspector David Toschi), Robert Downey Jr. (Paul Avery), Anthony Edwards (Inspector William Armstrong), Brian Cox (Melvin Belli), John Carroll Lynch (Arthur Leigh Allen)

In Vallejo, California, in the summer of 1969, an unknown assailant shoots a couple on "lover's lane." The killer sends letters to the *San Francisco Chronicle* that he wants published and gives his name as Zodiac. Robert Graysmith, a political cartoonist for the paper, becomes interested in the case, but crime reporter Avery dismisses his ideas. On September 27, 1969, Zodiac attacks a couple near Napa (17:43 to 23:12). Zodiac kills a cabbie in San Francisco and detectives Dave Toschi and Bill Armstrong are put on the case. Zodiac says he will call a TV show and wants to talk to lawyer Melvin Belli, but Zodiac does not call. Zodiac takes credit for the attempted kidnapping of a woman and her baby. Mr. Cheny in Torrence gives the police a tip about Arthur Leigh Allen, but the police can't tie him to the murders. Avery leaves the *Chronicle*. Graysmith becomes obsessed with the case and believes the killer must have known Darlene Ferrin, the first victim. Graysmith interviews Darlene's sister, who says her sister was afraid of "Leigh" and that other facts tie Allen to the case. Then the man who survived the first shooting reappears.

A compelling story based on true events. The characters are well developed and the plot is sharp.

Alternate Film: *Somebody Up There Likes Me*

28
AMELIE
Year: 2001
Genre: Romantic Comedy
Run Time: 2 hours 2 minutes
Date Revealed in Film: 1:56:15
Availability: Blu-ray (Lionsgate Films), DVD (Miramax)
Director: Jean-Pierre Jeunet; **Screenplay**: Guillaume Laurant and Jean-Pierre Jeunet
Cast: Audrey Tautou (Amelie Poulain), Matthieu Kassovitz (Nino Quincampoix), Rufus (Raphael Poulain), Serge Merlin ("the Glass Man"), Isabelle Ganty (Georgette), Claire Maurier (Suzanne), Dominique Pinon (Joseph), Jamel Debbouze (Lucien)

Amelie's eccentric parents homeschool her because they wrongly think she has a heart condition. Childhood events make Amelie an imaginative and thoughtful young woman who works at a café in Paris that is home to a quirky staff and idiosyncratic customers. Her neighbors include the "glass man," who re-creates Renoir's painting *Luncheon of the Boating Party* each year. Shock at the news of Princess Di's death leads her to find a tin box filled with a boy's childhood mementos hidden in the wall of her apartment. Amelie resolves to start doing good deeds to help others. She tracks down the owner of the box and surreptitiously returns it to him. She ends up with the photo album of a man who hangs around rail station photo booths. Amelie steers a customer, Joseph, off of annoying his ex-girlfriend Gina and into a relationship with Georgette. When Mr. Collignon, the greengrocer who is always insulting his assistant, accidentally leaves his key in the door, Amelie makes a copy and uses it to set up a series of delayed action practical jokes on the man. Amelie leaves a trail for Nino, the owner of the photo album, to follow and returns the book without talking to him, but inviting him to the café. Amelie performs good deeds for the glass man, her father, and the concierge of her apartment building. When Nino comes to the café, Amelie chickens out and doesn't talk to him, but with the help of those she has helped, finally overcomes her timidity. On September 28, 1997, Nino and Amelie celebrate their new love on a motorbike ride (1:56:14 to 1:57:26).

This is a very inadequate description of this wonderful film. It is too quirky and unusual to easily synopsize.

Awards: *Academy Award Nominations*: Best Art Direction, Best Cinematography, Best Foreign Language Film, Best Original Screenplay, and Best Sound. *Golden Globe Nomination*: Best Foreign Language Film

Alternate Film: *Looker*

29

CHINATOWN

Year: 1974

Genre: Crime Drama

Run Time: 2 hours 10 minutes

Date Revealed in Film: 16:20

Availability: Blu-ray (Warner Home Video), DVD (Paramount Home Video)

Director: Roman Polanski; **Screenplay**: Robert Towne

Cast: Jack Nicholson (Jake Gittes), Faye Dunaway (Evelyn Mulwray), John Huston (Noah Cross), John Hillerman (Russ Yelburton), Diane Ladd (Ida Sessions), Darrell Zwerling (Hollis I. Mulwray), Roy Jenson (Claude Mulvihill), Bruce Glover (Duffy)

A woman calling herself Mrs. Evelyn Mulwray hires L.A. private eye Jake Gittes to trail her husband, Hollis Mulwray, head of the water department, and Jake photographs Mulwray with a girl. On September 29, 1937 (16:20 to 33:23), the photos appear in the newspaper. Jake learns that the Mrs. Mulwray who hired him was fake and that Mulwray's drowned body was found in a reservoir. Jake learns Mulwray and Noah Cross, who is also Evelyn's father, were joint owners of the water system until Mulwray's belief that the system should belong to the public caused a split. Cross hires Jake to find the woman who hired him. Jake investigates suspicious land purchases. He has a one-night stand with Evelyn and meets her sister, Katherine. The police suspect Evelyn of her husband's murder and want Jake to produce her. After a confrontation where Jake learns who Katherine really is, Jake solves the crime and arranges a confrontation to bring things to a head.

A modern film noir classic. Told entirely from Jake's point of view, we see nothing he doesn't. You have to pay attention with this film's complex plot.

Awards: *Academy Award Win*: Best Original Screenplay. *Academy Award Nominations*: Best Picture, Best Director, Best Actor (Jack Nicholson), Best Cinematography, Best Actress (Faye Dunaway), Best Film Editing, Best Art Direction, Best Sound Mixing, Best Costume Design, and Best Original Score. *Golden Globe Wins*: Best Motion Picture–Drama, Best Director–Motion Picture, Best Motion Picture Actor–Drama (Nicholson), and Best Screenplay–Motion Picture. *Golden Globe Nominations*: Best Motion Picture Actress–Drama (Dunaway), Best Supporting Actor–Motion Picture (John Huston), and Best Original Score

Alternate Film: *Pride of the Yankees*

30
THE YEAR OF LIVING DANGEROUSLY

Year: 1983
Genre: Romantic Drama
Run Time: 1 hour 55 minutes
Availability: DVD (Warner Home Video), VHS (MGM/UA Home Video)
Director: Peter Weir; **Screenplay**: C. J. Koch, Peter Weir, and David Williamson, based on C. J. Koch's novel
Cast: Mel Gibson (Guy Hamilton), Sigourney Weaver (Jill Bryant), Linda Hunt (Billy Kwan), Michael Murphy (Pete Curtis), Bill Kerr (Colonel Henderson), Noel Ferrier (Wally O'Sullivan), Paul Sonkkila (Kevin Condon), Bembol Rocco (Kumar)

Guy Hamilton arrives in Jakarta, Indonesia, as the representative of the Australian Broadcasting Service. He meets Billy Kwan, a dwarf who does photography and introduces him to all the right people, including Jill Bryant, who works at the British embassy, with whom Guy starts an affair. Guy tries to confirm a communist uprising and Sukarno's police kill Kwan. When the army launches its coup d'état on September 30, 1965, Guy goes to the presidential palace to get the story, but he is beaten and his left eye is injured. Finally later that day he goes to the airport and with a mix of persuasion and boldness gets on the last plane out (1:38:32 to 1:51:25).

On the one hand it's a romance, on the other an exploration of how we should respond to poverty and suffering. Works as both.

Awards: *Academy Award Win*: Best Supporting Actress (Linda Hunt). *Golden Globe Nomination*: Best Performance by an Actress in a Supporting Role in a Motion Picture (Linda Hunt)

Source: Ricklefs, M. C. *A History of Modern Indonesia*. Stanford, CA: Stanford University Press, 2001. This book at page 338 gives the coup date.

Alternate Film: *Come Back to the Five and Dime, Jimmie Dean, Jimmie Dean*

October

1

THE KING AND I

Year: 1956

Genre: Romantic Musical

Run Time: 2 hours 13 minutes

Availability: Blu-ray and DVD (Fox Home Video)

Director: Walter Lang; **Screenplay**: Ernest Lehman, based on Oscar Hammerstein II and Richard Rodgers's musical and Margaret Landon's book *Anna and the King of Siam*

Cast: Deborah Kerr (Anna Leonowens), Yul Brynner (Mongkut), Rita Moreno (Tuptim), Terry Saunders (Lady Thiang), Martin Benson (Kralahome), Rex Thompson (Louis Leonowens), Patrick Adiarte (Prince Chulalongkorn), Alan Mowbray (Sir John Hay)

Widowed schoolteacher Anna Leonowens arrives in Siam with her son to teach the children of Mongkut, king of Siam. She almost leaves when told she must live in the palace. The king's wives are curious about her and Anna learns the newest wife, the Burmese Tuptim, is in love with Lun Tha, the man who brought her to Siam. Anna's lessons cause some controversy, and she argues with the king about the custom that no one's head should be higher than his. Later she helps Lun Tha and Tuptim's plans to elope. Anna helps the king undercut reports that he is a barbarian by holding a successful European-style banquet for the British ambassador. Then Tuptim, who has run away, is caught and the king prepares to whip her, but Anna calls him a barbarian and he cannot do it. After some months of not seeing the king, Anna packs up to leave Siam, but Lady Thiang begs her to see the king, who is dying. They are reconciled and Prince Chulalongkorn becomes king, abolishing slavery and the custom of bowing to the king as Mongkut dies on October 1, 1867 (1:56:52 to 2:12:59).

A musical from Hollywood's golden age. This is pure entertainment. Brynner and Kerr have fantastic on-screen chemistry that brings this film to life.

Awards: *Academy Award Wins*: Best Actor (Yul Brynner), Best Art Direction, Best Color Costume Design, Best Music, and Best Sound Recording. *Academy Award Nominations*: Best Picture, Best Director, Best Actress (Deborah Kerr), and Best Color Cinematography. *Golden Globe Wins*: Best Motion Picture–Musical/Comedy and Best Motion Picture Actress–Comedy/Musical (Kerr). *Golden Globe Nominations*: Best Motion Picture Actor–Comedy/Musical (Brynner) and Best Film Promoting International Understanding

Source: Landon, Margaret. *Anna and the King of Siam*. New York: Harper-Perennial, 2000. This book at page 389 gives the date of Mongkut's death.

Alternate Film: *Auntie Mame*

2
ONE FLEW OVER THE CUCKOO'S NEST

Year: 1975
Genre: Drama
Run Time: 2 hours 13 minutes
Availability: DVD and VHS (Warner Home Video)
Director: Miloš Forman; **Screenplay**: Lawrence Hauben and Bo Goldman, based on Ken Kesey's novel
Cast: Jack Nicholson (Randle McMurphy), Louise Fletcher (Nurse Ratched), William Redfield (Dale Harding), Will Sampson ("Chief" Bromden), Brad Dourif (Billy Bibbit), Danny DeVito (Martini), Christopher Lloyd (Max Taber), Dean Brooks (Dr. John Spivey)

In Oregon in 1963, Randle McMurphy, a criminal, is transferred to a mental institution for evaluation, as he hopes to serve the rest of his sentence in a hospital rather than jail. Inflexible nurse Mildred Ratched, who employs humiliation and a rigid routine to keep the patients cowed, runs McMurphy's ward. McMurphy makes himself the leader of a disparate group of patients and McMurphy and Ratched enter into a battle of wills, including voting on whether to watch the first game of the World Series on October 2, 1963 (31:36 to 39:27). McMurphy tries to encourage the other patients and engineers an escape where he and his group go deep-sea fishing. McMurphy and Ratched's battle of wills continues, culminating in a wild Christmas party. The aftermath changes McMurphy and the rest of the patients forever.

A tale about nonconformity and hope. Nicholson and Fletcher give classic performances in this outstanding battle of wills.

Awards: *Academy Award Wins*: Best Picture, Best Director, Best Actor (Jack Nicholson), Best Actress (Louise Fletcher), and Best Adapted Screenplay. *Academy Award Nominations*: Best Supporting Actor (Brad Dourif), Best Cinematography, Best Film Editing, and Best Original Music Score. *Golden Globe Wins*: Best Motion Picture–Drama, Best Acting Debut in a Motion Picture–Male (Dourif), Best Motion Picture Actress–Drama (Fletcher), Best Director–Motion Picture, Best Screenplay–Motion Picture, and Best Motion Picture Actor–Drama (Nicholson)

Source: Enders, Eric. *100 Years of the World Series*. New York: Barnes & Noble Books, 2003. This book at page 160 gives the game date.

Alternate Film: *Black Hawk Down*

3
LAWRENCE OF ARABIA

Year: 1962
Genre: Biographical Drama
Run Time: 3 hours 36 minutes
Availability: Blu-ray and DVD (Sony Pictures)
Director: David Lean; **Screenplay**: Robert Bolt and Michael Wilson
Cast: Peter O'Toole (T. E. Lawrence), Alec Guinness (Prince Faisal), Anthony Quinn (Auda abu Tayi), Jack Hawkins (General Allenby), Omar Sharif (Sherif Ali ibn el Kharish), José Ferrer (Turkish Bey), Anthony Quayle (Colonel Harry Brighton)

The film opens with Major T. E. Lawrence's motorcycle accident. We flash back to 1916 Cairo, where T. E. Lawrence is a British lieutenant who knows the Bedouin. He is sent by Gen. Allenby to see if Prince Faisal can successfully revolt against the Turks. After a defeat Maj. Brighton, Lawrence's superior, urges retreat, while Lawrence urges an attack on Aqaba. The surprise attack takes them across the worst desert. When Lawrence goes back alone to save a lost Bedouin, he gains even the respect of Sherif Ali, Faisal's second in command. Lawrence tricks the local tribe into supporting the attack, but has to shoot the very man he saved when that man almost causes a blood feud. Lawrence leads the Arabs in a guerilla war against the Turks. Lawrence is captured and beaten, but returns to lead the Arabs into Damascus. The British Army, led by Gen. Allenby, arrives on October 3, 1918 (3:25:34 to 3:27:26).

One of the most breathtaking films ever made. The cinematography is spectacular. The film gives a look at a very complex man and an insight into the Arab world.

Awards: *Academy Award Wins*: Best Picture, Best Director, Best Art Direction, Best Cinematography, Best Original Music Score, Best Film Editing, and Best Sound. *Academy Award Nominations*: Best Actor (Peter O'Toole), Best Supporting Actor (Omar Sharif), and Best Adapted Screenplay. *Golden Globe Wins*: Best Motion Picture–Drama, Best Supporting Actor (Sharif), Best Motion Picture Director, and Best Cinematography–Color. *Golden Globe Nominations*: Best Motion Picture Actor–Drama (Anthony Quinn and Peter O'Toole) and Best Motion Picture Score

Alternate Film: *A Painted House*

4

EIGHT MEN OUT

Year: 1988
Genre: Sports/Drama
Run Time: 1 hour 59 minutes
Date Revealed in Film: 1:07:16
Availability: DVD (Metro-Goldwyn-Mayer), VHS (Orion Home Video)
Director: John Sayles; **Screenplay**: John Sayles, based on Eliot Asinof's book
Cast: Jace Alexander (Dickey Kerr), John Anderson (Kennesaw Mountain Landis), Bill Irwin (Eddie Collins), Michael Lerner (Arnold Rothstein), Christopher Lloyd (Bill Burns), David Strathairn (Eddie Cicotte), D. B. Sweeney (Shoeless Joe Jackson)

At a game against St. Louis where the Chicago White Sox win the pennant, two gamblers, "Sleepy" Bill Burns and Billy Maharg, discuss which Sox players might be willing to throw games for money. The Sox think Charles Comisky, the owner, underpays them, and several players agree to throw games for cash. Burns and Maharg propose to Arnold Rothstein, a prominent gambler, that he bankroll the fix. Rothstein plays a double game, making the players think they're going to be rich, while betting against the Sox. Some reporters start to suspect something's up. In game one of the series, Cicotte hits the first batter with a pitch, the agreed-upon signal that "the fix is on." The Sox lose game one and game two, but win game three. The Sox lose game four on October 4, 1919 (1:07:15 to 1:08:28), and five, but win six and seven. Before the deciding game eight, the gamblers threaten the life of "Lefty" Williams's wife, so he throws the game and the Sox lose the series. Reporters start printing stories about the fix and the players go on trial. The outcome is good news and bad news for the players.

Mainly sticks to the facts, with only a few alterations for dramatic purposes. Holds your interest with good performances.

Alternate Film: *Northwest Passage*

5

OCTOBER SKY

Year: 1999
Genre: Biographical Drama
Run Time: 1 hour 48 minutes
Date Revealed in Film: 2:55
Availability: DVD and VHS (Universal Studios)
Director: Joe Johnston; **Screenplay**: Lewis Colick, based on Homer Hickam's biography *Rocket Boys*
Cast: Jake Gyllenhaal (Homer Hickam), Chris Cooper (John Hickam), Laura Dern (Miss Frieda Riley), Chris Owen (Quentin Wilson), William Lee Scott (Roy Lee Cooke), Chad Lindberg (Sherman O'Dell), Natalie Canerday (Elsie Hickam), Chris Ellis (John Turner)

This film is set in Coalwood, West Virginia, where John Hickam, a mine superintendent, lives with his wife and two sons. The younger son, Homer, hears about the launch of *Sputnik* on October 5, 1957, and becomes interested in rockets (00:01 to 9:03). He teams up with Quentin, the school's science geek, and two other boys, Roy Lee and O'Dell. Their first rockets crash or explode, but eventually they shoot off several that work. Then one of their rockets is accused of starting a forest fire. Homer has to drop out of school to work in the mine and hates it. He discovers their rocket could not have caused the fire. The boys resume making rockets and enter the National Science Fair in Indianapolis. The school can only afford to send Roy, who has a big fight with his father about his and the town's future before he goes. At the science fair, their rocket is stolen. Roy's father has to decide how far he is willing to go to show he supports Roy.

A good biographical film. The characters actually act the way you think they would, which doesn't happen often in movies. One of the very, very few films that could use more romance. Homer doesn't even kiss his girlfriend! **Alternate Film**: *In the Name of the Father*

6

TRUE GRIT
Year: 1969
Genre: Western/Adventure
Run Time: 2 hours 8 minutes
Date Revealed in Film: 2:05:10
Availability: Blu-ray (Warner Home Video), DVD (Paramount Pictures)
Director: Henry Hathaway; **Screenplay**: Marguerite Roberts, based on Charles Portis's novel
Cast: John Wayne (Rooster Cogburn), Kim Darby (Mattie Ross), Glen Campbell (La Boeuf), Jeremy Slate (Emmett Quincy), Robert Duvall (Lucky Ned Pepper), Dennis Hopper (Moon), Strother Martin (Col. G. Stonehill), Jeff Corey (Tom Chaney)

On October 6, 1880, Frank Ross goes to Ft. Smith, Arkansas, with Tom Chaney, a hired man who shoots him and flees to the Indian Territory (04:15 to 05:12). Frank's daughter, bookish tightwad Mattie Ross, arrives in Ft. Smith to collect her father's body and have Chaney brought to justice. She thinks U.S. Marshal "Rooster" Cogburn might be the man to do the job. A Texas Ranger, La Boeuf, worms his way into their expedition to capture Chaney. The three journey to a cabin occupied by two suspicious characters, one of whom says that "Lucky" Ned Pepper's gang (Chaney is thought to be a member) is coming there. Rooster sets an ambush, but "Lucky" Ned has a miraculous escape. Then Mattie meets and shoots Chaney, injuring him, but is caught by Pepper and used as a hostage to force Cogburn and La Boeuf to leave. The gang abandons Mattie and Chaney. Rooster takes out Pepper's gang, but Chaney knocks out La Boeuf. Mattie shoots Chaney, but falls in a pit, breaking her arm. She is bitten by a rattlesnake. Things look bad, but Cogburn, Mattie, and La Boeuf are tougher than they appear.

The very last of the classic old-school westerns. The good guys are good and the bad guys are bad. As good today as it was forty years ago.

Awards: *Academy Award Win*: Best Actor (John Wayne). *Academy Award Nomination*: Best Original Song. *Golden Globe Win*: Best Motion Picture Actor–Drama (Wayne). *Golden Globe Nominations*: Most Promising Newcomer (Glen Campbell) and Best Original Song

Alternate Film: *Midnight Express*

7

THE BIG CHILL

Year: 1983
Genre: Comedy/Drama
Run Time: 1 hour 45 minutes
Availability: Blu-ray (Criterion)
Director: Lawrence Kasdan; **Screenplay**: Lawrence Kasdan and Barbara Benedek
Cast: Tom Berenger (Sam Weber), Glenn Close (Sarah Cooper), Jeff Goldblum (Michael Gold), William Hurt (Nick Carlton), Kevin Kline (Harold Cooper), Mary Kay Place (Meg Jones), Meg Tilly (Chloe), JoBeth Williams (Karen Bowens), Patricia Gaul (Annie)

Harold Cooper and his wife, Sarah, learn that their friend Alex has killed himself. At the funeral they meet their friends from college: Sam, an actor; Meg an attorney; Michael, a journalist; Nick, a Vietnam vet and radio host; Karen, a housewife, as well as Chloe, Alex's much younger girlfriend. Everyone decides to stay at the Coopers for the weekend. The next morning, October 7, 1983, we learn Sarah had an affair with Alex five years ago, but Harold had forgiven her (1:24:51 to 1:43:03). Meg tells Sarah she wants a child and plans to ask Sam to father it, but he declines. Sarah tells Karen about her affair with Alex and its negative consequences, subtly warning Karen off her idea to have an affair with Sam. Everyone watches the big Michigan–Michigan State football game. Karen still approaches Sam, and he pushes her away, but later they have sex. Nick and Chloe get together. Sarah lets Harold try to impregnate Meg. The next day everyone leaves, except for Nick and Chloe, who move into the guesthouse together.

Okay as a character study. Also, in my mind, this is evidence that all the "love and freedom" expressed in the sixties really didn't make anybody happier. None of the characters in this film really seems to be content with his or her life.

Awards: *Academy Award Nominations*: Best Picture, Best Supporting Actress (Glenn Close), and Best Original Screenplay. *Golden Globe Nominations*: Best Motion Picture–Comedy/Musical and Best Screenplay–Motion Picture

Source: Boyles, Bob, and Guido, Paul. *The USA Today College Football Encyclopedia*. New York: Skyhorse Publishing, 2008. This book at page 414 shows that the Michigan–Michigan State football game in 1983 was on October 8, so Richard leaves the day before.

Alternate Film: *The Sum of All Fears*

8

SERGEANT YORK

Year: 1941
Genre: Biographical Drama
Run Time: 2 hours 14 minutes
Date Revealed in Film: 1:39:03
Availability: DVD (Warner Home Video), VHS (MGM/UA Home Video)
Director: Howard Hawks; **Screenplay**: Harry Chandlee, Abem Finkel, John Huston, and Howard Koch
Cast: Gary Cooper (Alvin York), Walter Brennan (Pastor Rosier Pile), Joan Leslie (Gracie Williams), Stanley Ridges (Major Buxton), Margaret Wycherly (Mother York), Dickie Moore (George York), Ward Bond (Ike Botkin), Noah Beery Jr. (Buck Lipscomb)

In the mountains of Tennessee in 1916, Alvin York is a disappointment to his religious mother, as he drinks and carouses. Alvin spots Gracie Williams and takes a liking to her. Alvin's efforts to buy a piece of farmland are thwarted by circumstance. Alvin goes back to carousing, but when he gets struck by lightning, and lives, Alvin has a conversion. When the United States enters World War I Alvin joins up and is sent to France. On October 8, 1918, in an attack York's outfit gets behind the German lines. York single-handedly kills 20 Germans and helps capture 132 (1:39:05 to 1:57:05). York wins the Congressional Medal of Honor, returning to a hero's welcome. Alvin turns down Hollywood and goes back to Tennessee, where the state has bought him the farm he wanted.

A melodramatic film, but not too bad for the era. Interesting that the film is very sympathetic to York's earlier pacifist leanings. A good Hollywoodized biopic.

Awards: *Academy Award Wins*: Best Actor (Gary Cooper) and Best Film Editing. *Academy Award Nominations*: Best Picture, Best Director, Best Supporting Actor (Walter Brennan), Best Supporting Actress (Margaret Wycherly), Best Original Screenplay, Best Cinematography–Black-and-White, Best Original Music Score, Best Sound, and Best Art Direction

Alternate Film: *A Waltz Through the Hills*

9

FAR FROM THE MADDING CROWD

Year: 1967
Genre: Period Drama
Run Time: 2 hours 48 minutes
Date Revealed in Film: 2:12:17–27
Availability: DVD (Warner Home Video), VHS (MGM/UA Home Video)
Director: John Schlesinger; **Screenplay**: Frederic Raphael, based on Thomas Hardy's novel
Cast: Julie Christie (Bathsheba Everdene), Terence Stamp (Frank Troy), Peter Finch (William Boldwood), Alan Bates (Gabriel Oak), Prunella Ransome (Fanny Robin)

Shepard Gabriel Oak proposes to beautiful Bathsheba Everdene, but she refuses him. Disaster forces Gabriel to look for employment and he ends up working for Bathsheba. On her wedding day, simple Fanny Robin, who works for Bathsheba, goes to the wrong church, angering her fiancé, Frank Troy, who sends her away, not knowing she is pregnant with his child. Bathsheba toys with the affections of an older and lonely, but wealthy, nearby farmer, William Boldwood. Bathsheba meets Frank Troy and they elope, resulting in Boldwood being humiliated. Troy is a rake with no concern for Bathsheba or her farm. On October 9, 1868, Fanny Robin meets Troy, who promises to give her money, but she dies that night while giving birth to Troy's child (1:49:47 to 1:59:27). Her death causes Troy to reveal to Bathsheba that he loved Fanny more than her. Troy is apparently drowned. After a year, Boldwood proposes again to Bathsheba, but when Troy shows up, Boldwood kills him. This forces Bathsheba to finally recognize her true feelings toward Gabriel.

A story of passion, pride, and anger. Bathsheba's failure to recognize the true devotion of Gabriel is what drives this very enjoyable film.

Awards: *Academy Award Nomination*: Best Music Score. *Golden Globe Nominations*: Best Motion Picture–Drama, Best Motion Picture Actor–Drama (Alan Bates), and Best Supporting Actress (Prunella Ransome)

Alternate Film: *The Other End of the Line*

10
MOONRISE KINGDOM

Year: 2012
Genre: Romantic Comedy
Release Date: May 16, 2012
Date Revealed in Film: 1:24:17
Run Time: 1 hour 34 minutes
Availability: DVD, Blu-ray (Universal Studios Home Entertainment)
Director: Wes Anderson; **Screenplay**: Wes Anderson and Roman Coppola
Cast: Jared Gilman (Sam Shakusky), Kara Hayward (Suzy Bishop), Bruce Willis (Captain Duffy Sharp), Edward Norton (Scout Master Randy Ward), Bill Murray (Walt Bishop), Frances McDormand (Laura Bishop), Tilda Swinton (Social Services)

In September 1965, on New Penzance Island off the New England coast, the Khaki Scouts at Camp Ivanhoe prepare for a Hullabaloo. It is discovered that Sam Shakusky, the least-liked scout in the troop, and Suzy Bishop, who lives on the island, have run away together. We see in a flashback that they met last year and fell in love. The scouts catch up with Sam and Suzy, but they escape. Sam and Suzy reach a secluded beach, where they spend a fun day together and share some kisses. The next morning they are discovered. Suzy is taken home, while Sam is put in Captain Sharp's custody until Social Services can pick him up. The Khaki Scouts regret that they hated Sam and decide to help him. They smuggle Suzy out of her house and rescue Sam. A hurricane is approaching the island. Everyone heads to the storm shelter in the church. When Social Services arrives, Sam and Suzy climb on the roof in the storm and are about to jump. However, Suzy's parents come up with a plan to save the day. By October 10, 1965 (1:24:15–1:24:41), Scoutmaster Ward and his troop are well on their way to rebuilding the camp.

A refreshing and unusual film. This movie defies the Hollywood clichés and comes up with the unexpected. Definitely worth seeing.

Awards: *Academy Award Nomination*: Best Original Screenplay. *Golden Globe Nomination*: Best Motion Picture–Comedy or Musical

Alternate Film: *Walk Don't Run*

11

MAN ON THE MOON

Year: 1999

Genre: Biographical Drama

Run Time: 1 hour 58 minutes

Availability: DVD (Universal Studios), VHS (Cinehaus)

Director: Miloš Forman; **Screenplay**: Scott Alexander and Larry Karaszewski

Cast: Jim Carrey (Andy Kaufman/Tony Clifton), Danny DeVito (George Shapiro), Courtney Love (Lynne Margulies), Paul Giamatti (Bob Zmuda/Tony Clifton), Vincent Schiavelli (Maynard Smith), Gerry Becker (Stanley Kaufman), Jerry Lawler (himself)

At a young age Andy Kaufman starts out performing for his sister. He gets fired from his first job but eventually appears on *Saturday Night Live* on October 11, 1975 (18:06 to 20:18). Andy gets a job on the TV show *Taxi*, which he later comes to hate. Andy often appears as his alter ego, Tony Clifton, an obnoxious stand-up comic. Andy starts wrestling women for laughs, and is fired from *Fridays* after refusing to do drug humor. Andy is voted off *SNL* and *Taxi* is canceled. Andy says he has cancer, but even members of his family wonder if that is just another publicity stunt, and after his death, people wonder if he is really dead.

A strange movie about a strange guy. I was never a big fan, but after seeing the movie I admire him more for being determined to do things his way. Carey gives an excellent performance.

Awards: *Golden Globe Win*: Best Performance by an Actor in a Motion Picture–Comedy/Musical (Jim Carrey). *Golden Globe Nomination*: Best Motion Picture–Comedy/Musical

Source: Zmuda, Bob. *Andy Kaufman Revealed!* New York: Little, Brown & Co., 1999. This book at page 59 gives the date of his appearance on *SNL*.

Alternate Film: *The Big Miracle*

12
UNSTOPPABLE

Year: 2010
Genre: Action/Adventure
Run Time: 1 hour 38 minutes
Date Revealed in Film: 12:06
Availability: Blu-ray and DVD (Fox Home Video)
Director: Tony Scott; **Screenplay**: Mark Bomback
Cast: Denzel Washington (Frank Barnes), Chris Pine (Will Colson), Rosario Dawson (Connie Hooper), Lew Temple (Ned Oldham), Ethan Suplee (Dewey), Kevin Dunn (Oscar Galvin), Kevin Corrigan (Scott Werner), Jessy Schram (Darcy Colson)

On October 12, 2010, new conductor Will Colson and railroad engineer Frank Barnes don't mesh. At the Fuller rail yard Dewey makes a mistake and allows engine 777, pulling a train full of hazardous cargo, to become a runaway, rolling down the track with no one on board. Yardmaster Connie Hooper and her boss, Oscar Galvin, argue about how to stop the train and Galvin's plan fails. After just missing being hit by the runaway, Frank and Will start chasing it down, in spite of threats by Galvin. Galvin's plan to derail the train fails and fears arise that 777 will derail at the Stanton Curve, crash into several fuel storage tanks, and cause a major disaster. Frank and Will catch up to the runaway. Will injures his foot while coupling their engine to the rear car. Frank goes out onto the train and engages each car's handbrake. The train just manages to keep on the rails as it speeds through the Stanton curve. Ned Oldham, a railroad worker who has been trailing 777 at Connie's orders, appears and enables the end of the crisis.

A fantastic action film with plenty of thrills.

Awards: *Academy Award Nomination*: Best Sound Editing
Alternate Film: *Born on the Fourth of July*

13
50 FIRST DATES

Year: 2004
Genre: Romantic Comedy
Run Time: 1 hour 39 minutes
Date Revealed in Film: 24:14–15
Availability: Blu-ray and DVD (Sony Pictures)
Director: Peter Segal; **Screenplay**: George Wing
Cast: Adam Sandler (Henry Roth), Drew Barrymore (Lucy Whitmore), Sean Astin (Doug Whitmore), Blake Clark (Marlin Whitmore), Dan Aykroyd (Dr. Keats), Rob Schneider (Ula), Amy Hill (Sue), Missi Pyle (Noreen), Lusia Strus (Alexa)

Henry is a marine veterinarian who lives in Hawaii and only dates tourists who return to the mainland so he can avoid commitment. He is restoring a sailboat so he can go to the Arctic and study the under-ice lives of walruses. One day the mast cracks, so he goes ashore and while waiting for the Coast Guard in a café sees a young blonde woman, to whom he is attracted. He returns the next day and contrives to meet her. Her name is Lucy and they agree to meet at the café again tomorrow for breakfast. Sue, the owner of the café, tries to run him off, and after Lucy appears not to know him, Sue tells Henry that last October 13, Lucy and her father were in a car accident (22:49 to 23:31). Her father had only minor injuries, but Lucy suffered a major head injury that each night when she goes to sleep causes her to forget everything that happened that day, so she keeps reliving (or so she thinks) October 13. Her father and brother conspire to make Lucy think it's the same day by having her do the same things each day. Henry eventually develops a relationship with Lucy. Henry gets her father to follow his plan of playing a tape for Lucy each morning that reveals her condition to her. Lucy eventually ends this and tells Henry to go live his life without her. However, Henry no longer wants to avoid commitment.

It's very improbable, but very good. Henry, who tried to avoid commitment like the plague, becomes a guy who takes on a special commitment. Every day he has to get Lucy to fall in love with him all over again.

Alternate Film: *The Chant of Jimmie Blacksmith*

14

THE ENGLISH PATIENT

Year: 1996
Genre: Period Drama
Run Time: 3 hours 42 minutes
Date Revealed in Film: 9:23
Availability: Blu-ray and DVD (Lionsgate Films)
Director: Anthony Minghella; **Screenplay**: Anthony Minghella, based on Michael Ondaatje's novel
Cast: Ralph Fiennes (Count László Almásy), Juliette Binoche (Hana), Willem Dafoe (David Caravaggio), Kristin Scott Thomas (Katharine Clifton), Naveen Andrews (Kip), Colin Firth (Geoffrey Clifton), Jürgen Prochnow (Major Muller)

During World War II the Germans shoot at a biplane carrying a man and a woman flying over the desert. It catches on fire and crashes. The burned pilot is found by a group of Arabs. Meanwhile, at a Canadian Army Hospital in Italy, a nurse, Hana, learns her fiancé has been killed. On October 14, 1944, the burned pilot, who is now at Hana's hospital, is questioned about his identity (9:00 to 10:41). Hana decides to stay at an abandoned monastery to care for the dying pilot. The pilot flashes back and we learn he is Hungarian Count László de Almásy. It is before the war and along with the Englishman Madox he is involved in mapping and exploring the Sahara Desert. They are joined by Geoffrey and Katharine Clifton. The count and Katharine start an affair, but of course her husband finds out about it. Katharine ends their affair at the outbreak of the war. The plane that is to be given to the count so he can leave Egypt is piloted by Geoffrey, who fails to kill the count by crashing the plane into him, and instead kills himself and injures Katharine. What the count does next leads back to the events shown at the start of the film.

This film does have excellent cinematography and the actors are really good, but its jumbled story line makes for an inferior film, it seems to me. Not really Best Picture quality.

Awards: *Academy Award Wins*: Best Picture, Best Supporting Actress (Juliette Binoche), Best Set Decoration, Best Cinematography, Best Costume Design, Best Director, Best Film Editing, Best Original Dramatic Score, and Best Sound. *Academy Award Nominations*: Best Adapted Screenplay, Best Actor (Ralph Fiennes), and Best Actress (Kristin Scott Thomas). *Golden Globe Wins*: Best Motion Picture–Drama and Best Original Score–Motion Picture. *Golden Globe Nominations*: Best Director–Motion Picture, Best Performance by an Actress in a Motion Picture–Drama (Kristin Scott Thomas), Best Performance by an Actor in a Motion Picture–Drama (Ralph Fiennes), Best Performance by an Actress in a Supporting Role in a Motion Picture (Juliette Binoche), and Best Screenplay–Motion Picture

Alternate Film: *Flight*

15

FREQUENCY

Year: 2000
Genre: Science Fiction
Run Time: 1 hour 58 minutes
Date Revealed in Film: 1:16:47
Availability: Blu-ray (Warner Home Video), DVD (New Line Cinema)
Director: Gregory Hoblit; **Screenplay**: Toby Emmerich
Cast: Dennis Quaid (Francis Patrick Sullivan), Jim Caviezel (John Francis Sullivan), Andre Braugher (Satch DeLeon), Elizabeth Mitchell (Julia "Jules" Sullivan), Shawn Doyle (Jack Shepard), Noah Emmerich (Gordon "Gordo" Hersch)

In October 1969, Francis Sullivan is a fireman married to Jules, a nurse, living in Queens, New York, with their six-year-old son, John. Thirty years later John assembles a ham radio set that belonged to his father, who died in a fire in 1969. John in 1999 talks on the radio to his father in 1969. Francis doesn't believe him, but John tells him how he will die in a fire the next day. With this knowledge Francis escapes the fire, visits the hospital where his wife works, and she saves a man who died in the previous timeline. In 1999 John is now aware that his mother was a victim of the "Nightingale" serial killer. Francis is able to prevent the next murder. However, when Francis tries to save Sissy Clark on October 15, 1969 (1:13:27 to 1:20:29), he is assaulted by the killer, who steals his driver's license. John tells Frank to hide his wallet for thirty years so John is able to lift fingerprints off it, identifying the killer as detective Jack Shepard. Shepard plants evidence implicating Francis, but his knowledge of the future convinces his friend Detective Satch DeLeon that his story about Shepard is true. Francis finds evidence linking Shepard to the killings and Francis thinks he's killed Shepard. However, the danger to John and his family is a long way from being over.

A sci-fi film with a human touch. This one is about people, not gadgets. You care about these characters and what happens to them. Don't think too hard about the many time lines in this story or your head may start to hurt.

Awards: *Golden Globe Nomination*: Best Original Song–Motion Picture
Alternate Film: *The Woman in White*

16

MARIE ANTOINETTE

Year: 1938
Genre: Period Drama
Run Time: 2 hours 29 minutes
Availability: DVD (Warner Home Video), VHS (MGM/UA Home Video)
Director: W. S. Van Dyke; **Screenplay**: Donald Ogden Stewart, Ernest Vajda, and Claudine West, based on Stefan Zweig's biography *Marie Antoinette: The Portrait of An Average Woman*
Cast: Norma Shearer (Marie Antoinette), Robert Morley (King Louis XVI), Tyrone Power (Count Axel von Fersen), John Barrymore (King Louis XV), Anita Louise (Princesse de Lamballe), Joseph Schildkraut (Duke Phillipe d'Orleans)

Vivacious Marie Antoinette is married to dullard Louis, heir to the French throne. She has to deal with not having a son, as well as the hostility of Madame du Barry, mistress of King Louis XV. The king wants to annul the marriage, but Louis defends Marie. Meanwhile, Marie and Count Axel von

Fersen begin an affair. The king dies, so Louis becomes Louis XVI and Marie becomes queen. They finally have a son. Conditions in the country are getting worse. Marie gets mixed up in the "Affair of the Necklace," where she ends up publicly humiliated. The French Revolution begins and the royal family is the target of the revolutionaries. The royal family tries to flee abroad but is caught and jailed. Louis is executed and Marie's son is taken from her. Marie is guillotined on October 16, 1793 (2:33:32 to 2:35:17).

A somewhat fictionalized biopic from the golden age. Surprising that it sticks as close to the facts as it does. If you want to know more about the "Affair of the Necklace" watch the movie of that name.

Awards: *Academy Award Wins*: Best Supporting Actor (Robert Morley), Best Art Direction, and Best Original Score. *Academy Award Nomination*: Best Actress (Norma Shearer)

Source: Haslip, Joan. *Marie Antoinette*. New York: Weidenfeld & Nicolson, 1987. This book at page 290 gives her death date.

Alternate Film: *When Harry Met Sally*

17

AWAKENINGS

Year: 1990

Genre: Biographical Drama

Run Time: 2 hours 1 minute

Date Revealed in Film: 1:07:40

Availability: Blu-ray and DVD (Image Entertainment)

Director: Penny Marshall; **Screenplay**: Steven Zaillian, based on Oliver Sacks's book

Cast: Robert De Niro (Leonard Lowe), Robin Williams (Dr. Malcolm Sayer), John Heard (Dr. Kaufman), Ruth Nelson (Mrs. Lowe), Julie Kavner (Eleanor Costello), Penelope Ann Miller (Paula), Max von Sydow (Dr. Peter Ingham)

Introverted Dr. Malcolm Sayer comes to work at Bainbridge mental hospital in the Bronx, in spite of having no experience dealing with patients. He becomes interested in a group of patients who appear to be in a frozen-like state, staring and never moving or talking. He learns they will respond to various stimuli such as catching a thrown ball, music, or a human touch. Sayer also learns that they all previously had encephalitis. Sayer gets the hospital to pay for a trial of a new drug L-dopa. One patient, Leonard Lowe, "wakes up," becoming fully functional for the first time in thirty years. Dr. Sayer persuades the hospital to let him try L-dopa on all his patients. It is a success, as they wake up on October 17, 1969 (1:08:10 to 1:11:24). The revived patients try to adjust to losing so many years. However, the good times don't continue for very long.

A very touching film. Has moments of great joy and sadness. Great performances by both De Niro and Williams.

Awards: *Academy Award Nominations*: Best Picture, Best Adapted Screenplay, and Best Actor (Robert De Niro). *Golden Globe Nomination*: Best Performance by an Actor in a Motion Picture–Drama (Robin Williams)

Alternate Film: *Fever Pitch* (2005)

18

SUMMER OF SAM

Year: 1999

Genre: Drama

Run Time: 2 hours 22 minutes

Availability: Blu-ray (Disney/Buena Vista), DVD (Touchstone Pictures)

Director: Spike Lee; **Screenplay**: Spike Lee, Victor Colicchio, and Michael Imperioli

Cast: John Leguizamo (Vinny), Adrien Brody (Richie), Mira Sorvino (Dionna), Jennifer Esposito (Ruby), Anthony LaPaglia (Detective Petrocelli), Michael Rispoli (Joey), Bebe Neuwirth (Gloria), Patti LuPone (Helen), Ben Gazzara (Luigi)

In New York 1977, Vinny realizes that he may have seen the "Son of Sam" serial killer while committing adultery with his wife's cousin. Richie returns to the neighborhood, having become a part of the punk scene, and gets the cold shoulder from his old pals, but ends up in a relationship with Ruby, Vinny's half sister, even though Richie makes his drug money by dancing and being a male prostitute at a gay nightclub. The vice squad asks local crime lord Luigi for help in catching the killer. Both Luigi and a group of locals compile lists of possible suspects. Richie has a confrontation with his stepfather and leaves home. After Vinny convinces his wife, Dionna, to participate in an orgy, she leaves him. The men in the neighborhood begin to suspect Richie is the killer as the city suffers through a blackout. They talk Vinny into luring Richie into a trap, and he reluctantly goes along with this. Richie is being beaten up on the way to being lynched, when the last person he expects to support him saves his life. After the real killer is arrested, life goes on, with Reggie Jackson hitting three home runs, helping the Yankees win the deciding game six of the World Series on October 19, 1977 (2:15:06–2:15:31).

A fine character-driven, slice-of-life film.

Alternate Film: *Bride of the Wind*

19
CONGO

Year: 1995
Genre: Action/Adventure
Run Time: 1 hour 49 minutes
Date Revealed in Film: 46:02
Availability: Blu-ray and DVD (Warner Home Video)
Director: Frank Marshall; **Screenplay**: John Patrick Shanley, based on Michael Crichton's novel
Cast: Laura Linney (Dr. Karen Ross), Dylan Walsh (Dr. Peter Elliot), Ernie Hudson (Captain Munro Kelly), Tim Curry (Herkermer Homolka), Grant Heslov (Richard), Joe Don Baker (R. B. Travis), Adewale Akinnuoye-Agbaje (Kahega)

Charlie Travis, ex-fiancé of Karen Ross, finds a blue diamond in the Congo that he uses to test a communications laser. While reporting back via a satellite link several dead bodies are seen before something destroys the camera. Karen leads an expedition to look for Charlie, not the diamonds. Her team includes Peter Elliott, a primatologist, and Amy, a talking gorilla. On October 18, 1994 (34:14 to 48:26), the team parachutes into the jungle, but Amy accidentally destroys their radio. R. B. sends another expedition by air. Karen's team sails down river to Zanj and finds the crashed plane of the third expedition. In the city they are attacked by a gray gorilla and find paintings showing the city's inhabitants training gorillas to guard the mine. The team enters the blue diamond mine and the gorillas attack again. Things look bleak, but then a fortunate discovery and a natural disaster enable Karen's team to have a fighting chance of escape.

A good action film. Much better than some critics have portrayed it.
Alternate Film: *Hilary and Jackie*

20

SLUMDOG MILLIONAIRE
Year: 2008
Genre: Romantic Drama
Run Time: 2 hours
Date Revealed in the Film: 1:50:11
Availability: Blu-ray and DVD (Fox Home Video)
Director: Danny Boyle; **Screenplay:** Simon Beaufoy, based on Vikas Swarup's novel
Cast: Dev Patel (Jamal Malik), Ayush Mahesh Khedekar (Youngest Jamal), Tanay Chheda (Teenage Jamal), Freida Pinto (Latika), Rubina Ali (Youngest Latika), Tanvi Ganesh Lonkar (Teenage Latika), Madhur Mittal (Salim Malik)

Jamal, his brother Salim, and their friend Latika are Mumbai slumdogs who have many adventures growing up that involve autographs, riots, begging, and murder. As adults, Jamal works at a call center, Salim is lieutenant to Javed, an underworld crime boss, and Latika is Javed's mistress. Jamal tracks down Latika and makes contact with her, but she reluctantly pushes him away. Jamal becomes a contestant on *Who Wants to Be a Millionaire* as part of a plan to reconnect with Latika. He easily answers most of the questions, so the host suspects Jamal is committing fraud somehow. Jamal is detained by the police, who torture and question him, and he tells them the story of his life and how his experiences have given him the answers to the questions. He returns to the show on October 20, 2005 (1:35:15 to 1:53:14), where his experiences won't help him with the final question.

Has comedy, drama, romance, and pathos. All the pieces come together to create a film in which there are really no wasted scenes. Just about every minute of this film contributes toward the resolution. A must see.

Awards: *Academy Award Wins:* Best Picture, Best Director, Best Adapted Screenplay, Best Cinematography, Best Editing, Best Original Score, Best Original Song ("Jai Ho"), and Best Sound Mixing. *Academy Award Nomi-*

nations: Best Original Song ("O . . . Saya") and Best Sound Editing. *Golden Globe Wins*: Best Motion Picture–Drama, Best Director–Motion Picture, Best Screenplay–Motion Picture, and Best Original Score–Motion Picture
Alternate Film: *The Game*

21
ENEMY AT THE GATES
Year: 2001
Genre: War/Drama
Run Time: 2 hours 11 minutes
Date Revealed in Film: 35:16
Availability: Blu-ray (Warner Home Video), DVD (Paramount Home Video)
Director: Jean-Jacques Annaud; **Screenplay**: Jean-Jacques Annaud and Alain Godard, based on William Craig's book *Enemy at the Gates: The Battle for Stalingrad*
Cast: Jude Law (Vassili Zaitsev), Ed Harris (Erwin König), Rachel Weisz (Tania Chernova), Joseph Fiennes (Danilov), Bob Hoskins (Nikita Khrushchev), Ron Perlman (Koulikov), Eva Mattes (Mother Filipov), Gabriel Thomson (Sacha Filipov)
The Germans attack ships bringing reinforcements to Stalingrad, among those on board are Vassili Zaitsev and Tania Chernova, who speaks German. Commissar Danilov meets Vassili, who impresses him by killing five Germans with five bullets. Danilov prepares leaflets touting this. Khrushchev comes to Stalingrad and agrees to Danilov's proposal to promote heroes to bolster morale. Vassili is made a sniper and lives in the basement of the Filipov family, the mother, her son Sasha, and Tania. On October 21, 1942, König, head of the German sniper school, arrives to get Vassili (35:15 to 37:05). Vassili and König engage in a life-and-death, cat-and-mouse game through the ruins of Stalingrad. But who is the cat and who is the mouse? At the same time Tania, Vassili, and Danilov become caught up in a classic love triangle.

An old-time *High Noon* western drawdown with two men interested only in each other. Also explores love, jealousy, and manipulation.
Alternate Film: *That Hamilton Woman*

22

THIRTEEN DAYS

Year: 2000
Genre: Historical Drama
Run Time: 2 hours 25 minutes
Availability: Blu-ray and DVD (New Line Cinema)
Director: Roger Donaldson; **Screenplay**: David Self, based on Ernest R. May and Philip D. Zelikow's book *The Kennedy Tapes: Inside the White House During the Cuban Missile Crisis*
Cast: Kevin Costner (Kenneth O'Donnell), Bruce Greenwood (John F. Kennedy), Stephanie Romanov (Jacqueline Kennedy), Steven Culp (Robert F. Kennedy), Dylan Baker (Robert McNamara), Lucinda Jenney (Helen O'Donnell)

After a U2 spy plane discovers that the Soviets are putting offensive missiles into Cuba, the EXCOM committee is set up to find a solution. They discuss various options, including invasion. Many oppose this, fearing that a Soviet response elsewhere would lead to World War III. Secretary of Defense Robert McNamara finally suggests a blockade or quarantine of Cuba. JFK meets with the Soviet ambassador, who denies the Soviets are putting offensive weapons in Cuba. JFK orders a blockade. Adlai Stevenson, the UN representative, proposes a backdoor deal to remove American missiles in Turkey in return for getting the Soviet ones out of Cuba. On October 22, 1962, JFK tells the nation about the missiles and the quarantine (45:16 to 52:19). Low-level reconnaissance flights are ordered to gather intelligence for the invasion that has been set for next week unless a deal can be reached. JFK has to deal with an aggressive American military as well as the duplicitous Soviets. When a U2 spy plane is shot down, the world teeters on the edge of a nuclear abyss.

The film takes some liberties with its portrayal of the characters. However, it's still a tense, watchable film. Very good real-life political thriller.

Source: Dobbs, Michael. *One Minute to Midnight*. New York: Alfred A. Knopf, 2008. This book at page 49 gives the date of Kennedy's speech.

Alternate film: *Blast from the Past*

23
ALIVE

Year: 1993
Genre: Action/Adventure
Run Time: 2 hours
Availability: DVD and VHS (Touchstone Home Video)
Director: Frank Marshall; **Screenplay:** John Patrick Shanley, based on Piers Paul Read's book *Alive: The Story of the Andes Survivors*
Cast: Ethan Hawke (Nando Parrado), Vincent Spano (Antonio Balbi), Josh Hamilton (Roberto Canessa), Bruce Ramsey (Carlitos Paez), John Haymes Newton (Antonio Vizintin), Diana Barrington (Eugenia), John Malkovich (Narrator)

A Uruguayan rugby team is flying to Chile to play a game, but they crash high in the Andes. Some are killed outright, some are injured, and some just have scratches. After a while when they aren't rescued they decide to walk out, but they are now so weak from hunger they have to give up. They decide to resort to cannibalism to survive, eating the bodies of those killed in the crash to stay alive. On October 23, 1972, they launch an unsuccessful expedition to find the tail of the aircraft, which had broken off in the crash (1:06:07 to 1:08:16). An avalanche occurs and a few more people are killed. Another group is sent out and they find the tail. They bring the plane's radio there and hook it up to batteries in the tail, but it still won't work. However, the survivors launch another effort to walk out.

An amazing true story. A great film that shows the power of the will to survive. Also interesting as a character study.

Source: Read, Piers Paul. *Alive*. New York: Harper Perennial, 2005. At page 76 we are told that it was October 22 when they first discussed cannibalism and that it was the next day (pp. 84, 87) that a group of three left to try to find the tail.

Alternate Film: *Lust for Life*

24
HENRY V

Year: 1989
Genre: Biographical Drama
Run Time: 2 hours 17 minutes

Availability: DVD (MGM Home Entertainment), VHS (CBS/Fox Video)
Director: Kenneth Branagh; **Screenplay:** Kenneth Branagh, based on William
Shakespeare's play
Cast: Kenneth Branagh (Henry V of England), Simon Shepherd (Humphrey,
Duke of Gloucester), James Larkin (John, Duke of Bedford), Brian Blessed
(Thomas Beaufort), Emma Thompson (Catherine of Valois), Judi Dench
(Mistress Quickly)
The Archbishop of Canterbury explains in a council with King Henry V
that the current king of France bases his claim on a line of descent through
a woman, so the French can't complain when Henry claims the French
throne on the same basis. Three knights conspire to kill the king, but they
are detected and sentenced to death. Diplomacy fails to resolve the conflict.
Henry invades France and captures Harfleur. Henry decides to take the army
and march through French territory to the English possession of Calais. The
French king orders an attack on Henry. The march is difficult in heavy rain
on October 24, 1415, but the French are eager for battle (59:02 to 1:09:29).
Henry walks among his troops in disguise in order to judge morale. The
outnumbered English are attacked by the French in the Battle of Agincourt.
    An excellent film. Preserves Shakespeare's wonderful dialogue. The battle
scenes of Agincourt are well done.
Awards: *Academy Award Win:* Best Costume Design. *Academy Award Nomi-
nations:* Best Actor (Kenneth Branagh) and Best Director
Source: Dupuy, R. Ernest, and Dupuy, Trevor N. *The Encyclopedia of Military
History from 3500 B.C. to the Present.* New York: Harper & Row, 1977.
This book at page 413 gives the date of the day before the battle.
Alternate Film: *D.C. Sniper: 23 Days of Terror*

25
HEAVEN CAN WAIT
Year: 1943
Genre: Romantic Comedy
Run Time: 1 hour 52 minutes
Date Revealed in Film: 1:37:05
Availability: DVD (Criterion), VHS (CBS/Fox Video)
Director: Ernst Lubitsch; **Screenplay:** Samson Raphaelson, based on Leslie
Bush-Fekete's play *Birthday*

Cast: Gene Tierney (Martha), Don Ameche (Henry Van Cleve), Charles Co-
burn (Hugo Van Cleve), Marjorie Main (Mrs. Strable), Laird Cregar (His
Excellency), Spring Byington (Bertha Van Cleve), Allyn Joslyn (Albert Van
Cleve), Eugene Pallette (E. F. Strable)

Henry Van Cleve arrives in Hell and has to convince "His Excellency" (the
devil) of his suitability to enter the place. Henry does this by telling his life
story. Henry came from a rich family and grew up into a playboy, with many
incidents occurring on his birthday, October 25. He gets drunk at age fifteen
and at age twenty-six, elopes with his cousin's fiancée, Martha. (16:31–35:50,
40:35–49:10). However, after ten years of marriage, Martha leaves him, since
she thinks he's seeing other women. He pursues her to her parents' home
and on their tenth anniversary and his thirty-sixth birthday persuades her to
return to him (1:10:03–1:1:23:15). Fifteen years later Henry pretends to romance a showgirl to keep her away from his son, but later pays her off. Henry
and Martha celebrate their silver wedding anniversary (1:31:25–1:37:34), but
Martha soon dies. Henry celebrates his sixtieth birthday, but resumes an ac-
tive social life, much to the dismay of his son. Henry reaches his seventieth
birthday (1:44:10–1:44:38), but dies soon thereafter. His Excellency makes a
ruling on Henry's petition for admission to Hell.

A funny period comedy.

Awards: *Academy Award Nominations*: Best Picture, Best Director, and Best
Color Cinematography

Alternate Film: *The Charge of the Light Brigade* (1936)

26

MY DARLING CLEMENTINE

Year: 1946
Genre: Western/Romance
Run Time: 1 hour 37 minutes
Availability: DVD and VHS (Fox Home Video)
Director: John Ford; **Screenplay**: Winston Miller and Samuel G. Engel, based
on Stuart Lake's biography *Wyatt Earp: Frontier Marshal*
Cast: Henry Fonda (Wyatt Earp), Victor Mature ("Doc" Holliday), Cathy
Downs (Clementine Carter), Linda Darnell (Chihuahua), Walter Brennan
(Old Man Clanton), Tim Holt (Virgil Earp), Ward Bond (Morgan Earp),
Jane Darwell (Kate Nelson)

The Earps are driving a herd of cattle to California and they stop near Tombstone, Arizona. They meet Old Man Clanton and his son Billy. Wyatt, Virgil, and Morgan go into town and Wyatt is offered the job of town marshal, which he accepts after finding out his younger brother, James, was killed by rustlers. Marshal Earp reaches an accommodation with "Doc" Holliday, the town gambler. Clementine Carter arrives, having tracked Holliday from Boston. Wyatt escorts Clementine to a dance and dinner, but Doc doesn't like this. Chihuahua, Doc's Mexican girlfriend, and Doc tell Clementine to leave town. Chihuahua has a cross that belonged to James Earp and eventually admits she got it from Billy Clanton, who kills Chihuahua. Virgil goes after Billy and kills him, but is in turn killed by Old Man Clanton. The Clantons ride in and tell Wyatt they're waiting for him. On the morning of October 26, 1881, Wyatt, Morgan, and Doc Holliday go to the O.K. Corral for a showdown with the Clantons (1:24:56 to 1:34:22).

One of the great classic westerns. It has both action and romance as well as that fantastic final shootout at the O.K. Corral. The great acting here blends with the great cinematography to create a timeless classic.

Source: Luber, Steven. *Murder in Tombstone*. New Haven, CT: Yale University Press, 2004. This book at page 3 gives the date of the gunfight.

Alternate Film: *Jim Thorpe: All-American*

27

THE TIME TRAVELER'S WIFE

Year: 2009

Genre: Science Fiction/Romance

Run Time: 1 hour 47 minutes

Availability: Blu-ray and DVD (New Line Cinema)

Director: Robert Schwentke; **Screenplay**: Bruce Joel Rubin, based on Audrey Niffenegger's novel

Cast: Eric Bana (Henry DeTamble), Rachel McAdams (Clare Abshire DeTamble), Ron Livingston (Gomez), Jane McLean (Charisse), Stephen Tobolowsky (Dr. David Kendrick), Arliss Howard (Richard DeTamble), Michelle Nolden (Annette DeTamble)

Henry is a young boy who sees his mom die in a car crash and learns he can time travel. An older Henry appears in a library, where he meets Clare, who says she first met him when she was six. They talk and later have an amorous interlude. The next morning, October 27, 2009, Clare finds evidence of a prior girlfriend in Henry's medicine cabinet (16:37 to 18:47). Henry and Clare get married, but on their wedding day he jumps back to an early meeting with Clare. Their married life is affected by his time travel, being gone for long periods, but on the upside Henry enables Clare to win the lottery. Clare has to trick Henry in order to have child with him. Henry travels to the future and meets his daughter, Alba, who gives him some bad news.

This is a good movie, but a confusing one. Many questions are left unanswered. For instance, does Henry have a job? If so how does he keep it when he keeps disappearing? Still, it's a fun movie as long as you don't take it too seriously.

Source: Niffenegger, Audrey. *The Time Traveler's Wife*. San Francisco: Mac-Adam/Cage, 2003. This book at pp. 7–24 gives the date.

Alternate Film: *The Deer Hunter*

28

SWEET LAND

Year: 2005
Genre: Romantic Drama
Run Time: 1 hour 50 minutes
Date Revealed in Film: 7:40
Availability: DVD (Fox Home Video)
Director: Ali Selim; **Screenplay**: Ali Selim, based on Will Weaver's short story "A Gravestone Made of Wheat"
Cast: Elizabeth Reaser (Inge), Tim Guinee (Olaf Torvik), Alan Cumming (Frandsen), Alex Kingston (Brownie Frandsen), John Heard (Reverend Sorrensen), Lois Smith (older Inge), Patrick Heusinger (Lars), Ned Beatty (Harmo), Paul Sand (older Frandsen)

Inge Torvik dies with her grandson Lars by her side. Lars recalls his grandfather Olaf, who had immigrated to Minnesota from Norway and was married to Inge for forty-eight years. On October 28, 2004, Lars signs a contract to sell the farm so it can become a subdivision (2:34 to 3:26; 7:13 to 7:50, 1:39:42 to 1:40:25). In a flashback Olaf's parents send Inge Altenburg to marry him. Olaf and his more loquacious friend Frandsen take her to the church to get married. The revelation that she is German and a member of the Socialist Party prevents both a church and civil wedding. Inge stays with Frandsen's family for a while, but eventually she moves into Olaf's house and bears the disapproval of the minister and their neighbors. Inga almost leaves, but is finally able to break through Olaf's fiercely pragmatic outer shell. The two of them harvest Olaf's corn crop alone since none of the neighbors will help. Then Frandsen's farm is auctioned off for not paying the mortgage and Olaf is the high bidder for $7,000, which he doesn't have and only has one day to get or he will lose his own farm. The couple are surprised when the last person they expected to help comes to their rescue.

Almost unbelievable that this film did not receive a single Oscar nod, but since it's not full of gratuitous sex and violence and instead has good storytelling and acting, that fact really doesn't surprise me. See this wonderful film. **Alternate Film**: *The Perfect Storm*

29

A CRY IN THE DARK

Year: 1988
Genre: Crime Drama
Run Time: 2 hours
Availability: DVD and VHS (Warner Home Video)
Director: Fred Schepisi; **Screenplay**: Robert Caldwell and Fred Schepisi, based on John Bryson's book *Evil Angels*
Cast: Meryl Streep (Lindy Chamberlain), Sam Neill (Michael Chamberlain), Bruce Myles (Ian Barker, Q.C.), Neil Fitzpatrick (John Phillips, Q.C.), Charles Tingwell (Justice James Muirhead), Maurie Fields (Justice Denis Barritt)

Seventh-Day Adventist pastor Michael Chamberlain; his wife, Lindy; their two sons and baby girl, Azaria, go camping at Ayers Rock. While they are eating supper a cry is heard. Lindy returns to check on Azaria and sees a dingo running with something in its mouth. She finds the baby gone from the tent and she is not found. An inquest rules that a dingo carried off Azaria and killed her. Then the investigation is reopened and a lot of forensic evidence is produced. Lindy is charged with murder. On October 29, 1982, she is found guilty of murder (1:41:25 to 1:44:56). However, three years later she gets a lucky break.

A great movie of justice. Reminds me of another great movie, *The Ox-bow Incident*. There, as in this movie, people are quick to rush to judgment, relying on their prejudices instead of real facts.

Awards: *Academy Award Nomination*: Best Actress (Meryl Streep). *Golden Globe Nominations*: Best Motion Picture–Drama, Best Director–Motion Picture, Best Performance by an Actress in a Motion Picture–Drama (Streep), and Best Screenplay–Motion Picture

Source: Howe, Arian. *Lindy Chamberlain Revisited*. Canada Bay, NSW, Australia: LhR Press, 2005. This book at page 104 gives the date of her conviction.

Alternate Film: *True Lies*

30

RADIO DAYS

Year: 1987

Genre: Comedy/Drama

Run Time: 1 hour 28 minutes

Availability: Blu-ray (Twilight Time), DVD (Metro-Goldwyn-Mayer)

Director: Woody Allen: **Screenplay**: Woody Allen

Cast: Woody Allen (narrator), Mia Farrow (Sally White), Jeff Daniels (Biff Baxter), Michael Tucker (father), Julie Kavner (mother), Seth Green (Joe), Dianne Wiest (Aunt Bea), Josh Mostel (Uncle Abe), Renee Lippen (Aunt Ceil), Diane Keaton (singer)

The narrator's mother listens to Irene and Roger's society gossip show and he listens to *The Masked Avenger* on the radio. His home is full of his quirky relatives. Mr. Manulis takes the narrator's Aunt Bea on a date on October 30, 1938, but runs out of gas in the fog. When they hear Orson Welles's *War of the Worlds* broadcast he becomes terrified and runs off (13:57 to 18:42). We are treated to stories of the radio stars interspersed with stories about the narrator, his family, and his pals. A lengthy plot line involves Sally, the cigarette girl, and how a (lucky?) break got her into broadcasting.

A cute and funny coming-of-age story. Woody Allen's droll narration makes the film. Also has a great soundtrack of songs from the 1930s and 1940s.

Awards: *Academy Award Nominations*: Best Art Direction and Best Screenplay

Source: Callow, Simon. *Orson Welles: The Road to Xanadu*. New York: Viking, 1995. This book at page 401 gives the date of the *War of the Worlds* broadcast.

Alternate Film: *The Shining* (1980)

31

TO KILL A MOCKINGBIRD

Year: 1962

Genre: Drama

Run Time: 2 hours 9 minutes

Availability: Blu-ray and DVD (Universal Studios)

Director: Robert Mulligan; **Screenplay**: Horton Foote, based on Harper Lee's novel

Cast: Gregory Peck (Atticus Finch), Mary Badham ("Scout" Finch), Phillip Alford ("Jem" Finch), Robert Duvall ("Boo" Radley), John Megna ("Dill" Harris), Brock Peters (Tom Robinson), Estelle Evans (Calpurnia)

In Depression-era Alabama, widowed attorney Atticus Finch lives with his two children: son Jem and daughter Scout. He gets appointed to represent a black man, Tom Robinson, who has been charged with rape. The children, and their friend Dill are scared of and fascinated with their reclusive neighbor "Boo" Radley. Other children and Bob Ewell, the alleged victim's father, take a disliking to the Finch family. Atticus and Tom Robinson are saved from a lynching by the unexpected appearance of the children at the jail. At the trial we learn Tom Robinson supposedly raped Mayella Ewell, but Atticus brilliantly proves that there was no rape and that her own father, upset since she had become friends with Tom Robinson, beat her up. Tom Robinson is found guilty anyway, and is killed trying to escape. On Halloween night, October 31, 1936, Jem and Scout experience real fear, but find salvation in an unexpected source (1:51:02 to 2:09:00).

One of the great classics. On the one hand it is a sweet coming-of-age story, and on the other a tale of racism and violence. It works on both levels.

Awards: *Academy Award Wins*: Best Actor (Gregory Peck), Best Art Direction, and Best Adapted Screenplay. *Academy Award Nominations*: Best Picture, Best Director, Best Cinematography–Black-and-White, Best Actress in a Supporting Role (Mary Badham), and Best Music Score. *Golden*

Globe Wins: Best Motion Picture Actor–Drama (Peck), Best Motion Picture Score, and Best Film Promoting International Understanding. *Golden Globe Nominations*: Best Motion Picture–Drama and Best Motion Picture Director

Alternate Film: *Monster House*

November

1

E.T. THE EXTRA-TERRESTRIAL

Year: 1982

Genre: Adventure/Science Fiction

Run Time: 1 hour 55 minutes

Availability: Blu-ray and DVD (Universal Studios Home Entertainment)

Director: Steven Spielberg; **Screenplay**: Melissa Mathison

Cast: Henry Thomas (Elliott), Robert MacNaughton (Michael), Drew Barrymore (Gertie), Dee Wallace (Mary), Peter Coyote ("Keys"), K. C. Martel (Greag), Sean Frye (Steve), C. Thomas Howell (Tyler), Erika Eleniak (girl Elliott kisses in class)

Ten-year-old Elliott finds an alien (whom he calls E.T.) who was left behind by his ship. Elliott only tells his older brother, Michael, and younger sister, Gertie. On Halloween Elliott sneaks E.T. (disguised as a ghost) to the forest, where E.T. uses a device he constructed from odds and ends to "phone home." The next day, November 1, 1981, when Elliott wakes up, he finds E.T. gone and returns home (1:14:39 to 1:21:56). Michael goes to the forest, finds E.T., and brings him home, but both E.T. and Elliott appear to be dying, as they share a psychic connection. The kids tell their mom about E.T. and they start to leave, when government agents invade the house. They set up a medical facility and try to save E.T., but he dies and Elliott recovers. Elliott is left alone with the body when E.T. revives. Elliott and Michael put a daring plan into effect to save E.T.

A sweet sci-fi movie. One of the first sci-fi comedy movies, with an alien invasion that is portrayed positively. Drew Barrymore is very good in her first movie role.

Awards: *Academy Award Wins*: Best Sound Effects Editing, Best Visual Effects, Best Original Score, and Best Sound. *Academy Award Nominations*: Best Cinematography, Best Director, Best Film Editing, Best Picture, and Best Original Screenplay. *Golden Globe Wins*: Best Original Score–Motion Picture and Best Motion Picture–Drama. *Golden Globe Nominations*: Best Director–Motion Picture, New Star of the Year in a Motion Picture–Male (Henry Thomas), and Best Screenplay–Motion Picture

Alternate Film: *The Apartment*

2

YANKEE DOODLE DANDY

Year: 1942

Genre: Biographical Musical

Run Time: 2 hours 6 minutes

Availability: DVD (Warner Home Video), VHS (CBS Fox Video)

Director: Michael Curtiz; **Screenplay**: Robert Buckner and Edmund Joseph

Cast: James Cagney (George M. Cohan), Joan Leslie (Mary Cohan), Eddie Foy Jr. (Eddie Foy), Walter Huston (Jerry Cohan), Richard Whorf (Sam Harris), Irene Manning (Fay Templeton), George Tobias (Dietz), Rosemary DeCamp (Nellie Cohan)

Just after the Broadway premiere of "I'd Rather Be Right" on November 2, 1937, George M. Cohan receives a summons to the White House. Upon meeting the president, he tells his life story (1:12 to 3:26). He was born to two vaudevillians and they along with George's younger sister Josie toured as the "Four Cohans." Years pass and George meets Mary, who goes on tour with the Cohans. George goes to New York and tries to sell his songs with no luck, but he is able to bamboozle a producer into putting on his musical play "Little Johnnie Jones" and it is a big hit. George and Mary get married and he writes many popular Broadway shows, but a serious drama bombs. When World War I breaks out, George tries to enlist but is turned down, as he is too old, but he contributes by writing "Over There." After the war he continues writing Broadway shows for a time and then retires. George writes "I'd Rather Be Right" as a comeback.

One of the great Hollywoodized biopics of the 1930s and 1940s. Not a great stickler for factual accuracy. However, it does make for an entertaining enough film.

Awards: *Academy Award Wins*: Best Actor (James Cagney), Best Original Music Score, and Best Sound. *Academy Award Nominations*: Best Supporting Actor (Walter Huston), Best Director, Best Film Editing, Best Picture, and Best Original Screenplay

Source: McCabe, John. *George M. Cohan: The Man Who Owned Broadway.* Garden City, NY: Doubleday & Co., Inc., 1973. This book at page 279 gives the date of the summons.

Alternate Film: *The Path to War*

3

GOODFELLAS

Year: 1990 (Warner Bros.)
Genre: Biographical Drama
Run Time: 2 hours 26 minutes
Availability: Blu-ray and DVD (Warner Home Video)
Director: Martin Scorsese; **Screenplay**: Martin Scorsese and Nicholas Pileggi, based on Nicholas Pileggi's book *Wiseguy: Life in a Mafia Family*
Cast: Ray Liotta (Henry Hill), Robert De Niro (Jimmy Conway), Joe Pesci (Tommy DeVito), Lorraine Bracco (Karen Hill), Paul Sorvino (Paul Cicero), Chuck Low (Morrie Kessler), Frank DiLeo (Tuddy Cicero), Frank Sivero (Frankie Carbone)

Henry Hill admires the gangsters in his neighborhood, and even though he's only half Italian, he works his way into the Mob and uses his connections to impress Karen, whom he marries. Tommy kills recently released mobster Billy Batts, and Henry and his pal Jimmy help him dispose of the body. Henry takes a mistress, and this causes problems in his marriage and with the Mob. He goes to Florida to collect a debt for the Mob, but the guy's sister works for the FBI! Henry is arrested and on November 3, 1972, sentenced to ten years (1:18:58 to 1:19:15). His prison time is tolerable due to his Mob connections.

When he gets out, his Mob boss, Pauli, warns him not to sell drugs, but Henry does anyway and helps in a big robbery from Lufthansa. Mafioso Jimmy starts killing anyone involved in the job to eliminate any witnesses, and Tommy is killed by the Mob for murdering Billy Batts. Henry is arrested for drug trafficking, and he thinks Jimmy is going to have him killed. So Henry makes an equally dangerous and unexpected choice.

A film that seems much more factual that the overly dramatic *Godfather* trilogy. Ray Liotta is very good as Henry Hill.

Awards: *Academy Award Win*: Best Supporting Actor (Joe Pesci). *Academy Award Nominations*: Best Supporting Actress (Lorraine Bracco), Best Picture, Best Director, Best Film Editing, and Best Adapted Screenplay. *Golden Globe Nominations*: Best Motion Picture–Drama, Best Director–Motion Picture, Best Performance by an Actress in a Supporting Role in a Motion Picture (Bracco), Best Performance by an Actor in a Supporting Role in a Motion Picture (Pesci), and Best Screenplay–Motion Picture

Source: Pileggi, Nicholas. *Wiseguy: Life in a Mafia Family*. New York: Pocket Books, 1985. This book at page 160 gives the date of his sentencing.

Alternate Film: *Big*

4

V FOR VENDETTA

Year: 2005
Genre: Science Fiction/Thriller
Run Time: 2 hours 12 minutes
Date Revealed in Film: 9:37
Availability: Blu-ray and DVD (Warner Home Video)
Director: James McTeigue; **Screenplay**: Larry Wachowski and Andy Wachowski, based on David Lloyd and Alan Moore's graphic novel
Cast: Hugo Weaving (V), Natalie Portman (Evey Hammond), Stephen Rea (Eric Finch), John Hurt (High Chancellor Adam Sutler), Stephen Fry (Gordon Deitrich), Tim Pigott-Smith (Peter Creedy), Rupert Graves (Dominic Stone), Roger Allam (Lewis Prothero)

In a future dystopian London, V, a mysterious figure, blows up the Old Bailey on November 4 and rescues Evey Hammond (2:24 to 10:38). When Evey helps V escape after making a broadcast attacking the dictatorial government, he takes her to his secret base. V kills several high government officials. V got super abilities from an experimental cure for a pandemic virus. Evey joins V's crusade. Finch, the policeman tracking V and Evey, figures out that conservatives used the fear created by the virus to take over the government. V tells Creedy, the head of the security services, that if he will deliver the High Chancellor, Sutler, to him, V will give himself up. Creedy delivers Sutler, who is killed by V. When Creedy tries to arrest V, he kills Creedy and his men, but is mortally wounded. He returns to Evey, dying, and confesses his love for her. Finch reaches Evey just as she is about to send off the explosive-laden train with V's body on board, leading to the dramatic climax.

A rich portrayal of a nightmare, dystopian world. There are some major plot holes, but the suspension of disbelief is worth it. This film does carry a message for today and it's from Benjamin Franklin, "Those who would give up essential liberty to purchase a little temporary safety deserve neither liberty nor safety."

Alternate Film: *Mockingbird Don't Sing*

5

BACK TO THE FUTURE

Year: 1985
Genre: Science Fiction/Comedy
Run Time: 1 hour 56 minutes
Date Revealed in the Film: 37:07
Availability: Blu-ray and DVD (Universal Home Video)
Director: Robert Zemeckis; **Screenplay**: Bob Gale and Robert Zemeckis
Cast: Michael J. Fox (Marty McFly), Christopher Lloyd (Doc Brown), Crispin Glover (George McFly), Lea Thompson (Lorraine McFly), Thomas F. Wilson (Biff Tannen), Claudia Wells (Jennifer Parker), James Tolkan (Mr. Strickland)

Marty McFly's father, George, is bullied by his boss, Biff Tannen. His mom tells how she met George when her father hit him with their car. Marty meets his friend, eccentric inventor Doc Brown, and learns Doc built a time machine into a DeLorean motor car using plutonium, which he conned a Libyan terrorist group into stealing for him. Doc Brown sets the destination coordinates for the day he got the idea for time travel. Then the Libyan terrorists show up and start shooting. After seeing Doc Brown shot and apparently killed, Marty gets in the DeLorean and takes off. When he reaches 88 miles per hour, the time circuits activate and he is sent back to November 5, 1955 (31:27 to 52:10). He meets his father, but Marty is hit by the car and not his father, so his mother becomes infatuated with Marty instead. Marty convinces Doc Brown that he is really from the future. The plutonium is depleted and only the fact that Marty has a handbill that his girlfriend gave him provides some hope. Marty's very existence is endangered by the fact that he interfered with his parents' meeting. Marty has to arrange for his parents to fall in love and get "back to the future."

A rare and truly funny sci-fi film. It doesn't take itself too seriously. So just relax and enjoy it.

Awards: *Academy Award Win*: Best Sound Editing. *Academy Award Nominations*: Best Song and Best Original Screenplay. *Golden Globe Nominations*: Best Motion Picture–Comedy/Musical, Best Performance by an Actor in a Motion Picture–Comedy/Musical (Michael J. Fox), Best Screenplay–Motion Picture, and Best Original Song–Motion Picture

Alternate Film: *Time after Time*

6

THE ARTIST

Year: 2011
Genre: Comedy-Drama
Run Time: 1 hour 40 minutes
Date Revealed in Film: 9:57
Availability: Blu-ray and DVD (Sony Pictures)
Director: Michel Hazanavicius; **Screenplay**: Michel Hazanavicius
Cast: Jean Dujardin (George Valentin), Bérénice Bejo (Peppy Miller), John Goodman (Al Zimmer), James Cromwell (Clifton), Penelope Ann Miller (Doris Valentin), Malcolm McDowell (Peppy's Butler), Beth Grant (Peppy's maid), Ed Lauter (Peppy's chauffeur)

After the premiere of his new silent film, in which he plays a roguish hero, George Valentin kisses Peppy Miller. The next day, Sunday, November 6, 1927, their picture appears on the front page of *Variety* with the caption "Who's That Girl?" which upsets Valentin's wife (9:51 to 26:01). Peppy goes to Kinograph Studios and with help from Valentin works her way up from extra to star. Two years later Valentin and the studio head part ways over the introduction of sound in film. Valentin decides to produce his own silent film *Tears of Love*. His film and Peppy's new movie *Beauty Spot* premiere the same day. The crowds flock to see Peppy and not George. George returns home to find his wife is kicking him out. Bankrupt, George is forced to auction off his effects, sets fire to his film collection, and is almost overcome by smoke. Peppy, now a major star, takes care of Valentin while he recuperates. She stops him from killing himself and has an idea that restores Valentin's will to live.

It's a history lesson disguised as a love story. Many silent stars weren't able to transition to the talkies, as their voices were not suitable. However, those silent stars had to be great actors, as they had to show everything with their faces and gestures since they couldn't tell the story with words.

Awards: *Academy Award Wins*: Best Picture, Best Director, Best Actor (Jean Dujardin), Best Original Score, and Best Costume Design. *Academy Award Nominations*: Best Supporting Actress (Bérénice Bejo), Best Original Screenplay, Best Art Direction, Best Cinematography, and Best Film Editing. *Golden Globe Wins*: Best Performance by an Actor in a Motion Picture–Comedy or Musical (Dujardin), Best Original Score–Motion Picture, and Best Motion Picture–Comedy/Musical. *Golden Globe Nominations*: Best Performance by an Actress in a Supporting Role in a Motion Picture (Bejo), Best Director–Motion Picture, and Best Screenplay–Motion Picture

Alternate Film: *The Music Lovers*

7

REDS

Year: 1981
Genre: Biographical Drama
Run Time: 3 hours 15 minutes
Availability: Blu-ray and DVD (Paramount Home Video)
Director: Warren Beatty; **Screenplay**: Warren Beatty and Trevor Griffiths
Cast: Warren Beatty (John Reed), Diane Keaton (Louise Bryant), Edward Herrmann (Max Eastman), Jack Nicholson (Eugene O'Neill), Maureen

Stapleton (Emma Goldman), Paul Sorvino (Louis C. Fraina), Nicolas Coster (Paul Trullinger)

In 1912 Portland, unconventional Louise Bryant meets Jack Reed, and runs away with him. He's involved in radical socialist causes, and she has an affair with Eugene O'Neill. Jack finds out about the affair and she leaves for France. He follows her and they travel on to Russia. They participate in pro-Bolshevik demonstrations and are personally reconciled. They are involved in the takeover of the Winter Palace on November 7, 1917 (1:42:07 to 1:42:29). They return to the United States, where she testifies in front of the Senate and Jack writes his book, *Ten Days That Shook the World*, about the Russian Revolution. Jack founds an American Communist Party and sneaks into Russia to try and get recognition of his group as the "official" American Communist Party, but the Comintern refuses to recognize his group. Reed is arrested in Finland as a Soviet spy. Eventually Lenin trades some imprisoned Finns for Reed. He is sent to Baku to help spread communism and on his return is reunited with Louise.

A biopic about an unconventional person caught up in events that changed the course of history.

Awards: *Academy Award Wins*: Best Supporting Actress (Maureen Stapleton), Best Cinematography, and Best Director. *Academy Award Nominations*: Best Actor (Warren Beatty), Best Supporting Actor (Jack Nicholson), Best Actress (Diane Keaton), Best Art Direction, Best Costume Design, Best Film Editing, Best Picture, Best Sound, and Best Original Screenplay. *Golden Globe Win*: Best Director–Motion Picture. *Golden Globe Nominations*: Best Motion Picture–Drama, Best Motion Picture Actress–Drama (Keaton), Best Motion Picture Actor–Drama (Beatty), Best Motion Picture Actress in a Supporting Role (Stapleton), Best Motion Picture Actor in a Supporting Role (Nicholson), and Best Screenplay–Motion Picture

Source: Gorman, Robert F. *Great Events from History: The 20th Century 1901–1940, Vol. 3 1915–1923*. Pasadena, CA: Salem Press, 2007. This book on pages 1393–95 says the Bolsheviks entered the Winter Palace in the early morning hours of November 7, 1917.

Alternate Film: *She Wore a Yellow Ribbon*

8
THE ADJUSTMENT BUREAU
Year: 2011
Genre: Fantasy/Romance
Run Time: 1 hour 46 minutes
Date Revealed in Film: 1:38, 1:55, and 4:00
Availability: Blu-ray and DVD (Universal Pictures)
Director: George Nolfi; **Screenplay**: George Nolfi, based on the Philip K. Dick short story "The Adjustment Team"
Cast: Matt Damon (David Norris), Emily Blunt (Elise Sellas), Anthony Mackie (Harry Mitchell), John Slattery (Richardson), Michael Kelly (Charlie Traynor), Terence Stamp (Thompson), Donnie Keshawarz (Donaldson), Anthony Ruivivar (McCrady)

Congressman David Norris loses the 2006 New York United States Senate race. Early the next morning, November 8, 2006 (6:56 to 14:15), while preparing to concede the election, he meets Elise Sellas in the men's bathroom of the Waldorf-Astoria Hotel, who inspires him to make an unusually honest concession speech, which makes him an early favorite for the 2010 election. A month later Harry is tasked by his boss, Richardson, to stop David from meeting Elise again, he but fails. At work David finds his colleagues frozen in time being scanned by men in suits, who take him to a warehouse, where he is told a romance with Elise is "not in the plan," to forget her and never mention the Adjustment Bureau. For three years David rides the same bus and finally meets Elise again. The Adjustment Bureau tries to sabotage their relationship, but David outwits them and spends the night with Elise. It is revealed that David and Elise were meant to be together until "the plan" was changed. Thompson is brought in to break them up. He tells David that he will not become president and Elise will not become a famous choreographer if they are together. David leaves her to prevent this from happening. However, David can't forget Elise, and eleven months later defies the Adjustment Bureau to try to have a future with Elise.

A sci-fi romance film. David has to fight very hard for his girl. Hopefully she appreciates his efforts.
Alternate Film: *Rudy*

9
THE PICTURE OF DORIAN GRAY

Year: 1945
Genre: Fantasy/Drama
Run Time: 1 hour 50 minutes
Date Revealed in Film: 1:03:25–26
Availability: DVD (Warner Home Video), VHS (MGM/UA Home Video)
Director: Albert Lewin: **Screenplay**: Albert Lewin, based on Oscar Wilde's novel
Cast: George Sanders (Lord Henry Wotton), Hurd Hatfield (Dorian Gray), Donna Reed (Gladys Hallward), Angela Lansbury (Sibyl Vane), Peter Lawford (David Stone), Lowell Gilmore (Basil Hallward), Richard Fraser (James Vane), Lydia Bilbrook (Mrs. Vane)

Dorian Gray is sitting for a portrait by Basil Hallward when he meets Lord Henry Wotton, who says that life isn't worth living unless it's devoted to the pursuit of pleasure. Dorian wishes the portrait could age instead of him. Dorian meets Sybil Vane, and they are engaged. Wotton persuades Dorian to pursue a hedonistic life, so Dorian breaks it off with Sybil, who later commits suicide. Dorian locks the picture up and goes on to live a dissolute and self-indulgent life. Twenty years later Dorian meets Hallward's niece Gladys and they are attracted to each other. On November 9, 1904 (1:03:24 to 1:15:41), Dorian meets Hallward and shows him the portrait, which has changed into a hideous image reflecting the state of Dorian's soul. Fearful he will tell Gladys, Dorian kills Hallward. Dorian proposes to Gladys and she accepts. David Stone, who was attracted to Gladys and jealous of Dorian, takes steps to expose Dorian's tragic secret.

A scary, but in some ways profound, film. Dorian's secret sins, even though not outwardly visible to the world, still have consequences for his inner self.

Awards: *Academy Award Win*: Best Black-and-White Cinematography. *Academy Award Nominations*: Best Black-and-White Interior Art Direction and Best Supporting Actress (Angela Lansbury). *Golden Globe Win*: Best Supporting Actress (Lansbury)

Alternate Film: *Where Were You When the Lights Went Out?*

10
CONTACT
Year: 1997
Genre: Science Fiction
Run Time: 2 hours 30 minutes
Date Revealed in Film: 1:02:37
Availability: Blu-ray and DVD (Warner Home Video)
Director: Robert Zemeckis; **Screenplay**: James V. Hart and Michael Golden-
berg, based on Carl Sagan's novel
Cast: Jodie Foster (Dr. Ellie Arroway), Jena Malone (young Ellie Arroway),
Matthew McConaughey (Palmer Joss), James Woods (Michael Kitz), Tom
Skerritt (David Drumlin), John Hurt (S. R. Hadden), David Morse (Theo-
dore Arroway)

Ellie Arroway is a radio astronomer who goes to work at the Arecibo radio
telescope to conduct SETI (Search for Extra-Terrestrial Intelligence) research.
Ellie reflects back on the death of her father on November 10, 1974, from a
heart attack, as a result of which she became an atheist (21:15 to 23:05). Dr.
David Drumlin from the NSF ends her research, but mysterious billionaire S.
R. Hadden pays to lease the very large array of radio telescopes in New Mexico. Four years later, with Drumlin again threatening to end her research, Arroway picks up a signal from Vega. Haddon hacks into Arroway's computers
and deciphers 60,000 pages of data that give the schematics to build a travel
machine. The world combines to build the machine. Arroway is rejected as
passenger because she's an atheist and Drumlin is picked instead, but a group
of religious fanatics blows it up, killing Drumlin. A second machine was built
in secret and Arroway is picked as the passenger. Arroway travels through a
series of wormholes to Vega. She encounters an alien, who tells her this is just
the first step. She returns to a surprising and confusing reception.

A sci-fi film that also works as a political thriller. However, it does use the
old mysterious-billionaire plot device to act as a deus ex machina.

Awards: *Academy Award Nomination*: Best Sound. *Golden Globe Nomina-
tion*: Best Performance by an Actress in a Motion Picture–Drama (Jodie
Foster)
Alternate Film: *The Court-Martial of Billy Mitchell*

11
THE CURIOUS CASE OF BENJAMIN BUTTON
Year: 2008
Genre: Romantic Drama
Run Time: 2 hours 46 minutes
Date Revealed in Film: 8:04–05
Availability: Blu-ray and DVD (Criterion)
Director: David Fincher; **Screenplay**: Eric Roth, based on F. Scott Fitzgerald's short story
Cast: Brad Pitt (Benjamin Button), Cate Blanchett (Daisy Fuller), Taraji P. Henson (Queenie), Julia Ormond (Caroline Fuller), Jason Flemyng (Thomas Button), Mahershalalhashbaz Ali (Tizzy Weathers), Tilda Swinton (Elizabeth Abbott)

In 2005 New Orleans, Daisy Fuller is dying. Her daughter, Caroline, starts reading Benjamin Button's diary. He was born on Armistice Day, November 11, 1918, with the appearance and maladies of an old man (7:57 to 17:51). When his mother dies in childbirth, his father, Thomas Button, abandons him at a nursing home, where Queenie, a black woman, decides to raise him. A faith healer gets Benjamin out of his wheelchair and he meets six-year-old Daisy, whose grandmother lives in the home. Benjamin joins the Merchant Marine and goes to Murmansk, Russia. Daisy goes to New York and joins the ballet. A U-boat sinks Benjamin's ship, but he survives. After the war he returns to New Orleans and passes up a chance to pursue a relationship with Daisy. He meets Thomas Button again, who now reveals he's Benjamin's father and leaves everything to Benjamin when he dies. In 1957 a series of chance events lead to a career-ending injury for Daisy. He goes to see her in Paris, but she tells him to go away. In 1962 they meet again and move in together. Daisy opens a dance studio and they have a child, Caroline, who reading the diary now learns Benjamin Button is her real father. He leaves and travels the world while Daisy marries someone else. He returns, appearing younger, and they have one night stand. In 1991 Daisy gets a call from social workers about Benjamin, who appears to be 12 but has dementia. She cares for him as he continues to get mentally older and physically younger.

Reflects on the absurdities of life and how the biggest changes often have a tiny beginning. While Benjamin starts out physically old, he doesn't start with the wisdom that comes with age. He makes mistakes like everybody else.

Awards: *Academy Award Wins*: Best Art Direction and Best Visual Effects. *Academy Award Nominations*: Best Picture, Best Director, Best Actor (Brad Pitt), Best Supporting Actress (Taraji P. Henson), Best Adapted Screenplay, Best Editing, Best Cinematography, Best Costume Design, Best Makeup, Best Original Score, and Best Sound. *Golden Globe Nominations*: Best Motion Picture–Drama, Best Performance by an Actor in a Motion Picture–Drama (Pitt), Best Director–Motion Picture, Best Screenplay–Motion Picture, and Best Original Score–Motion Picture
Alternate Film: *War Horse*

12

BACK TO THE FUTURE PART II

Year: 1989
Genre: Science Fiction
Run Time: 1 hour 48 minutes
Date Revealed in Film: 1:01:20
Availability: Blu-ray and DVD (Universal Home Video)
Director: Robert Zemeckis; **Screenplay**: Robert Zemeckis and Bob Gale
Cast: Michael J. Fox (Marty McFly Sr./Marty McFly Jr./Marlene McFly), Christopher Lloyd (Dr. Emmett L. "Doc" Brown), Thomas F. Wilson (Biff and Griff Tannen), Lea Thompson (Lorraine Baines McFly/Tannen), Elisabeth Shue (Jennifer Parker McFly)

Immediately after the end of *Back to the Future*, Doc Brown returns and picks up Marty McFly and his girlfriend, Jennifer Parker. In 2015 Doc hypnotizes Jennifer, while Marty impersonates his son, Marty Jr., so he can refuse the offer from Griff Tannen that led to Marty Jr. and his sister being arrested. Marty buys a sports almanac for 1950–2000. He tosses it after being rebuked by Doc, but old Biff Tannen, who has been watching, takes it. Jennifer is found by the police and taken to her future home, where she learns things aren't ideal due to an auto accident her husband, Marty, was in years ago. Doc and Marty retrieve Jennifer and return to 1985. They learn that in this alternate 1985 Biff has taken over the town, killed Marty's father, and forced his mother to marry him. Doc has been committed. They trace the change to the sports almanac and deduce that old Biff "borrowed" the DeLorean and gave the almanac to his younger self. When confronted Biff says he got the book on the day of the

"Enchantment under the Sea" dance in 1955. He tries to kill Marty and Doc, but they escape to November 12, 1955, where they retrieve the book from Biff, restoring the timeline. However, the lightning storm that damaged the clock tower causes more problems (1:02:22 to 1:42:25).

Not as good as the first one, but still better than a lot of films. Funny and quirky, but you better pay attention. You might want to remember some things for *Part III*!

Awards: *Academy Award Nomination*: Best Visual Effects
Alternate Film: *Inn of the Sixth Happiness*

13

BACK TO THE FUTURE PART III

Year: 1990
Genre: Science Fiction
Run Time: 1 hour 58 minutes
Date Revealed in Film: 5:25–29
Availability: Blu-ray and DVD (Universal Home Video)
Director: Robert Zemeckis; **Screenplay**: Robert Zemeckis and Bob Gale
Cast: Michael J. Fox (Marty and Seamus McFly), Christopher Lloyd ("Doc" Brown), Mary Steenburgen (Clara Clayton), Thomas F. Wilson ("Mad Dog" and Biff Tannen), Lea Thompson (Maggie and Lorraine Baines McFly), Elisabeth Shue (Jennifer Parker)

Just after Doc Brown has sent Marty McFly back to the future, the Marty who was left in 1955 at the end of *Part II* comes running up and Doc is so surprised he passes out. The next day, November 13, 1955, Marty and Doc discuss his letter that tells where the time machine is hidden and how to repair it (3:58 to 10:29). They retrieve the DeLorean, but after Marty finds Doc's grave showing he died on September 7, 1885, he travels to 1885, using the name "Clint Eastwood." Marty and Doc plan to use a train to push the out-of-gas DeLorean up to 88 mph on a spur line out to Shonash ravine and then into the future on the yet-to-be-built railroad bridge. Doc saves the new schoolmarm, Clara Clayton, from crashing into the ravine. Buford "Mad Dog" Tannen threatens Doc at a dance and when Marty saves him, Tannan challenges Marty to a duel the morning they plan to return to the future. Doc at first decides to stay with Clara but changes his mind and tells her he's leaving. Clara gets on the train to leave town. Doc takes one drink in the saloon and passes out. Clara learns that Doc really loved her and races after him. Marty uses a trick he learned to win the duel with Tannen. Doc and Marty stop the train, steal the locomotive, and start the run to the ravine, with Marty in the DeLorean. When Clara appears in the locomotive's cab, Doc and Marty have to use some innovative thinking to save Clara and get back to the future. Back in 1985, Marty shows that time travel has taught him something.

An action-packed conclusion to one of the greatest science-fiction trilogies. Innovative in introducing comedy to science fiction. Before this, almost all sci-fi films were sooo serious. These films made sci-fi fun.

Alternate Film: *Silkwood*

14
THE LAST PICTURE SHOW

Year: 1971
Genre: Romantic Drama
Run Time: 1 hour 58 minutes
Date Revealed in Film: 15:47
Availability: DVD (Criterion), VHS (RCA/Columbia Pictures Home Video)
Director: Peter Bogdanovich; **Screenplay**: Peter Bogdanovich and Larry Mc-
    Murtry, based on Larry McMurtry's novel
Cast: Ben Johnson (Sam the Lion), Jeff Bridges (Duane Jackson), Timothy
    Bottoms (Sonny Crawford), Cybill Shepherd (Jacy Farrow), Cloris Leach-
    man (Ruth Popper), Ellen Burstyn (Lois Farrow), Eileen Brennan (Gen-
    evieve), Randy Quaid (Lester Marlow)

Best friends Sonny Crawford and Duane Jackson live in the dying small town of Anarene, Texas. Duane is dating the rich and beautiful Jacy Farrow. Sonny breaks up with Charlene. On November 14, 1951 (14:56 to 23:20), the high school English class discusses Keats. Jacy's mother is having an affair with Abilene, who works for her husband. At the town's Christmas dance, Lester Marlow invites Jacy to a nude swim party, which upsets Duane. Sonny and Ruth Popper, wife of the gay high school sports coach, start an affair. While Sonny and Duane are in Mexico on a road trip Sam the Lion dies, leaving his pool hall to Sonny. Jacy has a number of sexual encounters with Duane, Abilene, and Sonny. Duane returns and beats up Sonny, since he still considers Jacy his girl. Sonny and Jacy try to elope, but they are stopped and taken back to Anarene. Duane enlists in the army. They see the last picture show at the movie theater, which is closing. Sonny returns to Ruth for comfort.

This town is the Peyton Place of the southwest. None of these characters really have any moral compass. They just do what feels good regardless of the consequences or harm to others or themselves.

Awards: *Academy Award Wins*: Best Supporting Actor (Ben Johnson) and Best Supporting Actress (Cloris Leachman). *Academy Award Nominations*: Best Cinematography, Best Supporting Actor (Jeff Bridges), Best Supporting Actress (Ellen Burstyn), Best Director, Best Picture, and Best Adapted Screenplay. *Golden Globe Win*: Best Supporting Actor–Motion Picture (Johnson). *Golden Globe Nominations*: Best Motion Picture–Drama, Best Director–Motion Picture, Best Supporting Actress–Motion Picture (Burstyn), Best Supporting Actress–Motion Picture (Leachman), and Most Promising Newcomer–Female (Cybill Shepherd)

Alternate Film: *We Are Marshall*

15

ANIMAL HOUSE

Year: 1978
Genre: Comedy
Run Time: 1 hour 49 minutes
Date Revealed in Film: 1:00:31–33
Availability: Blu-ray and DVD (Universal Home Video)
Director: John Landis; **Screenplay**: Harold Ramis, Douglas Kenney, and Chris Miller
Cast: John Belushi (Bluto), Tim Matheson (Otter), Peter Riegert (Boon), Tom Hulce (Pinto), Stephen Furst (Flounder), James Widdoes (Robert Hoover), Bruce McGill (D-Day), James Daughton (Greg Marmalard), John Vernon (Dean Wormer)

In 1962 at Faber College nerdy Larry Kroger and obese Kent Dorfman are ignored when they attend an Omega Theta Pi fraternity rush party. Kent is a legacy of Delta Tau Chi fraternity and they are accepted as pledges and given the nicknames Pinto and Flounder. The Omegas are obnoxious and the Deltas are party animals and pranksters. They leave a dead horse in the dean's office, start food fights, become peeping Toms, and try to cheat on tests. The events of the Delta's toga party outrage both Dean Wormer and the mayor. On November 15, 1962 (57:36 to 1:03:26), a disciplinary hearing held by the Pan-Hellenic Council revokes the charter of Delta Tau Chi. The boys take a road trip to Emily Dickinson College, where they use an outrageous but effective technique to get dates, but later abandon them. "Babs" Jansen, an overly perky sorority girl, tries to get Greg Marmalard, president of Omega, for her boyfriend, which leads to Otter getting beaten up by a gang of Omegas. Since their grades are awful, Dean Wormer expels all the Deltas from Faber. However, the Deltas don't take this lying down, leading to the hilarious and disastrous climax.

A funny, over-the-top film. This movie has many genuinely hilarious scenes. Don't take it too seriously. It is only wishful thinking on the part of the film's creators that students with a 0.0 GPA ever become U.S. senators.
Alternate Film: *Miss Potter*

16
GOSFORD PARK
Year: 2001
Genre: Mystery/Drama
Run Time: 2 hours 17 minutes
Date Revealed in Film: 1:42:11
Availability: DVD and VHS (Universal Home Video)
Director: Robert Altman; **Screenplay**: Julian Fellowes
Cast: Maggie Smith (Countess of Trentham), Kelly MacDonald (Mary), Jeremy Northam (Ivor Novello), Bob Balaban (Morris Weissman), Helen Mirren (Mrs. Wilson), Ryan Phillippe (Henry Denton), Kristin Scott Thomas (Lady Sylvia McCordle)

The Countess of Trentham and her maid, Mary, go to a house party at Gosford Park, home of Sir William and Lady Sylvia McCordle. A large group of friends and relations of the McCordles and their servants also arrive to spend the weekend. Sir William says he is going to stop investing in his brother-in-law, Mr. Meredith's, business and end Lady Trentham's allowance. Mary is attracted to Lord Stockbridge's valet, Parks, who was raised in an orphanage. After dinner, when the others go to the drawing room, Sir William goes to the library, where an unidentified man stabs him. After the body is found, incompetent Inspector Thomas and the competent Constable Dexter arrive to investigate. It is discovered that Sir William was already dead from poison when he was stabbed. The next day, November 16, 1932, they question various suspects (1:29:05 to 1:59:05). Mrs. Croft, the cook, reveals what Sir William did about girls who worked in his factory that got pregnant and this enables Mary to solve the case.

A period piece whodunit that is more about class differences than the murder. A lot of undercurrents here, not all of which are thoroughly explored.

Awards: *Academy Award Win*: Best Original Screenplay. *Academy Award Nominations*: Best Actress in a Supporting Role (Maggie Smith and Helen Mirren), Best Set Direction, Best Costume Design, Best Director, and Best Picture. *Golden Globe Win*: Best Director–Motion Picture. *Golden Globe Nominations*: Best Motion Picture–Comedy or Musical, Best Performance by an Actress in a Supporting Role in a Motion Picture (Helen Mirren and Maggie Smith), and Best Screenplay–Motion Picture

Alternate Film: *Infamous*

17
THE CAT'S MEOW
Year: 2001
Genre: Period Drama
Run Time: 1 hour 54 minutes
Date Revealed in Film: 4:28
Availability: DVD (Lionsgate Home Entertainment)
Director: Peter Bogdanovich; **Screenplay**: Steven Peros, based on his play
Cast: Kirsten Dunst (Marion Davies), Edward Herrmann (W. R. Hearst), Eddie Izzard (Charlie Chaplin), Cary Elwes (Thomas H. Ince), Jennifer Tilly (Louella Parsons), Joanna Lumley (Elinor Glyn), Claudia Harrison (Margaret Livingston)

Tom Ince's funeral becomes a Hollywood media event. One of the attendees, writer Elinor Glyn, thinks back to the events surrounding Ince's death. Newspaper baron William Randolph Hearst hosted a birthday party for Ince on his yacht the *Oneida*, with a select guest list. Ince proposes a merger of their studios to Hearst, but Hearst rejects this. Charlie Chaplin tries to seduce

Marion, Hearst's mistress. There is a lavish birthday party for Ince. Several things convince Hearst that Marion and Chaplin are having an affair. Hearst shoots a man he thinks is Chaplin, but it turns out to be Ince. The next day, on November 17, 1924 (1:25:38 to 1:43:12), Ince is taken off the ship and later dies. Hearst confronts Chaplin and Marion, and Marion decides to stay with Hearst. Louella Parsons, who saw the shooting, blackmails Hearst into a lifetime contract in exchange for keeping mum. Hearst swears all the other guests to silence.

An interesting Hollywood mystery. Takes the whispers and creates a coherent, plausible story. There are several outstanding performances in this film, especially Jennifer Tilley as Louella Parsons and Edward Herrmann as W. R. Hearst.

Alternate Film: *A Simple Twist of Fate*

18

LES MISÉRABLES

Year: 2012
Genre: Musical/Drama
Run Time: 2 hours 38 minutes
Date Revealed in Film: 4:15
Availability: Blu-ray and DVD (Universal Studios)
Director: Tom Hooper; **Screenplay**: William Nicholson, Alain Boublil, Claude-Michel Stronberg, and Herbert Kretzmer, based on Victor Hugo's novel
Cast: Hugh Jackman (Jean Valjean), Russell Crowe (Javert), Anne Hathaway (Fantine), Amanda Seyfried (Cosette), Eddie Redmayne (Marius Pontmercy), Helena Bonham Carter (Madame Thénardier), Sacha Baron Cohen (Thénardier)

On November 18, 1815, Jean Valjean is released on parole (00:39 to 5:26) and, after an unexpected act of kindness, goes straight, becoming a factory owner. His former guard Javert vows to return him to jail. When his identity is exposed, Valjean promises the dying Fantine that he will care for her daughter, Cosette. He gets her from the unscrupulous Thénardier, evades Javert, and takes her to Paris. Nine years later, Marius, a student, sees Cosette, now a young woman, and they fall in love with each other. The Thénardiers' plot to have Valjean arrested fails. Valjean decides to flee with Cosette, and Marius leaves a letter for her. At the funeral of Jean Lamarque, an official sympathetic to the poor, students start an uprising. Javert tries to join the rebels as a spy but is unmasked. Valjean reads Marius's letter to Cosette, then joins the rebels to protect him. He is told to kill Javert, but lets him go. The army wipes out the rebels. Valjean saves an unconscious Marius. Javert tries to stop him, but finally lets Valjean go, causing such internal conflict that he commits suicide. Cosette nurses Marius back to health. Valjean reveals his past to Marius, but begs him never to tell Cosette. At Marius and Cosette's wedding reception, they learn some crucial information about Valjean.

One of the better musical dramas. The songs and performances in this version are very good. A classic tale of love, hope, and second chances.

Awards: *Academy Award Wins*: Best Supporting Actress (Anne Hathaway), Best Makeup and Hairstyling, and Best Sound Mixing. *Academy Award Nominations*: Best Picture, Best Actor (Hugh Jackman), Best Original Song, Best Costume Design, and Best Production Designs. *Golden Globe Wins*: Best Motion Picture–Comedy or Musical, Best Performance by an Actor in a Motion Picture–Comedy or Musical (Jackman), and Best Performance by an Actress in a Motion Picture–Comedy or Musical (Hathaway). *Golden Globe Nomination*: Best Original Song–Motion Picture

Alternate Film: *Gia*

19

12 MONKEYS

Year: 1995
Genre: Science Fiction
Run Time: 2 hours 9 minutes
Date Revealed in Film: 44:55
Availability: Blu-ray and DVD (Universal Studios)
Director: Terry Gilliam; **Screenplay**: David Peoples and Janet Peoples
Cast: Bruce Willis (James Cole), Madeleine Stowe (Kathryn Railly), Brad Pitt (Jeffrey Goines), Christopher Plummer (Dr. Goines), Jon Seda (Jose), Christopher Meloni (Lt. Halperin), David Morse (Dr. Peters), Frank Gorshin (Dr. Fletcher)

James Cole, a jailed convict living in a future where a virus killed five billion people in 1997, is sent to the past in order to win a pardon by getting a pure sample of the virus so a cure can be devised. However, Cole arrives in 1990, not 1996, and is put in a mental institution, where he meets Jeffrey Goines, before Cole is returned to the future. There a voice message left in the past is played, giving the location of the "Army of the Twelve Monkeys," a terrorist group that supposedly developed and spread the virus. Cole is sent back to 1996, where on November 19 he kidnaps Railly, a doctor who examined him in 1990 (44:41 to 53:10). He confronts Goines, who denies any involvement with the virus even though his father is a famous virologist. Railly finds proof that Cole has traveled in time and leaves the voice message heard in the future. She and Cole plan to run away together, but Cole's effort to complete his mission leads to tragedy.

An uneven film. Great action and characterization.

Awards: *Academy Award Nominations*: Best Costume Design and Best Supporting Actor (Brad Pitt). *Golden Globe Win*: Best Performance by an Actor in a Supporting Role in a Motion Picture (Pitt)

Alternate Film: *Sherlock Holmes*

20

THE LAST STATION

Year: 2009
Genre: Biographical Drama
Run Time: 1 hour 52 minutes
Availability: Blu-ray and DVD (Sony Pictures)
Director: Michael Hoffman; **Screenplay**: Michael Hoffman, based on Jay Parini's novel
Cast: Christopher Plummer (Leo Tolstoy), Helen Mirren (Sofya Tolstaya), Paul Giamatti (Vladimir Chertkov), James McAvoy (Valentin Fedorovich Bulgakov), Anne-Marie Duff (Sasha), Kerry Condon (Masha), Patrick Kennedy (Sergeyenko)

Vladimir Chertkov, head of the Tolstoyan Society and under house arrest in Moscow, hires Valentin Bulgakov as Tolstoy's private secretary. Valentin steps into simmering arguments between Tolstoy; his wife, Sofya; their daughter, Sasha; and Chertkov about Tolstoy's will. When Tolstoy signs a new secret will leaving the copyright on his works to the Russian people, Sofya is very angry. Tolstoy sneaks away in the middle of the night and Sofya is so upset she tries unsuccessfully to drown herself. Sasha and Valentin join

Tolstoy. Tolstoy gets off the train at Astropova, which becomes his last station on November 20, 1910 (1:38:36 to 1:45:45).

A good biopic with insight into the characters even though this film only covers six months. Has beautiful, lush cinematography.

Awards: *Academy Award Nominations*: Best Actress (Helen Mirren) and Best Supporting Actor (Christopher Plummer). *Golden Globe Nominations*: Best Performance by an Actress in a Motion Picture–Drama (Mirren) and Best Performance by an Actor in a Motion Picture–Drama (Plummer)

Source: Troyat, Henri. *Tolstoy*. New York: Doubleday & Co., 1967. This book at page 725 gives the date of Tolstoy's death.

Alternate Film: *The Iron Lady*

21

BRIDGET JONES'S DIARY

Year: 2001

Genre: Romantic Comedy

Run Time: 1 hour 37 minutes

Availability: Blu-ray (Lionsgate Home Entertainment), DVD (Miramax)

Director: Sharon Maguire; **Screenplay**: Helen Fielding, Andrew Davies, and Richard Curtis, based on Helen Fielding's novel

Cast: Renée Zellweger (Bridget Jones), Hugh Grant (Daniel Cleaver), Colin Firth (Mark Darcy), Gemma Jones (Mrs. Jones), Jim Broadbent (Mr. Jones), Celia Imrie (Una Alconbury), James Faulkner (Uncle Geoffrey), Embeth Davidtz (Natasha Glenville)

Bridget Jones is a neurotic, single thirty-something. At her parents' for Christmas, she meets and ends up in a mutual hate fest with Mark Darcy. Bridget flirts with her boss, womanizer Daniel Cleaver, who reinforces her bad opinion of Mark Darcy. Bridget and Daniel's relationship ends when she finds him with another woman, Lara. Daniel and Lara get engaged and Bridget quits her job. Bridget meets Mark again and this time he helps her with her new job. On November 21, Bridget's dinner party for her friends ends in a fistfight between Daniel and Mark (1:00:13 to 1:13:50). At Christmas Bridget is horrified to learn that Daniel committed adultery with Mark's wife and that's why they hate each other. Bridget confesses her feelings for Mark, just as it is announced that he and his fiancée, Natasha, are taking jobs in New

York. However, Mark later returns and though he reads what Bridget wrote about him in her diary, all may not be lost.

A funny romantic comedy. Zellweger, Firth, and Grant are all very good. An amusing tale partly inspired by the Jane Austen classic *Pride and Prejudice*. **Awards**: *Academy Award Nomination*: Best Actress (Renée Zellweger). *Golden Globe Nominations*: Best Motion Picture–Comedy or Musical and Best Performance by an Actress in a Motion Picture–Comedy or Musical (Renée Zellweger) **Source**: Fielding, Helen. *Bridget Jones's Diary*. New York: Viking, 1996. This book at pages 233–37 gives the date of the party. **Alternate Film**: *Brittanic*

22

BATMAN
Year: 1989
Genre: Action/Adventure
Run Time: 2 hours 6 minutes
Date Revealed in the Film: 14:46
Availability: Blu-ray and DVD (Warner Home Video)
Director: Tim Burton; **Screenwriter**: Sam Hamm and Warren Skaaren
Cast: Michael Keaton (Batman), Jack Nicholson (The Joker), Kim Basinger (Vicki Vale), Robert Wuhl (Alexander Knox), Billy Dee Williams (Harvey Dent), Tracey Walter (Bob), Pat Hingle (Commissioner Gordon), Jack Palance (Carl Grissom)

On November 22 in Gotham City Batman stops two crooks trying to rob a family (2:31 to 12:18). Mayor Borg appoints Harvey Dent as the new DA, with the job of getting rid of "Boss" Grissom, the local organized crime leader. Boss Grissom betrays his subordinate Jack Napier, when he learns Napier was having an affair with Grissom's mistress. After apparently dying in a vat of toxic chemicals, Napier returns as The Joker and replaces Grissom. Meanwhile, Vicki Vale, famous photographer, gets close to millionaire Bruce Wayne and Batman, after he saves her life. The city wants to postpone its bicentennial celebration, but The Joker says he will release $20 million in cash, so people show up anyway. The Joker also plans to release toxic gas at the celebration. Batman has to save the day, since no one else can.

One of the better superhero movies. Examines the split personality issues of both Batman and The Joker. The action sequences are great!

Awards: *Academy Award Nomination*: Best Set Decoration. *Golden Globe Nomination*: Best Performance by an Actor in a Motion Picture–Comedy/ Musical (Jack Nicholson)

Alternate Film: *Mermaids*

23

WEIRD SCIENCE

Year: 1985
Genre: Fantasy/Comedy
Run Time: 1 hour 34 minutes
Date Revealed in Film: 16:53
Availability: Blu-ray and DVD (Universal Home Video)
Director: John Hughes; **Screenplay**: John Hughes
Cast: Anthony Michael Hall (Gary Wallace), Ilan Mitchell-Smith (Wyatt Donnelly), Kelly LeBrock (Lisa), Bill Paxton (Chet Donnelly), Suzanne Snyder (Deb), Judie Aronson (Hilly), Robert Downey Jr. (Ian), Robert Rusler (Max), John Kapelos (Dino)

Gary and Wyatt are geeks who decide to create a virtual girl on Wyatt's computer by hacking into a military supercomputer. A lightning strike transforms a Barbie doll into "Lisa," a real live 3D fantasy woman. They go out on the town on November 23, 1984 (3:41 to 27:14). Lisa sets up a party at Wyatt's house and hundreds of people show up. Wyatt and Gary meet and like Hilly and Deb. The party is really crazy, with an attempt to duplicate Lisa that nearly destroys the house. Wyatt's grandparents and bikers both show up. Wyatt and Gary hook up with Hilly and Deb. Wyatt's brother, Chet, threatens to expose Wyatt, but Lisa changes him into a disgusting creature. Lisa leaves and almost everything returns to normal.

One of the funnier 1980s teen comedies. Touches on some serious themes such as believing in yourself, dreams versus reality, and love. Very funny!

Alternate Film: *The Hunt for Red October*

24

HONEY, I SHRUNK THE KIDS

Year: 1989
Genre: Fantasy/Adventure
Run Time: 1 hour 33 minutes
Date Revealed in Film: 57:32
Availability: DVD (Disney/Buena Vista), VHS (Walt Disney Home Video)
Director: Joe Johnston, **Screenplay**: Stuart Gordon, Brian Yuzna, Ed Naha, and Tom Schulman
Cast: Rick Moranis (Wayne Szalinski), Matt Frewer (Russell Thompson Sr.), Marcia Strassman (Diane Szalinski), Thomas W. Brown (Russell Thompson Jr.), Amy O'Neill (Amy Szalinski), Jared Rushton (Ron Thompson), Robert Oliveri (Nick Szalinski)

Eccentric "inventor" Wayne Szalinski has been trying to develop a "shrink ray," but all test subjects just explode. His neighbor's son Ron hits a baseball through the attic window, accidentally lodging in the machine, acting as a filter, causing it to now work properly. The machine accidentally shrinks Ron, his older brother, Russ, and the Szalinski kids to a quarter of an inch high. Wayne enters the room and in anger smashes the machine, sweeps up the kids into a garbage bag, and dumps it at the back of the lot. The kids leave the bag and head for the house. They have many adventures crossing the lawn to get back to the house. Wayne repairs the machine and enables the two families to celebrate an unusual Thanksgiving on November 24, 1988 (1:29:15 to 1:29:51).

A cute film with good special effects. The parent in both families seem to be somewhat stereotyped. Keeps your interest, as the kids have one narrow escape after another.

Source: Johnson, Otto T., ed. *The 1986 Information Please Almanac*. Boston: Houghton Mifflin, 1986. This gives the date of Thanksgiving 1988 at page 351.

Alternate Film: *Ruby*

25

NORTH BY NORTHWEST

Year: 1959
Genre: Action/Adventure
Run Time: 2 hours 16 minutes
Date Revealed in Film: 38:41
Availability: Blu-ray and DVD (Warner Home Video)
Director: Alfred Hitchcock; **Screenplay:** Ernest Lehman
Cast: Cary Grant (Roger Thornhill), Eva Marie Saint (Eve Kendall), James Mason (Phillip Vandamm), Leo G. Carroll (The Professor), Jessie Royce Landis (Clara Thornhill), Martin Landau (Leonard), Philip Ober (Lester Townsend)

Roger Thornhill is a self-absorbed advertising executive who lives in New York and gets mistaken for someone named George Kaplan. He is kidnapped by people who try to kill him, since they think he's Kaplan, but he escapes. On the next day, November 25, 1958 (21:25 to 1:00:11), Thornhill's efforts to prove he was kidnapped fail, and he ends up accused of murder. Kaplan is an imaginary person created by U.S. intelligence to divert suspicion from the real agent who is watching Vandamm, an enemy spy and Thornhill's kidnapper. Thornhill sneaks on board the train for Chicago in pursuit of Kaplan. An attractive young woman, Eve Kendall (who, unknown to Thornhill, is an associate of Vandamm's), hides him and they have an amorous interlude. In Chicago Thornhill has two close escapes. Thornhill learns he has put the government's real agent, Eve Kendall, in danger. Thornhill, who has fallen for her, agrees to help save her. At Mount Rushmore, Thornhill's murder by Eve is staged. She is going to leave the country with Vandamm to continue spying on him. Thornhill escapes and learns Vandamm knows she is a double agent and plans to kill her. He is able to warn her and they flee over the face of Mount Rushmore, pursued by Vandamm's thugs.

One of Hitchcock's best films. The crop duster attack and the flight across Mount Rushmore are classic scenes. The growth of Thornhill's character is interesting. The date of November 25 may be a continuity error, since the film seems to take place earlier in the year.

Awards: *Academy Award Nominations*: Best Set Decoration (Color), Best Film Editing, and Best Original Screenplay
Alternate Film: *Must Love Dogs*

26
PRIDE AND PREJUDICE
Year: 2005
Genre: Romantic Drama
Run Time: 2 hours 9 minutes
Availability: Blu-ray and DVD (Universal Home Video)
Director: Joe Wright; **Screenplay**: Deborah Moggach, based on Jane Austen's novel
Cast: Keira Knightley (Elizabeth Bennet), Matthew MacFadyen (Mr. Darcy), Donald Sutherland (Mr. Bennet), Judi Dench (Lady Catherine de Bourgh), Rosamund Pike (Jane Bennet), Penelope Wilton (Mrs. Gardiner), Simon Woods (Mr. Bingley)

The Bennet family of Regency England are members of the landed gentry who live on their estate of Longbourn. When the rich and amiable Mr. Bingley moves into the area, Mrs. Bennet is ecstatic, as she thinks he will marry one of her five daughters. At a dance, Mr. Bingley and Jane, the oldest Bennet sister, are instantly attracted to each other. His friend, the haughty and very wealthy Mr. Darcy, insults her younger sister, Elizabeth, who takes an instant dislike to him, reinforced when George Wickham tells her Darcy cheated him. On November 26, 1811 (33:17 to 45:35), Mr. Bingley holds a ball. Mr. Collins, who will inherit Longbourn, proposes to Elizabeth, but she says no. Mr. Bingley returns to London instead of proposing to Jane as expected. Elizabeth visits her best friend, Charlotte Lucas, who married Mr. Collins, who is the parson on the estate of Lady Catherine de Bourgh, Mr. Darcy's aunt. Elizabeth learns Mr. Darcy separated Bingley and Jane, so she rejects Mr. Darcy's proposal. Darcy writes her a letter that refutes all her misconceptions about him. On a tour, Elizabeth meets Mr. Darcy again, but her younger sister Lydia runs away with Wickham. When they don't get married social disaster looms for the Bennets. Rescue comes from an unexpected source.

A good period drama. The actors all put an interesting spin on their characters, while the costumes and sets are very well done. The soundtrack is good and appropriate for the film.

Awards: *Academy Award Nominations*: Best Actress (Keira Knightley), Best Art Direction, Best Costume Design, and Best Original Score. *Golden Globe Nominations*: Best Motion Picture–Comedy or Musical and Best

Performance by an Actress in a Motion Picture–Comedy or Musical (Knightley)

Source: Austen, Jane. *Pride and Prejudice*. New York: Barnes & Noble Classics, 2003. This book at page 255 gives the date of the ball.

Alternate Film: *Planes, Trains and Automobiles*

27

LITTLE BIG MAN

Year: 1970

Genre: Western/Comedy

Run Time: 2 hours 19 minutes

Availability: Blu-ray and DVD (Paramount Home Video)

Director: Arthur Penn; **Screenplay**: Calder Willingham, based on Thomas Berger's novel

Cast: Dustin Hoffman (Jack Crabb), Faye Dunaway (Mrs. Pendrake), Chief Dan George (Old Lodge Skins), Martin Balsam (Mr. Merriweather), Richard Mulligan (Gen. George Armstrong Custer), Jeff Corey (Wild Bill Hickok), Aimée Eccles (Sunshine)

Jack Crabb, a 121-year-old man, is being interviewed. In a long flashback, he tells his life story. When he was ten, the Pawnee attack his family's wagons. He and his sister are captured by the Cheyenne, but she soon escapes. He is adopted into the tribe and named "Little Big Man." He is captured by whites and lives with the Pendrakes. He works for a patent medicine salesman, becomes a gunfighter, and gets married. He goes bankrupt trying to run a store, meets Custer, and loses his wife when she is abducted by the Cheyenne. He joins the army to look for her and later rejoins the tribe to do the same thing, but stops when he learns she married a fellow brave. On November 27, 1868, at the Washita River, Custer attacks, destroying the village. Little Big Man is spared by Custer (1:28:41 to 1:37:46). He is a trapper for a while. He becomes a scout for the army, but Custer believes he is a liar and decides to do the exact opposite of what Jack advises. This doesn't turn out well for Custer.

Veers between comedy and action. A good portrayal of the Cheyenne lifestyle.

Awards: *Academy Award Nomination*: Best Supporting Actor (Chief Dan George). *Golden Globe Nomination*: Best Actor in a Supporting Role (Chief Dan George)

Source: Hatch, Thom. *The Custer Companion: A Comprehensive Guide to the Life of George Armstrong Custer and the Plains Indian Wars*. Mechanicsburg, PA: Stackpole Books, 2002. This book at pages 77–78 gives the date of this action.

Alternate Film: *The Sound of Music*

28

THE AMERICAN PRESIDENT

Year: 1995
Genre: Romantic Drama
Run Time: 1 hour 54 minutes
Date Revealed in Film: 43:42
Availability: Blu-ray and DVD (Warner Home Video)
Director: Rob Reiner; **Screenplay**: Aaron Sorkin
Cast: Michael Douglas (President Andrew Shepherd), Annette Bening (Sydney Ellen Wade), Martin Sheen (A. J. MacInerney), Michael J. Fox (Lewis Rothschild), Anna Deveare Smith (Robin McCall), Richard Dreyfuss (Senator Bob Rumson)

Widower President Andrew Shepherd decides to use his 63 percent popularity rating to push a crime bill (minus an assault weapons ban) through Congress, but to recommend only a 10 percent reduction in CO_2 emissions, as he thinks that's all that can get passed, and that these bills will help his upcoming reelection campaign. Sydney Ellen Wade, a lobbyist hired by the Global Defense Council to push their agenda, including a 20 percent CO_2 reduction, meets the president, and he makes a deal with her to get a 20 percent reduction passed. Shepherd asks her to attend a state dinner with him, and invites her to dinner with his daughter the next evening. On November 28, 1998, Sydney comes to dinner. They kiss, but he leaves to deal with a foreign policy crisis (48:35 to 55:47). Later, after a date, Sydney spends the night at the White House, and she and Shepherd become a couple. His Republican opponent starts a "family values" smear campaign against Shepherd. Even though Sydney performed her part of the deal, Shepherd agrees to table the environmental bill. Sydney is angry and leaves, forcing Shepherd to rethink his priorities.

An almost sickeningly sweet romantic comedy. However, Michael Douglas and Annette Bening do it justice.

Awards: *Academy Award Nomination*: Best Original Score. *Golden Globe Nominations*: Best Motion Picture–Comedy/Musical, Best Director–Motion Picture, Best Performance by an Actress in a Motion Picture–Comedy/Musical (Annette Bening), Best Performance by an Actor in a Motion Picture–Comedy/Musical (Michael Douglas), and Best Screenplay–Motion Picture

Alternate Film: *Where the Lilies Bloom*

29

THE GODFATHER, PART II

Year: 1974

Genre: Crime Drama

Run Time: 3 hours 20 minutes

Date Revealed in Film: 1:03:26–28

Availability: Blu-ray and DVD (Paramount Home Video)

Director: Francis Ford Coppola; **Screenplay**: Francis Ford Coppola and Mario Puzo

Cast: Al Pacino (Michael Corleone), Robert Duvall (Tom Hagen), Diane Keaton (Kay Adams-Corleone), Robert De Niro (Young Vito Corleone), Michael V. Gazzo (Frank Pentangeli), Talia Shire (Connie Corleone), Lee Strasberg (Hyman Roth)

In 1901 Sicily, the local Mafia boss, Don Ciccio, kills Vito Andolini's family. Vito flees to America, changing his surname to Corleone. In 1958 Don Michael Corleone, head of the Corleone crime family, argues with Senator Pat Geary about his refusal to agree to a gambling license for a newly purchased casino. Jewish gangster Hyman Roth attempts a hit on Michael. In 1917 New York, Vito Corleone becomes a low-level Mafia member. On November 29, 1958 (1:00:11 to 1:05:04), Michael Corleone meets Hyman Roth in Miami and lulls Roth into a false sense of security. Senator Geary is blackmailed into supporting Michael's plans. Michael learns his brother Fredo betrayed him to Roth. Michael's attempt to have Roth killed fails. In 1920 Vito Corleone kills Don Fanucci. The Senate crime committee thinks Frank Pentangi's testimony will enable them to get Michael, but Michael scares him into denying his sworn statements. In the 1920s Vito Corleone becomes a feared Mafia boss. Both Michael and Vito Corleone get their revenge.

An epic award-winning film. However, it just doesn't seem to have the oomph of the first *Godfather* film.

Awards: *Academy Award Wins*: Best Picture, Best Director, Best Adapted Screenplay, Best Supporting Actor (Robert De Niro), Best Art-Direction–Set Decoration, and Best Original Dramatic Score. *Academy Award Nominations*: Best Actor (Al Pacino), Best Supporting Actor (Michael V. Gazzo), Best Supporting Actor (Lee Strasberg), Best Supporting Actress (Talia Shire), and Best Costume Design. *Golden Globe Nominations*: Best Motion Picture–Drama, Best Director–Motion Picture, Best Motion Picture Actor–Drama (Pacino), Most Promising Newcomer (Lee Strasberg), Best Screenplay–Motion Picture, and Best Original Score

Alternate Film: *Spider-Man*

30
THE BUDDY HOLLY STORY

Year: 1978

Genre: Biographical Drama

Run Time: 1 hour 54 minutes

Availability: Blu-ray (Twilight Time), DVD (Sony Home Video)

Director: Steve Rash; **Screenplay**: Robert Gittler, based on John Goldrosen's biography *Buddy Holly: His Life and Music*

Cast: Gary Busey (Buddy Holly), Don Stroud (Jesse Charles), Charles Martin Smith (Ray Bob Simmons), William Jordan (Riley Randolph), Conrad Janis (Ross Turner), Maria Richwine (Maria Elena Holly), Paul Mooney (Sam Cooke)

Buddy Holly and two pals from Lubbock, Texas, form a band called the Crickets. Buddy wants to play rock-and-roll songs he has written, but gets pushback from radio sponsors and Nashville record producers. When a song of theirs is accidentally pressed as a record, Buddy is able to convince Coral Records to let him control their recording sessions. Buddy starts dating Maria, a secretary at Coral. They become the first white act to appear at the Apollo Theater and tour with Sam Cooke. Tensions arise because Jesse and Ray Bob want to go back to Lubbock, while Buddy wants to stay in New York. On November 30, 1957, Buddy and the Crickets rehearse for their appearance the next day on the *Ed Sullivan Show* (1:15:33 to 1:16:28). Just before their appearance, Buddy and Jesse have a huge fight and after the show the band breaks up. Buddy and Maria get married, but he is persuaded to go on a promotional tour because he needs the money, leading to tragedy.

A very entertaining biography. Like many biographies about musicians, it is not very factual. However, if looked at as entertainment and not history, it isn't disappointing. The movie will certainly hold the viewer's interest for two hours.

Awards: *Academy Award Win*: Best Original Song Score and Its Adaptation or Adaptation Score. *Academy Award Nominations*: Best Actor (Gary Busey) and Best Sound. *Golden Globe Nomination*: Best Motion Picture Actor–Musical/Comedy (Busey)

Source: Amnurn, Ellis. *Buddy Holly: A Biography*. New York: St. Martin's Press, 1995. This book at pages 113–14 gives the date of their rehearsal.

Alternate Film: *The Adventures of Mark Twain*

December

1

ANNIE HALL

Year: 1977
Genre: Romantic Comedy
Run Time: 1 hour 33 minutes
Date Revealed in Film: 3:57
Availability: Blu-ray and DVD (Metro-Goldwyn-Mayer)
Director: Woody Allen; **Screenplay**: Woody Allen and Marshall Brickman
Cast: Woody Allen (Alvy "Max" Singer), Diane Keaton (Annie Hall), Paul Simon (Tony Lacey), Shelley Duvall (Pam), Christopher Walken (Duane Hall), Colleen Dewhurst (Mrs. Hall), Janet Margolin (Robin), Carol Kane (Allison Portchnik)

Comedian Alvy Singer can't understand why his relationship with Annie Hall ended. Alvy thinks back to his childhood, including an episode on December 1, 1942 (3:53 to 5:26), when he kissed a girl in class. As a child Alvy was very depressed and neurotic. Alvy had a poor sexual relationship with his first two wives and doesn't do any better with Annie. Alvy thinks all his problems are caused by anti-Semitism. He and Annie have a very unusual relationship and they live together for a time. A visit to her family is a disaster and they break up after Alvy finds her arm in arm with one of her professors. Alvy asks strangers on the street about the nature of relationships. Alvy and Annie reunite and vow to stay together forever, but after a trip to California they agree their relationship is not working. Alvy flies to Los Angeles and proposes to her. She refuses. He writes a play about their relationship, but in it she accepts his proposal. He meets Annie again when both have moved on to other people.

This is Woody Allen at his best. His portrayal of the neurotic, emotionally unstable Alvy is a classic. Diane Keaton is fantastic as the title character. A funny movie that dispenses a few real nuggets of wisdom about life. Funny also for its many breaking-the-fourth-wall scenes.

Awards: *Academy Award Wins*: Best Picture, Best Director, Best Actress (Diane Keaton), and Best Original Screenplay. *Academy Award Nomination*: Best Actor (Woody Allen). *Golden Globe Win*: Best Motion Picture Actress–Musical/Comedy (Keaton). *Golden Globe Nominations*: Best Motion Picture–Musical/Comedy, Best Director–Motion Picture, Best Motion Picture Actor–Musical/Comedy (Allen), and Best Screenplay–Motion Picture

Alternate Film: *The Great Gatsby* (2013)

2

CASABLANCA
Year: 1942
Genre: Romantic Drama
Run Time: 1 hour 42 minutes
Date Revealed in Film: 8:56
Availability: Blu-ray and DVD (Warner Home Video)
Director: Michael Curtiz; **Screenplay**: Julius Epstein, Philip Epstein, and Howard Koch, based on Murray Burnett and Joan Alison's play, *Everybody Comes to Rick's*
Cast: Humphrey Bogart (Rick Blaine), Ingrid Bergman (Ilsa Lund), Paul Henreid (Victor Laszlo), Claude Rains (Captain Louis Renault), Conrad Veidt (Major Heinrich Strasser), Sydney Greenstreet (Signor Ferrari), Peter Lorre (Signor Ugarte)

American expatriate Richard "Rick" Blaine runs a bar in Casablanca, Morocco, in 1941 catering to refugees trying to reach Lisbon, the gateway to the United States. Two German couriers are murdered and relieved of letters of transit that allow whoever possesses them to get to Lisbon. The letters are passed to Rick for safekeeping and become his when the police under Maj. Renault kill the owner on December 2, 1941. Victor Laszlo, a prominent anti-Nazi, arrives with his wife in Casablanca (2:01 to 36:13). Via a flashback we learn that prior to the war Rick and Ilsa were lovers at a time when she believed her husband was dead. On the day they were to flee Paris, she learned her husband was alive and stayed behind to care for him. She didn't tell Rick why she stayed. Both Laszlo and Ilsa try to get the letters from Rick. The police arrive and arrest Laszlo on a minor charge. Rick persuades the police to release Laszlo, promising to get evidence to convict Laszlo on a more serious charge. When Renault tries to re-arrest Laszlo this sets up a classic tear-jerker farewell scene and the final showdown, where Rick and Renault are forced to show their true colors.

What can you say? One of the greatest movies ever made, even though the story is so clichéd it shouldn't work, but somehow it does. Bergman and Bogart have all those great lines.

Awards: *Academy Award Wins*: Best Adapted Screenplay, Best Director, and Best Picture. *Academy Award Nominations*: Best Actor (Humphrey Bogart), Best Supporting Actor (Claude Rains), Best Cinematography–Black-and-White, Best Film Editing, and Best Music

Alternate Film: *Into the Wild* (2007)

3

THE DEVIL WEARS PRADA

Year: 2006

Genre: Comedy/Drama

Run Time: 1 hour 49 minutes

Date Revealed in Film: 1:38:59

Availability: Blu-ray and DVD (Fox Home Video)

Director: David Frankel; **Screenplay**: Aline Brosh McKenna, based on Lauren Weisberger's novel

Cast: Anne Hathaway (Andrea "Andy" Sachs), Meryl Streep (Miranda Priestly), Emily Blunt (Emily Charlton), Stanley Tucci (Nigel), Simon Baker (Christian Thompson), Adrian Grenier (Nate Cooper), Daniel Sunjata (James Holt), Tracie Thoms (Lily)

Andrea Sachs applies for a job as assistant to the assistant of Miranda Priestly, the domineering editor of *Runway*, a haute couture fashion magazine. Even though Andy is not a fashionista and has never heard of Miranda before, she is hired. Andy is thrown into this high-pressure job to sink or swim while having to deal with Miranda's snide comments and Emily's laughing at her fashion sense. The stress starts to get to Andy, but with the help of Nigel, an editor, she revamps her appearance. After she botches an assignment, Miranda decides to get rid of Andy by giving her a truly impossible task: get a copy of the unpublished *Harry Potter and the Deathly Hallows* for her twin girls to read. However, Andy defies expectations and succeeds. Even Miranda is (grudgingly) impressed. Andy misses her boyfriend's birthday party due to work. Miranda decides to take Andy instead of Emily with her to Paris fashion week and threatens to fire her and sabotage her future journalistic career plans if she refuses. Andy begins to feel like she has sold her soul to the devil when she and Nate break up over her job and she has to tell Emily she's going to Paris instead of her. In Paris Andy tries and fails to warn Miranda that she's going to be fired, but Miranda outmaneuvers her boss, at the cost of Nigel's dreams. Andy is upset at this, but Miranda points out that she did the same thing to Emily. Andy decides she's had enough and on December 3, 2005, she tosses her cell phone into a fountain and quits (1:28:21 to 1:39:17). Back in New York she makes up with Nate. When she applies for a job at a newspaper Andy is surprised when Miranda gives her a good reference.

A quirky film with an interesting mix of romance and workplace comedy. Both Streep and Hathaway live their roles, and you can't imagine anyone else in these parts. A very watchable film.

Awards: *Academy Award Nominations*: Best Actress (Meryl Streep) and Best Costume Design. *Golden Globe Win*: Best Performance by an Actress in a Motion Picture–Comedy or Musical (Streep). *Golden Globe Nominations*: Best Motion Picture–Comedy or Musical and Best Performance by an Actress in a Motion Picture–Comedy or Musical (Emily Blunt)

Alternate Film: *Murder in the First* (1995)

4

CITIZEN KANE

Year: 1941
Genre: Mystery/Drama
Run Time: 1 hour 59 minutes
Date Revealed in Film: 1:34:41
Availability: Blu-ray and DVD (Warner Home Video)
Director: Orson Welles; **Screenplay:** Herman J. Mankiewicz and Orson Welles
Cast: Orson Welles (Charles Foster Kane), William Alland (Jerry Thompson), Ray Collins (Jim W. Gettys), Dorothy Comingore (Susan Alexander Kane), Joseph Cotten (Jedediah Leland), George Coulouris (Walter Parks Thatcher), Paul Stewart (Raymond)

Charles Foster Kane, reclusive multimillionaire, dies alone at his Florida mansion uttering his last word, "Rosebud." A newspaper reporter is hired to find out what he meant by interviewing everyone associated with Kane. Kane was born in poverty in Colorado, but his mother, who owned a boardinghouse, got the title to a mine when a roomer died with an unpaid bill. She became rich when the mine was found to actually be stuffed with gold. Young Charles is playing outside on his sled when told he is to go live in the east. While still a young man he buys the *New York Enquirer* and relaunches it as a purveyor of "yellow journalism." He works for progressive causes and acquires a lot of enemies among his fellow millionaires. He marries the niece of the president of the United States, but they gradually become distant. He runs for governor, but one week before the election his opponents threaten to reveal he has been having an affair with Susan Alexander unless he bows out. Kane refuses and is defeated and divorced by his wife. Kane marries Susan and sets out to make her a famous opera star, but her talent does not support that effort. She performs in many operas, including one in Washington on December 4, 1919 (1:34:38 to 1:34:45), but has a breakdown and gives up singing. Kane builds Xanadu mansion for her, but she doesn't like it there. They later break up. When Kane dies, the executors burn a lot of junk Kane had collected.

A true classic. Clearly shows the truth of the old adage "You can't buy happiness." His money brought him nothing but sorrow and he was happiest as the young boy playing in the snow on his favorite sled.

Awards: *Academy Award Win*: Best Original Screenplay. *Academy Award Nominations*: Best Picture, Best Director, Best Actor (Orson Welles), Best Art Direction–Black-and-White, Best Film Editing, Best Cinematography, Best Score, and Best Sound Recording
Alternate Film: *The Children of Men* (2006)

5

AMADEUS

Year: 1984
Genre: Biographical Drama
Run Time: 2 hours 40 minutes
Availability: Blu-ray and DVD (Warner Home Video)
Director: Miloš Forman; **Screenplay**: Peter Shaffer, based on his play
Cast: F. Murray Abraham (Antonio Salieri), Tom Hulce (Wolfgang Amadeus Mozart), Elizabeth Berridge (Constanze Mozart), Roy Dotrice (Leopold Mozart), Simon Callow (Emanuel Schikaneder), Jeffrey Jones (Joseph II), Christine Ebersole (Costanza)

In 1823 Salieri attempts suicide and is put in an insane asylum. There he confesses to a priest. In his youth he vowed to stay celibate if he could devote his life to music. The death of his father, who wanted him to go in to business, allows him to pursue his dream. He becomes court composer for Joseph II. When Mozart arrives in Vienna, Salieri doesn't like him. He thinks Mozart is lewd and irreverent, but talented. Salieri refuses to accept the idea of God "speaking" through Mozart's talent and laughing at his own mediocrity. Mozart's eventual success begins to wane and Salieri sees his chance for revenge. Salieri, in disguise, commissions Mozart to write a Requiem Mass, with the idea that Salieri will steal the piece and kill Mozart, thus receiving the credit for writing a "great" piece. Mozart works on the Requiem and *The Magic Flute* together, driving himself to exhaustion, and his wife leaves. He collapses when *The Magic Flute* is premiered. Salieri pushes him to complete the Requiem, but Mozart's wife returns and locks up the score. Mozart dies on December 5, 1791. Salieri does not get the score of the Requiem (2:22:40 to 2:28:55).

A well-done if somewhat unconventional biopic. It focuses as much on Salieri as on Mozart. Almost operates as a dual biography. And of course the music is fantastic.

Awards: *Academy Award Win*: Best Picture, Best Actor (F. Murray Abraham), Best Director, Best Costume Design, Best Adapted Screenplay, Best Art Direction, Best Makeup, and Best Sound. *Academy Award Nominations*: Best Cinematography, Best Film Editing, and Best Actor (Tom Hulce). *Golden Globe Wins*: Best Director–Motion Picture, Best Performance by an Actor in a Motion Picture–Drama (Abraham), Best Screenplay–Motion Picture, and Best Motion Picture–Drama. *Golden Globe Nominations*: Best Performance by an Actor in a Motion Picture–Drama (Hulce) and Best Performance by an Actor in a Supporting Role in a Motion Picture (Jeffrey Jones)

Source: Wates, Roye E. *Mozart: An Introduction to the Music, the Man and the Myths*. Milwaukee, WI: Amadeus Press, 2010. This book at page 238 gives his death date.

Alternate Film: *Swearing Allegiance*

6

FROM HERE TO ETERNITY

Year: 1953
Genre: Romantic Drama
Run Time: 1 hour 58 minutes
Date Revealed in Film: 1:40:12
Availability: Blu-ray and DVD (Sony Pictures)
Director: Fred Zinneman; **Screenplay**: Daniel Taradash, based on the James Jones novel
Cast: Burt Lancaster (1st Sergeant Milton Warden), Montgomery Clift (Pvt. Robert E. Lee Prewitt), Deborah Kerr (Karen Holmes), Donna Reed ("Lorene" Burke), Frank Sinatra (Pvt. Maggio), Philip Ober (Capt. Holmes), Ernest Borgnine ("Fatso" Judson)

Pvt. Prewitt transfers to G Company at Schofield Barracks, giving up a corporal's rank to do so. Captain Holmes wants him to box so he can win the regimental tournament, but Prewitt refuses. Sgt. Warden really runs things, not Holmes. Karen Holmes, who is estranged from her husband, starts an affair with Warden, leading to the iconic "surf scene." Prewitt meets Lorene. Sgt. Judson, a non-com at the stockade, and Maggio get in a fight. Maggio goes AWOL and is arrested, court-martialed, and sent to the stockade, where Judson abuses him. Prewitt proposes to Lorene, but she refuses. Capt. Holmes finds out about the affair. Karen asks Warden to apply for officer's training school so she can divorce her husband and marry him. He refuses and she ends their affair. Sgt. Galovitch goads Prewitt into a fight, but Holmes lets Galovitch off. This incident is witnessed by the base commander, who orders an investigation. Maggio escapes, but dies. Prewitt kills Judson. Prewitt goes AWOL and hides at Lorene's house. When the results of Holmes's treatment of Prewitt are presented to the commanding general, Holmes is told to choose either resignation or court-martial, and he quits. Capt. Ross replaces Holmes on December 6, 1941, and demotes Galovitch (1:39:00 to 1:43:23). The Japanese attack. Prewitt tries to return at night and is shot. Karen and Lorene meet on a ship leaving for the mainland. Karen recognizes that Lorene was Prewitt's girlfriend.

A passable melodrama. On the whole a real movie about real people. Nobody here is pure good or evil, but believable. Well worth watching

Awards: *Academy Award Wins*: Best Picture, Best Director, Best Writing–Adapted Screenplay, Best Supporting Actor (Frank Sinatra), and Best Supporting Actress (Donna Reed). *Academy Award Nominations*: Best Actor (Montgomery Clift), Best Supporting Actor (Burt Lancaster), Best Actress (Deborah Kerr), Best Costume Design, and Best Score. *Golden Globe Wins*: Best Motion Picture Director and Best Supporting Actor (Sinatra)

Alternate Film: *The Lovely Bones* (2009)

7

TORA! TORA! TORA!

Year: 1970

Genre: War/Drama

Run Time: 2 hours 24 minutes

Date Revealed in Film: 1:10:48

Availability: Blu-ray and DVD (Fox Home Video)

Directors: Richard Fleischer, Kinji Fukasaku, and Toshio Masuda; **Screenplay**: Larry Forrester, Ryuzo Kikushima, and Hideo Oguni, based on Gordon W. Prange's book and Ladislaus Farago's *The Broken Seal*

Cast: Martin Balsam (Admiral Kimmel), Joseph Cotton (Henry L. Stimson), E. G. Marshall (Colonel Bratton), James Whitmore (Admiral Halsey), Jason Robards (General Short), Richard Anderson (Captain Earle), George Macready (Cordell Hull)

Yamamoto assumes command of the Japanese fleet. Japan sends Nomura and Kurusu to Washington as special emissaries. The American military is reading Japanese coded diplomatic messages. Yamamoto wonders if Japan could use new shallow-running torpedoes to attack the American fleet at Pearl Harbor, while Admiral Kimmel dismisses the possibility of a torpedo attack, as the harbor is too shallow for conventional torpedoes. Gen. Short has his airplanes bunched together, as he considers sabotage more likely than an air attack. Japanese commander Genda devises a plan to attack the American fleet in Pearl Harbor. Japan sends a fourteen-part message to its embassy in Washington, but holds the last part until December 7, 1941, telling the ambassador to submit the message at exactly 1:00 PM that day. That Sunday morning Col. Bratton can't reach Gen. Marshall, and Adm. Stark, chief of naval operations, instead of calling Adm. Kimmel in Hawaii, calls the president. The Japanese launch their planes. Gen. Marshall sends a warning message to Gen. Short as an ordinary telegram. The Japanese attack begins and the message, "Air Raid Pearl Harbor, This Is No Drill" is sent. Six battleships are torpedoed and bombed. A lucky bomb hit sinks the *Arizona*. Secretary of State Hull receives Nomura and Kurusu after learning of the attack and blasts them out. The Japanese commander doesn't send a third attack. Gen. Short finally gets the warning message from Gen. Marshall. Yamamoto says that as the attack occurred before the delivery of the message Americans will think this was a sneak attack (1:10:45 to 2:33:34).

Another all-star, docudrama war epic. I feel sorry for poor Col. Bratton, who does everything in his power to try to save the day, but circumstances defeat him.

Awards: *Academy Award Wins*: Best Special Effects and Best Cinematography. *Academy Award Nominations*: Best Art Direction–Set Decoration, Best Sound, and Best Film Editing

Alternate Film: *Donovan's Reef* (1963)

8

THE INSIDER
Year: 1999
Genre: Drama/Thriller
Run Time: 2 hours 37 minutes
Date Revealed in Film: 1:56:49

Availability: Blu-ray (Disney/Buena Vista), DVD (Touchstone Pictures)

Director: Michael Mann; **Screenplay**: Eric Roth and Michael Mann, based on Marie Brenner's article "The Man Who Knew Too Much"

Cast: Al Pacino (Lowell Bergman), Russell Crowe (Jeffrey Wigand), Renee Olstead (Deborah Wigand), Christopher Plummer (Mike Wallace), Lindsay Crouse (Sharon Tiller), Michael Gambon (Thomas Sandefur), Diane Venora (Liane Wigand)

In Louisville, Kentucky, Jeffrey Wigand is fired from his job at Brown and Williamson Tobacco Company. Lowell Bergman, Mike Wallace's assistant, gets a box of documents from inside Phillip Morris and is referred to Wigand as someone who can help him interpret them. Wigand tells Bergman that tobacco company executives lied when they told Congress they did not know nicotine was addictive. Bergman learns that if Wigand testifies in a court case, what he said would be public record and Brown and Williamson could not sue him for violating the confidentiality agreement he was forced to sign. Wigand testifies in the state of Mississippi's lawsuit against the tobacco companies, but his wife leaves him. At CBS, fear of a lawsuit by Brown and Williamson makes them show an edited version of Wigand's interview. Wigand discovers that the tobacco companies have started a smear campaign against him on December 8, 1995 (1:51:55 to 1:59:24). Bergman proves most of the allegations are distorted or untrue. After the edited interview is broadcast, Bergman tips off the *New York Times*, which does a story accusing CBS of caving. The unedited interview finally airs, but Bergman quits.

A very important movie. It shows the danger of allowing corporations to own news sources. Wigand is what Bergman called him: a hero.

Awards: *Academy Award Nominations*: Best Picture, Best Director, Best Adapted Screenplay, Best Actor (Russell Crowe), Best Cinematography, Best Film Editing, and Best Sound. *Golden Globe Nominations*: Best Motion Picture–Drama, Best Director–Motion Picture, Best Performance by an Actor in a Motion Picture–Drama (Crowe), Best Screenplay–Motion Picture, and Best Original Score–Motion Picture

Alternate Film: *The Notebook*

9

20,000 LEAGUES UNDER THE SEA

Year: 1954
Genre: Action/Adventure
Run Time: 2 hours 7 minutes
Date Revealed in Film: 11:52–53
Availability: DVD (Disney/Buena Vista)
Director: Richard Fleischer; **Screenplay**: Earl Felton, based on Jules Verne's novel
Cast: Kirk Douglas (Ned Land), James Mason (Captain Nemo), Paul Lukas (Professor Pierre Aronnax), Peter Lorre (Conseil), Robert J. Wilke (*Nautilus*'s First Mate), Ted de Corsia (Captain Farragut), Carleton Young (John Howard), J. M. Kerrigan (Billy)

In 1868 a mysterious monster sinks a number of ships. The U.S. government recruits Professor Pierre Aronnax; his assistant, Conseil; and expert harpooner Ned Land to go on an expedition on the USS *Abraham Lincoln* to hunt for the monster. The ship is attacked by the monster and sunk. On December 9, 1868 (20:00 to 52:15), Aronnax, Conseil, and Land go on board the *Nautilus*, a fantastic submarine commanded by the mysterious Captain Nemo. He decides not to kill them and lets Land and Conseil go on an underwater hunt with the *Nautilus*'s crew. Ned becomes interested in the vast treasure Nemo has collected. Nemo takes them to the prison island of Rura Penthe, where the inmates mine phosphates for use in munitions and Nemo tells Aronnax he used to be a prisoner there, until he escaped. The *Nautilus* attacks and sinks a ship carrying phosphates from the island. Nemo justifies this act saying he prevented the deaths of many in war. Ned learns the location of Vulcania, Nemo's secret island base, and puts the location in bottles that he throws overboard. Their adventures include fighting off cannibals and a giant squid, during which Ned saves Nemo's life. At Vulcania, they find it ringed by warships and Marines already ashore. Nemo's response leads to the exciting climax.

A pretty good action/adventure film, if a little dated. Kirk Douglas should be glad he never tried to make a go of it as a singer.

Awards: *Academy Award Wins*: Best Color Art Direction and Best Special Effects. *Academy Award Nomination*: Best Film Editing
Alternate Film: *The Last Days of Patton*

10

A BEAUTIFUL MIND

Year: 2001

Genre: Biographical Drama

Run Time: 2 hours 15 minutes

Availability: Blu-ray and DVD (Universal Studios)

Director: Ron Howard; **Screenplay:** Akiva Goldsman, based on Sylvia Nasar's book

Cast: Russell Crowe (John Forbes Nash Jr.), Jennifer Connelly (Alicia Nash), Paul Bettany ("Charles Herman"), Ed Harris ("William Parcher"), Anthony Rapp (Bender), Christopher Plummer (Dr. Rosen), Judd Hirsch (Helinger)

At Princeton in 1947 mathematical genius John Nash meets his roommate, Charles Herman. Nash is a total geek, but brilliant. He develops a theory that since no one likes to be second best, competition may not be the best way for everyone to maximize their outcome. Five years later Nash is recruited by FBI agent William Parcher to find coded messages in magazines about an atom bomb the Soviets are smuggling into the United States. At Princeton he teaches calculus. A student, Alicia, approaches him for a date and they later get married. Nash thinks he's being watched by the Soviets and tries to quit working for the FBI. At a lecture he freaks out, is chased down, and committed. We learn that Parcher does not exist and the whole program to scan magazines for codes only existed only in Nash's mind. He tries to recover his sanity, but he stops taking his medicines and has more delusions. Charles Herman does not exist either. Nash makes a breakthrough as he realizes that Herman's young niece "Marcee," whom he met years ago, has not aged at all and thus cannot be real. He returns to Princeton. Nash still sees his delusions, but ignores them. He wins the Nobel Prize in economics, which is presented to him on December 10, 1994 (2:04:59 to 2:08:30).

An unusual film because a lot of what we see happens only in Nash's mind. Russell Crowe does an excellent job of making Nash's delusions believable.

Awards: *Academy Award Wins*: Best Picture, Best Adapted Screenplay, Best Director, and Best Supporting Actress (Jennifer Connelly). *Academy Award Nominations*: Best Makeup, Best Actor (Russell Crowe), Best Film Editing, and Best Original Score. *Golden Globe Wins*: Best Performance by an Actor in a Motion Picture–Drama (Crowe), Best Performance by an Actress in a Supporting Role in a Motion Picture (Connelly), Best Screenplay–Motion Picture, and Best Motion Picture–Drama. *Golden Globe Nominations*: Best Director–Motion Picture and Best Original Score–Motion Picture

Alternate Film: *Operation Petticoat*

11

PSYCHO

Year: 1960
Genre: Horror/Mystery
Run Time: 1 hour 49 minutes
Date Revealed in Film: 2:20
Availability: Blu-ray and DVD (Universal Studios)
Director: Alfred Hitchcock; **Screenplay**: Joseph Stefano, based on Robert Bloch's novel
Cast: Anthony Perkins (Norman Bates), Janet Leigh (Marion Crane), Vera Miles (Lila Crane), John Gavin (Sam Loomis), Martin Balsam (Det. Milton Arbogast), Simon Oakland (Dr. Fred Richmond), John McIntire (Sheriff Chambers)

On December 11, 1959 (1:55 to 13:35), Marion Crane is involved in a sexual relationship with Sam Loomis, but they can't marry due to his financial situation. She works at a real estate office, from which she steals $40,000 and runs. The next evening she stops at the Bates Motel run by momma's boy clerk, Norman Bates, who watches her undress through a peephole. While she is in the shower an indistinct figure stabs her to death. Norman disposes of all signs of this crime. Marion's sister Lila and Sam Loomis start looking for Marion, but Arbogast, a private eye who's been hired to find the money, approaches them. Arbogast's search eventually brings him to the Bates Motel, where Norman says she stayed one night and left. Arbogast calls and tells this to Lila and Sam. He goes back to talk to Norman's mother in the house located on a ridge overlooking the hotel, but a figure stabs him to death. When he does not call back Lila and Sam go to the Bates Motel and check in. When Lila decides to try and talk to Norman's mother, what she finds exposes the source of the horror at the Bates Motel.

One of Hitchcock's scariest! The famous shower scene is an icon of cinematography. This film created the whole genre of the modern "slasher" film. **Awards**: *Academy Award Nominations*: Best Director, Best Supporting Actress (Janet Leigh), Best Art Direction, and Best Cinematography–Black-and-White. *Golden Globe Win*: Best Supporting Actress (Leigh). **Alternate Film**: *Wallis and Edward*

12

WAKE ISLAND

Year: 1942
Genre: War/Drama
Run Time: 1 hour 27 minutes
Date Revealed in Film: 1:08:07
Availability: DVD (Universal Studios), VHS (MCA Home Video)
Director: John Farrow; **Screenplay**: W. R. Burnett and Frank Butler
Cast: Brian Donlevy (Major Bruce Caton), Albert Dekker (Shad McClosky), MacDonald Carey (Bruce Cameron), William Bendix (Aloysius K. Randall), Robert Preston (Private Joe Doyle), Walter Abel (Commander Roberts), Mikhail Rasumny (Ivan Probenzky)

In November 1941 the small Marine garrison on Wake Island gets a new commander, Major Caton, known as a "hardnose" by some in the command. McClosky is the new foreman of the civilian workers who are strengthening the fortifications. A Japanese envoy passes through on his way to Washington. On the morning of December 8 they learn of the attack on Pearl Harbor and suffer through an air raid. A few days later, they don't fire back, luring the Japanese landing force in close, where they blast it with their guns. On December 12, 1941, the garrison suffers through another air raid (1:07:26 to 1:08:13). When a cruiser arrives that can stand off and blast them to dust, a Marine pilot flies out and sinks it. However, the Japanese are not about to give up.

An interesting piece of American World War II propaganda with the defenders compared to prior heroes of Custer's last stand and the lost battalion. A lot of the movie is taken up by comical confrontations between two Marines. Also the garrison surrendered and didn't fight to the last man. **Awards**: *Academy Award Nominations*: Best Picture, Best Actor in a Supporting Role (William Bendix), Best Director, and Best Original Screenplay **Alternate Film**: *Recount*

13

THE TRUMAN SHOW

Year: 1998
Genre: Comedy/Drama
Run Time: 1 hour 43 minutes
Date Revealed in Film: 30:41
Availability: Blu-ray (Warner Home Video), DVD (Paramount Pictures)
Director: Peter Weir; **Screenplay**: Andrew Niccol
Cast: Jim Carrey (Truman Burbank), Laura Linney (Meryl Burbank/Hannah Gill), Ed Harris (Christof), Noah Emmerich (Marlon/Louis Coltrane), Natascha McElhone (Lauren Garnend/Sylvia), Paul Giamatti (Simeon), Peter Krause (Lawrence)

Truman Burbank lives in Seahaven, an ideal town, working as an insurance agent. Actually, his life is a continuous reality TV show and all the other residents of the domed city of Seahaven are actors. One day a lighting fixture falls from the sky, but it is explained as having come from an airplane. Truman never leaves the island, as he is terrified of crossing water since his father drowned at sea in a storm. Truman sees a hobo he thinks is his father, but the man is hustled away. In college Truman met his wife, Meryl, but he was attracted to Lauren. Lauren tried to tell him he's on TV, but she was taken away and Truman never saw her again. On December 13 the car radio starts describing his actions (29:27 to 36:56). Truman now wants to leave, but his efforts are frustrated. The show's creator, Christof, gives an interview, telling how Truman was the first infant to be legally adopted by a corporation. Truman tunnels out and escapes. The show is suspended while the town turns out to search for him. Truman heads to sea in a small boat. Christof sends a huge storm to frighten Truman, but he presses on and Christof finally ends the storm. Truman reaches the edge of the dome and finds the exit door. Christof tries to talk him into staying, but Truman leaves as Sylvia (Lauren) races to join him. The show ends.

A film that touches on the nature of reality and free will. A satire on today's world of shrinking privacy and exhibitionism. It also has some genuinely comic moments.

Awards: *Academy Award Nominations*: Best Supporting Actor (Ed Harris), Best Director, and Best Original Screenplay. *Golden Globe Wins*: Best Performance by an Actor in a Motion Picture–Drama (Jim Carrey), Best

Performance by an Actor in a Supporting Role in a Motion Picture (Harris), and Best Original Score–Motion Picture. *Golden Globe Nominations*: Best Motion Picture–Drama, Best Director–Motion Picture, and Best Screenplay–Motion Picture
Alternate Film: *Great Balls of Fire!*

14

KNUTE ROCKNE: ALL-AMERICAN

Year: 1940
Genre: Biography
Run Time: 1 hour 38 minutes
Date Revealed in Film: 44:21
Availability: DVD (Warner Brothers), VHS (MGM/UA Home Video)
Director: Lloyd Bacon; **Screenplay**: Robert Buckner
Cast: Pat O'Brien (Knute Rockne), Ronald Reagan (George Gipp), Gale Page
     (Bonnie), John Qualen (Lars), Donald Crisp (Father Callahan)
Knute Rockne, son of Norwegian immigrants, plays football from an early age, works in the post office, and attends Notre Dame. Knute and Gus Dorais develop the forward pass and use it to beat Army, the powerhouse of the day. After graduation Rockne teaches chemistry at Notre Dame and works with the football team. Knute gets married and starts a family. Rockne becomes football coach and recruits George Gipp.

After winning games, Gipp falls ill. Before dying on December 14, 1920, Gipp asks Rockne to tell the team someday when they're down to "win just one for the Gipper" (44:20 to 47:38). After the team goes undefeated Rockne takes them to a show and gets the idea of the shift at the line of scrimmage. Rockne and his players, "the Four Horsemen," dominate football for three years. Before the next Army game, Rockne says they can't lose, but they do anyway. They still get a big welcome when they come home.

Rockne develops phlebitis and has to coach the Army game from a wheelchair. At halftime they are losing, so he tells them the story about Gipp and they come back to win. Rockne speaks in favor of football in front of a congressional committee. He takes his family on a long planned vacation to Florida, but Rockne has to fly to California. The plane crashes and he is killed.

A great biopic of the 1940s. Some parts seem contrived, but overall it is pretty good. Famous for Ronald Reagan's "win one for the Gipper" scene. **Alternate Film**: *Reach for the Sky*

15

THE GLENN MILLER STORY

Year: 1953
Genre: Biographical Drama
Run Time: 1 hour 55 minutes
Availability: DVD (Universal Studios), VHS (MCA Home Video)
Director: Anthony Mann; **Screenplay**: Valentine Davies and Oscar Brodney
Cast: James Stewart (Glenn Miller), June Allyson (Helen Burger Miller), Harry Morgan (Chummy MacGregor), Charles Drake (Don Haynes), George Tobias (Si Schribman), Barton MacLane (Gen. Henry H. Arnold), Marion Ross (Polly Haynes)

Glenn Miller works at odd jobs and plays trombone in dance bands while trying his hand at arranging music. He is hired to play and arrange on tour with a popular band. Glenn gets reacquainted with Helen Burger. He goes to New York. Glenn calls Helen and proposes to her and they get married. He quits his band job and studies composition. Glenn has a hit with "Midnight Serenade" and forms his own touring band. Helen miscarries and can't have any more children. Glenn writes a string of popular hits. Glenn and Helen adopt a boy and a girl. When World War II begins he joins the army, but he hates directing marches. Glenn gets permission to form a swing band that travels around entertaining the troops. On December 15, 1944, Glenn takes off to fly to Paris. The plane is never heard from again (1:44:59 to 1:46:18).

A somewhat fictionalized biopic from the end of the "golden age of the biopic." Jimmy Stewart's and June Allyson's performances make this picture. An entertaining enough film.

Awards: *Academy Award Win*: Best Sound. *Academy Award Nominations*: Best Screenplay and Best Score
Source: Waterkeyn, Xavier. *Air and Space Disasters of the World*. London: New Holland Publishers, 2007. This book at page 210 gives the crash date.
Alternate Film: *Mrs. Fitzherbert*

16
BATTLE OF THE BULGE

Year: 1965
Genre: War/Drama
Run Time: 2 hours 47 minutes
Availability: Blu-ray and DVD (Warner Home Video)
Director: Ken Annakin; **Screenplay:** Bernard Gordon, John Melson, Milton Sperling, and Philip Yordan
Cast: Henry Fonda (Lt. Col. Kiley), Robert Shaw (Col. Hessler), Robert Ryan (Gen. Grey), Dana Andrews (Col. Pritchard), Charles Bronson (Wolenski), Hans Christian Blech (Conrad), James MacArthur (Lt. Weaver), Telly Savalas (Sgt. Guffy)

U.S. intelligence officer Kiley flies a reconnaissance plane over enemy lines and buzzes a German staff car. Col. Hessler, the German officer in the car, reaches his destination, a bunker where he is briefed on a secret offensive. Kiley tries to convince his superiors that the Germans are about to attack, but they don't believe him. On December 16, 1944, the Germans attack, achieving surprise everywhere (39:04 to 1:16:34). Germans dressed as Americans have infiltrated behind the lines. Kiley discovers the Germans are short of fuel. The Germans surround Ambleve, where the Americans are making a last stand. Hessler is ordered to bypass the town, but he refuses and captures it, with a few Americans escaping. Kiley goes on a reconnaissance flight and almost crashes in the fog, but discovers the location of the Germans. The outnumbered American tanks engage in a fighting retreat, forcing the Germans to use extra fuel. An American fuel dump the Germans are trying to reach so they can refuel is ordered destroyed, but German infiltrators intercept the order. An American at the dump recognizes them as Germans and kills them. As the Germans arrive, Kiley and others roll burning fuel drums down the hill and destroy the German panzers. Hessler is killed and the Germans retreat.

Has some good action sequences. However, it takes liberties with the facts and the terrain. Still a watchable film.

Awards: *Golden Globe Nominations*: Best Supporting Actor (Telly Savalas) and Best Original Score

Source: MacDonald, Charles B. *A Time for Trumpets: The Untold Story of the Battle of the Bulge.* New York: William Morrow and Company, Inc., 1985. This book at page 117 gives the date of the German attack.
Alternate Film: *Johnny Tremaine*

17
THE ASSASSINATION BUREAU
Year: 1969
Genre: Black Comedy
Run Time: 1 hour 50 minutes
Date Revealed in Film: 3:03
Availability: DVD and VHS (Paramount Home Video)
Director: Basil Dearen; **Screenplay:** Michael Relph and Wolf Mankowitz, based on Jack London and Robert L. Fish's novella, *The Assassination Bureau, Ltd.*
Cast: Oliver Reed (Ivan Dragomiloff), Diana Rigg (Sonya Winter), Telly Savalas (Lord Bostwick), Curt Jürgens (General von Pinck), Philippe Noiret (Monsieur Lucoville), Warren Mitchell (Herr Weiss), Beryl Reid (Madame Otero)
After several suspicious deaths, including that of Count Kissen on December 17 (1:23 to 1:50), journalist Sonya Winter uncovers the existence of an organization that will kill anyone for a price. She hires the group to kill its own leader, Ivan Dragomiloff. He decides to use this situation to return the group to its idealistic original principles of only killing those who deserve death and issues a challenge to the other members: kill him or he will kill them. Dragomiloff and Miss Winter tour Europe as he avoids the plots of his cohorts and eliminates many of them. What neither Dragomiloff nor Miss Winter realize is that they are both being used as pawns in a much bigger and deadlier international game.
An imaginative black comedy.
Awards: *Golden Globe Nomination:* Best English-Language Foreign Film
Alternate Film: *The Enigma of Kaspar Hauser*

18
STALAG 17
Year: 1953
Genre: War/Drama
Run Time: 2 hours

Date Revealed in Film: 2:15–20

Availability: Blu-ray (Warner Home Video), DVD (Paramount Home Video)

Director: Billy Wilder; **Screenplay**: Edwin Blum and Billy Wilder

Cast: William Holden (Sefton), Don Taylor (Lt. Dunbar), Otto Preminger (Von Scherbach), Robert Strauss ("Animal" Kasava), Harvey Lembeck (Harry Shapiro), Sig Ruman (Sgt. Schulz), Peter Graves (Price), Neville Brand (Duke)

The film opens on December 18, 1944, as two American prisoners try to escape through a tunnel from Stalag 17. They are shot as they emerge (00:01 to 9:31). The POWs are convinced they have a traitor among them and suspicion falls on Sefton, who barters with the Germans for food. Later when a newly arrived prisoner, Dunbar, is hauled off to solitary after he told the other prisoners he had blown up an ammo train on the way to the camp, Sefton is accused of being the spy, beaten, and robbed of his property. He decides to catch the spy to clear himself. By hiding in the barracks during an air raid he discovers that the spy is Price, head of security. The prisoners free Dunbar and hide him. Price volunteers to take Dunbar out, but Sefton tricks Price into revealing that he is a German plant. A tied-up Price is thrown out into the yard bedecked with tin cans and killed by the guards. In the confusion Sefton and Dunbar escape.

Presents a somewhat sanitized version of POW life. It works as a mystery film in a way. Who is the spy? The cynical Sefton is presented almost as an antihero. He is looking out for himself.

Awards: *Academy Award* Win: Best Actor (William Holden). *Academy Award Nominations*: Best Director and Best Supporting Actor (Robert Strauss)

Alternate Film: *Thirty Days of Night*

19

ROBINSON CRUSOE

Year: 1997

Genre: Action/Adventure

Run Time: 1 hour 45 minutes

Availability: DVD (Echo Bridge Entertainment), VHS (Buena Vista Home Entertainment)

Directors: Rod Hardy and George T. Miller; **Screenplay**: Christopher Lofton, Tracy Keenan Wynn, and Christopher Canaan, based on Daniel Defoe's novel

Cast: Pierce Brosnan (Robinson Crusoe), William Takaku (Friday), Polly Walker (Mary McGregor)

Defoe is persuaded to write Crusoe's story. Crusoe's family fortunes decline, so his girl is forcibly betrothed to his best friend. They duel, his friend is killed, and Crusoe flees to sea. His vessel is in a storm and shipwrecks. Crusoe is washed up on an island alone. He retrieves useful items and a dog from the ship. Crusoe daydreams about his girl and builds a monument to his arrival. He finds footprints and a canoe. Crusoe saves a native from being sacrificed and calls him "Friday." They eventually become friends, after agreeing to disagree about religion. They blow up the cannibals when they return, but the dog is killed. They start building a boat and persevere even through a hurricane. The natives return, but they fight them off. They leave the island on December 19, 1686 (1:12; 08 to 1:12:58), and reach Friday's island, where they aren't happy to see him. They force Crusoe and Friday to fight. Crusoe says he won't kill Friday, but Europeans arrive, who kill Friday and save him. Crusoe returns home and marries his girl.

A moderately good adaptation. Creates an interesting backstory for Crusoe. The interactions between Crusoe and Friday are very good, with Friday not acting like a native in one of those bwana movies of the forties. Brosnan is very good as Crusoe.

Source: Defoe, Daniel. *Robinson Crusoe*. New York: Penguin Group, 1980.
This book at page 270 gives date he left the island.

Alternate Film: *Birdman of Alcatraz*

20

POCAHONTAS

Year: 1995
Genre: Adventure/Drama
Run Time: 1 hour 21 minutes
Availability: Blu-ray and DVD (Buena Vista Home Entertainment)
Directors: Mike Gabriel and Eric Goldberg; **Screenplay**: Carl Binder, Susannah Grant, and Phillip LaZebnik

Cast: Mel Gibson (John Smith), David Ogden Stiers (Gov. Ratcliffe), Linda Hunt (Grandmother Willow), Irene Bedard (Pocahontas), Russell Means (Powhatan), Christian Bale (Thomas)

On December 20, 1606, English settlers sail to Virginia (00:22 to 1:49), among them are John Smith and Gov. Ratcliffe. In Virginia, Chief Powhatan wants his daughter Pocahontas to marry Kokoum, a stern warrior, but she doesn't. The English land and start digging for gold. Smith and Pocahontas meet and she convinces him her people aren't savages. There is a skirmish and Powhatan says the English are dangerous. Smith learns there is no gold, but Gov. Ratcliffe doesn't believe him. Pocahontas and Smith sneak off to meet. Kokoum sees them kiss, attacks, and is killed by the man who, at Ratcliffe's request, was spying on Smith. The man runs and warriors seize Smith, thinking he is the killer. A rescue mission attacks as Smith is about to be executed. Pocahontas says she loves Smith and her father spares him. Ratcliffe orders his men to kill Powhatan, but they refuse. Ratcliffe tries to shoot the chief, but Smith steps in the way. Ratcliffe is sent to England for trial and Smith goes along to get treatment for his wound.

A typical Disney renaissance film. Takes great liberty with the facts. Tries to produce a politically correct version of history. Still, it is entertaining enough.

Awards: *Academy Award Wins*: Best Original Song and Best Original Score. *Golden Globe Win*: Best Original Song–Motion Picture. *Golden Globe Nomination*: Best Original Score–Motion Picture

Source: Wooley, Benjamin. *Savage Kingdom.* New York: HarperCollins, 2007. This book at page 34 gives the date they left.

Alternate Film: *White Christmas*

21

HOME ALONE

Year: 1990
Genre: Comedy/Drama
Run Time: 1 hour 43 minutes
Availability: Blu-ray and DVD (Fox Home Video)
Director: Chris Columbus; **Screenplay**: John Hughes
Cast: Macaulay Culkin (Kevin McCallister), Joe Pesci (Harry Lyme), Daniel Stern (Marv Merchants), Roberts Blossom (Old Man Marley), Catherine

O'Hara (Kate McCallister), John Heard (Peter McCallister), Devin Ratray (Buzz McCallister), John Candy (Gus Polinski)

The McCallisters are preparing on December 21 to go to France for Christmas. Kevin is told that his neighbor, Mr. Morley, is a serial killer. Kevin acts rude and has to sleep in the attic (1:03 to 12:11). The power goes out, they oversleep, and due to a mix up, Kevin is left behind and this isn't discovered until they are halfway to Paris. Kevin thinks the wish he made last night to never see his family again has been granted, and he likes it at first, as he does everything he's usually not allowed to do. Burglars arrive to case the joint, but leave when they hear Kevin inside. The next day the burglars learn no one is at home, but Kevin creates the illusion of a party and scares them off. His mom finally gets a flight back to the States. The crooks visit and figure out he's home alone. His mom gets a lift in a truck from a polka band to get home. Kevin starts missing his family and sets traps to defend the house. When the burglars try to break in, his traps beat them up. They chase him to a neighbor's house and almost get him, but Mr. Morley saves him and the burglars are arrested. On Christmas morn his family returns, to Kevin's delight.

A cute film that kind of grows on you. Kevin starts out as a brat, but learns to be careful of what you wish for. You might find you don't really like what you get.

Awards: *Academy Award Nominations*: Best Original Song and Best Original Score. *Golden Globe Nominations*: Best Motion Picture–Comedy/Musical and Best Performance by an Actor in a Motion Picture–Comedy/Musical (Macaulay Culkin)

Source: Counting the days back from Christmas reveals the first night is the 21st.

Alternate Film: *Coco before Chanel*

22

BATTLEGROUND

Year: 1949
Genre: War/Drama
Run Time: 1 hour 58 minutes
Availability: DVD (Warner Home Video)
Director: William Wellman; **Screenplay**: Robert Pirosh

Cast: Van Johnson (Holley), John Hodiak (Jarvess), Ricardo Montalban (Roderigues), George Murphy (Pop Stazak), Marshall Thompson (Jim Layton), Jerome Courtland (Abner Spudler), Don Taylor (Standiferd), James Whitmore (Kinnie)

Jim Layton and his pal Hooper are replacements assigned to different companies of the U.S. 101st Airborne. They are sent to Bastogne and ordered to dig in. Layton, as the new man, must dig alone. When they are almost through, they are moved to a new spot and have to start over. Layton, Holley, and Kippton stand guard at a roadblock. Germans dressed as GIs infiltrate and later blow up a bridge. Layton's visit to see Hooper ends in tragedy as he learns Hooper has been killed. Roderigues, Holley, and Jarvess are sent out on patrol. They encounter the infiltrators. Roderigues is wounded and has to be left behind; he freezes to death. The squad learns that they are surrounded. The squad is attacked and Holley, the squad leader, starts to sneak off, but when Layton follows him, he is embarrassed and leads a successful counterattack. On December 22, 1944 (1:27:07 to 1:32:19), while on guard duty, they receive the German mission to Gen. McAuliffe asking for surrender, to which McAuliffe replies, "Nuts." They are running out of supplies and the town is bombed. They are sent out to make a last stand, but the skies clear, allowing resupply. The squad goes to the rear for well-earned R&R.

A tough, realistic combat film. No super "gung-ho" guys here, just real men who are actually worried about being in combat. Well-developed characters.

Awards: *Academy Award Wins*: Best Cinematography and Best Original Screenplay. *Academy Award Nominations*: Best Picture, Best Director, Best Film Editing, and Best Supporting Actor (James Whitmore). *Golden Globe Wins*: Best Supporting Actor (Whitmore) and Best Screenplay

Source: McDonald, Charles B. *A Time for Trumpets*. New York: William Morrow and Company, 1985. This book at pages 511–13 gives the date of the "Nuts" reply.

Alternate Film: *Mansfield Park* (1999)

23

LETHAL WEAPON

Year: 1987
Genre: Crime Drama
Run Time: 1 hour 50 minutes

Date Revealed in Film: 59:20, 1:51:45
Availability: Blu-ray and DVD (Warner Home Video)
Director: Richard Donner; **Screenplay**: Shane Black
Cast: Mel Gibson (Martin Riggs), Danny Glover (Roger Murtaugh), Gary
    Busey (Mr. Joshua), Mitchell Ryan (Gen. Peter McAllister), Tom Atkins
    (Michael Hunsaker), Darlene Love (Trish Murtaugh), Jackie Swanson
    (Amanda Hunsaker)
LAPD detective Roger Murtaugh gets a message from Michael Hunsaker, a
Vietnam War buddy whom he hasn't seen in twelve years. He investigates
a suicide and is horrified to learn that it is Amanda Hunsaker, his friend's
daughter. Detective Martin Riggs, suicidal over the death of his wife, is
made Murtaugh's partner. Amanda Hunsaker's death is ruled a murder.
Hunsaker had contacted Murtaugh to get help in getting his daughter out
of her druggie prostitute existence. The partners investigate Amanda's pimp
and engage in a gunfight, during which Riggs saves Murtaugh's life. On December 23, 1986, the partners deduce that a prostitute named Dixie was the
one who killed Amanda, but her house blows up as they arrive to question
her. They find witnesses who link the bomb to ones used by Special Forces
in Vietnam, with whom Riggs served in that war. They confront Hunsaker
and learn he is involved in money laundering for a heroin smuggling operation, but before they can get the details, Hunsaker is killed. The smugglers
believe that they have killed Riggs and then kidnap Murtaugh's daughter
(1:00:48 to 1:23:00). Murtaugh and Riggs are captured the next day when
they try to free her. Murtaugh and Riggs are tortured, but Riggs escapes
and frees the two Murtaughs. Mr. Joshua, the smuggler's hit man, escapes
and tries to take revenge on Murtaugh's family, leading to an explosive final
confrontation.

   A story of redemption. Murtaugh gives Riggs a reason to live, while Riggs
gives Murtaugh new enthusiasm for the job. Busey gives a great performance
as Mr. Joshua.
Awards: *Academy Award Nominations*: Best Sound Effects and Best Sound
    Effects Editing
Alternate Film: *Miracle on 34th Street*

24
IT'S A WONDERFUL LIFE

Year: 1946
Genre: Fantasy/Drama
Run Time: 2 hours 10 minutes
Date Revealed in Film: 1:17:04
Availability: Blu-ray and DVD (Paramount Home Video)
Director: Frank Capra; **Screenplay:** Frances Goodrich, Albert Hackett, Jo
    Swerling, and Frank Capra, based on Philip Van Doren Stern's short story
    "The Greatest Gift"
Cast: James Stewart (George Bailey), Donna Reed (Mary Hatch Bailey),
    Henry Travers (Clarence Odbody), Lionel Barrymore (Mr. Potter),
    Thomas Mitchell (Uncle Billy Bailey), Beulah Bondi (Ma Bailey), Frank
    Faylen (Ernie Bishop), Ward Bond (Bert)

In response to numerous prayers, Heaven decides to send Clarence, an apprentice angel who has not yet earned his wings, to help George Bailey get through a crisis in his life. In a long flashback, Clarence is shown the major events of George's life in preparation for his mission. George is an unsung hero, saving lives and, after his father's death, running his building and loan company that is the only thing standing in the way of greedy Mr. Potter taking over the idyllic town of Bedford Falls. George marries his childhood sweetheart, Mary Hatch, and gives up his dream of traveling the world. He settles into domesticity, while his younger brother goes to college and later becomes a war hero, winning the Congressional Medal of Honor. On December 24, 1945 (1:16:40 to 2:09:34), George's absent-minded uncle Billy, who works with him, loses $8,000 in company funds the day a bank examiner arrives in town to conduct an audit. George's fear of arrest and disgrace lead him to attempt suicide. Clarence prevents this, but when George says everybody would be better off without him, Clarence grants his wish. Clarence shows George that the world would have been much worse off if George had never been born. George agrees to return to reality. His problems aren't over yet, but the many people George helped over the years pitch in to create the satisfying conclusion.

A fantastic film. Just right for the holiday season. Won't be dated one hundred years from now.

Awards: *Academy Award Win*: Technical Achievement. *Academy Award Nominations*: Best Picture, Best Director, Best Actor (Stewart), Best Film Editing, and Best Sound Recording. *Golden Globe Win*: Best Motion Picture Director (Frank Capra)
Alternate film: *Die Hard*

25

THE GREATEST STORY EVER TOLD
Year: 1965
Genre: Biblical Drama
Run Time: 3 hours 45 minutes
Availability: Blu-ray and DVD (Metro-Goldwyn-Mayer)
Director: George Stevens; **Screenplay**: George Stevens and James Lee Barrett
Cast: Max Von Sydow (Jesus), Charlton Heston (John the Baptist), José Ferrer (Herod Antipas), Dorothy McGuire (Mary), Claude Rains (Herod the Great), Telly Savalas (Pontius Pilate), Martin Landau (Caiaphas), David McCallum (Judas Iscariot)

Jesus is born (traditionally) on December 25 (5:45 to 6:15). Magi follow his star and meet with King Herod, then go to Bethlehem with gifts. Joseph is warned to flee to Egypt. Herod sends troops to kill all male infants. Herod dies. The Holy Family returns to Nazareth and the Romans annex Judea. Years pass and John the Baptist appears, preaching and baptizing. One day Jesus appears to be baptized and then goes into the desert, where Satan unsuccessfully tempts him. Jesus gathers his disciples and teaches them with parables. Pilate is made governor. Jesus performs various miracles such as healing and resurrection. John the Baptist is arrested and then beheaded at the behest of Salome. Jesus is anointed and enters Jerusalem on Palm Sunday. Jesus cleanses the temple and Judas meets with the Sanhedrin to betray Jesus. Jesus and his disciples have their Last Supper and Jesus is arrested. He is tried by the Sanhedrin and brought before Pilate and Herod Antipas. The crowd tells Pilate to "crucify him," so Pilate orders this. Jesus is nailed to a cross and dies. He is buried in a tomb. On Easter Sunday the tomb is found empty, as Jesus has been resurrected and later appears to the disciples.

A good but subdued telling of this story. Von Sydow plays Jesus as intense but unemotional. Has some great sequences, especially the resurrection of Lazarus.

Awards: *Academy Award Nominations*: Best Musical Score, Best Cinematography–Color, Best Art Direction, Best Costume Design, and Best Visual Effects
Alternate Film: *A Christmas Carol* (1984)

26
THE SEARCHERS
Year: 1956
Genre: Western/Drama
Run Time: 1 hour 59 minutes
Availability: Blu-ray and DVD (Warner Home Video)
Director: John Ford; **Screenplay**: Frank S. Nugent, based on Alan Le May's novel
Cast: John Wayne (Ethan Edwards), Jeffrey Hunter (Martin Pawley), Vera Miles (Laurie Jorgensen), Ward Bond (Rev. Capt. Samuel Johnson Clayton), Natalie Wood (Debbie Edwards), Harry Carey Jr. (Brad Jorgensen), Lana Wood (Debbie Edwards [young])

Three years after the end of the Civil War Ethan Edwards returns to the west Texas ranch of his brother, Aaron, and his wife, Martha. Their three children, Lucy, who is being courted by neighbor Brad Jorgensen; Debbie; and Ben, live with them along with orphan Martin Pawley. The Jorgensens' cattle are rustled, and the Texas Rangers, including Ethan, ride out and learn that it was Comanche that stole the cattle. They return, but the Comanche have attacked the Edwards homestead, killing Aaron, Martha, and Ben, but carrying off Lucy and Debbie as captives. The Rangers give chase, and Ethan reveals an implacable hatred for Indians. Eventually only Ethan and Martin continue the search for Debbie. They learn a Comanche chief named Scar is holding her. Martin and Ethan encounter the cavalry, and on December 26, 1868 (1:10:59 to 1:12:26), they ride through a Comanche village that the army has just burned. An incognito visit to Scar's camp reveals that Debbie identifies as Comanche now, and she asks them to leave. Ethan tries to kill her but is stopped by Martin. Ethan and Martin return to the Jorgensens, but a cavalry detachment arrives with the location of Scar's new camp. Martin sneaks in to rescue Debbie just before the camp is attacked. Ethan kills Scar but carries Debbie back to the care of the Jorgensens instead of trying to kill her. Ethan walks away alone.

One of the all-time classic westerns. Has plenty of action, but also delves into the psychology of the characters. The film has some fantastic cinematography. **Source**: Washburn, Wilcomb E. *Handbook of North American Indians, Vol. 4: History of Indian–White Relations.* Washington, DC: Smithsonian Institution, 1988. This book at page 175 says that on December 25, 1868, Maj. Evans beat Comanche Chief Black Horse at Soldier Spring.
Alternate Film: *Gorillas in the Mist*

27

FINDING NEVERLAND
Year: 2004
Genre: Biographical Drama
Run Time: 1 hour 46 minutes
Date Revealed in Film: 1:06:34
Availability: Blu-ray and DVD (Miramax)
Director: Marc Forster; **Screenplay**: David Magee, based on Allan Knee's play
Cast: Johnny Depp (J. M. Barrie), Kate Winslet (Sylvia Llewelyn Davies), Julie Christie (Emma du Maurier), Radha Mitchell (Mary Ansell Barrie), Dustin Hoffman (Charles Frohman), Freddie Highmore (Peter Llewelyn Davies), Eileen Essell (Mrs. Snow)
After the failure of his play *Little Mary*, playwright J. M. Barrie meets widow Sylvia Davies and becomes a father figure to her sons. His wife eventually leaves him, while Sylvia's mother objects to their relationship and Sylvia gets weaker from disease. Barrie writes *Peter Pan* based on his relationship with the children. His producer reluctantly puts on the play. On opening night, December 27, 1904, Barrie puts children from an orphanage in the audience. Their enthusiasm infects the adults and creates a huge success (1:05:40 to 1:22:47). Sylvia was too ill to attend the premiere, so a scaled-back version is presented to her at home. She soon dies, leaving custody of her boys to Barrie.

A very watchable movie. You feel like you get to know the characters and their motivations. An interesting look behind the scenes of the origin of *Peter Pan*.
Awards: *Academy Award Win*: Best Original Music Score. *Academy Award Nominations*: Best Picture, Best Adapted Screenplay, Best Actor (Johnny Depp), Best Art Direction, Best Costume Design, and Best Film Editing
Alternate Film: *The Kite Runner*

28

SILVER LININGS PLAYBOOK

Year: 2012
Genre: Romance/Drama
Run Time: 2 hours 2 minutes
Availability: Blu-ray and DVD (Starz/Anchor Bay)
Director: David O. Russell; **Screenplay**: David O. Russell, based on Matthew
Quick's novel *The Silver Linings Playbook*
Cast: Bradley Cooper (Pat Solitano Jr.), Jennifer Lawrence (Tiffany Maxwell),
Robert De Niro (Pat Solitano Sr.), Jackie Weaver (Dolores Solitano), Chris
Tucker (Danny McDaniels), Anupam Kher (Dr. Cliff Patel), Julia Stiles
(Veronica)

Pat Solitano Jr. is released into his parents' custody from a mental hospital,
where he was committed after almost beating his wife's lover to death. Pat has
bipolar disorder but won't take medication. His father lost his job and is using
illegal bookmaking to get enough cash to start a restaurant. Pat wants to get
in shape and reconcile with Nikki. He meets his best friend Ronnie's sister-
in-law, Tiffany, an unemployed widow, and she tells him why she lost her
job. She agrees to give a letter to Nikki if he will be her partner in an upcoming dance contest. Nikki's reply hints she might be willing to reconcile. Pat
refuses to recognize that he's attracted to Tiffany. Pat's dad bets all his money
on the Eagles–Giants football game. He persuades Pat to attend as a good
luck charm for the team. Pat skips dance practice with Tiffany to go, but gets
in a fight and the Eagles lose. Pat Sr. bets a friend that if the Eagles beat the
Cowboys and Tiffany and Pat score at least 5 out of 10 in the dance contest,
Pat Sr. will win back all the money he lost. Pat agrees to go to the contest when
he learns Nikki will be there. On December 28, 2008 (1:37:14 to 1:54:29), at
the dance contest Nikki actually is there. Pat and Tiffany score 5.0. Since the
Eagles won, his dad wins the bet. Pat Sr. gives his son some advice that leads
to the satisfying conclusion.

A pleasing romantic drama. Some parts are funny, some parts are sad, all
parts are revealing. Cooper and Lawrence both give moving performances as
real people.

Awards: *Academy Award Win*: Best Actress (Jennifer Lawrence). *Academy
Award Nominations*: Best Picture, Best Actor (Bradley Cooper), Best Supporting Actor (Robert De Niro), Best Director, Best Supporting Actress

(Jackie Weaver), Best Adapted Screenplay, and Best Film Editing. *Golden Globe Win*: Best Performance by an Actress in a Motion Picture–Comedy or Musical (Lawrence). *Golden Globe Nominations*: Best Motion Picture–Comedy or Musical, Best Performance by an Actor in a Motion Picture–Comedy or Musical (Cooper), and Best Screenplay–Motion Picture

Source: "Eagles-Cowboys between the Tackles." *Philadelphia Daily News*, December 29, 2008. This article gives the date of the game

Alternate Film: *The Amityville Horror* (1979)

29

BECKET

Year: 1964

Genre: Biographical Drama

Run Time: 2 hours 28 minutes

Availability: Blu-ray and DVD (MPI Media Group)

Director: Peter Glenville; **Screenplay**: Edward Anhalt, based on Jean Anouilh's play

Cast: Richard Burton (Thomas Becket), Peter O'Toole (King Henry II of England), John Gielgud (King Louis VII of France), Paolo Stoppa (Pope Alexander III), Martita Hunt (Empress Matilda), Pamela Brown (Queen Eleanor), Siân Phillips (Gwendolen)

King Henry II relies on his Saxon page, Thomas À Becket, to arrange drunken debaucheries. When the Archbishopric of Canterbury becomes vacant Henry appoints Becket to the post, thinking he can control him. Becket instead becomes a very pious archbishop. Henry had argued with the previous bishop, who refused to allow taxation of church property to support Henry's wars in France. Becket adopts the same position and Henry is outraged. A plot to force Becket's resignation by creating a scandal fails, but Becket flees. He travels to Rome and asks the pope to be allowed to resign as archbishop and become a monk. The pope refuses this request. A truce is arranged and Becket returns to England. Becket's popularity with the commons worries Henry and in a drunken rage he asks, "Will no one rid me of this troublesome priest?" Three knights take him seriously and kill Becket on December 29, 1170 (2:15:12 to 2:22:59). Monks whip Henry as penance. Becket was made a saint.

The film takes some factual liberties. These are to drive the plot by making Becket a Saxon who is opposed by the Normans. Still, great acting and a watchable film.

Awards: *Academy Award Win*: Best Adapted Screenplay. *Academy Award Nominations*: Best Actor (Richard Burton and Peter O'Toole), Best Picture, Best Supporting Actor (John Gielgud), Best Art Direction, Best Costume Design, Best Director, Best Editing, Best Score, and Best Sound. *Golden Globe Wins*: Best Motion Picture–Drama and Best Motion Picture Actor–Drama (O'Toole). *Golden Globe Nominations*: Best Motion Picture Director, Best Motion Picture Actor–Drama (Burton), and Best Original Score

Source: Guy, J. *Thomas Becket*. New York: Random House, 2012. This book at page 312 gives his death date.

Alternate Film: *Marley and Me*

30
ZERO DARK THIRTY
Year: 2012
Genre: Drama/Thriller
Run Time: 2 hours 37 minutes
Date Revealed in Film: 54:40
Availability: Blu-ray and DVD (Sony Pictures)
Director: Kathryn Bigelow; **Screenplay**: Mark Boal
Cast: Jessica Chastain (Maya), Jason Clarke (Dan), Jennifer Ehle (Jessica), Kyle Chandler (Joseph Bradley), Joel Edgerton (Patrick), Mark Strong (George), Édgar Ramírez (Larry), James Gandolfini (CIA Director)

Two years after 9/11, Maya, a young CIA operative, works in Pakistan with Dan, who uses torture to extract from Ammar al-Baluchi that Abu Ahmed is a courier for Osama bin Laden. Abu Faraj is arrested and tortured, but denies knowing anything about Abu Ahmed. Maya interprets this as him trying to hide the importance of Abu Ahmed. Dan returns to Washington and Maya starts working with Jessica, another CIA case officer. Jessica goes to Afghanistan to meet with a supposed high-level mole inside al-Qaeda, but on December 30, 2009, Jessica is killed in a car bomb attack and Maya vows revenge (54:35 to 1:04:05). The CIA is told Abu Ahmed is dead, but they think that actually his brother was killed. Dan bribes a Kuwaiti prince into giving him the phone number of Abu Ahmed's mother. The CIA taps her phone and locates a compound where Abu Ahmed seems be in Abbottabad, Pakistan. Maya has become mystical, believing she was spared in a hotel bombing and assassination attempt so she can finish the job. In spite of top-level doubts that bin Laden is at the compound, a mission to get him is approved. Maya briefs Navy SEALs about the mission. The SEALs go in and kill bin Laden and capture intelligence information. Maya confirms that the body brought back is bin Laden's. She gets on a plane home, but cannot give the pilot a destination as she starts weeping as a release from years of tension.

A nuts-and-bolts look at the world of espionage. I fear the world of real spies is much closer to *Zero Dark Thirty* than any of the James Bond films.

Awards: *Academy Award Win*: Best Sound Editing. *Academy Award Nominations*: Best Picture, Best Actress (Jessica Chastain), Best Film Editing, and Best Original Screenplay. *Golden Globe Win*: Best Performance by an Actress in a Motion Picture–Drama (Chastain). *Golden Globe Nominations*: Best Motion Picture–Drama, Best Director–Motion Picture, and Best Screenplay–Motion Picture

Source: *Times Almanac 2011*. New York: Encyclopaedia Britannica, 2011. This book on page 20 gives the date of Jessica's death.

Alternate Film: *The Deliberate Stranger*

31

THE POSEIDON ADVENTURE

Year: 1972

Genre: Disaster

Run Time: 1 hour 57 minutes

Date Revealed in Film: 1:50

Availability: Blu-ray and DVD (Twentieth Century Fox)

Director: Ronald Neame and Irwin Allen; **Screenplay**: Wendell Mayes and Stirling Silliphant, based on Paul Gallico's novel

Cast: Gene Hackman (Reverend Scott), Ernest Borgnine (Mike Rogo), Red Buttons (James Martin), Carol Lynley (Nonnie Parry), Shelley Winters (Belle Rosen), Jack Albertson (Manny Rosen), Roddy McDowall (Acres), Stella Stevens (Linda Rogo)

The SS *Poseidon* is capsized by a tsunami in the Mediterranean at midnight on New Year's Eve, December 31, 1972 (00:01 to 24:42). The radical Rev. Scott tries to lead a disparate group to safety. They climb up through the overturned ship, having many narrow escapes along the way and losing a few of their group. The survivors reach the propeller shaft room, where a rescue team from a helicopter cuts through the hull and saves the remaining ones.

One of the best of the disaster flicks. One interesting point: the Mediterranean is one of the few places on Earth where this story *might* be able to occur. Due to the shallow seabed, a rogue wave could reach an incredible height.

Awards: *Academy Award Wins*: Best Original Song and a Special Achievement Award for Visual Effects. *Academy Award Nominations*: Best Actress in a Supporting Role (Shelley Winters), Best Cinematography, Best Art Direction–Set Decoration, Best Costume Design, Best Sound, Best Film Editing, and Best Original Score. *Golden Globe Win*: Best Supporting Actress–Motion Picture (Winters). *Golden Globe Nominations*: Best Motion Picture–Drama, Best Original Score, and Best Original Song

Alternate Film: *While You Were Sleeping*

Index

Aaron, Caroline 145
Aaron, Quinton 124
Abdi, Barkhad 90, 91
Abel, Jake 173
Abel, Walter 372
Above and Beyond 236
Abraham, F. Murray 364, 365
Abramowsky, Klaus 127
The Accused 65
Adams, Amy 57, 241, 263
Adams, Jane 41
Adams, Nick 161
Adiarte, Patrick 295
The Adjustment Bureau 334
Adler, Robert 163
Adonis, Frank 74
The Adventures of Mark Twain 358
The Adventures of Robin Hood 91
The Affair of the Necklace 153
Affleck, Ben 27, 160, 270
Agar, John 51
The Age of Innocence 256
Agutter, Jenny 17

Ahmed, Faysal 90
Air Force One 286
Akinnuoye-Agbaje, Adewale 254, 313
The Alamo 51
Albert, Eddie 171
Albert, Edward 178
Albertson, Jack 391
Alda, Alan 203, 204
Alexander, Caroline 15
Alexander, Jace 298
Alexander, Jane 276, 277
Alexander, Nathan 217
Alexander, Scott 305
Alford, Phillip 324
Ali 52
Ali, Mahershalalhashbaz 338
Ali, Rubina 314
Alison, Joan 360
Alive 317
All the Kings Men (1947) 251
All the President's Men 276
Allam, Roger 330
Alland, William 363

Allen, Debbie 190
Allen, Irwin 391
Allen, Jack 264
Allen, Joan 139, 140
Allen, Nancy 38
Allen, Steve 15
Allen, Woody 323, 359, 360
Al's Lads 116
Allyson, June 375
Almagor, Gila 193
Altman, Robert 343
Amadeus 364
Amazing Grace 162
Ameche, Don 319
Amelia 82
Amelie 290
The Americanization of Emily 171
The American President 355
Amis, Suzy 111
Amistad 52
The Amityville Horror (1979) 389
Amnurn, Ellis 358
Anastasia 113
And Starring Pancho Villa as Himself 140
Anders, Sean 103
Anderson, Doris 223
Anderson, Herbert 15
Anderson, John 298
Anderson, Maxwell 24
Anderson, Michael 17, 218
Anderson, Richard 366
Anderson, Robert Woodruff 179
Anderson, Wes 304
Andoh, Adjoa 175
Andrew, Sylvia 45
Andrews, Dana 376
Andrews, Harry 245

Andrews, Julie 158
Andrews, Naveen 308
The Andromeda Strain 35
Angela's Ashes 250
Anger Management 160
Anhalt, Edward 389
Animal House 342
Annakin, Ken 171, 376
Annaud, Jean-Jacques 315
Anne of the Thousand Days 23
Annie Hall 359
Anouilh, Jean 389
Anousaki, Eleni 7
Antin, Steve 65
Antonio, Lou 201
Anzio 22
The Apartment 328
Apollo 13 110
Applegate, Christina 232
Apted, Michael 9, 162
Arahanga, Julian 48
Arch, Jeff 42
Archer, Anne 20
Ardrey, Robert 25
Arend, Geoffrey 142
Argenziano, Carmen 65
Argo 27
Arkin, Alan 27, 28
Arnett, Will 158
Aronson, Judie 350
Around the World in Eighty Days 218
Arquette, David 232
Arquette, Patricia 240
Arsan, Emmanuelle 179
Arthur, Jean 200
The Artist 332
Ashcroft, Peggy 97, 98
Asinof, Eliot 298

The Assassination Bureau 377
*The Assassination of Jesse James by the
    Coward Robert Ford* 173
The Assassination of Richard Nixon 50
Astin, Mackenzie 204
Astin, Sean 11, 59, 79, 149, 307
Atkins, Tom 383
Atkinson, Rick 206, 272
Atkinson, Rowan 131
Atonement 165
Attanasio, Paul 183
Attenborough, Richard 3, 29, 87, 105,
    133, 179, 180, 204, 274, 280
Auberjonois, René 247
Auclair, Michel 257
The Audrey Hepburn Story 203
August, John 31
Auntie Mame 296
Austen, Jane 189, 282, 349, 353
Austin, Michael 287
Auto Focus 195
Avatar 151
The Aviator 203
Avildsen, John G. 1
Avnet, Jon 18
Awakenings 311
Aykroyd, Dan 27, 106, 307

Babe, Thomas 232
Bacall, Lauren 22
Bacall, Michael 119
Back to the Future 331
Back to the Future, Part II 339
Back to the Future, Part III 340
Bacon, Kevin 110, 150
Bacon, Lloyd 10, 374
Badel, Alan 257
Badham, Mary 324

Baer, Buddy 215
Bailey, Charles W., II 146
Bailey, Robert, Jr. 44
Baker, Carroll 102
Baker, Diane 163, 234
Baker, Dylan 183, 317
Baker, Joe Don 313
Baker, Paul R. 191
Baker, Ray 283
Baker, Simon 154, 252, 361
Baker, Stanley 21
Balaban, Bob 155, 343
Baldwin, Alec 34, 203
Bale, Christian 239, 380
Balfour, Katherine 67
Ball, John 275
Ballard, J. G. 239
Balsam, Martin 146, 276, 354, 366, 371
Bamber, David 217
Bana, Eric 320
Bancroft, Anne 62, 107
Banderas, Antonio 224
Banerjee, Victor 97
Banks, Elizabeth 61
Bannen, Ian 235
Baranski, Christine 17, 156
Barash, Olivia 33
Barile, Anthony 152
Barkin, Ellen 232
Barrett, James Lee 385
Barrington, Diana 317
Barry Lyndon 180
Barrymore, Drew 255, 307, 327
Barrymore, John 310
Barrymore, Lionel 223, 384
Baruchel, Jay 104
Barzman, Ben 245
Basaraba, Gary 20

Basinger, Kim 349

Bass, Ronald 82, 108

Bassermann, Albert 117

Bassett, Angela 49

*Bat*21* 110

Bates, Alan 7, 303, 304

Bates, Harry 278

Bates, Kathy 18, 111, 124

Bates, Michael 221

Batman 349

Batteer, Joe 181

Battle at Apache Pass 209

Battle of Britain 244

Battle of the Bulge 376

Battleground 381

Bavier, Frances 278

Baxter, Anne 10, 120

Beach, Adam 181

Bean, Sean 11, 20, 173

Bearman, Joshuah 27

Beatty, Ned 197, 321

Beatty, Warren 37, 222, 333, 334

Beaufoy, Simon 128, 263, 314

A Beautiful Mind 370

Beaven, Ellie 238, 239

Becker, Gerry 305

Becket 389

Beckinsale, Kate 203

Becoming Jane 15

Bedard, Irene 380

Bedelia, Bonnie 96

Beery, Noah, Jr. 248, 302

Begley, Louis 36

Beharie, Nicole 288

Behrman, S. N. 215

Béja, Xavier 213

Bejo, Bérénice 332, 333

Bell, Jamie 167

Bell, Marshall 184

Bellows, Gil 71

Belushi, John 342

Bendix, William 372

Benedek, Barbara 301

Bening, Annette 37, 355, 356

Bennett, Alan 121, 204

Bennett, Charles 168

The Benny Goodman Story 15

Ben-Porat, Benjamin 193

Benson, Martin 295

Benton, Robert 197, 222, 227, 283

Berenger, Tom 200, 301

Berenson, Marisa 180

Beresford, Bruce 27, 54

Bergen, Candice 29, 179, 180

Berger, Thomas 354

Bergin, Patrick 20

Bergman, Ingrid 122, 360

Bergren, Eric 107

Berkeley, Xander 286

Bernard, Carlo 28

Bernstein, Carl 276

Berridge, Elizabeth 364

Berti, Marina 215

Bertolucci, Bernardo 229

Besson, Luc 134

Bettany, Paul 370

Beymer, Richard 234

Beyond Rangoon 240

Beyond the Sea 145

Bickford, Charles 39, 40, 63

Biehn, Michael 143

Bieri, Ramon 35

Bierko, Craig 84

Big 330

The Big Chill 301

The Big Miracle 306

The Big Red One 205
Bigelow, Kathryn 390
Bilbrook, Lydia 336
Billy Budd 259
Binder, Carl 379
Binoche, Juliette 308, 309
Birch, Thora 20
Birdman of Alcatraz 379
Birinski, Leo 223
Birken, Andrew 134
Bishop, Julie 51
Bishop, Stephen 258
Bissell, Whit 5
Black, Lucas 34
Black, Shane 383
Black August 252
Black Hawk Down 297
Black Sunday 18
Black Swan 41
Blade Runner 7
Blair, Betsy 185, 186
Blake, Amanda 63
Blake, Katherine 24
Blake, Michael 125, 126
Blanchett, Cate 203, 204, 338
Blast from the Past 316
Blech, Hans Christian 66, 376
Blessed, Brian 318
Bleszynski, Nick 55
Blethyn, Brenda 145
The Blind Side 124
Bloch, Robert 371
Bloom, Orlando 11, 59, 79
Blossom, Roberts 380
Blow 237
Blucas, Mark 52
Blum, Edwin 378
Blumenson, Merlin 221

Blunt, Emily 334, 361, 362
Boal, Mark 390
Boatman, Michael 152
Bobby Jones: Stroke of Genius 208
Boen, Earl 143, 260
Bogarde, Dirk 280
Bogart, Humphrey 360, 361
Bogdanovich, Peter 227, 341, 344
Bohem, Leslie 51
Boland, Bridget 24
Bolt, Robert 6, 14, 202, 297
Bomback, Mark 306
Bond, Casey 258
Bond, Ward 71, 138, 269, 302, 319, 384, 386
Bondi, Beulah 384
Bonnie and Clyde 222
Bonucci, Emilio 204
Boone, Pat 163
Boone, Richard 22
Boorman, John 123, 240
Booth, James 21
Boothe, Powers 139
Borgnine, Ernest 185, 186, 365, 391
Born on the Fourth of July 307
Bose: The Forgotten Hero 127
Boston, Rachel 142
Boswall, John 99
Bosworth, Kate 145
Bottoms, Timothy 341
Boublil, Alain 345
Boulle, Pierre 89, 144
The Bounty 14
The Bourne Identity 253
Bowens, Malick 13
Bower, David 131
Boyd, Billy 214
Boyd, William 105

Boyens, Philippa 11, 59, 79
Boyle, Danny 128, 314
Boyle, Peter 132
Boyles, Bob 302
The Boys from Brazil 45
Brach, Gérard 101
Brackett, Charles 163
Bracco, Lorraine 329, 330
Bradford, Richard 277
Bradley, James 51
Bradley, Omar 221
Branagh, Kenneth 217, 318
Brand, Neville 378
Brand, Russell 158
Brandauer, Klaus Maria 13, 14
Brando, Marlon 182, 183, 197, 255, 256
Bratt, Benjamin 28
Braugher, Andre 309
Braveheart 235
Breach 46
The Break Up 196
Breaker Morant 54
The Breakfast Club 86
Breen, Patrick 287
Breen, Richard L., 161
Brega, Mario 104–5
Brennan, Eileen 268, 341
Brennan, Walter 302, 303, 319
Brenner, Marie 368
Breuer, William B. 28
Brian's Song (2011) 274
Brickman, Marshall 359
Bride of the Wind 313
Bridesmaids 227
The Bridge 126
The Bridge at Remagen 66
Bridge on the River Kwai 144
A Bridge Too Far 279

Bridges, Jeff 60, 232, 261, 341
Bridges, Lloyd 225
Bridget Jones's Diary 348
Bright Star 54
Brighton Beach Memoirs 285
Briley, John 28, 274
The Brink's Job 19
Brittanic 349
Broadbent, Jim 210, 287, 348
Brocksmith, Roy 184
Broderick, James 253
Brodney, Oscar 375
Brody, Adrien 2, 154, 231, 232, 312
Bronson, Charles 87, 376
Bronte, Charlotte 167, 168
Brooke, Sorrell 227
Brooks, Dean 296
Brooks, Mel 132
Brosnan, Pierce 37, 379
Brown, Bryan 54
Brown Christy 169
Brown, Clancy 71
Brown, Harry 50
Brown, James 63
Brown, Joe E. 43
Brown, John 214
Brown, Pamela 389
Brown, Ralph 239
Brown, Rob 288
Brown, Thomas W. 350
Browne, Roscoe Lee 17
Brownjohn, John 101
Broyles, William, Jr. 110
Bruce, Duncan A. 236
Bruno, Chris 88
Bruno, Dylan 195
Brusati, Franco 212
Brynner, Yul 295, 296

Bryson, John 322
The Buccaneer 8
Buchanan, Edgar 200
Buchman, Sidney 242
Bugsy 186
Buffalo Bill 246
Buckner, Robert 328, 374
The Buddy Holly Story 357
Buffini, Moira 167
Bujold, Genevieve 24
Buker, Rick 104
Bullock, Sandra 124, 125, 204, 273
Burke, Billy 226
Burnett, Murray 360
Burnett, W. R. 87, 372
Burns, Edward 174
Burrell, Ty 211
Burstyn, Ellen 341, 342
Burton, Jeff 89
Burton, Kate 128
Burton, LeVar 53
Burton, Richard 24, 99, 243, 389, 390
Burton, Tim 31, 349
Busey, Gary 357, 358, 383
Busfield, Timothy 147
Bush-Fekete, Leslie 218
Buster 238
Butch Cassidy and the Sundance Kid 166
Butler, Frank 372
Butler, Gerard 272
Butterworth, Jez 211
Butterworth, John-Henry 211
Buttons, Red 391
Byington, Spring 319
Byrne, Gabriel 124

Caan, James 255, 256, 280
Cabot, Sebastian 5

Cacoyannis, Michael 7
Cage, Nicholas 181
Cagney, James 138, 190, 328, 329
Cahill, Eddie 50
Caine, Michael 21, 244, 246, 280
The Caine Mutiny 229
Caldwell, Robert 322
Caldwell, Zoe 273
Calhern, Louis 122
Callow, Simon 131, 324, 364
Cameron, James 111, 143, 151, 260
Campbell, Alan 63
Campbell, Cheryl 207
Campbell, Glen 300, 301
Campbell, John 10
Canaan, Christopher 379
Candy, John 381
Canerday, Natalie 299
Cannon, J. D. 201
Cantinflas 218, 219
Caplan, Lizzy 128
Capobianco, Carissa 93
Capra, Frank 69, 384, 385
Capricorn One 78
Capshaw, Kate 37
Captain Phillips 90
Carabastos, James 152
Cardinal, Tantoo 126
Carell, Steve 158
Carey, Harry, Jr. 386
Carey, Helen 241
Carey, MacDonald 372
Carey, Philip 138
Cariou, Len 281
Carley, Christopher 38
Carlin, John 175
Carlito's Way 249
Carlyle, Robert 250

Carnovsky, Morris 36
Caron, Glenn Gordon 37
Carradine, John 22, 218
Carradine, Keith 232
Carradine, Robert 205
Carrey, Jim 41, 42, 305, 306, 373
Carrington 21
Carroll, Leo G. 352
Carroll, Tim 88
Carson, Jack 63, 269
Carson, Robert 63
Carter, Helena Bonham 31, 216, 265, 266, 345
Carter, Joseph 74
Casablanca 360
Casadesus, Gisèle 213
Cash, Johnny 12
Cassel, Vincent 134
Cassell, Alan 55
Cassell, Wally 51
Cassidy, Ted 166
Cast a Giant Shadow 147
Castellano, Richard S. 255
Casualties of War 239
Cates, Phoebe 287
Caton-Jones, Michael 148
The Cat's Meow 344
Cauffiel, Jessica 88
Caviezel, James 2, 55, 209, 252, 309
Cazale, John 253
Cera, Michael 119
Chancellor, Anna 131
Chandlee, Harry 302
Chandler, Kyle 27, 390
Channing, Stockard 195
The Chant of Jimmie Blacksmith 308
Chaplin 105
Chaplin, Ben 2

Chaplin, Charlie 105
Chaplin, Geraldine 6, 106
The Charge of the Light Brigade (1936) 319
Chariots of Fire 72, 207
Charisse, Cyd 85
Charleson, Ian 29, 207
Charlie and the Chocolate Factory 31
Charlie Wilson's War 111
Chastain, Jessica 177, 178, 390, 391
Chayefsky, Paddy 185
Cheadle, Don 152
Cheah, Johnny 240
Chen, Joan 229
Chernus, Michael 90
Chheda, Tanay 314
Chicago 156
A Child's Wish 35
The Children of Men (2006) 364
Childs, Julia 241
Chinatown 291
Chitty Chitty Bang Bang 204
Chocolat 85
Chong, Felix 75
Chong, Marcus 48
Christie, Julie 6, 303, 387
Christie, Morven 214
A Christmas Carol (1984) 386
The Chronicles of Narnia: The Voyage of the Dawn Treader 275
Church, Thomas Haden 196
Cimarron 120
Cimmino, Giovani 272
Cinderella Man 83
Ciolli, Augusta 185
Citizen Kane 363
A Civil Action 132
Clancy, Tom 20

Clark, Blake 307
Clarke, Jason 390
Clarkson, Patricia 50, 68, 277
Clavell, James 87
Clay, Nicholas 123
Cleckley, Hervey 251
Clements, John 264
Clennon, David 20
Cleopatra 242
Cleveland, Christopher 81
Clift, Montgomery 64, 65, 365, 366
Clooney, George 68
Close, Glenn 17, 286, 301, 302
Close Encounters of the Third Kind 154
Cloverfield 155
Coal Miner's Daughter 9
Cobb 215
Cobb, Lee J. 39, 219, 220, 251
Cobb, Thomas 261
Coburn, Charles 191, 319
Coburn, James 178
Cochrane, Rory 160
Cocks, Jay 210
Coco before Chanel 381
Coffin, Pierre 158
Cohen, Sacha Baron 345
Colasanto, Nicholas 74
Colbert, Claudette 45
Cold Mountain 228
Cold Turkey 163
Cole, Gary 46
Coleman, Dabney 47
Colicchio, Victor 312
Colick, Lewis 34, 145, 299
Colicos, John 24
Collette, Toni 189
Colley, Don Pedro 83
Collier, James L. 16

Collin, John 101
Collins, Lilly 124
Collins, Phil 238
Collins, Ray 363
Colman, Ronald 69
The Color of Freedom 40
Columbus, Chris 173, 380
Comden, Betty 85
Come Back to the Five and Dime, Jimmie Dean, Jimmie Dean 292
Comingore, Dorothy 363
The Company You Keep 29
Condon, Bill 156
Condon, Kerry 250, 347
Congo 313
Connaughton, Shane 169
A Connecticut Yankee in King Arthur's Court 187
Connelly, Jennifer 370, 371
Connelly, Marc 153
Connery, Sean 277, 278, 280
Connick, Harry 149
Conroy, Frank 278
Considine, Paddy 84
Considine, Robert 116
Conspiracy 44
The Conspirator 134
Contact 337
Conti, Bill 2
Conway, Kevin 200
Coogan, Steve 173
Cooke, Alistair 251
Cool Hand Luke 201
Cooper, Bradley 388, 389
Cooper, Chris 46, 60, 247, 254, 261, 299
Cooper, Gary 225, 226, 302, 303
Cooper, Gladys 39, 40
Cooper, Jackie 197

Cooper, James Fenimore 233, 234
Coppola, Francis Ford 221, 255, 356
Coppola, Roman 304
Coraline 44
Corbett, Michael 176
Corey, Jeff 300, 354
Corrigan, Kevin 306
Cosgrove, Miranda 158
Cosmo, James 189
Costa, Ricardo 122
Coster, Nicolas 334
Costner, Kevin 125, 126, 147, 277, 317
Cotton, Joseph 363, 366
Cotton, Oliver 259
Coulouris, George 363
Coulson, Bernie 65
The Count of Monte Cristo 55
Courage under Fire 53
The Court Martial of Billy Mitchell 337
Courtenay, Tom 6
Courtland, Jerome 382
Cox, Ashley 17
Cox, Brian 214, 254, 280, 289
Cox, Ronny 184
Coyote, Peter 327
Craig, William 315
Cranston, Bryan 27
Crazy Heart 261
Cregar, Laird 319
Crenna, Richard 179
Crewson, Wendy 286
Crichton, Michael 35, 183, 184, 313
Crime of the Century 3
Crisp, Donald 36, 374
Cromwell 4
Cromwell, James 93, 206, 262, 332
Cronyn, Hume 243
Cross, Ben 207

Cross, David 41
Cross, Shauna 255
Crouse, Lindsay 283, 368
Crowe, Cameron 196
Crowe, Christopher 233
Crowe, Russell 78, 79, 84, 345, 368, 370, 371
The Crucible 282
Crudup, Billy 226
Cruise, Tom 108, 150, 151, 217
Cry Freedom 274
A Cry in the Dark 322
Cuddy, William 82
Cukor, George 63
Culkin, Kieran 119
Culkin, Macaulay 380, 381
Culp, Nancy 251
Culp, Steven 317
Cumberbatch, Benedict 162, 165
Cumming, Alan 189, 321
Cunningham, John W. 225
Curie, Eve 117
The Curious Case of Benjamin Button 338
Currie, Finlay 128, 215
Curry, Tim 313
Curtis, Alan 248
Curtis, Richard 23, 131, 348
Curtis, Tony 43
Curtiz, Michael 91, 328, 360
Cusack, Cyril 99, 257
Cusack, John 2
Czarniak, Henry 193

Daddario, Alexandra 173
Dafoe, Willem 186, 308
Dahl, Arlene 163
Dahl, John 28

Dahl, Roald 31
Daldry, Stephen 273
The Dam Busters 148
D'Amico, Masolino 212
Damon, Matt 75, 174, 175, 196, 254, 334
Dances with Wolves 125
D'Angelo, Beverly 9, 10
Daniels, Jeff 68, 190, 200, 323
Danning, Sybil 193
Danson, Ted 174
Darabont, Frank 71, 206
Darby, Kim 300
Dark Blue 62
Darnell, Linda 319
Darvas, Lili 120
Darwell, Jane 319
Daughton, James 342
Daurio, Ken 158
David, Keith 44, 195
David, Thayer 163
Davidtz, Embeth 73, 348
Davies, Andrew 348
Davies, Gerald 176
Davies, Valentine 15, 375
Davis, Andrew 77
Davis, Judy 97, 98
Davis, Viola 177, 273
Davison, Bruce 46
Dawn Anna 118
Dawson, Rosario 306
Day, Doris 168
Day of the Jackal 256
The Day the Earth Stood Still 278
Dayan, Assi 193
Day-Lewis, Daniel 14, 29, 30, 170, 210, 211, 233
Days of Thunder 46
Dazed and Confused 160

D.C. Sniper: 23 Days of Terror 318
De Banzie, Brenda 169
de Corsia, Ted 369
de Elia, Tomas 224
de Havilland, Olivia 113, 114
De Niro, Robert 74, 75, 277, 311, 312, 329, 356, 357, 388
De Palma, Brian 277
de Rosnay, Tatiana 213
De Vore, Christopher 107
De Vries, Kelly 135
De Wilde, Brandon 200, 201
The Dead Zone 25
Dean, Loren 110
Dean, Quentin 275, 276
Dearen, Basil 377
Death on the Nile 36
Dearden, Basil 25
Debbouze, Jamel 290
DeCamp, Rosemary 328
Deep Impact 141
The Deer Hunter 321
Deezen, Eddie 38
Defoe, Daniel 379
DeFore, Don 116
Dekker, Albert 372
Delany, Dana 33
The Deliberate Stranger 391
Delpy, Julie 127
Dempster, Derek 244
Dench, Judi 167, 270, 271, 318, 353
Deneuve, Catherine 94
Denham, Maurice 257
Denison, Michael 3
Dennehy, Brian 96
Dennis, Gill 12
Denton, Kit 54
The Departed 75

DePaul, Tony 209
Depp, Johnny 31, 32, 387
Dern, Bruce 232
Dern, Laura 299
Dershowitz, Alan 16, 17
Deschanel, Emily 91
Deschanel, Zooey 142
Desmond, Florence 45
DeSoto, Rosanna 33
Despicable Me 158
The Devil Wears Prada 361
DeVito, Danny 296, 305
Devlin, Alan 57
Devlin, Dean 199
Dewhurst, Colleen 359
Dexter, Brad 271
Dexter, Pete 232
Dhavernas, Caroline 46
Di Cicco, Bobby 38, 205
Diamond, I. A. L. 43
The Diary of Anne Frank 234
Diaz, Cameron 210, 211
DiCaprio, Leonardo 75, 76, 111, 112, 203, 204, 210
Dick, Philip K. 8, 184, 334
Dickens, Charles 128
Dickens, Kim 125
Die Hard 385
Diesel, Vin 174
Dieterle, William 36
Dietrich, Marlene 64
Diffring, Anton 246
DiLeo, Frank 329
Dillane, Stephen 281
Dillman, Bradford 66
Dillon, Melinda 155
Dinesen, Isak 14
Dirty Harry 96

Disclosure 183
District 9 242
The Diving Bell and the Butterfly 122
Dobbs, Michael 316
Doctor Zhivago 5
Doctorow, E. L. 190
Dog Day Afternoon 252
Doherty, Edward 10
Dominczyk, Dagmara 56
Donachie, Ron 214
Donald, James 87, 144
Donaldson, Roger 14, 88, 317
Donat, Robert 95, 96
Donen, Stanley 85
Donlevy, Brian 372
Donner, Richard 197, 383
D'Onofrio, Vincent 176
Donohoe, Amanda 121
Donovan, Tate 68, 149
Donovan's Reef 367
Doomsday Gun 83
The Doors 200
Dotrice, Roy 364
Douchant, Mike 81
Douglas, Kirk 146, 369
Douglas, Michael 136, 137, 183, 355, 356
Dourif, Brad 186, 190, 296, 297
Downey, Robert, Jr. 68, 106, 289, 350
Downfall 118
Downs, Cathy 319
Doyle, Shawn 309
Doyle-Murray, Brian 32
Dr. No 5
Drago, Billy 277
Dragon: The Bruce Lee Story 32
Drake, Charles 375
Dreamchild 26
Drescher, Fran 190

Dreyfuss, Richard 155, 355
Drivas, Robert 201
Driving Miss Daisy 25
A Dry White Season 182
Duchaussoy, Michel 213
The Duchess 153
Ducommun, Rick 32
Duel 174
Duff, Anne-Marie 347
Dujardin, Jean 332, 333
Duke, Patty 62
Dumas, Alexandre 55, 56
Dun, Dennis 230
Dunaway, Faye 134, 222, 291, 292, 354
Duncan, David 5
Duncan, Michael Clarke 206, 207
Dunkirk 143
Dunlop, Lesley 107
Dunn, Kevin 306
Dunst, Kirsten 41, 344
Duprez, June 264
Dupuy, R. Ernest 25, 237, 240, 247, 265, 318
Dupuy, Trevor 25, 237, 240, 247, 265, 318
Duriez, Colin 4
Durning, Charles 253, 268
Dutton, Charles S. 288
Duvall, Robert 83, 141, 255, 256, 261, 300, 324, 356
Duvall, Shelley 359
Dwan, Allan 50
Dye, Dale 28

East of Eden (1956) 102
Eastwood, Clint 38, 104, 175
Ebb, Fred 156
Ebersole, Christine 364

Eccles, Aimée 354
Eccleston, Christopher 82
Echevarría, Emilio 52
Ed Wood 247
Eddie and the Cruisers 76
Edgar, David 216
Edgerton, Joel 390
Edwards, Anthony 289
Efron, Marshall 83
Ehle, Jennifer 157, 265, 390
Eichinger, Bernd 118
Eight Men Out 298
El Cid 208
Eleni 259
Eleniak, Erika 327
The Elephant Man 107
Elisofon, Eliot 25
Elfont, Harry 57
Elizabeth 176
Elizabeth: The Golden Age 37
Elliott, Chris 32
Elliott, Peter 187
Ellis, Chris 110, 299
Ellis, Nelsan 288
Ellis, Novalyne Price 176
Ellman, Richard 157
Elwes, Cary 216, 344
Emery, Gilbert 223
Emma 189
Emmanuel, Takis 7
Emmerich, Noah 50, 182, 211, 309, 373
Emmerich, Roland 199, 247
Emmerich, Toby 309
Emond, Linda 241
Empire of the Sun 239
Enders, Eric 297
Endfield, Cy 21
Enemy at the Gates 315

Engel, Joel 281
Engel, Samuel G. 319
The English Patient 308
*The Englishman Who Went Up a Hill
  and Came Down a Mountain* 188
The Enigma of Kaspar Hauser 377
Enright, Ray 248
Ephron, Delia 47
Ephron, Nora 42, 47, 241
Epstein, Julius 360
Epstein, Philip 360
Ermey, R. Lee 186
Erskine, Marilyn 237
Erwin, Bill 195
Escape from Alcatraz 178
Esposito, Jennifer 312
Essell, Eileen 387
Estevez, Emilio 86
E.T.: The Extraterrestrial 327
Eternal Sunshine of the Spotless Mind 41
Europa, Europa 126
Evans, Bruce A. 266
Evans, Estelle 324
Evans, Maurice 89
Eve, Alice 104
Everett, Rupert 121
Evers-Wiliams, Myrlie 178
Evita 224
Excalibur 123
The Executioner's Song 17
Exodus 219
The Express 288
Extremely Loud & Incredibly Close 273
Eyre, Peter 288

Fabian 171
Fair Game 211

The Falcon and the Snowman 16
Fallon, Jimmy 255
Fanning, Dakota 44
Fanning, Elle 196
Fantoni, Sergio 271
Far and Away 279
Far from the Madding Crowd 303
Farago, Ladislaus 221, 366
Farmiga, Vera 75
Farrell, Colin 261
Farrell, Nicholas 207
Farrow, John 218, 372
Farrow, Mia 323
Fassbender, Michael 167
Faulkner, James 348
Fawcett, Farrah 17
Faylen, Frank 384
The FBI Story 161
Federici, Blanche 223
Feldman, Corey 266
Feldman, Marty 132
Fellowes, Julian 3, 343
Felton, Earl 369
Felton, Verna 267
Ferber, Edna 120
Ferch, Heino 118
Ferrer, José 297, 385
Ferrier, Noel 292
Fest, Joachim 118
Fever Pitch (2005) 312
A Few Good Men 149
Field, Betty 267
Field, Sally 30, 172, 195, 283
Field of Dreams 134, 147
Fielding, Helen 348, 349
Fields, Maurie 322
Fiennes, Joseph 28, 270, 315

Fiennes, Ralph 73, 74, 308, 309
50 First Dates 307
55 Days at Peking 245
The Fighter 71
The Fighting Sullivans 10
Finch, Peter 303
Fincher, David 289, 338
Finding Neverland 387
Finkel, Abem 302
Finlay, Frank 231
Finney, Albert 162
Firth, Colin 23, 265, 266, 270, 308, 348
Firth, Peter 101, 281
Fish, Robert L. 377
Fishburne, Laurence 48
Fisher, Frances 33, 111
Fisher, Gregor 23, 99
Fisher, Michael 94
Fitzgerald, F. Scott 338
Fitzgerald, Geraldine 191
Fitz-Gerald, Lewis 54
Fitzgerald, Susan 250
FitzGerald, Tara 188
Fitzmaurice, George 223
Fitzpatrick, Neil 322
(500) Days of Summer 142
Flagg, Fannie 18, 19
Flags of Our Fathers 48
Fleder, Gary 288
Fleet, James 131
Fleischer, Richard 366, 369
Fleming, Victor 113
Flemyng, Jason 338
Fletcher, Louise 296, 297
Flight 309
Flight of the Intruder 273
Flight of the Phoenix (1965) 79
Flight 90: Disaster on the Potomac 13

Flitter, Josh 281
Flushed Away 206
The Flying Scotsman 214
Flynn, Erroll 91, 269
Foer, Jonathan 273
Fonda, Henry 102, 138, 171, 178, 319, 376
Foote, Horton 324
Forbes, Bryan 105
Ford, Colin 196
Ford, Glenn 120, 178, 197
Ford, Harrison 8, 20, 77, 78, 96, 286
Ford, John 70, 102, 138, 319, 386
Foreman, Carl 144, 225
Forlani, Claire 209
Forman, Miloš 190, 296, 305, 364
Forrest Gump 171
Forrester, Larry 366
Forster, E. M. 97
Forster, Marc 387
Forsyth, Frederick 8, 257
Forsyth, Rosemary 183
Forsythe, William 33
44 Minutes: The North Hollywood Shootout 56
42nd Street 260
Fosse, Bob 156
Foster, Jodie 65, 337
The Four Feathers 264
Four Weddings and a Funeral 131
Fowler, William M., Jr. 234
Fox, Edward 14, 29, 257, 280
Fox, Emilia 231
Fox, James 20,
Fox, Michael J. 331, 332, 339, 340, 355
Foxx, Jamie 53, 100, 101
Foy, Eddie, Jr. 328
Frain, James 3, 55, 195

Fraley, Oscar 277
Francher, Hampton 8
Francis, Alec B. 223
Franco, James 28, 128
Frank, Anne 234
Frank, Melvin 236
Frankel, David 361
Frankenheimer, John 146
Franks, Kenny A. 121
Franz, Arthur 51
Franzero, Carlo Maria 242
Franzoni, David 78
Fraser, Laura 214
Fraser, Richard 336
Frawley, William 269
Frazier, Charles 228
Frears, Stephen 262
Freeman, Al, Jr. 49
Freeman, Morgan 27, 71, 72, 141, 175
French, Dawn 44
French, Susan 195
Frequency 309
Frewer, Matt 350
Fricker, Brenda 170
Frida 280
Friday Night Lights 265
Fried Green Tomatoes 18
Froeschel, George 159
From Here to Eternity 365
From Russia with Love 176
Frost, Mark 209, 281
Frost/Nixon 91
Fry, Stephen 157, 158, 330
Frye, Sean 327
The Fugitive 77
Fukasaku, Kinji 366
Fukunaga, Cary 167
Fulford, Christopher 137

Full Metal Jacket 30
Fuller, Samuel 205
Furlong, Edward 260
Furst, Stephen 342
Furth, George 166
Futterman, Dan 40

Gable, Clark 113, 114
Gabriel, Mike 379
Gaiman, Neil 44
Gage, Nicholas 259
Gaghan Stephen 51
Gale, Bob 38, 331, 339, 340
Gallagher, Robert C. 288
Gallico, Paul 391
Gallipoli 237
Gallo, Mario 74
Gambon, Michael 162, 265, 368
The Game 315
Gandhi 29
Gandolfini, James 390
Gangs of New York 210
Ganty, Isabelle 290
Ganz, Bruno 118
Ganz, Lowell 195
Gaon, Yehoram 193
Garai, Romola 162, 165
Garber, Victor 27, 42
Garbo, Greta 223
García, Andy 277
Gardner, Ava 146, 245
Garland, Judy 63, 64, 65
Garner, James 87
Garner, Joe 50
Garr, Teri 132, 155
Garrick, Barbara 42
Garrow, David J. 26
Garson, Greer 95, 96, 117, 159

Gartner, James 81
Gates, Larry 237, 275
Gaul, Patricia 301
Gavin, John 371
Gazzara, Ben 66, 312
Gazzo, Michael V. 356, 357
Gearhart, Devon 209
Geer, Ellen 20
Gélin, Daniel 169
Genn, Leo 215, 216, 245
Gentleman Jim 269
Geoffrey, Paul 123
George, Chief Dan 354
Gere, Richard 82, 156, 157
Gerolmo, Chris 186
Gersten, Berta 15
Getchell, Robert 20
Gettysburg 199
Ghost 287
Ghosts of Mississippi 34
Gia 346
Giamatti, Paul 84, 85, 305, 347, 373
Gibson, Mel 14, 235, 238, 247, 292, 380,
    383
Gibson, William 62
Gidding, Nelson 35
Gideon, Raynold 266
Gielgud, John 29, 107, 218, 389, 390
Gilbert, Brian 157
Gilliam, Terry 346
Gilman, Jared 304
Gilmore, Lowell 336
Gilois, Bettina 81
Gilpin, Jack 17
Gilroy, Tony 253
Gish, Annabeth 139
Gittler, Robert 357
Giuffrè, Aldo 104

Gladiator 78
Glazer, Benjamin 223
Gleason, Paul 86
Gleeson, Brendan 210, 228, 235
Gleizer, Michele 127
The Glen Miller Story 375
Glenn, Scott 93, 135
Glenville, Peter 389
Globus, Ken 193
Glory 216
Glory Road 81
Glover, Bruce 291
Glover, Crispin 331
Glover, Danny 283, 383
Godard, Alain 315
The Godfather 255
The Godfather, Part II 356
Gods and Generals 141
Gods and Monsters 161
Golan, Menahem 193
Goldberg, Eric 379
Goldberg, Whoopi 34
Goldblum, Jeff 199, 301
Goldenberg, Michael 337
Goldfinger 288
Goldie, Gilbert 187
Goldman, Bo 296
Goldman, Gary 184
Goldman, William 166, 276, 280
Goldrosen, John 357
Goldsman, Akiva 84, 370
Golino, Valeria 108
Gondry, Michael 41
Gone with the Wind 72, 113
Gonzalez, Rick 280
The Good, the Bad and the Ugly 104
Good Morning Vietnam 285
Goodall, Caroline 73, 183

Goodbye, Mr. Chips 95
Goode, Matthew 57
Goodfellas 329
Gooding, Cuba, Jr. 150, 287
Goodman, David Zelag 17
Goodman, Henry 249
Goodman, John 20, 27, 145, 273, 332
Goodnight, and Good Luck 68
Goodrich, Frances 234, 384
Goodrich, Thomas 252
Goodwin, Doris Kearns 30
Goodwin, Ginnifer 12
Gordan, Bernard 245, 376
Gordon, C. Henry 223
Gordon, Hannah 107
Gordon, Michael B. 272
Gordon, Stuart 350
Gordon-Levitt, Joseph 30, 142, 143
Goring, Marius 133
Gorillas in the Mist 387
Gorman, Robert F. 334
Gorshin, Frank 346
Gosford Park 343
Gotti 74
Gould, Elliott 280
Gould, Harold 268
Gould, Jonathan 38
Gran Torino 38
Grant, Beth 332
Grant, Cary 122, 352
Grant, Hugh 23, 131, 132, 188, 282, 348
Grant, James Edward 50
Grant, Lee 275, 276
Grant, Rodney A. 126
Grant, Susannah 379
Graves, Peter 378
Graves, Rupert 121, 330
Gray, Billy 278

Gray, Donald 264
Gray, Spalding 115, 240
Graysmith, Robert 289
Great Balls of Fire! 374
The Great Escape 87
Great Expectations 128
The Great Gatsby (2013) 360
The Great Locomotive Chase 109
The Great Raid 28
The Greatest Game Ever Played 281
The Greatest Story Ever Told 385
Greatorex, William 244
Green, Adolph 85
Green, David 238
Green, Nigel 21, 25
Green, Seth 323
The Green Mile 206
Greene, Graham 126
Greengrass, Paul 90
Greenstreet, Sydney 360
Greenwood, Bruce 317
Gregg, Clark 142
Grenier, Adrian 361
Greswell, Edward 273
Griffith, Kenneth 188
Griffiths, Rachel 280
Griffiths, Trevor 333
Groff, Jonathan 249
Groom, Winston 172
Groundhog Day 32
Gruffudd, Ioan 162
Gryff, Stefan 259
Guadalcanal Diary 224
Gubler, Matthew Gray 142
Guerra, Jackie 54
Guffey, Cary 155
Guggenheim, Eric 50
Guido, Paul 302

Guillermin, John 66
Guinee, Tim 321
Guinn, Jeff 222
Guinness, Alec 6, 97, 128, 144, 145, 297
Guiry, Tom 252
Gung Ho! 248
Gunner, Robert 89
Gunton, Bob 27, 71
Guthrie, A. B., Jr. 200
Guy, J. A. 390
Guzmán, Luis 55
Gwynne, Fred 4
Gyllenhaal, Jake 289, 299
Gyllenhaal, Maggie 261

Haber, Eitan 193
Hackett, Albert 234, 384
Hackford, Taylor 100
Hackman, Gene 186, 187, 197, 222, 280, 391
Hagen, Jean 85, 86
Hagen, Uta 17
Hague, William 162
Haig, Sid 83
Hale, Alan, Sr. 91, 269
Hale, John 24
Hale, Scott 22
Haley, Alex 49
Haley, Brian 39
Hall, Albert 49
Hall, Anthony Michael 86, 350
Hall, Hanna R. 172
Hambleton, Georgina Louise 170
Hamburger Hill 152
Hamer, Robert 245
Hamill, Mark 205
Hamilton, Gay 180
Hamilton, Guy 244

Hamilton, Josh 317
Hamilton, Linda 143, 260
Hamilton, Murray 153, 161
Hamilton, Suzanna 99
Hamm, Sam 349
Hammerstein, Oscar, II 295
Hampton, Christopher 165
Han, Maggie 230
Hancock, John Lee 51, 124, 280
Hanks, Tom 42, 43, 47, 90, 91, 110, 172, 174, 206, 273
Hanly, Peter 235
Hanna 46
Hanna, Tim 89
Hannah, Daryl 8, 136
Hannah, John 131
Hannibal (2006) 233
Hanson, Bobby 50
Harden, Marcia Gay 255
Hardesty, Van 153
Harding, Lyn 95
Hardwicke, Cedric 192
Hardwicke, Edward 3
Hardy, Jonathan 54
Hardy, Robert 282
Hardy, Rod 379
Hardy, Thomas 101, 102, 303
Harfouch, Corinna 118
Hargreaves, John 274
Harker, Susannah 182
Harlow 173
Harris, Ed 20, 110, 111, 135,139, 283, 287, 315, 370,373, 374
Harris, Richard 55, 78
Harrison, Claudia 344
Harrison, Jim 109
Harrison, Linda 89
Harrison, Rex 243

Hart, Ian 188
Hart, James V. 337
Hart, Moss 63
Harwood, Ronald 231
Haslip, Joan 311
Hastings, Max 280
Hatch, Thom 167, 355
Hatcher, Teri 44
Hatfield, Hurd 336
Hathaway, Anne 345, 346, 361
Hathaway, Henry 102, 300
Hatten, Yankton 283
Hauben, Lawrence 296
Hauer, Rutger 8
Havelock-Allan, Anthony 128
Havers, Nigel 97, 207, 239
Havilland, Olivia de 91
Hawaii 264
Hawke, Ethan 317
Hawkins, Jack 21, 144, 297
Hawkins, Sally 167
Hawks, Howard 302
Haworth, Jill 220
Hawthorne, Nigel 121, 122
Hayakawa, Sessue 45, 144, 145
Haydn, Richard 132
Hayes, John Michael 168
Haysbert, Dennis 46
Hayward, Kara 304
Hazanavicius, Michel 332
Head, Jae 125
Headey, Lena 272
Healy, Raymond J. 279
Heard, John 311, 321, 381
Hearn, Ann 65
Hearts in Atlantis 125
Heath, Mark 193
Heaven Can Wait 318

Heavenly Creatures 187
Heavens Fall 90
Hecht, Ben 122, 242
Heflin, Van 200
Heggen, Thomas 138, 139
Helm, Levon 9, 135
Helmore, Tom 5
The Help 177
Henderson, Shirley 263
Hendrickson, Lance 253
Hengge, Paul 127
Henreid, Paul 95, 360
Henriksen, Lance 143
Henry, Buck 227
Henry of Navarre 223
Henry V 317
Henson, Darrin 288
Henson, Taraji P. 338, 339
Hepburn, Katherine 37
Her, Ahney 38
Herald, Heinz 36
Herczeg, Geza 36
Herman, Paul 261
Hernandez, Jay 280
Herrington, Rowdy 209
Herrmann, Edward 333, 344
Herron, William Blake 253
Hershey, Barbara 135
Heslov, Grant 68, 313
Heston, Charlton 25, 89, 178, 245, 385
Heusinger, Patrick 321
Heywood, Pat 212
Hibbert, Christopher 122, 216
Hickam, Homer 299
High Noon 225, 315
Highmore, Freddie 31, 387
Hilary and Jackie 314
Hill, Amy 307

Hill, Arthur 35
Hill, Bernard 111
Hill, George Roy 166, 268
Hill, Jonah 258, 259
Hill, Walter 232
Hillenbrand, Laura 60, 61
Hiller, Arthur 67
Hiller, Wendy 107, 202, 203
Hillerman, John 291
Hilton, James 69, 95, 159
The Hindenberg 137
Hinds, Ciarán 263
Hingle, Pat 349
Hirsch, Judd 199, 249, 370
Hirschbiegel, Oliver 118
Hitchcock, Alfred 122, 168, 352, 371
The Hoax 7
Hobbs, Peter 35
Hoblit, Gregory 309
Hobson, Valerie 128
Hodgman, John 44
Hodiak, John 382
Hoffman, Dustin 108, 109, 134, 276, 354, 387
Hoffman, Michael 347
Hoffman, Philip Seymour 228, 258
Hoffmann, Gaby 42, 147
Hofschneider, Marco 127, 137
Hofschneider, Rene 127
Holbrook, Hal 136, 178, 276
Holden, Gloria 36
Holden, William 144, 267, 378
Holiday, Johnny 12
Holland, Agnieszka 127
Hollingsworth, Cliff 84
Hollywoodland 182
Holm, Ian 121, 203, 207, 208
Holt, Jack 70

Holt, Tim 319
Home Alone 380
Honey, I Shrunk the Kids 350
Hooper, Tom 265, 345
Hope and Glory 266
Hopkins, Anthony 3, 14, 88, 106, 107, 109, 139, 140, 280
Hopkins, Bo 66
Hopper, Dennis 300
Hordern, Michael 24, 25, 180
Horn, Thomas 273
Horne, Geoffrey 144
Horton, Edward Everett 69
Hoskins, Bob 145, 315
Houdini 188
Hough, Richard 14
Hounsou, Djimon 78
How the West Was Won 102
Howard, Arliss 320
Howard, Bryce Dallas 177
Howard, Joe 88
Howard, Leslie 113
Howard, Ron 22, 84, 110, 370
Howard, Sidney 113
Howard, Trevor 29, 244, 271
Howe, Arian 323
Howe, Brian 39
Howell, C. Thomas 200, 327
Huband, David 84
Hubbard, Lucien 248
Huber, Gusti 234
Hudson, Ernie 313
Hudson, Hugh 207
Huggins, Roy 77
Hughes, Declan 214
Hughes, John 86, 350, 380
Hughes, Wendy 287
Hugo, Victor 345

Hulce, Tom 342, 364, 365
Humphreys, Michael Conner 172
The Hunchback of Notre Dame 6
Hunt, Bonnie 108, 206
Hunt, Linda 259, 292, 380
Hunt, Martita 128, 389
The Hunt for Red October 350
Hunter, Bill 238
Hunter, Jeffrey 386
Hunter, Kim 89, 133
Hurd, Gale Ann 143
Hurt, John 99, 107, 202, 232, 330, 337
Hurt, William 301
Hussey, Olivia 212, 213
Huston, John 246, 291, 292, 302
Huston, Walter 328, 329
Hutchison, Doug 206
Hytner, Nicholas 121

I Am Legend 272
I Shot Andy Warhol 168
I Wanna Hold Your Hand 37
Iliff, W. Peter 20
Immortal Beloved 137
Imperioli, Michael 312
Imrie, Celia 348
In Cold Blood 4
In Love and War 204
In the Heat of the Night 275
In the Name of the Father 300
In Which We Serve 157
Incrocci, Agenorre 104
Independence Day 198
Infamous 344
Inge, William 267
Inherit the Wind 219
Inn of the Sixth Happiness 340
Inside Daisy Clover 255

The Insider 367
Internal Affairs 75
Into the Wild (2007) 361
Introducing Dorothy Dandridge 93
Invictus 175
Ireland, Dan 176
Ireland, John 245
The Iron Lady 348
Irons, Jeremy 17
Ironside, Michael 184
Irvin, John 152
Irwin, Bill 298
Is Paris Burning? 238
Isaacs, Jason 247
It's a Wonderful Life 384
Ivanir, Mark 73
Ivey, Judith 226
Izzard, Eddie 344

J. Edgar 144
Jack the Ripper 262
Jackman, Hugh 345, 346
Jackson, Brandon T. 173
Jackson, Peter 11, 59, 79, 187
Jackson, Samuel L. 20
Jacobi, Derek 8, 78, 257
Jacobi, Lou 234
Jacobsson, Ulla 21
Jacquelina, Tiara 240
Jaffe, Sam 69, 278
James, Clifton 201
Jane Eyre 167
Janis, Conrad 357
Jarrott, Charles 24
Jarvis, Martin 239
Jaws 198
Jeayes, Allan 264
Jeffrey, Peter 8

Jenney, Lucinda 317
Jennings, Alex 262
Jenson, Roy 291
Jenson, Sasha 160
Jergens, Diane 161
Jerome, Edwin 251
Jeunet, Jean-Pierre 290
Jewel 252
Jewell, Isabell 69
Jewison, Norman 275
JFK 60
Jim Thorpe: All-American 320
Joffe, Roland 115
Johansson, Scarlett 196
John Paul Jones 286
Johnny Tremaine 377
Johnson, Ben 200, 341, 342
Johnson, Corey 90
Johnson, George Clayton 17
Johnson, Marek 33
Johnson, Nunnally 45, 251
Johnson, Otto T. 351
Johnson, Richard 25
Johnson, Van 116, 382
Johnson, Mel, Jr. 184
Johnstad, Kurt 272
Johnston, Joe 299, 350
The Jokers 189
Jolie, Angelina 40, 41
Joncour, Serge 213
Jones, Angus T. 280
Jones, Carolyn 102
Jones, Cherry 82
Jones, Eddie 61
Jones, Evan 81, 246
Jones, Freddie 107
Jones, Gemma 282, 348
Jones, James 365

Jones, James Earl 147
Jones, Jeffrey 364, 365
Jones, Jennifer 39, 40
Jones, Julian Lewis 175
Jones, Laura 250
Jones, Maggie Elizabeth 196
Jones, Robert 274
Jones, Tommy Lee 9, 10, 30, 67, 77, 78
Jordan, Richard 17
Jordan, William 357
Jory, Victor 62
Joseph, Edmund 328
Josephson, Matthew 36
Josephy, Alvin M. 105
Joslyn, Allyn 319
Journey to the Center of the Earth 162
Jovovich, Milla 134
Judd, Ashley 195
Judgment at Nuremburg 63
Judgment in Berlin 261
Juliá, Raúl 96
Julie and Julia 241
Julius Caesar (1953) 75
Junge, Traudl 118
Jurado, Katy 225, 226
Jürgens, Curt 171, 377

Kahn, Madeline 132, 133, 227, 228
Kanakaredes, Melinda 173
Kane, Carol 359
Kapelos John 86, 350
Kaplan, Deborah 57
Kaplan, Jonathan 65
Karaszewski, Larry 305
Karol: A Man Who Became Pope 57
Karyo, Tchéky 134
Kasdan, Lawrence 301
Kassovitz, Matthieu 290

Katsulas, Andreas 77
Kaufman, Charlie 41
Kaufman, Phillip 135
Kavner, Julie 311, 323
Kazan, Nicholas 17, 33
Kazantzakis, Nikos 7
Keating, Larry 237
Keaton, Diane 256, 323, 333, 334, 356,
    359, 360
Keaton, Michael 349
Kedrova, Lila 7
Keegan, John 103
Keener, Catherine 90
Keighley,William 91
Keir, Andrew 243
Keith, Agnes Newton 45
Keller, Helen 62
Kelly, David 31
Kelly, Gene 85
Kelly, Grace 225
Kelly, Michael 334
Kelly, Moira 106
Kelly, Paula 35
Keneally, Thomas 73
Kennaway, James 244
Kennedy, George 201, 202
Kennedy, Graham 115
Kennedy, Patrick 347
Kenney, Douglas 342
Kent, Diana 187
Kerr, Bill 292
Kerr, Deborah 215, 295, 296, 365, 366
Kerr, Schin A. S. 81
Kerrigan, J. M. 369
Kesey, Ken 296
Keshawarz, Donnie 334
Kestelman, Sara 216
Keuning, Mark 45

Kgoroge, Tony 175
Khan, Alyy 40
Khan, Irrfan 40
Khartoum 25
Khedekar, Ayush Mahesh 314
Kher, Anupam 388
Kidder, Margot 197
Kidman, Nicole 228
Kidnapped 193
Kikushima, Ryuzo 366
Kilburn, Terry 95
The Killing Fields 115
King, Henry 39, 191
King, Regina 100
King, Stephen 71, 72, 206, 266
The King and I 295
King Solomon's Mines (1950) 149
The King's Speech 265
The Kingdom of Heaven 283
Kingsley, Ben 29, 30, 73
Kingston, Alex 321
Kinnear, Greg 47
Kinsella, W. P. 147
Kinski, Klaus 193
Kinski, Nastassja 101, 102
Kirby, Bruno 285
Kit Carson 190
Kitchen, Michael 13
The Kite Runner 387
Klimt 35
Kline, Kevin 274, 287, 301
Kluge, P. F. 252
Kluger, Jeffrey 110, 111
Knebel, Fletcher 146
Knee, Allan 387
Knight, Steven 162
Knightley, Keira 23, 165, 353, 354
Knowles, Patric 45, 91

Knox, Alexander 25, 191, 192
Knute Rockne: All-American 374
Ko, U Aung 240
Koch, C. J. 292
Koch, Howard 302, 360
Köhler, Juliane 118
Konstantin, Leopoldine 122
Korda, Zoltan 264
Koteas, Elias 2, 281
Krabbé, Jeroen 77, 137
Kramer, Stanley 64
Kramer vs. Kramer 22
Krause, Peter 373
Kretschmann, Thomas 118, 231
Kretzmer, Herbert 345
Krige, Alice 207
Krüger, Hardy 180
Kubrick, Stanley 180
Kue, Choua 39
Kundun 94
Kushner, Tony 30
Kyriakou, Anna 7

La Bamba 32
LaBeouf, Shia 281
Łabonarska, Halina 127
Lacey, Ingrid 204
Ladd, Alan 200
Ladd, Diane 88, 291
The Lady 217
Lady Jane 216
Laffan, Pat 57
Laffan, Patricia 215
Lake, Stuart 319
The Lake House 207
Lamb, Larry 238
Lambert, Paul F. 121
LaMotta Jake 74

Lancaster, Burt 64, 146, 147, 365, 366
Landau, Martin 243, 352, 385
Landis, Jessie Royce 352
Landis, John 342
Landon, Joseph 271
Landon, Margaret 295, 296
Lane, Diane 93, 232
Lang, Stephen 151
Lang, Walter 295
Lange, Jessica 20, 21
Langella, Frank 68
Langton, Paul 71
Lansbury, Angela 336
LaPaglia, Anthony 312
Lapotaire, Jane 216
Lara, Alexandra Maria 118
Larkin, James 318
Larson, Brie 119
Lasker, Alex 240
The Last Days of Patton 369
The Last Emperor 229
The Last King of Scotland 24
The Last of the Mohicans 233
The Last Picture Show 341
The Last Station 347
The Late Shift 154
Latifah, Queen 156, 157
Launer, Dale 4
Laurant, Guillaume 290
Laure, Carole 246
Lauter, Ed 332
Lavie, Arik 193
Law, Jude 157, 228, 229, 315
Lawford, Christopher 88
Lawford, Peter 219, 336
Lawler, Jerry 305
Lawrence, Jennifer 388, 389
Lawrence, Stephanie 238

Lawrence, Vincent 269
Lawrence of Arabia 297
Lawson, Leigh 101
Lawson, Ted 116
Lay, Beirne, Jr. 236
LaZebnik, Phillip 379
Le May, Alan 386
Leachman, Cloris 132, 133, 166, 341, 342
Lean, David 6, 97, 128, 144, 297
Lean on Me 103
Leap Year 56
Leavitt, Charles 288
LeBeau, Madeline 269
LeBrock, Kelly 350
Leder, Mimi 141
Lederer, Charles 153
Ledger, Heath 247
Lee, Ang 249, 252, 282
Lee, Christopher 11, 31, 59
Lee, Harper 324
Lee, Mark 238
Lee, Spike 49, 312
LeFrançois, W. S. 248
Legends of the Fall 109
Legge, Michael 250
Leguizamo, John 312
Lehman, Ernest 295, 352
Leigh, Janet 371, 372
Leigh, Vivien 113, 114
Lembeck, Harvey 378
Lemmon, Jack 43, 44, 138
Lennix, Harry J. 100
Lenny 65
Leone, Sergio 104
Leoni, Téa 141
Lerman, Logan 173
Lerner, Michael 298
LeRoy, Mervyn 116, 117, 138, 161, 215

Les Misérables 345
Leslie, Joan 302, 328
Lethal Weapon 382
Letters from Iwo Jima 89
Letts, Billie 195
Levene, Sam 248
Levien, Sonya 215
Levin, Henry 163
Levinson, Barry 108, 183, 285
Levy, Eugene 249
Lewin, Albert 336
Lewis, Michael 258
Leyton, John 271
The Life and Times of Judge Roy Bean
    108
Life as We Know It 220
The Life of Emile Zola 36
Liman, Doug 211, 253
Lincoln 30
The Linda McCartney Story 72
Lindberg, Chad 299
Lindbergh, Charles 153
Link, Arthur S. 192
Linklater, Richard 160
Linney, Laura 46, 313, 373
Liotta, Ray 147, 329
Lipman, Maureen 231
Lippen, Renee 323
List, Peyton 281
Litel, John 36
Lithgow, John 57, 149, 276, 288
Little Big Man 354
Liu, Lucy 156
Livesey, Roger 133
Livingston, Ron 320
Liz and Dick 235
Lloyd, Christopher 296, 298, 331, 339,
    340

Lloyd, David 330
Lloyd, Doris 5
Lockwood, Lewis 138
Lofton, Christopher 379
Logan, John 78, 203
Logan, Joshua 138, 267
Logan, Michael 43
Logan's Run 17
Loggia, Robert 199
Lombard, Karina 109
London, Jack 377
London, Jason 160
Lone, John 229, 230
Lonely Hearts 68
Lonergan, Kenneth 210
Long, Jodi 33
The Longest Day 170
Lonkar, Tanvi Ganesh 314
Lonsdale, Michael 257
Loo, Richard 69
Looker 291
Lopez, Jennifer 54
Lord, Walter 179
*The Lord of the Rings: The Fellowship of
    the Ring* 11
*The Lord of the Rings: The Return of the
    King* 79
The Lord of the Rings: The Two Towers
    59
The Lords of Discipline 101
Lorre, Peter 360, 369
The Lost Colony 249
Lost Horizon 69
The Lost Weekend 270
Loucky, Jaime 208
Louise, Anita 310
Love, Courtney 305
Love, Darlene 383

Love Actually 23
Love Affair 37
Love Story 67
Lovell, Jim 110, 111
The Lovely Bones 366
Low, Chuck 329
Löwitsch, Klaus 8
Luber, Steven 320
Lubitsch, Ernst 318
Lucas, George 83
Lucas, Josh 81
Ludlum, Robert 253
Luedtke, Kurt 14
Lukas, Paul 369
Luke, Derek 81
Lumet, Sidney 252
Lumley, Joanna 344
Lunghi, Cherie 124
LuPone, Patti 312
Lust for Life 317
Lutz, Adelle 240
Lydon, Michael 101
Lynch, David 107
Lynch, Jane 241
Lynch, John Carroll 289
Lynley, Carol 391
Lynn, Jonathan 4
Lynn, Loretta 9
Lynskey, Melanie 187

MacArthur 271
MacArthur, James 376
MacArthur, Hayes 104
Macchio, Ralph 4
MacDonald, Charles B. 377
MacDonald, Ian 225
MacDonald, Kelly 343
MacDougall, Ranald 242

MacDowell, Andie 32, 131, 132
Macfadyen, Angus 196, 235
MacFadyen, Matthew 353
Machine-Gun Kelly 289
Mackie, Anthony 334
Mackinnon, Douglas 214
MacLaine, Shirley 218
MacLane, Barton 375
MacLeod, Gavin 179
MacNaughton, Robert 327
Macready, George 366
Macy, William H. 60, 61, 286
Madame Curie 117
Madden, John 270
Madigan, Amy 147, 283
The Madness of King George 121
Madonna 224
Madsen, Virginia 34
Maffia, Roma 183
Magee, David 263, 387
Magee, Patrick 180
Maguire, Sharon 348
Maguire, Toby 60, 252
Mahin, John Lee 215
Main, Marjorie 319
Mak, Alan 75
Mako 179, 180
Malcolm X 49
Malcolm X, 49
Malden, Karl 221
Malkovich, John 93, 115, 134, 239, 259,
   283, 317
Malick, Terrence 2, 3
Malinger, Ross 42
Malone, Jena 337
Mamet, David 277
Mammone, Robert 28
A Man for All Seasons 202

The Man in the Iron Mask (1998) 268
Man of a Thousand Faces 259
Man on the Moon 305
The Man Who Knew Too Much 168
The Man Who Never Was 117
Mandel, Babaloo 195
Mangold, James 12
Manhattan Melodrama 181
Mankiewicz, Herman J. 363
Mankiewicz, Joseph L. 242
Mankowitz, Wolf 377
Mann, Abby 64
Mann, Anthony 120, 375
Mann, Delbert 185
Mann, Michael 53, 233, 368
Manning, Irene 328
Mansfield Park (1999) 382
Mantell, Joe 185, 186
Mara, Adele 51
Mara, Kate 128
Marable, Manney 178
Marceau, Sophie 235
March, Fredric 146, 147
Marcus, Stephen 281
Marie, Constance 54
Marie Antoinette 310
Margo 69
Margolin, Janet 359
Markowitz, Mitch 285
Markstein, George 8
Marley, John 67
Marley and Me 390
Marlowe, Andrew W. 286
Marlowe, Hugh 278
Mars, Kenneth 132, 166, 227
Marshall, E. G. 66, 366
Marshall, Frank 313, 317
Marshall, George 102

Marshall, Penny 311
Marshall, Rob 156
Marshall, Trudy 10
Martel, K. C. 327
Martin, Demetri 249
Martin, Lock 278
Martin, Mardik 74
Martin, Rosemary 101
Martin, Strother 166, 201, 300
Marton, Andrew 171
Marty 185
Marvin, Lee 205
Mary, Queen of Scots 39
Mary Shelly's Frankenstein 244
Maschwitz, Eric 95
Mason, A. E. W. 264
Mason, James 63, 163, 352, 369
Massey, Daniel 246
Massey, Raymond 133
Master and Commander: The Far Side of the World 146
Master of the World 128
Masterson, Mary Stuart 18
Mastroianni, Chiara 94
Masuda, Toshio 366
Mata Hari 223
Matewan 152
Matheson, Richard 194
Matheson, Tim 342
Mathison, Melissa Erika 327
The Matrix 48
A Matter of Life and Death 133
Mattes, Eva 315
Matthes, Ulrich 118
Matthews, Liesel 286
Mature, Victor 319
Maude, Joan 133
Maurier, Claire 290

Maxwell, Ronald F. 199
May, Ernest R. 317
May, Jodhi 233
Mayance, Mélusine 213
Mayes, Wendell 153, 271, 391
Mazer, Adam 46
Mazzello, Joseph 3
McAdams, Rachel 320
McAnally, Ray 170
McAuley, Alphonso 81
McAvoy, James 165, 166, 347
McBride, Danny R. 158
McCabe, John 329
McCall, Mary C., Jr. 10
McCallum, David 385
McCambridge, Mercedes 120
McCann, Sean 50
McClure, Marc 38
McComas, Francis 279
McConaughey, Matthew 160, 337
McCourt, Frank 250
McCoy, Horace 269
McCrory, Helen 262
McDaniel, Hattie 113, 114
McDermott, Dylan 152
McDonald, Charles B. 382
McDonald, Grace 248
McDonnell, Mary 126, 199
McDormand, Frances 186, 187, 240, 263, 304
McDowell, Malcolm 209, 332
McDowell, Roddy 89, 243, 391
McElhone, Natascha 373
McEnery, John 212
McEwan, Ian 165
McGill, Bruce 4, 84, 211, 342
McGillis, Kelly 65
McGinley, John C. 136

McGivern, Cecil 128
McGoohan, Patrick 235
McGovern, Elizabeth 190, 191
McGrath, Douglas 189
McGraw, Ali 67
McGraw, Tim 124
McGregor, Ewan 82, 189
McGuire, Dorothy 385
McIntire, John 371
McKellen, Ian 11, 12, 59, 79
McKenna, Aline Brosh 196, 361
McKenna, Siobhan 6
McKern, Leo 202
McKidd, Kevin 173
McKinnon, Ray 125
McLean, Jane 320
McLynn, Frank 79
McLynn, Pauline 250
McMullan, Tim 262
McMurtry, Larry 341
McNeice, Ian 188
McOmie, Maggie 83
McQuarrie, Christopher 217
McQueen, Butterfly 113
McQueen, Steve 87, 179, 180
McShane, Ian 44
McTavish, Graham 93
McTeigue, James 330
Meaney, Colm 188
Means, Russell 233, 380
Mee, Benjamin 196
Meet Me in St. Louis 129
Megna, John 324
Meisel, Kurt 8
Meloni, Christopher 346
Melson, John 376
Memphis Belle 148
Men in Black 138

Men of Honor 88
Mendez, Tony 27
Meneses, Alex 54
Merchant, Tamzin 157
Meredith, Burgess 1, 2
Merkerson, S. Epatha 260, 287
Merlin, Serge 290
Mermaids 350
Merrick, Monte 148
Merrison, Clive 187, 246
Messemer, Hannes 87
The Messenger: The Story of Joan of Arc 134
Messina, Chris 241
Meyer, Emile 200
Meyers, Jonathan Rhys 252
Michael Collins 253
Michalka, Amanda 93
Midnight Express 301
Midnight in the Garden of Good and Evil 254
Midway 178
A Mighty Heart 40
The Mighty Macs 81
Miles, Bernard 129, 169
Miles, Vera 161, 371, 386
Milland, Ray 67
Miller, Bennett 258
Miller, Chris 342
Miller, George T. 379
Miller, Jonny Lee 214
Miller, Omar Benson 288
Miller, Penelope Ann 311, 332
Miller, Seton 91
Miller, T. J. 104
Miller, Winston 319
Mills, John 95,128
Mimieux, Yvette 5

Mincotti, Esther 185
Mineo, Sal 220
Minghella, Anthony 228, 308
Miracle 50
Miracle on 34th Street 383
The Miracle Worker 62
Miro, Doug 28
Mirren, Helen 121, 122, 123, 262, 343, 344, 347, 348
Miss Pettigrew Lives for the Day 263
Miss Potter 343
Missing 277
Mississippi Burning 186
Mister Roberts 138
Mitchell, Elizabeth 309
Mitchell, George 35
Mitchell, Julian 157
Mitchell, Margaret 113, 114
Mitchell, Millard 85
Mitchell, Radha 387
Mitchell, Thomas 10, 69, 113, 191, 384
Mitchell, Warren 377
Mitchell-Smith, Ilan 350
Mitchum, Robert 116, 171, 248
Mittal, Madhur 314
Mockingbird Don't Sing 331
Modine, Matthew 149
Mofokeng, Patrick 175
Moggach, Deborah 353
Mokae, Zakes 182
Molen, Gerald R. 108
Mollà, Jordi 52
Möller, Ralf 78
Mommie Dearest 66
Monahan, William 75
Monday Night Mayhem 284
Moneyball 258
Monger, Christopher 188

Moniz, Lucia 23
Monroe, Marilyn 43, 44
Monster 9
Monster House 325
Montagu, Ashley 107, 108
Montalban, Ricardo 382
Monte, Rom 249
Montgomery, Robert 70
Mooney, Paul 357
Moonrise Kingdom 304
Moore, Alan 330
Moore, Demi 150, 183
Moore, Dickie 302
Moore, Joel David 151
Moore, Julianne 77
Moore, Kenny 226
Morales, Esai 33
Moranis, Rick 350
Morell, André 144
Moreno, Rita 85, 295
Moretz, Chloë Grace 142
Morgan, Gary 17
Morgan, Harry 22, 120, 375
Morgan, Jeffrey Dean 249
Morgan, Peter 262
Moriarty, Cathy 74, 75
Morison, Patricia 39
Morley, Karen 223
Morley, Robert 310, 311
Morris, Jim 281
Morris, John 103
Morris, Phyllis 45
Morrison, Samuel Elliott 3
Morrow, Barry 108
Morse, David 206, 337, 346
Mortensen, Viggo 11, 59, 79
Morton, Joe 260
Moscow, Alvin 33

Moss, Carrie-Ann 48
Mostel, Josh 323
Motta, Bess 143
Moua, Doua 38
Moustakas, Sotiris 7
Mouton, Benjamin 176
The Music Lovers 333
Mowbray, Alan 295
Mr. Saturday Night 38
Mrs. Brown 124
Mrs. Fitzherbert 375
Mrs. Miniver 159
Mulhare, Edward 271
Mulkey, Chris 287
Muller, Melissa 118
Mulligan, Richard 354
Mulligan, Robert 324
Mulock, Al 105
Mundin, Herbert 91
Muni, Paul 36
Munich 105
Murch, Walter 83
Murder in the First (1995) 362
Murdock, Jack 108
Murphy, Aaron J. 88
Murphy, George 382
Murphy, Michael 292
Murray, Bill 32, 304
The Music Man 221
Must Love Dogs 352
My Big Fat Greek Wedding 136
My Cousin Vinny 4
My Darling Clementine 319
My Girl 201
My Left Foot: The Story of Christy Brown
     169
Myers, Michael Scott 176
Myles, Bruce 322

Nack, William 93
Nagel, James 204
Naha, Ed 350
Nail, Jimmy 224
Nair, Mira 82
Nalluri, Bharat 263
Napier, Alan 163
Nasar, Sylvia 370
Nash, Jay Robert 233
Nation, Jack 261
Nava, Gregory 54
Neal, Patricia 278
Neame, Ronald 8, 128, 391
Ned Kelly 194
Neeson, Liam 14, 23, 73, 74, 210
Negulesco, Jean 45
Neill, Sam 322
Nelligan, Kate 259
Nelson, Craig T., 34, 115
Nelson, Hailey Anne 12
Nelson, Judd 86
Nelson, Ruth 311
Ness, Elliott 277
Neustadter, Scott 142
Neuwirth, Bebe 312
Newell, Mike 131
Newman, David 197, 222, 227
Newman, Leslie 197
Newman, Paul 166, 201, 202, 219,
     268
Newman, Susan Kendall 38
Newton, John Haymes 317
Newton, Robert 218
Ney, Richard 159
Ngor, Haing S. 115
Niccol, Andrew 373
Nicole, Jasika 104
Nichols, Austin 81

Nicholson, Jack 75, 76, 150, 151, 291, 292, 296, 297, 333, 334, 349, 350
Nicholson, William 3, 78, 345
Nielsen, Connie 28, 78
Niffenegger, Audrey 320, 321
Nighy, Bill 23, 217
Nineteen Eighty-Four 99
Niven, David 133, 218, 245
Nixon 139
Noiret, Philippe 377
Nolan, William F. 17
Nolden, Michelle 320
Nolfi, George 334
Nolte, Nick 2
Noonan, Tommy 63
Norgate, Kate 92
Norman, Marc 270
Norris, Dean 226
North, Edmund H. 221, 278
North by Northwest 352
Northam, Jeremy 189, 209, 343
Northwest Passage 299
Norton, Edward 304
The Notebook 368
Notorious 122
Novak, Kim 267
Novarro, Ramon 223
Noyce, Phillip 20
Nugent, Frank S. 138, 386
Nunn, Trevor 216
Nype, Russell 67

O Brother, Where Art Thou? 211
Oakland, Simon 371
Oates, Warren 275
O'Bannon, Dan 184
Ober, Philip 352, 365
O'Brien, Edmond 146, 147

O'Brien, Margaret 117
O'Brien, Pat 43, 374
O'Brien, Tom 65
O'Brien-Moore, Erin 36
O'Connell, Arthur 120, 267, 268
O'Connell, Jerry 266
O'Connor, Carroll 243
O'Connor, Donald 85, 86
O'Connor, Gavin 50
O'Connor, Simon 187
O' Conor, Hugh 170
October Sky 299
The Odd Couple 152
The Odessa File 8
O'Donnell, Chris 18, 204
O'Donnell, Rosie 42
O'Donovan, Noel 57
Oguni, Hideo 366
O'Hara, Catherine 380, 381
O'Hare, Denis 40
Oher, Michael 125
Oldman, Gary 137, 286
Oliveri, Robert 350
Olivier, Laurence 14, 25, 244
Olmos, Edward James 8, 54
Olsen, Christopher 168
Olsen, Moroni 122
Olson, James 35, 190
Olson, James S. 52
Olson, Kaitlin 57
Olstead, Renee 368
O'Malley, Bryan Lee 119
The Ωmega Man 236
On Her Majesties' Secret Service 276
Ondaatje, Michael 308
One Day 213
One Flew over the Cuckoo's Nest 296
127 Hours 127

The One That Got Away 23
O'Neal, Ryan 67,180, 227
O'Neil, Barbara 113
O'Neill, Amy 350
The Onion Field 69
Operation Daybreak 160
Operation Petticoat 371
Operation Thunderbolt 192
Orloff, John 40
Ormond, Julia 109, 338
Orwell, George 99
Osborn, Paul 117
O'Shea, Milo 212
The Other Boleyn Girl (2008) 63
The Other End of the Line 304
O'Toole, Peter 229, 297, 298, 389, 390
Otto, Miranda 59, 79
Out of Africa 13
Overton, Rick 32
Overy, Richard 266
Owen, Chris 299
Owen, Clive 254
Owen, Reginald 159
Owens, Ciaran 250
The Ox-Bow Incident 323

Pablo Queiroz, Juan 224
Pace, Lee 263
Pacino, Al 253, 255, 256, 356, 357, 368
Page, Ellen 255
Page, Gale 374
A Painted House 298
Pakula, Alan J. 96, 276
Pál, George 5
Palance, Jack 200, 201, 349
Palcy, Euzhan 182
Pallavisini, Alfredo 71, 249
Pallenberg, Rospo 123

Pallette, Eugene 91, 319
Palmer, Betsy 138
Paltrow, Gwyneth 189, 270, 271
Panama, Norman 236
Panettiere, Hayden 154
Panjabi, Archie 40
Pantoliano, Joe 33, 48, 77
Papas, Irene 7, 24
Paquet-Brenner, Gilles 213
Parini, Jay 158, 347
Paris, Jerry 185
Parker, Alan 186, 224, 250
Parker, Anthony Ray 48
Parker, Dorothy 63
Parker, Eleanor 237
Parker, Mary-Louise 18
Paronnaud, Vincent 94
Parsons, Estelle 222
The Party 205
A Passage to India 97
Pasternak, Boris 6
Patel, Dev 314
Paterson, Bill 115
The Path to War 329
Paton, Angela 32
Patric, Jason 52
Patrick, Robert 12, 260
The Patriot 246
Patriot Games 19
Patterson, James 275
Patton 220
Patton, Will 40
Patty Hearst 33
Paul, Cinco 158
Paxton, Bill 110, 111, 281, 350
Payne, Tom 263
Pearce, Donn 201
Pearce, Guy 55, 265

Pearl, Mariane 40
Pearson, Richard 101
Peck, Gregory 102, 324, 325
Peckham, Anthony 175
Peirse, Sarah 187
The Pelican Brief 166
Peña, Elizabeth 33
Pendleton, Austin 227
Penn, Arthur 62, 222, 354
Penn, Robin Wright 172, 173, 258
Penn, Sean 2, 94, 211
Pennell, Larry 161
Peoples, David 8, 346
Peoples, Janet 346
Peploe, Mark 229
Peppard, George 102
Peral, Solomon 127
Percy Jackson and the Olympians: The Lightning Thief 173
Perelman, S. J. 218
The Perfect Storm 322
Perkins, Anthony 371
Perkins, Millie 234
Perl, Arnold 49
Perlman, Ron 315
Peros, Steven 344
Perrine, Valerie 197
Persepolis 94
Pesci, Joe 4, 74, 75, 329, 330, 380
Peter-Kaiser, Eric 50
Peters, Brock 324
Petersen, Wolfgang 286
Phar Lap 82
Phelan, Anna Hamilton 82, 204
Phillippe, Ryan 46, 343
Phillips, Lou Diamond 33
Phillips, Richard 90
Phillips, Siân 389

Phoenix, Joaquin 12, 13, 78, 79
Phoenix, River 266
The Pianist 231
Pickles, Carolyn 101
Pickles, Christina 109
Pickup, Ronald 259
Picnic 267
Picnic at Hanging Rock 43
The Picture of Dorian Gray 336
Pidgeon, Walter 117, 159
Pierrot, Frédéric 213
Pierson, Frank 96, 201, 252
Pigg, Landon 255
Piggott-Smith, Tim 246, 330
Pike, Rosamund 353
Pileggi, Nicholas 329, 330
Pine, Chris 306
Pinon, Dominique 290
Pinto, Freida 314
Pirates of Silicon Valley 114
Pirosh, Robert 381
Pistilli, Juigi 105
Pitt, Brad 109, 110, 258, 259, 338, 339, 346, 347
Place, Mary Kay 301
A Place in the Sun 267
Places in the Heart 283
Plame, Valerie 211
Planes, Trains and Automobiles 354
Planet of the Apes 89
Platoon 2
Platt, Ruth 231
Pleasence, Donald 83
Plummer, Christopher 49, 194, 244, 346, 347, 348, 368, 370
Pocahontas 379
Poe, James 218
Poésy, Clémence 128

Poitier, Sidney 275, 276
Polanski, Roman 101, 231, 291
Pollack, Sydney 14
Pollard, Michael J. 222
Polk, Oscar 113
Poots, Imogeen 167
Pop, Iggy 94
Pork Chop Hill 116
Porter, Linda 217
Portis, Charles 300
Portman, Natalie 195, 228, 330
The Poseidon Adventure 391
Posey, Parker 47
Potente, Franka 254
Potter, Monica 226
Pounder, C. C. H. 151
Powell, Clifton 100
Powell, Julie 241
Powell, Michael 133
Powell, William 138
Power, Tyrone 310
Prange, Gordon W. 366
Pratt, Chris 258
Prebble, John 21
Preiss, Wolfgang 271
Preminger, Otto 219, 378
The President's Lady 162
Presnell, Harve 176
Pressburger, Emeric 133
Preston, Robert 372
Presumed Innocent 96
Price, Connor 84
Price, Vincent 39, 192
Pride and Prejudice 353
Pride of the Yankees 292
Primary Colors 20
The Prince and the Pauper (1937) 49

Princess Caraboo 287
Prine, Andrew 62
Prochnow, Jürgen 182, 308
The Producers (1967) 269
Prud'homme, Alex 241
Pryce, Jonathan 154, 224
Pryor, Bill 209
Psycho 371
Pugh, Robert 188
Pullman, Bill 42, 199
Pu-yi, Henry 229, 230
Puzo, Mario 197, 255, 256, 356
Pyle, Denver 222
Pyle, Missi 31, 307

Quaid, Dennis 52, 135, 199, 280, 288, 309, 341
Quaid, Randy 227
Qualen, John 374
Quayle, Anthony 24, 297
The Queen 262
The Queen's Sister 167
Quick, Matthew 388
The Quiet Earth 202
Quinlan, Kathleen 46, 110, 111
Quinn, Aidan 109, 209
Quinn, Anthony 7, 297, 298
Quiz Show 179
Quo Vadis 215

Radford, Michael 99
Radio 287
Radio Days 323
Raging Bull 74
Ragtime 190
Rain Man 107
Raine, Norman Reilly 36, 91

Rains, Claude 91, 122, 123, 360, 361, 385
Rajskub, Mary Lynn 241
Rameau, Hans 117
Ramirez, Édgar 390
Ramis, Harold 32, 342
Ramsey, Bruce 317
Ransome, Prunella 303, 304
Raphael, Frederic 303
Raphaelson, Samson 318
Rapp, Anthony 370
Rash, Steve 357
Rasumny, Mikhail 372
Rathbone, Basil 91
Ratray, Devin 381
Rau, Santha Rama 97
Rauch, Siegfried 205, 221
Ray 100
Ray, Billy 46, 90
Ray, Nicholas 245
Rea, Stephen 288, 330
Reach for the Sky 375
Read, Piers Paul 317
Reagan, Ronald 374
Reaser, Elizabeth 321
Recount 372
The Red Baron 119
Redfield, William 296
Redford, Robert 13, 166, 268, 269, 276
Redgrave, Vanessa 141, 157, 165
Redmayne, Eddie 345
Reds 333
Reed, Donna 15, 70, 336, 365, 366, 384
Reed, Oliver 78, 377
Reeve, Christopher 194, 197
Reeves, George 113
Reeves, Keanu 48
Reid, Beryl 377

Reid, Kate 35
Reilly, John C. 156, 157, 203
Reiner, Rob 34, 149, 266, 355
Reinert, Al 110
Reisch, Walter 163
Reisz, Karel 20
Relph, Michael 377
Renaud, Chris 158
Rennie, Michael 278
Revere, Anne 39, 40
Reversal of Fortune 16
Reynolds, Clarke 193
Reynolds, Debbie 85, 102
Reynolds, Kevin 55
Rhames, Ving 33
Rhys, Ieuan 188
Rhys-Davie, John 11, 59, 79
Ribisi, Giovanni 151
Rice, John 181
Rice, Tim 224
Rich, Mike 93, 280, 287
Richardson, Joely 154, 247
Richardson, Miranda 239
Richardson, Natasha 33
Richardson, Ralph 25, 219, 264
Richwine, Maria 357
Ricklefs, M. C. 292
Rickman, Alan 23, 282
Rickman, Thomas 9
Ride with the Devil 251
Ridges, Stanley 302
Ridings, Richard 134
Riegert, Peter 342
Rigg, Diana 377
The Right Stuff 135
Riley, Gary 266
Rimmer, Shane 13

Ringwald, Molly 86
Riordan, Rick 173
Riskin, Robert 69
Rispoli, Michael 312
Ritter, Krysten 104
Rivele, Stephen J. 53, 139
Robards, Jason 276, 277, 366
Robb, Annasophia 31
Robbins, Tim 71
Roberts, Dallas 12
Roberts, James B. 53, 75, 270
Roberts, Marguerite 300
Roberts, Michael D. 108
Roberts, Randy 52
Roberts, William 66
Robertson, Cliff 267
Robinson, Bartlett 153
Robinson, Bruce 115, 212
Robinson, David 105
Robinson, Edwards G., Jr. 43
Robinson, Phil Alden 147
Robinson Crusoe 378
Robinson Crusoe on Mars 218
Robson, Flora 245
Robson, Mark 271
Rocco, Bembol 292
Rockwell, Sam 206
Rocky 1
Rodat, Robert 174, 247
Rodriguez, Paul 88
Roëves, Maurice 233
Rogers, Richard 295
Rogue Trader 51
Rohr, Tony 57
Rolle, Esther 27
Rollins, Howard E., Jr. 190, 191
Roman Holiday 180
Romanov, Stephanie 317

Romeo and Juliet 212
Romero 87
Ronan, Saoirse 165, 166
Ronson, Peter 163
The Rookie 280
Rose, Bernard 137
Rose, Simon 214
Rosenberg, Stuart 201
Ross, Gary 60
Ross, Katherine 166
Ross, Kenneth G. 8, 54, 257
Ross, Marion 375
Rossellini, Isabella 137
Rossi, Leo 65
Roth, Eric 53, 172, 273, 338, 368
Rotko, William 46
Routh, Brandon 119
Rowlands, Gena 94
Royle, Selena 10
Rubenstein, Bill 240
Rubin, Bruce Joel 141, 320
Rubin, Danny 32
Ruby 351
Rudy 336
Ruffalo, Mark 41, 182, 289
Rufus 290
Ruivivar, Anthony 334
Ruman, Sig 378
Run Silent, Run Deep 230
Ruocheng, Ying 229
Rush 232
Rush, Geoffrey 265, 266, 270, 271
Rushton, Jared 350
Rusler, Robert 350
Russell, David O. 388
Russell, Kurt 50
Russell, Rosalind 267
Rutherford, Ann 113

Ryan, Cornelius 171, 280
Ryan, Edward 10
Ryan, Meg 42, 43, 47, 48
Ryan, Mitchell 383
Ryan, Robert 376

Sabrina (1954) 278
Sacks, Oliver 311
Sadler, William 71
Sagalle, Jonathan 73
Sagan, Carl 337
Saint, Eva Marie 219, 352
Saire, Warren 216
Sakamoto, Ryuichi 230
Saldana, Theresa 38, 74
Saldana, Zoe 151
Salmaggi, Cesare 71, 249
Sampson, Will 296
Sand, Paul 321
The Sand Pebbles 179
Sanders, George 336
Sanderson, William 8, 9
Sandler, Adam 307
Sands, Julian 115
Sands of Iwo Jima 50
Sanford, Donald S. 178
Sangster, Thomas 23
Santoro, Rodrigo 272
Sarah's Key 213
Sarandon, Chris 253
Sarandon, Susan 182
Sartain, Gailard 186
Satrapi, Marjane 94
Satterfield, John 11
Saunders, Jennifer 44
Saunders, Terry 295
Savage, Peter 74
Savalas, Telly 376, 377, 385

Saving Private Ryan 11, 174
Sayles, John 298
Scacchi, Greta 96, 145
Scarpelli, Furio 104
Schaefer, Jack 200
Schaffner, Franklin J. 89, 221
Schallert, William 275
Schamus, James 249, 252
Schell, Maria 8, 120
Schell, Maximilian 8, 64, 65, 141
Schenk, Nick 38
Schepisi, Fred 322
Schermer, Jules 10
Schiavelli, Vincent 305
Schiff, Zeev 193
Schildkraut, Joseph 36, 234, 235, 310
Schindler's List 73
Schlesinger, John 303
Schneider, Rob 307
Schrader, Paul 33, 74
Schram, Jessy 306
Schreiber, Liev 249
Schroeder, Barbet 17
Schulman, Arnold 120
Schulman, Tom 350
Schwartzman, Jason 119
Schwarzenegger, Arnold 143, 184, 260
Schweig, Eric 233
Schwentke, Robert 320
Sciorra, Annabella 17
Scofield, Paul 202, 203
Scorsese, Martin 74, 75, 203, 210, 329
Scott, Adam 57
Scott, Allan 204
Scott, George C. 221
Scott, Randolph 248
Scott, Ridley 8, 78
Scott, Tony 306

Scott, William Lee 299

Scott of the Antarctic 92

Scott Pilgrim vs. the World 119

Seale, Bobby 49

The Searchers 386

Seaton, George 39

Seabiscuit 60

Seboq-Montifiore, Hugh 160

Secretariat 93

Seda, Jon 54, 346

Seddon, Corina 99

Segal, Erich 67

Segal, George 66

Segel, Jason 158

Segal, Peter 307

Seidler, David 265

Selena 53

Self, David 317

Selick, Henry 44

Selim, Ali 321

Sense and Sensibility 282

September Dawn 86

Sergeant York 302

Serling, Rod 89, 146

Serpico 33

Seven Days in May 146

1776 139

Sewell, Rufus 162

Seyfried, Amanda 345

Seymour, Jane 194

Seymour, Ralph 108

Shaara, Michael 199

Shackleton 123

Shadowlands 3

Shaffer, Peter 364

Shakespeare, William 212, 318

Shakespeare in Love 270

Shanley, John Patrick 313, 317

Shandling, Garry 37

Shane 200

Sharif, Omar 6, 297, 298

Sharp, Michael D. 250

Sharpton, Al 49

Shaw, Fiona 170

Shaw, Kim 104

Shaw, Robert 202, 203, 244, 268, 376

Shaw, Stan 18

Shawkat, Alia 255

The Shawshank Redemption 71

She Wore a Yellow Ribbon 334

Shearer, Norma 310, 311

Sheedy, Ally 86

Sheen, Charlie 136

Sheen, Martin 29, 75, 136, 200, 355

Sheen, Michael 157, 262

Shelton, Marley 139

Shepard, Sam 135, 136, 211

Shepherd, Cybill 341, 342

Shepherd, John 209

Shepherd, Simon 318

Sheridan, Jim 169

Sheridan, Kirsten 170

Sherlock Holmes 347

Sherriff, R. C. 95, 264

She's Out of My League 103

Shilliday, Susan 109

Shindler, Colin 238

Shine 257

The Shining (1980) 324

Shipman, Pat 223

Shire, Talia 1, 2, 256, 356, 357

The Shootist 22

Shorter, Frank 226

Shue, Elisabeth 339, 340

Shusett, Ronald 184

Shyer, Charles 154

Sides, Hampton 28
Siegel, Don 22
Siemaszko, Casey 266
Sienkiewicz, Henryk 215
Sigal, Clancy 204
Silkwood 341
Silliphant, Stirling 275, 391
Silver, Ron 17, 53
Silver Linings Playbook 388
Silver Streak 104
Simmons, Jean 128
Simon, Josette 274
Simon, Mary 93
Simon, Paul 359
Simon, Robert F. 15
A Simple Twist of Fate 345
Sinatra, Frank 271, 365, 366
Since You Went Away 12
Sinclair, Stephen 59
Singer, Bryan 217
Singin' in the Rain 85
Sinise, Gary 110, 172, 173
Sisto, Jeremy 226
Sivero, Frank 329
The Sixth Sense 134
'68 170
Sizemore, Tom 174
Skaaren, Warren 349
Skerritt, Tom 337
Skutt, Alexander G. 53, 75
Slate, Jeremy 300
Slater, Christian 182
Slattery, John 334
Sleepless in Seattle 42, 186
Slezak, Victor 240
Sloane, Lindsay 104
Slumdog Millionaire 314
Smight, Jack 178

Smith, Alexis 269
Smith, Anna Deveare 355
Smith, C. Aubrey 264
Smith, Charles Martin 277, 357
Smith, Francis G., Jr. 66
Smith, Jada Pinkett 53
Smith, Jim Field 103
Smith, Lane 4
Smith, Lois 321
Smith, Maggie 343, 344
Smith, Patricia 153
Smith, Riley 287
Smith, Will 53, 199
Snyder, Suzanne 350
Snyder, Zack 272
Sobieski, Carol 18
Sobieski, Leelee 141
The Social Network 34
Sofaer, Abraham 133, 215
Sokolove, Richard 24
Soles, P. J. 20
Some Like It Hot 43
Somebody Up There Likes Me 290
Someone Like You 214
Somewhere in Time 193
Sommer, Josef 155
Sondergaard, Gale 36
Song of Bernadette 39
A Song to Remember 11
Sonkkila, Paul 292
Sorkin, Aaron 149, 258, 355
Sorvino, Mira 312
Sorvino, Paul 329, 334
Soul Surfer 10
The Sound of Music 355
Space, Arthur 153
Spacek, Sissy 9, 10, 177
Spacey, Kevin 145, 146

Spall, Timothy 265
Spano, Vincent 317
Spencer, John 96
Spencer, Octavia 177
Sperber, A. M. 69
Sperber, Wendie Jo 38
Sperling, Milton 376
Sphere 199
Spider-Man 357
Spielberg, Steven 30, 73, 154, 174, 239,
    327
The Spirit of St. Louis 153
Spizzirri, Angelo 280
Stade, George 14
Stalag 17 377
Staley, James 20
Stallone, Sylvester 1, 2, 246
Stamp, Terence 136, 217, 303, 334
Stand by Me 266
Stanley, Kim 135
Stapleton, Jean 47, 333, 334
Star 80 245
A Star Is Born 63
Starkey, David 24
Starr, Michael S. 146
Staunton, Imelda 249
Steel Magnolias 98
Steele, Karen 185
Steenburgen, Mary 177, 190, 191, 340
Stefani, Gwen 203
Stefano, Joseph 371
Steinberg, David 241
Steiger, Rod 6, 275, 276
Stephens, Robert 212
Stern, Daniel 255, 380
Stern, Matt 175
Stern, Philip Van Doren 384

Stevens, David 54
Stevens, Fisher 17
Stevens, Gary L. 61
Stevens, George 200, 234, 385
Stevens, Stella 391
Stewart, Donald 20
Stewart, Donald Ogden 310
Stewart, James 22, 102, 153, 161, 168,
    375, 384, 385
Stewart, Patrick 124, 216
Stewart, Paul 363
Stiers, David Ogden 380
Stiles, Julia 254, 388
The Sting 268
Stockett, Kathryn 177
Stoltz, Eric 149
Stone, Emma 177
Stone, Lewis 223
Stone, Milburn 248
Stone, Oliver 136, 139, 224
Stone, Sharon 184
Stoppa, Paolo 389
Stoppard, Tom 239, 270
Stormare, Peter 181
The Story of Alexander Graham Bell 70
Stowe, Madeline 233, 346
Strasberg, Lee 356, 357
Strasberg, Susan 267
Strassman, Marcia 350
Strathairn, David 30, 68, 69, 149, 298
Strauss, Robert 378
Streep, Meryl 13, 14, 241, 242, 322, 323,
    361, 362
Streisand, Barbara 227
Stronberg, Claude-Michel 345
Strong, Mark 263, 390
Strong, Michael 221

Stroud, Don 357
Strus, Lusia 307
Struther, Jan 159
Stuart, Gloria 111, 112
Stuart, Jeb 77
Studi, Wes 233
Sturges, John 87
Suburban Madness 222
Sugarland Express 133
Sukapatana, Chintara 285
Sullivan, Francis L. 128
The Sum of All Fears 302
Summer of Sam 312
Sunderland, Scott 95
Sunjata, Daniel 361
Sunrise at Campobello 241
Superman 197
Suplee, Ethan 306
Sutherland, Donald 182, 183, 226, 227, 228, 353
Sutherland, Kiefer 150, 266
Suzman, Janet 182
Swank, Hilary 82, 154
Swanson, Jackie 383
Swarthout, Glendonn 22
Swarthout, Miles 22
Swarup, Vikas 314
Swearing Allegiance 365
Sweeney, D. B. 149, 298
Sweet, John 154
Sweet Dreams 20
Sweet Land 321
Swenson, Inga 62
Swerling, Jo 384
Swink, Kitty 33
Swinton, Tilda 304, 338
The Swiss Family Robinson 32

Sylvan, William C. 66
Syms, Sylvia 262
Szpilman, Wladysaw 231
Szwarc, Jeannot 194

Takaku, William 379
Taking Woodstock 249
Talk Radio 184
Talty, Stephen 90
Tamblyn, Amber 128
Tamblyn, Russ 120
Tamm, Mary 8
Tandy, Jessica 18, 19, 27
Taradash, Daniel 365
Taradash, William 267
Tate, Larenz 100
Tautou, Audrey 290
Taylor, Don 378, 382
Taylor, Dub 222
Taylor, Elizabeth 243
Taylor, Joyce 161
Taylor, Robert 215, 237
Taylor, Rod 5
Taylor, Tate 177
Temple, Juno 165
Temple, Lew 306
ter Steege, Johanna 137
The Terminator 143
Terminator 2: Judgment Day 260
Terrio, Chris 27
Terry, Nigel 123
Tesich, Steve 259
Tess 101
Testimony 65
Thackeray, William 180
That Hamilton Woman 316
That Thing You Do! 185

Thaw, John 274
Thaxter, Phyllis 116
The Thin Red Line 2
The Time Machine 5
They Died with Their Boots On 191
They Were Expendable 70
Thigpen, Corbett 251
Thirteen Days 317
13 Going on 30 159
Thirty Days of Night 378
Thirty Seconds over Tokyo 116
Thoeren, Robert 43
Thomas, Henry 109, 327, 328
Thomas, Kristin Scott 131, 213, 308,
    309, 343
Thompson, Emma 23, 282, 283, 318
Thompson, Jack 54
Thompson, Lea 331, 339, 340
Thompson, Marshall 71, 382
Thompson, Rex 295
Thompson, Sophie 189
Thompson, Susanna 34
Thoms, Tracie 361
Thomson, Gabriel 315
Thornton, Billy Bob 52
Three Came Home 45
The Three Faces of Eve 250
300 272
Thunderball 158
Thurman, Judith 14
Thx 1138 83
Tiber, Elliot 249
Ticotin, Rachel 184
Tiernan, Andrew 272
Tierney, Gene 319
Tilly, Jennifer 344
Tilly, Meg 301
Time after Time 332

The Time Traveler's Wife 320
Timeline 100
Tingwell, Charles 322
Titanic 111
Titley, Craig 173
To Hell and Back 145
To Kill a Mockingbird 324
Tobias, George 328, 375
Tobolowsky, Stephen 32, 186, 320
Tolkan, James 331
Tolkien, J. R. R. 11, 12, 59, 60, 79, 81
Tolkin, Michael 141
Tollin, Mike 287
Tom and Huck 183
Tombstone 81
Tomei, Marisa 4, 106
Topor, Tom 65
Tora! Tora! Tora! 366
Torrence, Nate 104
Total Recall 184
Towne, Robert 37, 226, 291
Tracy, Spencer 64, 116
Tran, Tung Thanh 285
Travers, Henry 117, 159, 384
The Treasure of the Sierra Madre 250
Treves, Frederick 107
Trotti, Lamar 191
Troyat, Henri 348
True Grit 300
True Lies 323
Truffaut, François 155
The Truman Show 373
Trumbo, Dalton 116, 219
Trzebinski Errol 14
Tucci, Stanley 241, 361
Tucker, Anand 57
Tucker, Chris 388
Tucker, Forrest 51

Tucker, Michael 323
Turkel, Joe 8, 179
Turner, Sheldon 93
Turow, Scott 96
12 Monkeys 346
24 Hour Party People 169
20,000 Leagues under the Sea 369
Twist, John 161
Twohy, David 77
Tyldesley, Joyce 243
Tyler, Liv 59, 79
Tyson, Cicely 18

Uhry, Alfred 27
Ulrich, Skeet 252
An Ungentlemanly Act 97
Unstoppable 306
The Untouchables 277
Urban, Karl 79
Uris, Leon 219
Ustinov, Peter 17, 215, 216

V for Vendetta 330
Vajda, Ernest 310
Valdez, Luis 33
Valkyrie 217
Van Cleef, Lee 104, 225
Van Dyke, W.S. 310
van Eyck, Peter 66
Van Fleet, Jo 201
Van Peebles, Mario 53
Vance, Courtney B. 152
Vance, Jeffrey 106
Vanderbilt, James 289
Vang, Bee 38
Vargas, Jacob 54
Vaughn, Robert 66
Veidt, Conrad 360

Venora, Diane 368
The Verdict 49
Verhoeven, Paul 184
Verne, Jules 163, 218, 219, 369
Vernon, John 342
Veronica Guerin 192
Vibert, Ronan 231
The Victors 30
Victory 246
Victory at Entebbe 193
Villard, Henry 204
Vincent, Frank 74
Vincenzoni, Luciano 104
Vitali, Leon 180
Viva Zapata! 106
Vogel, Mike 104
Voight, Jon 8, 53, 81
Vollers, Margaret 35
Von Ryan's Express 271
Von Sydow, Max 246, 273, 374, 311, 385
Voskovec, Jiri 195
Voyadjis, Yorgo 7
Voyage of the Damned 151

W 28
Wachowski, Andy 48, 330
Wachowski, Larry 48, 330
Waddington, Steven 233
Wadham, Julian 121
Wager, Anthony 128
Wagner, Lou 89
Wahlberg, Mark 75, 76
Wake Island 372
Walk Don't Run 305
Walk the Line 12
Walken, Christopher 154, 359
Walker, James 99
Walker, Polly 189, 379

Walker, Robert 116
Walking Tall 244
Wall Street 136
Wallace, Dee 327
Wallace, Randall 93, 235
Wallach, Eli 104
Wallechinsky, David 208
Wallis & Edward 372
Walsh, Dylan 313
Walsh, Frances 11, 59, 79, 187
Walsh, J. T. 285
Walsh, M. Emmet 8
Walsh, Raoul 269
Walston, Ray 268
Walter, Tracey 349
Walters, Julie 238
A Waltz through the Hills 303
Wanninger, Ashley 127
War Horse 339
War of the Buttons 121
Ward, David 42, 268
Ward, Fred 135
Ward, Kelly 205
Ward, Sela 77
Ward, Sophie 167
Warden, Jack 276
Warner, David 111
Warner, H. B. 69, 70
Warren, Sharon 100
Warshofsky, David 90
Washburn, Wilcomb E. 387
Washington, Denzel 49, 274, 275, 306
Washington, Kerry 100
Washington Square 212
Wasikowska, Mia 82, 167
Waterkeyn, Xavier 33, 375
Waters, John 55
Waterston, Sam 115

Wates, Roye E. 365
Watkins, Maurine Dallas 156
Watson, Emily 250
Watson, Minor 269
Watson, Winifred 263
Watts, Naomi 211
The Way We Were 281
Wayne, David 35
Wayne, John 22, 51, 70, 171, 300, 301, 386
We Are Marshall 342
We Bought a Zoo 196
Wead, Frank 70
Weathers, Carl 1
Weaver, Jackie 388, 389
Weaver, Sigourney 151, 292
Weaver, Will 321
Weaving, Hugo 48, 330
Webb, Chloe 37
Webb, James R. 102
Webb, Marc 142
Weber, Michael H. 142
Weber, Steven 152
The Wedding Singer 234
Wedgeworth, Ann 20, 176
Weigley, Russell 229
Weir, Alison 203
Weir, Peter 237, 292, 373
Weird Science 350
Weisberger, Lauren 361
Weiser, Stanley 136
Weisz, Rachel 315
Welland, Colin 182, 207
Weller, Michael 190
Welles, Orson 202, 363, 364
Wellman, William 381
Wells, Claudia 331
Wells, John 287

Welsh, Kenneth 50

Wenham, David 272

Werfel, Franz 39

West, Claudine 95, 159, 310

West, Dominic 156, 272

Westerman, Floyd Red Crow 126

Westheimer, David 271

What Ever Happened to Baby Jane?
   240

What's Up Doc? 227

Wheaton, Wil 266

Whelan, Alison 170

When Harry Met Sally 311

Where the Heart Is 194

Where the Lilies Bloom 356

*Where Were You When the Lights Went
   Out?* 337

While You Were Sleeping 392

Whip It 254

Whitaker, Forest 285

White, James L. 100

White, William L. 70

White Christmas 380

Whitehead, Don 161

Whitfield, Mitchell 4

Whiting, Leonard 212, 213

Whitmore, James 71, 89, 237, 366, 382

Whittle, Annie 88

Whitty, May 117, 159

Who Is Clark Rockefeller? 226

The Whole Wide World 176

Whorf, Richard 328

Why Do Fools Fall in Love? 55

Wuhl, Robert 285

Wicki, Bernard 171

Widdoes, James 342

Widmark, Richard 64

Wiest, Dianne 323

Wiggins, Wiley 160

Wiig, Kristen 158, 255

Wild Bill 232

Wilde 157

Wilde, Andrew 99

Wilde, Oscar 336

Wilder, Billy 43, 153, 378

Wilder, Gene 132, 222

Wilke, Robert J. 369

Wilkinson, Christopher 53, 139

Wilkinson, Tom 41, 157, 217, 247,
   270

Willes, Jean 161

Williams, Billy Dee 349

Williams, Chris 88

Williams, JoBeth 301

Williams, Robin 285, 311, 312

Williams, Treat 128

Williams, Matt 195

Williamson, David 237, 292

Williamson, Nicol 123

Williamson, Mykelti 172

Willie, Roger 181

Willingham, Calder 354

Willis, Bruce 304, 346

Wilson 191

Wilson, Michael 89, 144, 297

Wilson, Patrick 52

Wilson, Renee 100

Wilson, Rita 42

Wilson, Thomas F. 331, 339, 340

Wilton, Penelope 274, 353

Wimperis, Arthur 159

Wincott, Michael 56

Windtalkers 181

Winfield, Paul 96, 143

Wing, George 307

Winger, Debra 3, 4, 287

Winslet, Kate 41, 42, 111, 112, 187, 282, 283, 387
The Winslow Boy 228
Winstead, Mary Elizabeth 119
Winterbottom, Michael 40
Winters, Shelley 234, 235, 391, 392
Wisdom, Tom 272
Wise, Greg 282
Wise, Robert 35, 179, 278
Wisher, William, Jr. 260
Witherspoon, Reese 12, 13
Without Limits 226
Wittliff, William 109
Wolfe, Ian 83
Wolfe, Tom 135
Wolpert, Jay 55
The Woman in White 310
Wong, Ellen 119
Wong, Victor 229, 230
Woo, John 181
Wood, Derek 244
Wood, Elijah 11, 41, 59, 79, 141
Wood, Natalie 386
Wood, Lana 386
Wood, Sam 95
Woodard, Alfre 287
Woodrell, Daniel 252
Woods, Donald 274
Woods, James 34, 139, 337
Woods, Simon 353
Woodward, Bob 276
Woodward, Edward 54
Woodward, Joanne 251
Woodward, Morgan 201
Wooley, Benjamin 380
Wooley, Sheb 225
Working Girl 61
A World Apart 135

The World's Fastest Indian 88
Worthington, Sam 28, 151
Wright, Edgar 119
Wright, Jeffrey 252, 273
Wright, Joe 165, 353
Wright, Teresa 159, 194
The Wrong Man 14
Wuhl, Robert 349
Wyatt, Jane 69
Wycherly, Margaret 302, 303
Wyler, William 159
Wyndham-Lewis, D. B. 168
Wynn, Ed 234, 235
Wynn, Tracy Keenan 379

Yablonsky, Yabo 246
Yankee Doodle Dandy 328
Yapp, Nick 239
Yates, Peter 259
Yates, Richard 66
The Year of Living Dangerously 292
Yordan, Philip 245, 376
York, Michael 17, 212
York, Susannah 202, 244
Young, Alan 5
Young, Burt 1
Young, Carleton 369
Young, Stephen 221
Young, Sean 8, 136
Young Bess 42
Young Frankenstein 132
You've Got Mail 47
Yuzna, Brian 350

Zahn, Steve 47
Zaillian, Steven 73, 210, 258, 311
Zane, Billy 111, 149
Zeffirelli, Franco 212

Zelikow, Philip D. 317
Zellweger, Renée 84, 156, 157, 160, 176, 228, 229, 348, 349
Zemekis, Robert 38, 172, 331, 337, 339, 340
Zerneck, Danielle von 33
Zero Dark Thirty 390
Zeta-Jones, Catherine 156, 157

Zinnemann, Fred 202, 225, 257, 365
Zmuda, Bob 306
Zodiac 289
Zorba the Greek 6
Zulu 21
Zweig, Stefan 310
Zwerling, Darrell 291
Zwick, Edward 109

About the Author

Ivan Walters graduated from college with a double major in history and political science. He now works as the sales representative for an industrial videography company. Mr. Walters has two children and lives in Rock Hill, South Carolina.

DATE DUE

FEB 1 5 2016	
MAR 1 6 2016	
JUL 0 6 2016	

PRINTED IN U.S.A.

28 Day Loan